# On Filmmaking

# On Filmmaking

*EDWARD DMYTRYK*

FOCAL PRESS
*Boston • London*

Focal Press is an imprint of Butterworth Publishers.


Copyright © 1986 by Butterworth Publishers.
All rights reserved.

**Library of Congress Cataloging in Publication Data**

Dmytryk, Edward.
  On filmmaking.

  Includes index.
  1. Moving-pictures.  I. Title.
PN1995.D56  1985     791.43     85–27381
ISBN 0–240–51760–1

Butterworth Publishers
80 Montvale Avenue
Stoneham, MA 02180


10  9  8  7  6  5  4  3  2  1

*Printed in the United States of America*

# Contents

# *Preface*

This book is written in the hope of informing, instructing, and entertaining, more or less in that order, students of the cinema and lovers of movies. It is a reasonably detailed exposition of the principles and techniques involved in four of the major creative areas of filmmaking—screenwriting, directing, *screen* acting, and film editing—each of which had originally been the subject of a separate volume. The process of consolidating the four previous volumes into this one, comprehensive volume has dictated some minor deletions, but if a few echoes remain it is only because the twice-told material is used in different contexts.

There is still some tendency to define filmmaking and television production as separate arts—mostly, I must confess, on the part of the filmmakers. But what may once have been a valid distinction is no longer true. As "live" staging disappeared so did the original video techniques, and only the "sit-com" now employs the paraphernalia of television's early days, including the use of multiple cameras. In the area of drama, comedy-drama, action, and melodrama, television now shares production techniques with its film "cousin." Much of it is even shot on film.

The means of presentation differ, of course, and because the "box" is still smaller than the screen, more close shots are used in films made for TV. But even that difference will diminish as the home screen increases in size to match (relative to viewer distance) the film screen's proportions, though whether the eventual recording system will be tape or film remains to be seen. As far as writing, directing, acting, and editing are concerned, an objective observer either now or in the future will find that the two "motion picture" forms are really one.

With this in mind, this book should be of value to students of both film and television. Essentially all the techniques and principles discussed here apply equally well to both arts.

The word "actor" is customarily applied to thespians of either sex, and it is so used in this book. The pronouns he, him, and his are also meant to apply equally to male or female actors, directors, or other crew members. Their use makes writing easier.

# On Filmmaking

# Book I

## ON SCREEN WRITING

# Introduction

There is no question that as far as any *good* film is concerned, the story is the thing. No matter how beautiful the photography, how clever the director's manipulation of the camera, how brilliant the acting, how breathtaking the settings, without a good story they become areas of purely parochial interest to the devotees of those particular crafts. I believe there can be little argument on this point. It follows that any book attempting to cover the art of filmmaking must begin with an analysis of the screen writer's craft.

Putting aside the considerations of the normal pains and aches of the creative process, writing a screenplay is still no easy undertaking. Even those few who have a talent for writing *for the screen* can find life difficult, and that, I believe, is because almost no one in the field squarely faces the screen-writing facts of life. Quite simply, fashioning a movie script is much more than most writers think it is and much less than they would like it to be.

Of all the contributors to that collective art called filmmaking, the screen writer is the one creator whose contribution is most frequently edited, controlled, revised, or discarded, and whose creative efforts are most often debated, denied, or subjected to arbitration. An actor may receive some degree of help from the director and, not infrequently, from the film editor, yet no one questions the source of his performance. The photographer's lighting is almost always a solo effort. In all but a few rare instances the director receives full credit for his work, whether it be good or inadequate. And critics, though usually ignorant of what really goes on in the cutting room, bend over backwards to laud the editor's expertise, not infrequently dishing out more credit than he deserves. But the screen writer's road to recognition is often marked by indecipherable sign posts, especially if the writing credit is shared by a number of scribblers. However, even as he steers around the pot holes, the rational writer will concede that there are a few valid reasons for this annoying state of affairs.

To begin with, unless he is not only the writer of a particular script but also its producer and/or director (in which case his problems are different but just as great) he is, at least in part, writing to someone else's taste, to someone else's order, appealing to someone else's judgment—first the producer, then the director, and occasionally, in these days of multimillion dollar stars, the actor. Each of these usually wants—demands—"input" into the script.

("Input" has become perhaps the most frightening and distasteful word in the artist's lexicon. It brings on convulsive shudders to directors, actors, and editors, but the screen writer suffers more from its implementation than the other three combined. For in this era of corporate boards, advisory commissions, and analytical committees, any attempt at ignoring "input" is considered the ultimate heresy.)

So, unless he is one of a very small elite, the screen writer must inure himself to writing with the ghost of "input" constantly at his shoulder; rarely does he have the opportunity to complete his version of a script uninterrupted, in the privacy of his own cubicle.

At the root of the problem is the nature of the screenplay itself. The truth is that it is rarely an original work to begin with. Most of the scenarios written for theatrical film production are derived from novels, short stories, plays, or earlier scripts. In each case the screen writer is really doing a re-write—an *adaptation*—not an original. In some instances, say *The Caine Mutiny* or *The Maltese Falcon*, little more than intelligent editing is called for. But in many adaptations of novels—*The Young Lions*, for instance, or *Raintree County*—a great deal of original characterization and story re-alignment must be created afresh. Rarely is the operation a completely happy one.

Scripts written by the authors of the original works, whether they be novels or plays, are frequently unsatisfactory. Quite simply, these artists, however talented in their own fields, rarely have any screen-writing expertise. If allowed an opinion, such a writer will hardly rhapsodize over another screen writer's reworking of his material. And that screenplay, in its turn, may be re-written a dozen times by another half-dozen writers, or teams of writers. By the time the average script arrives at the shooting stage, only expert and unbiased analysis can determine who wrote what and how much. Further credit complications arise from the re-writing which is frequently done on the set, or the sometimes effective editing performed on the moviola.

All this re-working of scripts may, on occasion, be senseless, but it is rarely willful. Just as, to quote the old Hollywood saw, "No one *wants* to make a bad movie," so no producer or director asks for a rewrite out of pure meanness. There are a number of reasons for the prevalence of so much rewriting and restructuring. Some are specious, growing out of the filmmakers' insecurities. A major one is that 19 out of 20 scripts are unreadable and 98 out of 100 just plain bad. Another remains valid and beyond debate: A film is (or should be) a *motion* picture, and though the medium is flexible enough to accommodate almost every other dramatic form,* the ideal *theatrical* film is not a novel, a short story, a documentary, or a play. It is a separate art form, demanding its own techniques—techniques which few writers have had the opportunity or the time to learn, fewer still to master.

A very competent novelist who develops his characters largely through literary exposition of their inner drives and desires is often incapable of developing these same characters in *cinematic* terms— he may even find it difficult to understand the special jargon of a director who has spent his life immersed in filmmaking. An excellent playwright, skilled at building drama and character through dialogue, may be at a loss when required to dramatize his ideas through action and reaction. Neither artist is conditioned to think in cinematic terms, and the transition is not an easy one, as many screenwriters have discovered to their dismay.

Skillful *adaptation* of good original material is the secret of fine screenplays, adaptation which takes full advantage of those techniques which film alone provides: varied and optimum camera positioning, effective change of audience point of view through competent film editing, and the ability to highlight dramatic transition by zeroing in on the *reaction*, thus affording the viewer a greater opportunity to understand, identify with, and interpret the attitudes and emotions of the people on the screen rather than just those of the author.

"Well, yes," most screen writers will say, "but those are the prerogatives and the responsibilities of the film director." And so they are—but not necessarily so. I have never met a director who knew it all. The more the writer can concern himself with the cinematic demands of the film, the sooner he will learn to understand, and use to advantage, the tremendous potential of the medium. How then can the quality of films fail to improve?

To such an end this book, while addressing itself to the basic requirements of screen writing, will pay special attention to the problems of adaptation.

---

*For example, a conversation piece such as the excellent *Dinner with Andre*.

# 1

# *First Steps*

Before we try the deep water let's get our feet wet with some of the basics, and the reasons for their existence. For some students this may be a review, but not entirely. It is important for writers to know what goes on in other areas of what is really an extremely complicated manufacturing process.

There are several stages in the building of a film script. The number varies, depending on the experience, the reputation, and the work habits of the writer.

First there is the short treatment, which, as the term implies, can be as brief as 2 pages or as long as 15 or more.* The short treatment is a basic outline of the plot. Dialogue is never included and characters are mentioned only briefly, with little or no development unless such development is the essential meat of the story.

This process, whether involving a novel or an original screenplay, is usually the function of a *"reader,"* who is employed by a literary agent or the producer's story editor.** "Readers" are regarded with suspicion by most writers who present original material for studio consideration, since they are usually quite young and inexperienced in filmmaking. To avoid this route many writers prepare their own short treatments, or synopses, when such a step is necessary.

Today, most studios and independent producers offer "step deals" when hiring a writer. As the term indicates, agreed-on payments are made to the writer in a series of steps, and the deal can be terminated

---

*I have known several such treatments, written by established writers, to be sold for prices well into five figures. I was personally involved with a 25-page treatment by Ben Hecht which R.K.O. bought for $25,000. The final script contained exactly one element of the original treatment—the title, *Cornered.*

**Throughout this book, the word "producer" can refer either to an individual, a producing company, or a studio.

by the producer at the completion of any one of them. For instance, a certain amount will be paid at the completion of the treatment, which usually means a *full* treatment. At this point the producer has the option of canceling the rest of the deal or of approving the next step in the contract, the writing of the first draft screenplay. The producer exercises the final option when the draft is completed. Again, he can cancel out at this stage or assign the writer to continue with a shooting script. This last step customarily includes the producer's right to an agreed-on number of rewrites, or "polishes"—usually no more than one or two. If the project is finally scheduled for production, such rewrites are usually carried out in collaboration with the director. After this final step the writer's engagement is terminated. In practice, of course, there are almost as many variations as there are lawyers, but some version of the above summary is the most common.

A few writers of established reputation and long experience opt to go directly into script form. Most, however, find it pays to write a full treatment. A few may indulge in a preliminary process, especially when working in tandem—they will construct a "step outline." The step outline, a very useful operation, consists of a numbered series of sentences or short paragraphs which describe a sequence-by-sequence development of the script's basic story line, as well as its subplot. It can be especially fruitful when adapting a novel in which the characters are well developed and which contains situations which easily lend themselves to cinematic reconstruction.

An example: The novel *Christ in Concrete* was a series of vignettes involving interesting, sympathetic, and amusing characters. It had a rich background and one powerful and tragic situation which was the essential root of the novel. But there was no linear plot on which to build the script. In one free-wheeling afternoon the writer, Ben Barzman, and I completed a three- or four-page step outline of a plot which Barzman, with little alteration, proceeded to develop into a full and very satisfactory script. If we had been faced with the need to develop new characters, or to change the old ones significantly, the job would have been much more difficult, and a full treatment would certainly have been required.

The full treatment can run from 75 to 200 pages, or more, depending on the inventiveness and the stamina of the writer. It develops the plot as well as the characters, their actions, and inter-relationships, in prose form. (See page 9.) An occasional dialogue scene may be included to give "flavor" to the treatment, especially if the writer feels the dramatic impact of such a scene will help to sell the project.

The character and style of writing in both the long treatment and the first draft are, in my opinion, extremely important. Both should be written to interest, excite, and inspire the producer. Many writers assume the producer wants only an extensive outline of the story with no frills included. They make that assumption because that's what the producers tell them. But to believe that shows a flawed awareness of human nature. No matter how "high" a producer may be on an original property, he still wants, and *needs*, to be sold on the *script*. Remember, at this stage the making of the film is never a certainty, and a flat, uninspired treatment or first draft can be a dreadful letdown and put the film in jeopardy. It is at this stage that many writers fail and their efforts are relegated to "the shelf," where the great majority die a musty death.

It is one of the anomolies of the movie business that at this stage the screen writer, whose techniques are quite different from those of the novelist, should find it advantageous to write like one. Not all producers know how to read a treatment or a rough draft, and even fewer financial backers have that capability. So the writer must keep in mind that these versions are meant to be *read*, not photographed. And even though he is describing images and actions, he should do so with all the *literary* skill at his command. There is little room for full-blown prose in a shooting script, but at the treatment stage it can be used to good effect. In fact, it can make the difference between a viable film or a dead project.

A treatment looks something like this:

FADE IN:

The year is 1938, it is New Year's Eve, and we are high in the Austrian Tyrol. At first we see only the towering mountains behind a broad, steeply sloping expanse of snow. The effect is awesome—cold, still, with thousands of stars in the early evening sky. The snow is still unmarked.

Suddenly, in the distance, a figure skis into the scene with a whoosh and a wild plume of snow, followed closely by another. With express speed they traverse the slope, finally flashing past close to the camera. Perhaps we can make out that the leading figure is that of a woman, the one bringing up the rear is a man.

A few quick shots take them down the mountain until the girl stems into a flying stop on a flat field of snow. The man swirls in behind her, showering her with a cloud of white crystals. They both shout with the exuberance of the moment, then trail off into laughter.

"You were brilliant," says the man, CHRISTIAN, after he stops laughing. "Tomorrow you are giving me lessons."

"Thank you," laughs the girl, MARGARET. Then she cocks her head to one side as she becomes aware of the slow lilt of a classic waltz coming from the not-too-distant ski lodge.

"What are they playing?" she asks. "Roslein," answers Christian, and he starts to sing the German lyrics. Margaret joins him briefly, then stumbles on the unremembered words. Christian helps her to finish the phrase, and they both laugh.

"Not bad," says Christian, "for an American."

And so on. . . .

A shooting script has a make-up all its own. It does not resemble a novel, a play, or even a normal video script, though some TV writers have adopted screenplay form. This form is based on a collection of conventions which, for good and sufficient reasons, have accumulated over a considerable period of time.

The script as we know it is written as much for the production department and the crew as it is for the actors and the director. It best serves a variety of purposes and is truly superior for none. If I were writing a script only for myself or the producer it would probably resemble an action novel.* If I were writing it for the actors, it would still follow the general structure of the novel, though the dialogue would be more clearly defined—more sharply separated from the descriptive material. But a film must be budgeted and scheduled. These two estimates are inextricably inter-related, and based on information contained in the shooting script—information which has only a little to do with plot and characterization.

On receiving a script, an experienced producer or director will glance at a few pages somewhere in its bowels, then turn to the last page. He is not trying to sneak a peek at the finish; he merely wants to determine the script's length. The last page number gives him that information and, if the scenes are also numbered (as they should be), those numbers and his glance at the earlier pages tell him how many set-ups have been arbitrarily written into the script and the ratio of dialogue to descriptive material. On the basis of this information he will estimate, with a fair degree of accuracy, how many minutes the finished film will run if the shooting closely follows the script.**

For example, if a script concentrates on master scenes and dialogue, 120 pages will approximate a two-hour film. If, on the other hand, it contains many cuts and much description, the same 120 pages will run perhaps an hour and forty minutes. Or, to put it another way, to fill a two-hour requirement the latter script may tolerate 135 to 140 pages.

Given a certain budget and a knowledge of the director's work habits, a production manager will arrive at an estimate of the schedule (the number of shooting days) by counting the pages of the script; and the more closely the writer has observed the script-writing conventions the more accurate that estimate will be. The specific script form

---

*With some deletions, *The Maltese Falcon* could be shot from the book, as could a good deal of Raymond Chandler. But so could a novella like Steinbeck's beautiful, non-action story, *The Red Pony.*

**The director is a modifying factor since one may shoot "close to the bone," achieving a fast pace, while another may favor a slower pace and the inclusion of many nuances. Physical difficulty involved in shooting action scenes is also an important variable.

appears on page 11, but a few general observations are in order. The script must be typed in pica 10 (or a comparable size). Elite accommodates a good deal more material per page than the conventions call for and is more difficult to read. Certain arbitrary spacing between lines, between separate scenes, and before and after descriptive passages should be observed. The length (i.e., the width across the page) of each line of dialogue should not exceed the given length, as the example indicates.

Some writers, trying to cram more of their deathless prose into a script, will occasionally try to cheat: They will decrease the spacing between lines, increase the length of each line of dialogue, and pack each page to the bottom edge. They deceive only themselves. An experienced filmmaker will spot the deception at once and will account for the distortion, but the skullduggery will not encourage admiration for the writer's contribution to his labors.

This is what a script should look like—in form, not in substance.*

1    FADE IN:

CLOSE SHOT    CHROME FIGURE    EXT. DESERT    NIGHT

We see a chrome figurine—a lady lifting her head to a strong breeze, her clothes sailing out behind her. CAMERA ZOOMS SLOWLY BACK to disclose the well-known radiator, then the full shape of a slightly off-white Rolls-Royce sedan.

Suddenly, there is a half-muffled MAN'S SCREAM, followed almost immediately by a barely discernible figure hurtling out of a sharply opened door on the passenger side. As the first figure rolls in the dust, a second shape hurls itself out of the car and throws itself on the first one. For a brief moment, the two shapes join in a frantic wrestling action in the dirt, then we get a close glimpse of a switch-blade knife opening with an angry "snick"—a split second later it is thrust forward sharply. The two figures separate, the larger one shuffling backwards, relentlessly pursued by the smaller one. Then the larger figure stumbles backward over a low, shining, white barricade and, with a GASPING SCREAM disappears downward into the night. For a short moment the small figure remains, looking down after the falling body; then it moves erratically, but swiftly, back to the car and climbs in. A

(CONTINUED)

*From Peter Allan Fields' adaptation of Bart Spicer's novel, *Act of Anger.*

1 (CONTINUED)

moment later the motor roars into action, there is a harsh
grinding of gears, and the car lurches forward INTO CAMERA.
As the figure on the radiator ZOOMS UP into a CLOSE UP and
freezes into a STILL PICTURE, we see the MAIN TITLE:

ACT OF ANGER

The CREDITS of the film continue through the last card, and

DISSOLVE THROUGH TO:

2        LONG SHOT        EXT. ROAD                        NIGHT

The long white ribbon shines palely in the false dawn,
stretching for a mile or more into the b.g. till it curves into
the barely seen range of mountains. In the not too distant left
F.G. stands a police car, vaguely lit by dim interior lights.

3        MED. CLOSE SHOT        INT. SHERIFF'S CAR        NIGHT

Two DEPUTIES sit lazily in the front seat. DEPUTY HOUSTON
SHRINER, the stringy, juiceless man who sits behind the
wheel, holds a stop watch. He looks over to see the second
deputy, MONTERO, slouched in the seat with his western-style
hat pulled down over his eyes. Shriner doesn't like that much.

                    SHRINER
          Hey, Mex . . .
                    (proffers stop watch)
          You take it for a while, eh?

Montero doesn't change his body position nor remove the hat
from his face. But he holds up his hand and raises a finger for
each of the following names:

                    MONTERO
                    (quietly)
          Deputy . . . Sheriff . . . Juan . . .
          Alonzo . . . Montero. That's five
          names to pick from . . .

                                              (CONTINUED)

3 (CONTINUED)

Only now does Montero sit upright, raise his hat to reveal his dark, well-angled face, and take the stop watch as he looks Shriner straight in the eye.

MONTERO (cont.)

. . . "Mex" isn't one of them.

As Shriner merely GRUNTS, there is suddenly the FLASH of REFLECTED LIGHT on their faces from the rear-view mirror. Simultaneously, we see two bright headlights in the distant b.g.


4      INSERT      STOP WATCH

Montero's hand clicks his thumb down on its stem, and the watch hand begins moving.


5      BACK TO TWO SHOT

MONTERO (cont.)

Boy, this one's moving some.

Shriner switches on the ignition and starts the motor.


6      LONG SHOT      EXT. ROAD      FAVORING ROLLS-ROYCE

The Rolls is barreling along at a frightening speed, and is having difficulty holding the road.

CUT TO:


7      MED. CLOSE      INT. SHERIFF'S CAR

As Shriner is yanking down the gearshift and releasing the brake, Montero stops the watch.

(CONTINUED)

7 (CONTINUED)

> MONTERO
>
> Better than ninety, and he's all
> over the road. Must be loaded or
> something. Watch yourself.

Montero presses the siren button. The Sheriff's car lurches
forward.

8      LONG SHOT        ROAD

The Sheriff's car bucks onto the concrete and burns rubber as
the Deputy pushes the accelerator to the floor. The top lights
flash red, the siren SCREAMS. Not too far behind now, the
speeding car tries to brake, and the tires WHINE agonizingly
as the car goes into a skid.

9      CLOSE SHOT       INT. SHERIFF'S CAR            (PROCESS)

Through the rear window the speeding car can be seen
swaying from side to side as the driver tries to fight the skid
and over-controls.

> MONTERO
>
> He ain't gonna make it . . .

10      FULL SHOT        SPEEDING CAR

It drops one wheel over the high concrete edge, reels as it
tries to recover, then rocks over on its side. Shrieking and
scattering sparks like a giant sparkler, it slides for fifty yards,
then rolls lazily onto its top, finally completing its turn to the
other side. It is a mess.

11      FULL SHOT        REVERSE ON SHERIFF'S CAR

It has come to a stop and is now backing quickly toward the
wreck. It comes to a halt off the road next to the wrecked car.

(CONTINUED)

11 (CONTINUED)

> Both deputies get out. Montero runs back up the road with a
> flare. Shriner moves to the car, climbs gingerly up on the side
> and starts prying open the door.

12     MED. SHOT          EXT. ROAD          FAVORING MONTERO

> He has set his flare, and is now returning toward the wreck.
> His foot kicks something metallic in the road. He picks it up
> without breaking stride.

13     MED. SHOT     REVERSE ON WRECK

> Shriner is already hauling a male body out of the car as
> Montero moves into SHOT. He helps lift the body down and lay
> it on the sand beside the road. CAMERA FOLLOWS and enables
> us to see now that the victim is a young, dark-haired boy. We
> will learn that his name is ARTURO CAMPEON.

                         SHRINER
                        (sourly)
              Mex kid. Where in hell did he get
              a car like that?

14     CLOSE SHOT     MONTERO AND ARTURO

> Montero straightens the boy's legs, and reaches into his shirt
> to feel for a heartbeat. His fingers find some Holy medallions.
> He turns over a gold St. Christopher.

15     INSERT     ST. CHRISTOPHER MEDAL

> On the back is the inscription: "ARTURO CAMPEON".

16     INTERCUTS   MONTERO AND ARTURO   SHRINER AT WRECK

> Arturo is breathing with the quick, shallow gulps of shock.
> Montero looks toward Shriner, who is stroking his hand over
> the underpinning of the wrecked car.

                              (CONTINUED)

16 (CONTINUED)

                         MONTERO
            Kid's still alive. Get a blanket, and
            radio for the ambulance.

                         SHRINER
            Look at this, will you? Chrome-
            plated underneath. You ever hear . . .

                         MONTERO
            Call an ambulance!

                         SHRINER
            I never heard of a car like this . . .

Before he can finish, Montero has risen to his feet and taken
an infuriated, menacing step toward Shriner, who takes a half-
step backward in alarm.

                         SHRINER (cont.)
            Okay . . . ! What the hell's the
            matter with you! He can wait a
            minute, can't he? I just want to
            see what kind of a car he stole . . .

Montero looks at the piece of metal he picked off the road, and
which he still holds. It's a Lady lifting her head into a strong
breeze, her clothes sailing out behind her. Montero goes back
to kneel down beside Arturo.

                         MONTERO
            I guess he stole it all right. It's a
            Rolls-Royce . . .
                    (harshly)
            . . . Call the ambulance . . . !
                    (quietly, to Arturo)
            Tough luck, Muchacho . . .
                    (face stiffens; bitterly)
            Tough luck, Mex.

                                        DISSOLVE TO:


    First, the spacing: The *scene number* is typed at 12 on the gage
bar. *Set-up directions* and *descriptive paragraphs* start at 18. *Lines of*
*spoken dialogue* start at 30 and run for no more than approximately
30 spaces (to 60)—lengths of words will necessitate some variance

here, but the difference should never be more than three or four spaces. *Parenthetical directions* in dialogue start at 37 and should run no longer than 14 or 15 spaces, as a rule. *Character names* indicating speakers of dialogue start at 44. Directions at bottoms of pages, for example (CONTINUED) and transition indicators at the finish of sequences such as (DISSOLVE TO) and (FADE OUT), start at approximately 60, though the choice is primarily aesthetic.

Directions, i.e., LONG SHOT, EXT. ROAD, NIGHT, are always in capital letters. Some writers prefer to underline the words in the direction line, but I find that an unnecessary labor. The *separation* between set-up description (LONG SHOT) and location description (EXT. ROAD) is usually 5 spaces. Time of day notation (NIGHT) is placed toward the end of the line. The positioning varies depending on the length of the time indication. LATE AFTERNOON, for instance, should be started much earlier on the line than DAY. The point is that the indication should end close to the right-hand margin. Time-of-day notation need only be indicated in the directions of the first scene of any sequence. When a location is changed or a transition (e.g., DISSOLVE) is indicated, the directions for the scene immediately following such a cut or transition should always include the time-of-day indication, even if it is the same as that of the preceding scene.

When directions are too lengthy for one line they are accommodated in the following fashion.

```
                                          INT. OFFICE
     MED. GROUP SHOT    BURT AND          LAWYERS LIBRARY
                        LAWYERS           LATE AFTERNOON
```

Second, the *line spacing:* There are two spaces between the directions, as in Scene 2, for instance, and the first line of description. The lines in the descriptive paragraphs are single-spaced, although, as shown in Scene 1, long descriptions can be broken up into short paragraphs for easier reading or to accentuate some particular action or description. These paragraphs are separated by two spaces.

*Scenes* are separated by three spaces (see end of Scene 2 and beginning of Scene 3). The same spacing is observed following transition directions such as DISSOLVE and CUT.

The dialogue speaker's name, always in CAPS, is separated from the preceding descriptive paragraphs by two spaces. *Dialogue* and *parenthetical directions* are single-spaced.

It is customary to capitalize names when they are introduced into the script. From then on, capitalization in script directions is a matter of choice.

Instead of placing the Glossary at the end of the book, as is customary, I would like to put it here so the reader will be familiar with the technical words and phrases as he continues with the following chapters. Quite a few professional writers have only a casual acquaintance with film vocabulary, but a thorough understanding of its contents is necessary for a clear communication with the script's potential readers.


GLOSSARY

**FADE IN**   The scene grows from total blackness to full exposure—usually in three or four feet of film.

**FADE OUT**   The reverse of a FADE IN. The image gradually darkens until it reaches total blackness.

**ANGLE**   One way of indicating *set-up* (the term I prefer). The term says absolutely nothing about the set-up to be used. If the scene description calls for *an angle, another angle, reverse angle*, etc., it is merely suggesting a different set-up. Such ambiguous directions are used by writers who recognize that set-ups are the director's prerogative and assume that any specific suggestions on their part will be ignored (more on this later.)

**VERY LONG SHOT, or (occasionally) V.L.S.**   The phrase is self-descriptive.

**LONG SHOT, or L.S.**   A *FULL SHOT*, showing one or more persons at full height. Obviously, the LONG SHOT can vary a great deal.

**MEDIUM LONG SHOT, or M.L.S.**   Self-descriptive, but too ambiguous for common use.

**GROUP SHOT**   A shot of many sizes, from a full shot of a group of many people, to a fairly tight shot, let us say *knee length*, of a group of three or four. It is used to indicate a shot in which the designated group is of special dramatic importance and should be isolated from others who might occupy a fuller shot.

**MEDIUM SHOT, or M.S.**   A shot of one or more persons, usually cut at about the knees.

**TWO SHOT**   A shot of two persons—size indeterminate—from waist figure to chest height.

**OVER SHOULDER, or O.S.**   A two shot which is shot over the shoulder of one of the two in the set-up and into a nearly full face of the second. It can also vary from a waist figure in which both persons are wholly on the screen to a very close O.S. in which only a slice of the cheek and a touch of the shoulder is visible.

**CLOSE SHOT, or C.S.**   Another ambiguous set-up, isolating one person, which can range from a waist figure to a "choker."

**CLOSE UP, or C.U.**   An individual, almost always chest high or higher.

**TIGHT CLOSE UP, or T.C.U.**   A close-up of the head.

**CHOKER**   A very tight close-up, usually cutting inside the chin and the hair-line.

**INSERT, or INS.**   A shot, usually close, of any inanimate object, usually the focus of someone's point of view. Letters, newspaper items, and bottles are examples of INSERTS.

**POINT OF VIEW, or POV**   A shot of anything an actor specifically looks at (usually out of shot) that we want the audience to see.

**INTERIOR, or INT.**   The *interior* of a set.

**EXTERIOR, or EXT.**   The great outdoors, whether rural or urban.

**DOLLY, or DOLLY SHOT**   Generally any movement of the camera as a whole. Also called *TRUCKING*, or *FOLLOW SHOT*, depending on the camera's movement.

**PAN SHOT**   A panoramic shot in which the camera head swings (usually slowly) from one side to the other as it follows some action, such as a football player running downfield. It can also pan across a vista. A camera can pan with an actor as he walks down a street, or it can truck with him, keeping him in relatively the same position to camera.

**WHIP PAN**   A very fast *PAN SHOT*, usually showing only a blur. Sometimes used as a transition from one cut to the next. The camera *whip pans* out of the first cut and *whip pans* into the second. The blurring effect hides the cutting point, giving the impression of one continuous shot.

**TILT**   Similar to a pan, but from bottom to top, or vice versa.

**ZOOM SHOT**   A move into or away from an object, a person, or persons by manipulating a special camera lens called a ZOOM LENS. The camera itself does not move.

**DISSOLVE**   A superimposition effect: Over a length of three or four feet (sometimes much longer) the outgoing scene fades away as the incoming scene, super-imposed, grows from nothing to full exposure. This is *not* a *fade out* and *fade in*.

**WIPE**   A form of dissolve in which one scene is *wiped* off the screen as the next is simultaneously wiped in. There are many trick forms of *wipes*. *All* dissolves are used for sequence transition.

**FREEZE FRAME**   A single frame of the film that is continued for any length of time. Occasionally used to end scenes, especially in comedy.

**MONTAGE**   A series of shots, usually without dialogue, cut together for a pictorial effect or to telescope a series of events in time.

**INTERCUTS**   Used when a scene is written as a master shot, to indicate the scene may be intercut between two or more set-ups, not indicated in the script, at the director's or cutter's pleasure.

**M.O.S.**   Without sound; silent.

**O.S.***   *Off Screen:* used for off-screen action or sound.

**V.O.**   *Voice Over:* an off-screen voice as in a narration or over a reacting close-up.

---

*The difference between O.S. (over shoulder) and O.S. (off screen) can easily be understood by the context in which they are used.

**PROCESS SHOT**   A *rear projection* or *front projection* shot. Example:
a person riding in a car with the roadside (projected onto a screen in
the B.G.) flashing by; or an interior of an office with the buildings or
action across the street projected onto a screen.
**B.G.**   Background.
**F.G.**   Foreground.

A number of terms, such as PULLS BACK, CLOSES IN, COMES
UP TO, HIGH SHOT, and FAVORING, are self-descriptive and need
no explanation.

# 2

# *In the Beginning . . .*

Skills vary—greatly. That is an obvious statement, yet an astounding number of people fail to take it into consideration when evaluating screen writers. Talent is important, of course, but most writers can also be placed into categories. For example, some writers are strong on plot contrivance but weak on character development. Others assemble groups of exciting, sometimes profound characters but can't imagine what to do with them. Some find it impossible to write a single scene from scratch but are able to flesh out a script with dramatic skill when given a solid story skeleton containing an interesting plot and honest characters. Which, obviously, is why so many films carry a multitude of screenplay credits.

A writer's particular bent will determine his approach to a script. I prefer those who start with characters and a situation. Good characters make a good film, even if the plot is rather thin. The reverse is rarely true.

Concentrating on character opens up plot possibilities to a great degree. Beginners in the field often complain about the extremely limited number of plots. That's true. So if you *start* with plot the odds are great that you will finish with a routine script. But there are as many characters to play with, to work with, and to investigate as there are people on earth. No two persons are exactly alike, not even identical twins.* When any two people get together, conflicts based on their differences in character and background are sure to arise, and *conflict*, as we shall see, is one of the most important ingredients in drama.

So, if a writer can develop a number of honest, empathetic characters (usually two or more), even a casual consideration of their areas

---

*As a matter of fact, Mark Twain wrote an interesting story bearing on that unusual situation—the conflicts of a pair of Siamese twins.

of similarities and differences will often render plot development an almost automatic procedure. Writers have frequently been quoted as saying, "The story wrote itself." Or, "The characters led—I followed." That would not have been possible if the right characters had not first been developed.

An aside: One of the reasons it was easier to write good scripts during Hollywood's golden era is that screenplays were often written, or stories selected, for *real* stars—players whose screen personalities established, or greatly modified, the characters in the script. In the film *Gone With the Wind*, Rhett Butler was not the character of the novel, but rather a more exciting Clark Gable. William Powell and Myrna Loy greatly enhanced the pleasure of *The Thin Man*. Humphrey Bogart made Captain Queeg live and breathe, and *Casablanca* might have been quite ordinary without Bogart and Bergman. Given Gary Cooper, the screenplay for *Mr. Deeds Goes to Town* was undoubtedly easier to write than if it had been fashioned for "Richard Roe."

Samuel Goldwyn is reported to have said, "Nobody walks out on a film in the first fifteen minutes." He meant, of course, that a film could enjoy a leisurely pace while it established the story's characters. To at least some extent that was true at a time when film viewers were not quite as sophisticated as they are today, but it is true no longer. Modern practice encourages us to grab the viewer as quickly as possible. This can be accomplished through a scene of action, of confrontation, or through the presentation of an unusual character or a pictorially effective incident.

The film *Crossfire* begins with a very short fight, seen only in shadow and lasting no more than a minute, but in this short time a man is murdered. In *Murder, My Sweet,* the camera simply moves in on a hot light, of the sort used in police interrogations, as the title cards roll on the screen. As the credits end we become aware of the off-screen questioning, and the camera pulls back to reveal the characters and the setting, a police department office. *Mirage* opens on a shot of an early evening New York skyline. A tall skyscraper dominates the scene. As the credits end, the background scene holds for a brief moment, then all the building's lights go out simultaneously. We cut to shots of dark corridors and their confused inhabitants, and the film is off and running.

A film can still open casually with character or background establishment, but the sooner you capture the viewer the more effectively you can manipulate him during the rest of the film—unless, of course, you've expended your total measure of cleverness on the first few minutes.

The overwhelming majority of stories are based on a *need*, a *problem*, an unusual *situation*, or all three of these elements combined. An easily understood example would be the average private eye melodrama. The *problem* is usually the commission of a crime—homicide, robbery, kidnapping, or a mysterious disappearance. The *need* is to solve the problem—to clear the innocent, to catch the killer, the thief, or the blackmailer, to recover the missing person or the loot. The *situations* are developed to set up *conflict*, to deepen the mystery and/or suspense, and to give the protagonist "man-size" obstacles to conquer. (If it is too easy it is not dramatic.)

There are, of course, more subtle and more powerful needs: the need to eliminate a physical or social danger, the need for love, for money, for success, for power, for self-fulfillment. These are often the burden of the subplot. The *satisfaction* of the need is usually delayed until the film's conclusion but, if it is achieved early in the story, *obstacles* must be created to delay its free use and enjoyment. Occasionally, the satisfaction of a need itself becomes the primary obstacle in the film and furnishes the material for its plot and character development. (See any "Three Wishes" story.)

A close relative of the latter is the "what if?" plot. A perfect example of this genre is the old, episodic film entitled *If I Had A Million*. The title says it all. Each of a number of randomly selected characters is given one million dollars—no strings attached—by an anonymous donor. The film's episodes are concerned with the manner in which the recipients survive the shock and conquer or fall victim to the problems growing out of such a windfall.

But *need* is undoubtedly the most common, the most useful, the most malleable, and the most easily understood and accepted basis for a story. A few examples will serve to clarify the concept. In *The African Queen* two completely diverse personalities are forced to ride the length of a dangerous African river in a dilapidated boat—that is the *situation*. Their *need* is twofold: first, to leave the territory, which is being occupied by the enemy, and second, to blow up the German gunboat at the end of their journey. The *conflict* is also twofold: first, that of two diametrically opposed characters, and second, their battles with the perils of the journey. By the end of the film they have conquered the *situation*, fulfilled their *needs*, and resolved both their physical and their personality *conflicts*.

*The Treasure of the Sierra Madre* is a much more complicated film, with more characters and more basic situations. But its one premise (and subplot) is the Biblical phrase, "Love of money is the root of all evil." The *need*, the *problem*, and the *situation* are all inherent in that one sentence; the story depends almost entirely on the development, the conflicts, and the relationships of the three oddly assorted characters and their *need* for, and love of, money.

None of these basic elements needs to be made clear at the film's beginning. With this in mind, let us analyze the four and a half opening pages of *Act of Anger*, as written in Chapter 1.

First, the "grabber." The opening scene is designed to precede the Main Title and the credits. It is written to be specifically pictorial—a montage—yet interesting to the *reader*. All the necessary action is spelled out, but breaking it up into set-ups might upset the reader's concentration and diminish the scene's dramatic impact. Although it is written to catch and hold the reader's attention, the language is simple and direct. This is one of the main differences between the novel and the screenplay. The material should be made as interesting as possible but circumlocution, fussiness, and embellishment should be avoided. The goal is to establish a reading pace that will closely match the eventual pace of the film.

The figures in the opening scene are kept purposely indistinct. We must comprehend the action, yet conceal the identities of the combatants. Although the viewer cannot at this point place either character into any definite plot context, the *situation* is vital enough to command his complete attention and to stimulate his interest. A preliminary *problem* has been set, though no immediate *need* has been established.

The rest of the sequence (scenes 2 through 16) develops the introductory situation and brings it to a quick conclusion. We know it will catapult us into the primary *problem* of the story. To avoid a drop in interest, it is possible that scenes of the car, barreling through the moon-lit countryside, could be incorporated into the background of the title cards.

The reader will notice that the script directions throughout the sequence describe the action in detail and indicate all the necessary basic set-ups. In other words, it could be shot as written. Any changes made by the director will be determined by the character of the location, the car-wrecking stunt (which can never be accurately foreseen), and possibly by his collaboration with the actors. (The "intercuts" indicated for scene 16 are completely at the director's discretion, since the need for them depends on his staging of the scenes.) The instructions, though "simple and direct," are written with as much style as possible with an eye to making the reading flow smoothly from direction to dialogue and back to direction again.

It is important to note two special features of the sequence, since they concern techniques which I will bring to the reader's attention time and again. Even though the deputies involved in this sequence are minor characters and only one of them will be seen again, time and effort are taken to develop them as fully as possible and this development is basically indirect.

Feature one: the *character*. One of the chief weaknesses of many scripts is the short shrift given the minor characters. Comments like "one dimensional human beings," or "cardboard characters," are perhaps the most common phrases seen in critical reviews. Any character who deserves to appear in a film deserves to be a "person." Only a little thought or effort is required to make him one. For instance, a ticket dispenser, whom we see only briefly as she delivers a customer's ticket and accepts his money, can be given some individual mannerism, a short remark, or an unusual reaction. She might, for instance, warn a customer that the film he is about to see lacks quality. That action alone establishes her as "someone," but the manner in which she delivers her message can tell us a good deal more. Does she say, "You may be disappointed" or "Save your money" or "It stinks"? Any of these expressions may get her fired, but she will be fired as a "person," not as a uniformed automaton. The more "persons" you have in your film, the more believable and acceptable it will be.

Feature two: development, or *exposition*. Overt exposition is another of a screenplay's great sins. All screen writers are aware of this, yet the sin is committed over and over again.

At the risk of beating a dead horse, let me make this clear. If a character must be established as a twenty-four-year-old Stanford graduate, married to a flashy blonde who is the daughter of the local banker, you cannot (or should not) write dialogue for the town's gossip which says, "Oh, he's about twenty-four, you know, with a Ph.D. from Stanford. He's married to the daughter of L.Q. Jordan, the banker. She's wealthy, of course, but intellectually far beneath him." This gives us a lot of information in a hurry, but oh, how dull! The same facts can be brought out, though less concisely, in more interesting, more cinematic ways. Most, if not all, of the information can be delivered in dramatic (or comic) scenes which will allow the viewer to make his own deductions and involve him more completely with the characters and the film. The sequence under consideration in this chapter furnishes us with an apt example.

Scene 3, which shows two unfamiliar deputies in a police car, could be dull; in this instance it is rendered interesting because we know a murder has been committed and police action is an anticipated part of the sequence, though the nature of that action cannot be assumed. The scene gives us time to introduce the deputies while building some suspense in anticipation of their confrontation with the speeding car.

. . . Montero raises a finger for each of the following names.

MONTERO
(quietly)
Deputy . . . Sheriff . . . Juan . . .
Alonzo . . . Montero. That's five
names to pick from . . .

> Only now does Montero sit upright, raise his hat to reveal his
> dark, well-angled face, and take the stop watch as he looks
> Shriner straight in the eye.
>
>                         MONTERO (cont.)
>                 . . . "Mex" isn't one of them.
>
> As Shriner merely GRUNTS,                    (and the scene continues.)

To begin with, "Hey, Mex. . .," the cue for Montero's answer,
is hardly standard modern behavior, and it allows Montero to deliver
*his* information in nonstandard fashion. Further, his speech is split
by a detailed direction instead of a simple "Montero sits upright." As
written, the directions give the actors and the director a good deal
more to work with. It is quite likely that these artists would come
up with the playing as suggested in the writer's directions on their
own; but if you're a conscientious writer, why take a chance?

However, the real purpose of this part of scene 3, its subplot as
some theorists might say, is not to identify one character by name
but to establish, lightly but definitely, the social environment of the
story—a milieu which will be essential to the film. Even though the
locale is not identified, it is immediately apparent that it is not a
friendly one for a Mexican, especially a Mexican who has just committed murder.

Another key aspect of the scene is that the information is given
through *conflict*. This word, this concept, appears again and again in
every dramatic form—man against man, man against nature, good
against evil, or even bad against worse. It pervades stories, sequences,
and scenes, whether in straight drama, melodrama, or comedy. In our
example, the information we have received so far—the murder and,
more positively, the identification of the locale's social environment—is delivered through conflict, whether active, in protest,
or subliminal.

The sequence continues in a riveting short scene of action—the
accident. Note that the car crash is not gratuitous but is brought about
through the intervention of the police car in its effort to prevent one.

After the crash the sequence is once more played against a background of conflict engendered by Shriner's callous disregard of the
injured driver as he finds the damaged car of greater interest than the
damaged driver. Montero's demands for help reach near physical confrontation before Shriner will pay attention to his job. Then Montero's
discovery of the boy's Mexican origin alerts us sharply to the difficulties and problems that lie ahead.

So here we have set up a *situation*, established at least part of a
*problem*, both physical and social, and in the first five minutes of the

film we have peopled it with exceptional characters who cannot help but set the tone for those who are yet to come.

The social environment is of major importance here since it sets up a conflict situation that will underlie the entire story. (In brief, the script's chief protagonist is a WASP lawyer who must confront the local ethnic attitudes and his own unwilling client [Arturo] while he plays detective in order to unravel the real reasons behind the boy's behavior and his crime.)

Bart Spicer, the author of the novel, is a master at creating conflict. His novel's theme—hero versus the rest of the world—is not unfamiliar, but his sharply defined characters and skillfully contrived situations made adaptation essentially a job of intelligent editing. Unfortunately, such is not always the case. Few good screen writers alter or invent needlessly—when they do, it is because there is little *cinematic* quality in the original work, and getting it into the script is their responsibility. That, and making certain that a novelist's description, or a playwright's exposition through dialogue, of inner character is communicated through the more pictorial technique of "action and reaction."

# 3

# *Who?*

A few—a very few—writers seem to have an inborn awareness of the nature of human character. Most of us have to study it and to learn about it through experience. A really good writer is an expert observer. Everything and everybody, whether routinely dull or exotically bizarre, is worthy of his attention. He will note and accumulate for future use odd or unusual names; he will also collect odd or unusual characters. But his greatest talent is his ability to scrutinize, without appearing to do so, *all* facets of human behavior, no matter how mundane some might seem to be. The ordinary behavior in one situation or environment may be totally eccentric in another. He will try to puzzle out the hidden implications of usual or unusual reactions, knowing that his conclusions will have little validity unless he can also read the reactors.

Curiosity and a talent for intelligent observation do not in themselves guarantee proper analysis and understanding of people. To develop such abilities a writer should study psychology, anthropology, sociobiology, and as many more of the behavioral sciences as he can accommodate. He should try to acquire a working knowledge of the genetic and the environmental influences on human personality and behavior. (Knowing a little about the behavior of other animals can't hurt, either.) Some writers have studied these areas formally, and most *good* writers continue to study them throughout their working lives; but too many average authors depend solely on their own "unerring instincts" in their delineation of the human psyche.

One of the things a film can do to perfection (although it rarely does) is to develop an honest, objective character. That is never the character as he would see himself nor, for that matter, as most others would see him—which is why it is so difficult to establish a character accurately through dialogue alone, either through the character's expressed opinions of himself or the articulated opinions of those around him. The average person finds it difficult, if not impossible, to view himself objectively. Subjectively, he is usually an olio of insecurity and daring, of buried failures and exaggerated successes, of bitter disappointments and high hopes, of self-blame and self-praise. No man is a hero to his wife or to himself nor, whatever the world says, does any honest woman consider herself another Helen of Troy.

All that is from the inside. But it is almost as difficult to view a person with true objectivity from the outside. How many first impressions have been eventually reversed! Since there is no such thing as a completely neutral standard, we judge others on the basis of *our* criteria, not theirs. To add to the problem, it is difficult to know what goes on *inside* that outside. Few people wear their hearts on their sleeves. Most put up a front—not always a totally false one— but the tough boss may be a pussy cat at home, and the sanctimonious do-gooder a nocturnal prowler.

"Bad" characters are easier to write than "good" ones, which is why gangster movies and film noire usually rate better reviews and greater box office than a *Little Lord Fauntleroy*. Most of us relate to a touch of evil, and it is indicative of viewers' tastes that the road to stardom has traditionally been trod by film heavies. Wally Beery, Clark Gable, James Cagney, Edward G. Robinson, Richard Widmark, and Humphrey Bogart, to name only a few, followed the crooked road to fame. Actors and actresses with a bit of the devil in them have always carried the greatest appeal for the general public. In *A Streetcar Named Desire*, Stanley Kowalski was hardly a role model but he made Marlon Brando a star. It may be a sad commentary on the human animal, but the good person, however praiseworthy, has always been considered a bit dull; whereas the moral, ethical, and legal rebel has always, even when hateful, captured the popular imagination. Al Capone has a place in American history, but no one remembers the name of the man who put him in jail. Few people, even in Russia, can identify the Metropolitan of the Orthodox Church; but Rasputin is known to everybody, and more for his faults than for his many great qualities.

All this can be explained as identification with, or admiration for, those with courage enough to break society's rules, many of which are irksome to most of us. On the whole, the average citizen is much more cynical today than he was in the Victorian era. Since most good writers are aware of this response, they color their characters some shade of gray rather than dead black or pure white. Remembering this as you develop your characters can help you to people your script with credible and empathetic personalities.

I often mention "honest" characters. By that I mean characters who are true to human nature, not ethically or morally blameless. If a character on the screen does, or says, something completely unbelievable—*for that character*—you lose touch with the viewer, often for the rest of the film. We do not expect a successful doctor to rob a bank, the contented husband to beat his wife (or vice versa), or a good, healthy Catholic to consider suicide. And yet . . .

Now and then a doctor *does* commit murder, an athlete risks his honor and his reputation by indulging in gambling or drugs, a wife shoots her beloved husband, and Scrooge suddenly exudes the milk of human kindness.* Such startling transitions in character behavior are indispensable to dramatic structure, but they must be made understandable, believable, and acceptable, no matter how unexpected, how surprising, they may seem at the moment. The viewer will always insist on asking, "Why?"

Just how does one convince the viewer that an honest character can honestly undergo a completely uncharacteristic transformation? One could, of course, introduce mind-altering drugs. Spy and sci-fi films have made this ploy acceptable and quite familiar, but it places the characters and their behavior outside the average viewer's experience and is therefore of limited value.** However, one mind-altering drug has been in general use from time immemorial—alcohol—and its application to character subversion in films is almost as common as its use. Everyone accepts that even the most pedestrian, sane, and law-abiding person may behave erratically when "under the influence." A character need not be a confirmed alcoholic to commit a crime or throw away a career or a happy marriage; a single night's spree can change his life and the lives of those around him irrevocably.

Alcohol-induced transformations are not always negative in character, especially in comedy. In *City Lights*, Chaplin's wealthy friend and benefactor became a benign and benevolent human being *only* when drunk. But most character changes are of a different order, and the only way to make them acceptable to the viewer is to prepare him for them, so that the unexpected, when it appears, is also "honest." Such preparation usually consists of bits of information showing subtly different behavior—an ambivalent remark or an off-beat decision, for instance—and it must be delicately engineered. As a rule (though not always) the viewer should not be aware that he is being conditioned to accept a change. An old dramatic axiom, "Inevitable but not obvious," works here. The transition should be largely unanticipated but, when it is disclosed, the viewer should think, "Of course! I should have known he would do that. Why didn't I see it?" Actually, as in a good detective story, the clues were there, but they were so cunningly

---

*At least three of these items have been reported in the news within the last few weeks of this book's writing.

**This stratagem originated long before modern science fiction. *Dr. Jekyll and Mr. Hyde* is an apt example.

incorporated into the drama that he accepted them as entities in their own right rather than as developmental sign posts.

Before we can deal with character changes, however, we must have distinct characters. These can be developed in a number of ways. One is by class. Classes still exist—even in the United States and even in the so-called classless societies of the socialist "republics." The truth is that a classless person is a nonperson; and, although classes tend more and more to lose their sharply defined edges, especially in the industrialized societies, it is still possible for John Le Carre to write about a present-day English public school teacher: "If it is vulgar to wear a pencil in the breast pocket of your jacket, to favour Fair Isle pullovers and brown ties, to bob a little, then Rode, beyond a shadow of doubt, was vulgar, for though he did not commit these sins, his manner implied them all."* (Of course, this also says something about the person making the observation.)

Le Carre here is describing class through clothes and manner. Very subtle and very true. He is also describing a snob, who is rarely a person of an elite class but usually a person of a lesser caste trying to behave as he believes the elitist behaves—and doing a bad job of it.

In this area the writer must be especially careful to avoid stereotyping. Exaggeration of class symbols results in caricature. But subtle coloration is most effective, and a complete character can hardly be realized without attention to class traits. The more skillfully they are developed the more believable are your characters.

Class characterization is a technique at which many American screen writers fail. They have been conditioned to believe that no such thing exists in the United States, and that if there are vestiges of it, they are necessarily bad and hardly worth their notice. Neither of these suppositions is true, and every intelligent author has learned to investigate class practices and attitudes to the fullest degree. Unfortunately, too many screen writers give them only passing and simplistic consideration.

Dress styles, male and female, are also potent character indicators. These are of routine value when used as passive reminders of a period, but they can gain added importance when used in an active manner. Dress modes can be changed—and not simply for camouflage, but in a serious attempt at personality alteration. The cliché, of course, is the mousey country girl who is given the total treatment in a fashion boutique and emerges a glamor queen. But, in a deeper vein, the *manner* in which a character goes about trying to change his *exterior* personality can give us an insight into his *interior* personality. *Characteristics* usually match *character*, and when a conscious attempt is

*John Le Carre, *A Murder of Quality*, Signet Books.

made to change them, some upheaval in the psyche is strongly indicated. Such variations of established traits can be used to alert the viewer to more dramatic developments to come.

The ease, or lack of it, with which a character wears a costume can also be a vivid indicator of character. This device has been frequently used in comedy (for instance, the squirming of a Huckleberry Finn accustomed to wearing overalls when he is forced to don his Sunday best), but it can also be employed effectively in every dramatic area. As do most of the things we have been discussing, it *shows* the viewer rather than telling him about it. Most people accept what they see much more readily than what they hear.

Attention to class mannerisms and the style of dress can be of more value in establishing a character's background than taking the easy way through dialogue or flashback. And actors will welcome the challenge and the opportunity to enrich their roles.

Another vein which rewards working is the description of a character's *immediate* milieu. The kind of quarters a person lives in, their state of order or disorder, the quality and taste of the home's adornment, are all signs which carry cinematic potential. Does your protagonist hang classics on his walls or centerfolds? If he is rich and can afford to display originals, are they good or are they tripe, avant garde or traditional? If he is poor and can afford only magazine reproductions, what is the quality of their contents? As you can see, the milieu can indicate character and financial state without a word of dialogue.

It can be said that this, too, is in the director's domain, something for him to take up with his art director or production designer. And so it is. But, as a director, I confess I miss a point here or there—so does the art director, the writer, and the actor. If we pool our varied skills at character analysis, each indicating his point of view in his own terms, we should arrive at a much more complete character than any one of us might create alone. At this particular stage of the game, "input", since it in no way pressures the director, is all to the good.

One of the more obvious means of establishing characterization is through dialogue—not so much by what the characters say as by how they say it, the words they use, the facility with which they use them, their grammar, and their tendency to veil the truth or to disclose it. However, film dialogue places a few constraints on the writer; it is not easy to come by.

Dialogue provides story information, reflects background, occupation, education, individuality, and attitude. All this is clear enough. The problems are not so much with the conception of the dialogue as with how it is written. The first requirement of a good "speech" is that it should have a natural flavor—natural for the person speaking it—and that it appear to be spontaneous. But because it is necessarily written, it often has a literary construction; and because it is usually edited and polished, sometimes endlessly, it can wind up sounding just like what it is—preconceived and prepared. Unless the dialogue is corrected on the set, it will develop artificial characters, characters who speak like the actors they are rather than the human beings they should be.

Unless one is creating a pompous pedant, the trick is to use a relatively small and simple vocabulary. Most scripts do very well with a pool of no more than a few thousand words, most of them monosyllabic and of Anglo-Saxon derivation. After all, the goal is to *reach* the viewer, not confuse him.

There are a few pitfalls to avoid: Except for a few simple question-and-answer exchanges ("Where is she?" "She just left for Philadelphia"), dialogue should avoid direct exposition, though indirection should not be pushed to the point of ridiculousness. Lines should not be too choppy—a technique sometimes used in a mistaken effort to establish a rapid pace—nor should they be too long. An overextended line can usually be broken up into a two-way exchange between the speaker and the listener that will sustain interest through variety without diminishing the value of the speaker's words. The following is an example of such a rearrangement.*

> HENRY
> I haven't done anything about it,
> but this letter has sat on my desk
> reminding me. It seems so silly,
> doesn't it, that I can trust Sarah
> absolutely not to read it, though
> she comes in here a dozen times
> a day, yet I can't trust————She's
> out for a walk now—a walk,
> Bendrix. . . .

He breaks off with a gesture of despair.

> BENDRIX
> I'm sorry.

> HENRY
> They always say, don't they, that
> a husband is the last person to
> know——

*From Lenore Coffee's script of *End of the Affair*, based on the novel by Graham Greene. A more complete analysis of this scene will be found in Book IV, Chapter 14.

                        (thrusts letter
                        toward Bendrix)
                Read it, Bendrix.

Bendrix takes the letter with no inkling of its contents, and
increasing surprise as he reads it aloud.

                        BENDRIX
                        (reading)
                'In reply to your inquiry, I would
                suggest you employ the services
                of a fellow called Savage, 159 Vigo
                Street. From all reports he has
                the reputation of being both able
                and discreet———'
                        (he reads on a bit,
                        then looks up,
                        genuinely startled)
                You mean that you want a
                private detective to follow Sarah?
                        (Henry nods)
                Really, Henry, you surprise me.
                One of His Majesty's most
                respected Civil Servants . . .
                        (Bendrix looks
                        incredulous)
                Funny—I imagined your mind
                was as neatly creased as your
                trousers.


A reworking of the above excerpt produces the following:

Henry thrusts the letter toward Bendrix.

                        HENRY
                Read it, Bendrix.

Bendrix takes the letter with no inkling of its contents. He
reads it aloud with increasing surprise.

                        BENDRIX
                        (reading)
                'In reply to your inquiry, I would
                suggest you employ the services

of a fellow called Savage, 159 Vigo
Street. From all reports he has
the reputation of being both able
and discreet———'
> (he reads on a
> bit, then looks
> up, startled)

HENRY
I haven't done anything about it,
but this letter has sat on my desk
reminding me. It seems so silly,
doesn't it, that I can trust Sarah
absolutely not to read it, though
she comes in here a dozen times
a day, and yet I can't trust———
She's out for a walk now—a walk,
Bendrix . . .

He breaks off with a gesture of despair.

BENDRIX
You mean *you* want a private
detective to follow Sarah?

HENRY
They always say, don't they, that
a husband is the last person to
know———

BENDRIX
Really, Henry, you surprise me.
One of his Majesty's most
respected Civil Servants . . .
> (Bendrix looks
> incredulous)
Funny—I imagined your mind
was as neatly creased as your
trousers.

(End of excerpt)


Introspective lines, i.e., a person talking to himself, should be
avoided at all costs; walking into a church for a one-way conversation
with God is not really an improvement. Repetition, for example:

> SPEAKER A
>
> I'm buying a car.
>
> SPEAKER B
>
> You're buying a car?
>
> SPEAKER A
>
> Yes, I'm buying a new car.

should also be avoided. This may seem rather silly, but I can't remember the number of times this ploy has been used to pad out a skimpy scene.

By long odds, the two most common sins are stiltedness, a literary quality incurred in the act of writing, and a sameness of expression, the result of the writer's inability to put himself into a character's being. In too many scripts the lines are obviously the writer's, not the character's. But a professor rarely speaks like the average bill collector, and a Pennsylvania steel worker expresses himself somewhat differently from an archbishop, though not necessarily less intelligently. A politician has a gobble-de-gook all his own and a mastery of buzz words few others can match.

In the average script most dialogue consists of straight, complete sentences, and the average actor will read them just like that. But in real life few people can organize their spontaneous thoughts that clearly or that grammatically. (I still hear supposedly well-trained and well-educated newscasters say, "between you and I.") So, a thorough effort should be made to write lines that fit each character, both in language used and in the manner of their utterance. For instance, a character might find a thought difficult to express because the appropriate words do not come easily to mind; his lines should be broken up to give him time for thought between phrases, and short repetitions may be supplied to imply self-correction or modification. Such characteristics would vary with each character as well as the particular thought that character is trying to express *spontaneously.*

The mastery of individual habits of speech is best achieved by listening to the real thing; and while a writer is studying people's behavior he should never forget to attune his ear to their *speech patterns.*

I am not referring to dialect. Dialect is almost impossible to write and, in view of the continuing battle against ethnic stereotyping, very dangerous. Lines meant to be spoken in dialect, whether in American or foreign idiom, should *always* be written straight. The dialect itself should be left to the actor—that is one of his skills, or should be. Those actors who cannot "do" dialect will be the first to tell you so. And where dialect is important to the character, the actor should be cast with that in mind. In the meantime, the greatest favor a writer can render the director (and himself) is to merely indicate the dialect desired and let it go at that.

Speech *patterns* are another matter. Though these, too, are often created on the set, it can do no harm, and might do a deal of good, to create them in the script. Recently I watched yet another rerun of *The Maltese Falcon.* I was struck (once more) by the amazingly effective delineation of Gutman (played by Sydney Greenstreet), achieved largely through speech patterns. I immediately went to the book. Here is what I found.

> Page 364—"We begin well, sir," the fat man purred, turning with a proffered glass in hand. "I distrust a man that says when. . . ."

> Spade—"I like to talk."
> Gutman—"Better and better! I distrust a close-mouthed man. . . . We'll get along, sir, that we will."

> "And I'll tell you right out that I'm a man who likes talking to a man who likes to talk."

> "You're the man for me, sir, a man cut along my own lines. . . . I like that way of doing business."

> Page 365—"That's wonderful, sir. That's wonderful. I do like a man who tells you right out he's looking out for himself."

> Page 375—"By Gad, sir, you're a chap worth knowing, an amazing character."

> Page 417—Gutman said fondly: "By Gad, sir, you're a character!"

> Page 426—"By Gad, sir, I believe you would. I really do. You're a character, sir, if you don't mind my saying so."

The excerpted lines, written by Dashiell Hammett, were transferred to the script verbatim. Spoken by an ordinary character they would have been stuffy and stilted, but they were perfect for the man Greenstreet was capable of playing. What intelligent producer, director, or adapter would care, or dare, to change lines like these—and what filmmaker, on reading them, could fail to *see* the character.

There is one creative right of which the writer is rarely deprived—the right to fashion a perfect scene. But screen writers rarely take the time (or are not allowed it) to develop effective speech mannerisms, except those of the most ordinary kind. They should try it more often.

Minor characteristics can also be a useful addition to the script, not only because of what they say about a character, but because many of them have become a part of folklore's common knowledge and are readily accepted by the viewer. For instance, a thoughtful, relaxed type smokes a pipe or knits a sweater; a tense, jittery type smokes cigarettes or chews his finger nails. A studious type wears glasses, a *funny* studious type wears *thick* glasses, and a vain type keeps them in his pocket until forced to use them, then he does so with a gesture of apologetic irritation.

You could, of course, show the nervous, jittery type smoking a pipe, but you would have to go to some length to make him believable; the stereotype would be accepted out of hand. Obviously, these are only starters, and shopworn, but the category is a lengthy one. Does she or he wear a hat, does she wear gloves when shopping, polish her toenails? Does he wear sandals or Gucci loafers? Does he like cats and/or dogs, or does he detest them both? How does he treat or react to a friend's baby? Once aware of the possibilities, one sees they are endless. It pays to remember this grab bag when you are working out your characters.

On a deeper level there is the possibility of establishing (indirectly) whether a behavior pattern has been influenced by genetic factors or by the environment. Psychologists continue to debate the relative importance of these two factors, but a writer is free to be dogmatic—to take the bull by the horns.

A few characteristics are fairly obvious. Intelligence is genetic; the opportunity to develop and use it optimally is environmental. A dialect is unquestionably a product of environment and, just because it can place him so specifically in a recognizably undesirable background, a character at some point in his life might be forced by genetic imperatives to change his manner of speech. Much more commonly, environmental imperatives such as economic pressures or a desire for self-improvement bring about the same decision. Though the dialect may be environmental, the gestures and phrasing accompanying it would most likely be hereditary. Certain basic traits such as self-control and a realistic or romantic outlook would probably have genetic origins, but political and social attitudes would unquestionably be the result of environmental pressures.

Personality traits are an important part of character development, especially when cinematically treated. Degrees of honesty, of shyness, of hypocrisy, of insecurity, are most effectively disclosed not by a person's private or public behavior, but by the *differences* between the two as captured by the camera. It is dramatically useful to understand that a person's genetic make-up may be incompatible with his environment, which presents another source of conflict—a conflict within the character himself.

Everything relating to character development applies to *all* characters, good and bad, major and minor. It is of prime importance that the antagonist(s) in any story be as well developed, as strong, as the protagonist(s). There is little drama in the conquest of a straw-man or the destruction of a tissue-paper situation. The creation of a strong "heavy" and of difficult obstacles make it easier to write more interesting and more powerful scenes.

Finally, two things must be borne in mind. First, no character in a film should lay himself psychologically bare (a most unnatural and uncommon occurrence): The film should do it for him by creating scenes of crisis, in reaction to which he unconsciously or unavoidably exposes his true self. In comedy, a self-professed hero panics when confronted by a baby bear. In serious drama, the manner in which a mother receives and accepts the news of an offspring's accidental death will tell us a great deal about her. Does she scream? Does she faint? Does she refuse to believe? Does she rant at God, or accept the Divine Will? Does she retreat or step forward to meet the situation? Does she think first of herself, of her husband, or of her other offspring? And how much time is involved in any of these reactions (very important)? Though the crisis remains the same, the *reactions* to it will decidedly change or color the character we thought we knew.

Almost every sequence in a film is in one way or another an opportunity—an obligation—to develop the story's characters—characters who need not say one word in self-analysis, nor require the verbal analysis of others in the film. This is where a film can shine, if you will permit it. A reaction to an unexpected crisis, even a small one like a toaster breaking down, will give us an honest glimpse into an honest person, while a two-minute opinion delivered by a character in the film tells us little that is verifiably true. It only forces us to examine the observer's motives, his observational ability, and his honesty. Such dialogue is, of course, useful in that context.

Second, character development is a *gradual*, continuing operation. We need not (indeed, I believe we should not) fully develop either our characters or our backgrounds in the first half hour of our film. On the contrary, our backgrounds should be seen only as our characters move through them or pause in them, and our characters need not be *fully* exposed or completely understood until the film's climactic scenes are played. Becoming acquainted with our people, sequence by sequence, is what keeps a film truly alive. It also makes it easier to write solid scenes with interesting and surprising exposures of both character and plot.

# 4

# *See How They Grow*

Whether you are inspired by a character, a concept, or a situation, sooner or later you will have to develop a story. You believe you have something to say and an extended anecdote just won't do. Every good film is built on an idea, and on the film-maker's desire to develop that idea into a film which will communicate it to as many others as he can possibly reach.

Most filmmakers are preachers, in a way. Whether through comedy, action, or drama, each has a message he wants to deliver. Those zany comedians, the Marx Brothers, spent their careers caricaturing high society (personified in Margaret Dumont) and got rich doing it. Charles Chaplin became the world's most recognizable figure by dramatizing society's "forgotten man." On the other hand, filmmakers like Griffith, Murnau, Ford, Capra, Renoir, and a good many others worked the more somber part of the spectrum. But, whatever they had to say, whether as simple as exhorting children to eat their spinach, or as difficult of realization as suggesting that people love one another, the message was always delivered entertainingly—that is, the film carrying the message had to engross the viewer. To do that, they were compelled to wrap their concepts in engrossing *stories*.

The development of a story usually depends on one of a limited number of tried and true plots; and its interest and attractiveness will depend on how skillfully the tried and true (and old hat) plot can, like a drab recipe, be camouflaged by exotic spices and sauces carefully and cleverly introduced.

One of the simplest but, when properly done, one of the most appealing and applicable plot forms is the "disaster" story. This is an old lode indeed; but though the vein has from time to time appeared to be completely worked out, some ingenious "prospector" always brings it back to pulsating life. Strange as it may seem, the disaster story depends far more on character than it does on the disaster itself. And whether that disaster takes place in only a few moments, as in *The Poseiden Adventure*, or remains a threat throughout the entire story, as in *Towering Inferno*, the overwhelmingly dominant element is the *behavior of the characters* in response to its effects, and in that area the writer has full freedom to function.

With only a little extrapolation, the disaster plot can serve as a basis for much more serious films. In *The Caine Mutiny*, for instance, the disaster is the U.S.S. CAINE itself and its maverick crew, whose crisis-provoking proclivities can unhinge any but the most stable of commanding officers.

To go somewhat further afield, even a "love story" quickly establishes some disaster, usually an emotional one—a misunderstanding, a social obstacle, or a moral problem—which presents those essential building blocks, *conflict* or *confrontation* and *conciliation* or *resolution*, usually in increasing order of difficulty, until all facets of the original disaster are cleared up and swept away to the satisfaction of the characters in the film and the viewer watching it.

A conscientious and able writer (two adjectives which do not always keep company) will, after establishing a playable situation, try to be as ingenious, as creative, as "different" as he can possibly be— *within the limits* of honesty and believability. And that's the rub, the occasion for brain-beating and long hours of torturous labor. If a woman walking down Fifth Avenue is suddenly confronted by a boa constrictor, you have a "different" scene; but it would most likely be a source of a guffaw rather than excitement, unless it could be made believable. And the effect would hardly be worth the effort.

As a director, given an acceptable plot and characters, I always spent the greatest amount of time and concentration trying to make each sequence and scene come alive—not only during the reworking of the script but throughout the shooting of the film, and in the cutting room. I would worry the setting, the movement, the dialogue, the motives, and the nature of the confrontations within each scene. I would search for the essential elements that might have been overlooked in the writing or lost in the rewriting. Occasionally, I would find one. It is nearly impossible to uncover all the useful aspects of a scene in the writing (or even in the realization or the editing), but one must always try. Given two writers of equal talent, the one who *never* gives up or takes the easy way out in a difficult situation will always create the better scripts.

It is difficult to analyze a story as a whole, except in the most general sense, so we will examine the various aspects of story development one segment at a time. First, let us analyze an adaptation in which theme, conflict, and character development are accomplished in a compact and "surprising" manner.

Our example is a short sequence from *The Young Lions*, a film I made at Twentieth Century Fox in 1957. In this particular scene, Noah Ackerman (Montgomery Clift), who has fallen in love with Hope Plowman (Hope Lange), comes to a small Vermont town to meet Hope's father. It is necessary to note that the last time we saw Hope and Noah together they had just met and, after making a complete fool of himself, Noah had fallen hopelessly in love. (See Chapter 9.) An extended sequence of Christian's encounter with a belligerent French girl, in occupied Paris, has intervened between these two scenes.

In the novel, this sequence occupies nine full pages and requires a reading time of seven or eight minutes (at a moderately fast pace). The contents and impressions in those nine pages are here summarized, then compared; first, with the original screenplay (not Irwin Shaw's, but written for our film), and second, with the filmed sequence as it appeared on the screen.

Chapter 11 starts:

> The train rattled slowly along between the drifts and the white hills of Vermont. Noah sat at the frosted window, with his overcoat on, shivering because the heating system of the car had broken down. He stared out at the slowly changing, forbidding, scenery, gray in the cloudy wastes of the Christmas dawn.

The paragraphs go on to describe the crowded train, the failure of the heating system, and the resulting day's growth of beard on Noah's face. His ebbing confidence is noted, as is a wild impulse to get off the train and head back to New York.

We learn that Hope has preceded him by two days to tell her father that she was getting married—and to a Jew. There is some material on his occupational training efforts, his feeling of guilt because of his 4-F status in the draft, then a description of Hope's father as a

> . . . . devout churchgoer, a hard-bitten Presbyterian elder, rooted stubbornly all his life in this harsh section of the world, and she would not marry without his consent.

He arrives at his station, where Hope, alone, is waiting for him.

> Then Hope hurried up to him. Her face was wan and disturbed. She didn't kiss him. She stopped three feet away from him. "Oh, my, Noah," she said, "you need a shave."
> "The water," he said, feeling irritated, "was frozen."

There is more description of platform activity, and Noah feels Hope is the bearer of bad news. After a few more perfunctory words. . . .

"Noah . . ." Hope said softly, her voice trembling with the effort to keep it steady. "Noah, I didn't tell them."

"What?" Noah asked stupidly.

"I didn't tell them. Not anything. Not that you were coming. Not that I wanted to marry you. Not that you're Jewish. Not that you're alive."

Noah swallowed. What a silly, aimless way to spend Christmas, he thought foolishly, looking at the uncelebrating hills.

After more "artificial" dialogue made in an effort to console Hope, she tries to explain.

"We came home from church and I thought I would be able to sit down in the kitchen with my father. But my brother came in. . . . They started to talk about the war, and my brother, he's an idiot anyway, my brother began to say that there were no Jews fighting in the war and they were making all the money, and my father just sat there nodding. . . ."

"That's all right," Noah kept saying stupidly, "that's perfectly all right." He moved his hands vaguely in their gloves because they were getting numb. I must get some breakfast, he thought. I need some coffee.

Hope excuses herself to go back to her father, then to accompany him to church. Noah takes a room at the local hotel to have breakfast, freshen up, and await the eleven o'clock meeting with the Plowmans. A space between paragraphs indicates a passage of time. There follows a page of internalizations about a number of things—the state of Noah's finances (low), the state of his mind concerning the division between Jew and Gentile, and a father's reluctance "to deliver his daughter over to a stranger."

The Plowmans are late, but at 12:30 Noah is finally called downstairs for the crucial meeting. He reviews all his shortcomings, and the contrast between himself—no family, a "common" accent, and low friends—and the proud, private, family and background-conscious New Englander he is about to meet.

As he finally faces Hope and her father, we are given a description of Plowman's appearance in some detail, and we are apprised of the sense of catastrophe that shows on Hope's face. She introduces them. . . .

"Father, this is Noah."

He put out his hand, though. Noah shook it. The hand was tough and horny. I'm not going to beg, Noah thought, no matter what. I'm not going to lie. I'm not going to pretend I'm anything much. If he says yes, fine. If he says no. . . . Noah refused to think about that.

"Very glad," her father said, "to make your acquaintance."

They stood in an uneasy group, with the old man who served as clerk watching them with undisguised interest.

"Seems to me," Mr. Plowman said, "might not be a bad idea for myself and Mr. Ackerman to have a little talk."

"Yes," Hope whispered, and the tense, uncertain, timbre of her voice made Noah feel that all was lost.

Mr. Plowman looked around the lobby consideringly. "This might not be the best place for it," he said, staring at the clerk, who stared back curiously. "Might take a little walk around town. Mr. Ackerman might like to see the town, anyway."

"Yes, Sir," said Noah.

"I'll wait here," said Hope.

There is a description of her sitting down in a squeaking rocker.

"We'll be back in a half hour or so, Daughter," Mr. Plowman said.

Noah winced a little at the "Daughter."

A paragraph takes the two men out of the hotel into the "harsh, windy cold." They walk two minutes in silence. Then Mr. Plowman speaks.

"How much," he asked, "do they charge you in the hotel?"

"Two-fifty," Noah said.

"For one day?" Mr. Plowman asked.

"Yes."

"Highway robbers," Mr. Plowman said. "All hotel-keepers."

Then he fell back into silence and they walked quietly once more. They walked past Marshall's Feed and Grain Store, past the drugstore of F. Kinne, past J. Gifford's Men's Clothing shop, past the law offices of Virgil Swift. . . .

. . . . and a few more mercantile establishments of that nature. Then . . .

Mr. Plowman's face was set and rigid, and as Noah looked from his sharp, quiet features, noncommittally arranged under the old-fashioned Sunday hat, to the storefronts, the names went into his brain like so many spikes driven into a plank by a methodical, impartial carpenter. Each name was an attack. Each name was a wall, an announcement, an arrow, a reproof. Subtly, Noah felt, in an ingenious quiet way, the old man was showing Noah the close-knit, homogenous world of plain English names from which his daughter sprang. Deviously, Noah felt, the old man was demanding, how will an Ackerman fit here, a name imported from the broil of Europe, a name lonely, careless, un-owned and dispossessed, a name without a father or a home, a name rootless and accidental.

Plowman points out the school that Hope attended. Noah reads its motto and thinks of the long historical background of this corner of the country.

"Cost twenty-three thousand dollars," Mr. Plowman said, "back in 1904. WPA wanted to tear it down and put up a new one in 1935. We stopped that. Waste of taxpayer's money. Perfectly good school."

As they continue walking, Noah notices the church a hundred yards down the road. . . .

That's where it's going to happen, Noah thought despairingly. This is the shrewdest weapon coming up. There are probably six dozen Plowmans buried in the yard, and I'm going to be told "in their presence."

But Plowman surprises him by suggesting they return to the hotel before they reach the church. On the way back Noah glances at the old man's face, and feels that he is searching painfully for the proper words with which to dismiss his daughter's lover. Plowman finally speaks. . . .

"You're doing an awful thing, young fellow," Mr. Plowman said, and Noah felt his jaw grow rigid as he prepared to fight. "You're putting an old man to the test of his principles. I won't deny it. I wish to God you would turn around and get on that train and go back to New York and never see Hope again. You won't do that, will you?" He peered shrewdly at Noah.

"No," said Noah. "I won't."

"Didn't think you would. Wouldn't've been up here in the first place if you would." The old man took a deep breath, stared at the cleared pavements before his feet, as he walked slowly at Noah's side. "Excuse me if I've given you a pretty glum walk through town," he said. "A man goes a good deal of his life living more or less automatically. But every once in a while, he has to make a real decision. He has to say to himself, now, what do I really believe, and is it good or is it bad? The last forty-five minutes you've had me doing that, and I'm not fond of you for it. Don't know any Jews, never had any dealings with them. I had to look at you and try to decide whether I thought Jews were wild, howling heathen, or congenital felons, or whatever. . . . Hope thinks you're not too bad, but young girls've made plenty of mistakes before. All my life I thought I believed one man was born as good as another, but thank God I never had to act on it till this day. Anybody else show up in town asking to marry Hope, I'd say, 'Come out to the house. Virginia's got turkey for dinner. . . .' "

They reach the hotel and Hope comes out to meet them. She and her father look at each other, while Noah feels intolerably burdened by the sights and the sounds of their walk. Then. . . .

"Well?" Hope said.

"Well," her father said slowly. "I just been telling Mr. Ackerman, there's turkey for dinner."

Slowly, Hope's face broke into a smile. She leaned over and kissed her father. "What in Heaven took so long?" she asked, and, dazedly, Noah knew it was going to be all right, although at the moment he was too spent and weary to feel anything about it.

"Might as well take your things, young man," Mr. Plowman said. "No sense giving these robbers all your money."

"Yes," said Noah. "Yes, of course." He moved slowly and dreamily up the steps into the hotel. He opened the door and looked back. Hope was holding her father's arm. The old man was grinning. It was a little forced and a little painful, but it was a grin.

"Oh," said Noah, "I forgot. Merry Christmas."

Then he went to get his bag.

*The Young Lions*, the novel, is 689 fully loaded pages of rather small type. If, following the book closely, it were made into a mini-series for television, it would probably run over 20 hours. The film version runs something over three hours. It is still one of Hollywood's five or six longest films. The script for that three-plus hours contained some 170 pages. Now, a page of script does not usually accommodate nearly as much material as a page of a book, so it can easily be seen that a tremendous (and merciless) editing job had to be done on the novel.

That's a customary procedure. Without it, few books would ever get to the screen, and more authors would be living in poverty. Except in the adaptation of an occasional short story, where expansion is called for, almost all novels, even normally short mystery stories, require a considerable amount of editing to bring them down to an acceptable screen time.

Irwin Shaw was quite probably the best short story writer of our time, if not of all time. This worked in our favor. The novel was essentially a series of short stories, of vignettes, which followed a selected group of characters through some five or six years of experiences on the home and battle fronts on both sides of the war. This construction made it possible to eliminate many chapters of the novel in their entirety.

Three basic story lines were laid down: Noah's, Michael's, and Christian's. The two Americans met, were separated, then reunited; and their personal stories, as in the example given, were never intertwined. Christian, as a German soldier, never met either of the Americans until he encountered Michael's bullet at the film's climax.

In adaptations, it is mandatory to clearly define the *theme*, the *characters*, and the *action* to be retained, and to determine what can be eliminated without damage to these three elements of the over-all story or of any particular part of it. An analysis of this selected sequence will demonstrate the process for one small section of the film, but the same analytical approach works for the film as a whole.

The following script version, written by Edward Anhalt, encom-

passes the scene in five pages—probably less than one-third the length
of the sequence in the novel. It stays close to Shaw's creation, since
a better one would be hard to come by, but it eliminates those parts
of the chapter which deal with Noah's troubled musings on the train,
in the hotel, and, finally, on the walk with Hope's father. Quite obviously, it would have been fruitless to dramatize those passages with
mostly painful portraits of Noah while we listened to his "voice-
overs"—a technique to be used only when under the pressure of extreme necessity—and though it is pleasant to savor them in the reading, they would be of no real value to the film.

At rare intervals it may be possible to relax and enjoy philosophical or psychological cerebration during the course of a film; but
in the overwhelming number of instances the demand of both filmmaker and viewer is, "Let's get on with it!" With this in mind, introductions to sequences, which are almost obligatory in a written
work, are automatically dispensed with in films, especially as the story
moves toward its climax. The same is true for the ends of sequences.
There should rarely be a "tag." (Even in comedy, where they are frequently seen, they are rarely fresh or clever but rather all too obvious.)
As soon as the necessary message has been delivered and the resultant
emotional reactions registered, a smooth transition by dissolve, or an
instantaneous one by cut, is in order. In a novel, the conclusions of
chapters tempt the reader to pause, to draw a breath, to ruminate.
Films offer few such occasions.

After the elimination of the opening section on the train, Hope's
confession of failure to communicate with her father is retained, but
no mention is made of the most important element in the sequence—
the fact that Noah is a Jew. This fact is the scene's most difficult
"obstacle" and source of conflict. Without it, there *is no scene*. The
film was released in 1958; but even in 1940, asking a father for his
daughter's hand was more often a source of comedy than a cause for
deep emotional concern. The question of a father's acceptance of a
son-in-law only serves to heighten the problem of ethnic acceptance,
a problem which has been with us for millenia and will probably stay
with us for some time to come.

So, if that is our "problem," the burden of our sequence, how
can it be set up in an indirect but dramatic scene rather than in
polemical fashion? Shaw solves the problem through Noah's anticipatory, self-torturing reverie on the train. He uses the same means to
develop the necessary counter-element, the Plowmans' New England,
Protestant background. But this technique is not suitable for a film,
and here, the two elements must be revealed through dialogue. A
montage treatment, with Noah's "voice-over", would be lengthy and
pretentious. But because Plowman announces the old, settled English

names without emphasis, the Gentile-Jewish conflict is brought into subtle, but sharp focus.

Scene (88) is a cut-away to Hope. It serves to keep her alive as a vitally interested character and to cut down the length of the men's walk. Incidentally, but importantly, it supplies the time needed for both Plowman and our viewers to absorb the effect of Noah's disclosure. (This is really an editing function, but it should be understood and anticipated by every writer.)

The cut back to Noah and Plowman gets to the meat of the sequence, substantially as in the novel but shortened. Noah finally makes his stand, mentions his ancestry in a less ambiguous manner, and we have only to wait for the hoped-for but by no means certain resolution. Before going any further, here is the scene as it appeared in Anhalt's script.

| 85 | EXT. RUTLAND STATION PLATFORM | DAY |

A steam engine puffs into the station hauling ancient day coaches. Noah can be seen through the window. He looks tired. There are only a few people waiting as the train jolts to a stop. Noah steps down, looks worriedly up and down the platform. Hope comes out of the waiting room doorway.

> HOPE
>> Noah.

Noah runs toward her. He bends to kiss her, but she kisses him quickly and perfunctorily.

> NOAH
> (with foreboding)
> What did your father say?

> HOPE
> (miserably)
> I didn't ask him.

> NOAH
>> Oh. . . .

She looks at Noah's hurt face.

> HOPE
> I've failed you, I've failed you.

(CONTINUED)

85 (CONTINUED)

                    NOAH
No, no. It's all right.

                    HOPE
I was afraid—I was afraid he'd
say no. He's so—ingrown. He
thinks people who live twenty
miles away are foreigners. He—
he's said things. . . .

                    NOAH
I understand, Hope.
            (taking over—the
            man of the
            house)
I'll talk to him.
            (looking at his
            watch)
What time is church out?

                    HOPE
He isn't in church this Sunday.
He's waiting for us in the
drugstore across the street.

Noah is appalled at the immediacy of this.

                    NOAH
    Now?

                    HOPE
    Oh, Noah . . .

Noah's courage is beginning to drain away. He sighs as a man
facing the inevitable.

                    NOAH
    Well . . .

He guides her o.s.

                                    DISSOLVE TO:

86     INT. DRUGSTORE        MED. FULL SHOT            DAY

The store is old-fashioned, with colored water in apothecary
jars and tall spindle-legged chairs in front of the small soda
fountain. MR. GRAHAM, the druggist, is behind the fountain.
MR. PLOWMAN stands in front of it, tall and stooped, with a
face that only New England could produce. They are both
looking up expressionlessly as Hope and Noah enter.

> HOPE
> Father, this is Noah Ackerman.

> MR. PLOWMAN
> Very glad to make your
> acquaintance.

Noah essays a smile as they shake hands. There is an uneasy
silence. Hope looks with embarrassment at Mr. Graham, who
takes the hint and starts to walk into the back of the store.
Noah makes it unnecessary.

> NOAH
> Mr. Plowman—the reason I'm
> here is—Hope and I—we want to
> be married.

Mr. Plowman gives no visible evidence that this is a surprise
to him.

> MR. PLOWMAN
> I see.
> (to Hope)
> Seems to me Mr. Ackerman and I
> might have a little talk.

> NOAH
> Certainly.

> MR. PLOWMAN
> Might take a walk around the
> town.

Noah is already moving toward the door. He opens it for Mr.
Plowman, who indicates that Noah is to go first. They go
outside.

87    EXT. STREET                                                    DAY

Mr. Plowman and Noah walk down the nearly empty street,
their collars up against the cold gusts of wind.

> MR. PLOWMAN
> Noah. That's a good old New
> England name.

> NOAH
> (softly)
> It's a good old Hebrew name, too,
> Mr. Plowman.

Mr. Plowman says nothing, reveals nothing. They pass a feed
store. The window is lettered: MARSHALL'S FEED STORE.

> MR. PLOWMAN
> Jack Marshall. I went to school
> with his father, and my father
> with his father.

Noah nods. Mr. Plowman points to a building across the
street.

> MR. PLOWMAN (cont.)
> Virgil Smith's law office.

A window on the second floor is lettered with the name.

> MR. PLOWMAN (cont.)
> One of his people did the legal
> work when they incorporated
> this town. 1750.

Noah says nothing, looks painfully interested. Mr. Plowman
hasn't looked at him, seems to ask no reply. They are passing
a church with a graveyard in front of it. Mr. Plowman stops,
points through a cluster of headstones to a granite plot
marker, simply labeled PLOWMAN.

> MR. PLOWMAN (cont.)
> Family plot. Seven generations of
> Plowmans there. Hope's mother,
> too.

Noah reacts to this quiet smugness with restrained anger.

88        INT. DRUGSTORE—HOPE AND MR. GRAHAM            DAY

He puts hot chocolate on the counter. Hope looks at it
unenthusiastically.

>                    HOPE
>           Mr. Graham, you know what I
>           could really use?

>                  MR. GRAHAM
>           What?

>                    HOPE
>           A slug of whiskey.

Mr. Graham looks at her sternly, then takes a medicine bottle
from under the counter, pours the contents into a coffee cup.
Hope looks dubiously at the label.

>                  HOPE (cont.)
>           It says liniment.

>                  MR. GRAHAM
>           Don't worry. It ain't liniment.

Hope picks up the cup, drains it, takes a deep breath.

89        EXT. STREET        NOAH AND MR. PLOWMAN          DAY

They are walking in the opposite direction, passing the
schoolhouse.

>                  MR. PLOWMAN
>           Went to school there. Hope.

He looks away from Noah to somewhere deep within himself.

>                MR. PLOWMAN (cont.)
>           You're doing an awful thing.
>           You're putting a man to the test
>           of his principles. I wish to heaven
>           you would turn around and get on
>           the train and never see Hope
>           again. You won't do that, will
>           you?

                                      (CONTINUED)

89 (CONTINUED)

Noah shakes his head.

>                    MR. PLOWMAN (cont.)
>                    Didn't think you would. Anybody
>                    from town ask to marry Hope, I'd
>                    say, "Come on out to the house.
>                    We've got turkey for dinner."

There is a long pause. Mr. Plowman is wrestling with his
unseen antagonist.

>                    MR. PLOWMAN (cont.)
>                    I never knew a Jew before. You
>                    go along all your life thinking a
>                    certain way and then someone
>                    jolts you and you have to look
>                    inside yourself. That's what
>                    you've made me do, and I'm not
>                    fond of you for it.

Noah slows, faces him.

>                    NOAH
>                    I know you'd like me to be solid
>                    and secure. I'm not. I make $35 a
>                    week, I'm 1-A in the draft, and all
>                    my ancestors were born in the
>                    ghetto—all the way back to
>                    Moses.
>                         (slowly and
>                          emphatically,
>                          and challengingly)
>                    I love Hope and I'll love her for
>                    all my life.

Hope comes out of the drugstore, stands waiting for them.
They walk toward her. Mr. Plowman's face is granite,
revealing nothing, but his eyes are suffering. Hope waits, her
face set and pained. As they come close, Mr. Plowman pushes
Noah gently forward.

                                          (CONTINUED)

89 (CONTINUED)

MR. PLOWMAN
(a wry smile)
I've just been telling Mr.
Ackerman. There's turkey for
dinner.

Then Hope is in her father's arms. Noah just stands there
grinning.

DISSOLVE TO:

It can be seen that the script version eliminates some of the difficulties involved in the adaptation, but it substitutes a number of others. First, the opening: It is difficult to believe that Hope, who has been established as an open, competent, and self-reliant young woman, would not prepare her father for the meeting. Allowing Noah to walk into this situation unwarned and unarmed is cruelty, or thoughtlessness, of the highest order; forcing her father to face a sudden attack from two unexpected quarters is even worse. (The criticism also holds true for the novel version, which does not even tell us *when* Plowman learns that Noah is Jewish. We must assume that Hope informs him during Noah's wait at the hotel.)

Plowman has a great deal of information to digest in a hurry: his daughter's desire to marry a stranger, and the fact that that stranger is a Jew. Either one of these emotional time bombs would, to say the least, give him pause. The two together are far too much to handle in a five-page scene—both for Plowman and for the screenwriter. The novel sets up the situation for the *reader* in the first page of the chapter, but it ignores the father. The script version doesn't set it up for the viewer or the father at all.

The solution was not too difficult. Sometimes, even in drama, it pays to be logical. And it was logical to assume that if Hope and her father were waiting for Noah, they would be waiting together; and if they were together, it was logical that they would be talking. Further, it seemed likely that the topic of their conversation would be Noah and the purpose of his visit, which diminished problem number one— the marriage. The rest was easy.

The scene was short and somewhat indirect, and it set up a far more dramatic means for presenting problem number two, both for Mr. Plowman and the viewer. Here the element of "sudden surprise" could be used most effectively.

Steam trains were hard to come by in 1957, and expensive. A bus was much easier and, because of Noah's deplorable financial condition, more logical. It also enabled us to stage the sequence within the closed environment of the town square, which was built on the "back lot."

As you will see, the intercutting (between Hope and the walking men) was changed, both in placement and in substance. It enabled us to negotiate the walk more efficiently and to stage the scene more dramatically. If, as the first script indicates (end of scene [87]) Noah reacts to the father's quiet smugness with restrained anger, it is better to use this emotion to inspire Noah's declaration to Plowman, rather than to let it dissipate during the cut-away. This is accomplished by cutting to Hope earlier in the sequence and getting back to Noah's scene in time to let us see his "restrained anger" develop to the point of retorting.

The substance of Hope's scene was completely altered. As it stands, the material furnishes a cheap and obvious laugh. It is also cliché. And though humor is always welcome, in this instance, and considering the content of the scene as a whole, it would have done more harm than good—again, because it is out of character. Whether or not you approve of imbibing, Hope has been established as a woman of solid substance who would not resort to alcohol as a means of calming her nerves.

However, as an example of what, in a very small way, rewriting is all about, let us examine the scene as if we wanted to retain the gist of it—to keep the humor without being too blatantly obvious. For example:

88      INT. DRUGSTORE—HOPE AND MR. GRAHAM                      DAY

> He puts hot chocolate on the counter. Hope looks at it
> unenthusiastically.

>                       HOPE
>           Mr. Graham, you know what I
>           could really use?

> Mr. Graham looks at her sternly, then breaks into a
> sympathetic smile. He knows what she's going through.
> Reaching under the counter, he brings out a medicine bottle,
> pours the contents into a coffee cup. Hope looks dubiously at
> the label.

>                       HOPE (cont.)
>           It says liniment.

>                                               (CONTINUED)

88 (CONTINUED)

MR. GRAHAM
Don't worry. It ain't liniment.

Hope picks up the cup, drains it, takes a deep breath.

CUT TO:


This version says the same thing as the original, but somewhat more subtly. It gets us our laugh but, because it allows the viewer to participate in the scene, to furnish his own substance, it is a more involved, and better, laugh. This is by no means a profound example, but it *is* an instance of the sort of re-examination that must constantly be made. However, there is a caveat, which will be discussed in its proper place.

It will be noted in the forthcoming scene that nowhere does Noah make mention of the "problem." His Jewishness is no problem to Noah; it is only a problem for Plowman. This is a very important distinction, which should probably be made more often.

Noah's one "position" statement is more appropriately placed in the scene, after a better build-up for it. We then leave the rest of the sequence to Hope's father. After all, it *is* Plowman's scene, *his* inner conflict, *his* decision. *He* creates the suspense. Giving Noah the final line before Plowman announces his decision greatly weakens it. Plowman must answer to his own conscience rather than react to Noah's stand.

A minor quibble, since this was not the final script, is a criticism of the last paragraph of the scene, which is written in "treatment" style. Here, there should be additional set-ups and scene numbers, since the action and reactions indicated could hardly be accommodated in one shot. Also, Plowman's action in pushing Noah toward Hope undercuts his final line, giving his decision away too early.

It is impossible to recall how much the final version came from the script and how much was improvised in rehearsals and on the set, but here is the scene as it appears in the film.


1     LONG SHOT      A SMALL NEW ENGLAND TOWN          DAY


2     TWO SHOT       INT. DRUGSTORE                    DAY

Hope and her father, MR. PLOWMAN, sit at the soda counter, coffee cups before them. Behind them, in the b.g., the TOWN
(CONTINUED)

2 (CONTINUED)

SQUARE can be seen through the store's open door and typical
jar-cluttered windows. Occasionally, throughout the scene,
Hope glances out at the street, as if expecting someone. She
seems apprehensive; her father quite at ease. When he speaks,
New England shows clearly in his accent.

> PLOWMAN
> (smiling)
> That's one of the hazards you run
> when you have a daughter. One
> day she's going to come to you
> and say, "I love him—I want to
> marry him."

> HOPE
> (smiling nervously)
> That's one of the hazards.

> PLOWMAN
> But you haven't told me anything
> about the man at all.

> HOPE
> Oh, he's gentle and he's clever—
> he's not just a man, he's a
> boy. . . .

> PLOWMAN
> . . . . and poor. . . .

> HOPE
> (a slight laugh)
> . . . . and poor.
> (a beat)
> He writes me a letter a day—even
> when we see each other in New
> York every night—and he's
> alone. . . .

Even as she speaks the last line, a Greyhound bus is seen
pulling around a corner in the distant b.g. and starting its
circuit of the square. As Hope finishes speaking she slides off
the stool and, after one final anxious look at her father, she
heads for the door.

3    M.L.S.    BUS    EXT. TOWN SQUARE    DAY

The bus pulls up to the curb, the door opens and Noah steps down to the pavement.


4    CLOSE TWO SHOT   HOPE AND PLOWMAN    AT DOOR
                                         OF STORE

They watch as Noah, off-scene, exits the bus. Then Hope turns quickly to her father.

                    HOPE
           He's Jewish, father.

And she escapes quickly toward Noah. Plowman stares off after her, his expression changing slowly to that of a man who has just been tagged with a baseball bat.


5    MEDIUM SHOT    HOPE AND NOAH    AT BUS

They embrace, then turn toward Plowman (off-scene). Hope takes Noah's arm and escorts him to the judge.


6    CLOSE GROUP SHOT    FAVORING PLOWMAN

Noah and Hope enter the shot. Plowman and Noah regard each other.

                    HOPE
           Father, this is Noah.

                   PLOWMAN
              (extends his hand)
           How do you do.

                    NOAH
                (taking it)
           How do you do, Sir.

There is a short pause, and then:

                                         (CONTINUED)

6 (CONTINUED)

> PLOWMAN
> Well, it seems to me that Mr.
> Ackerman and I might have a
> little talk.

> NOAH
> Certainly, Sir.

> PLOWMAN
> (to Hope)
> Why don't you finish your coffee,
> Hope—we won't be very long.

And with that ominous remark, he exits. Noah turns and
follows him, leaving a forlorn Hope gazing after them. Slowly
she turns and enters the drugstore.


7    FULL SHOT    DOLLY              EXT. TOWN SQUARE

Noah and Plowman walk into the shot, moving diagonally
across the street, which brings the b.g. buildings into full view.
As they walk, the CAMERA dollies ahead of them. With a nod
of his head, Plowman indicates one of the buildings.

> PLOWMAN
> That's Jack Marshall's. I went to
> school with his father—my father
> with his father.

Noah says nothing—looks a little glumly at the buildings.
Plowman, with another nod, continues.

> PLOWMAN (cont.)
> Virgil Smith's law office. One of
> his people did the work when
> they incorporated this town—
> 1750.


8    TWO SHOT  THE DRUGGIST AND HOPE      INT. DRUGSTORE

Seated on a stool at the counter, Hope looks off after the two
men (off-scene) as the druggist refills her coffee cup.

(CONTINUED)

8 (CONTINUED)

> DRUGGIST
> Well, looks like its going to be a
> nice day.

Hope nods absent-mindedly—continues to look off-camera.

9    LONG SHOT   TOWN SQUARE                HOPE'S POV

Noah and Plowman, their backs to us, are in the distant b.g.,
walking toward a church and its adjoining cemetery. The quiet
of the Vermont air is broken only by the sound of the church
choir, singing a Protestant hymn.

10   M.L.S.     ACROSS GRAVESTONES IN CEMETERY

Seen over the tombstones in the f.g., Plowman and Noah walk
up to the old wrought-iron fence.

11   TWO SHOT     NOAH AND PLOWMAN

They come to a stop at the fence and look over at the
headstones.

> PLOWMAN
> It's the family plot—seven
> generations of Plowmans
> there. . . .

12   P.O.V.    CLOSE SHOT                    HEADSTONES

> PLOWMAN'S VOICE (o.s.)
> Hope's mother, too.

13   BACK TO TWO SHOT

They turn and start away from the cemetery.

14      REVERSE TWO SHOT        DOLLY        PLOWMAN AND NOAH

The cemetery is now in the b.g. as they continue around the
square. Noah is beginning to seethe a little.

> PLOWMAN
> (somewhat flatly—
> playing for time)
> There's the school. . . .

Noah interrupts and, as he starts to speak, he stops walking.
Plowman is forced to swing around to face him, and the shot
becomes an OVER-SHOULDER angle on Noah.

> NOAH
> Mr. Plowman . . . uh . . .
> (stops walking)
> I don't have a family plot—I don't
> have a family. I earn $35 a week,
> and I'm 1-A in the draft. But I
> love Hope, and I shall love her for
> all my life.

15      OVER-SHOULDER (O.S.)                                      PLOWMAN

He regards Noah closely, then nods slowly, and turns away.

16      CONTINUE TWO SHOT DOLLY            NOAH AND PLOWMAN

For a moment they walk in silence. Plowman can stall no
longer.

> PLOWMAN
> You're doing an awful thing—
> putting a man to the test of his
> principles. . . .
> (a brief pause)
> I wish to heaven you'd turn
> around, get on that bus, and
> never see Hope again. . . .
> (a beat)
> But you won't do that, will you?

                                                      (CONTINUED)

16 (CONTINUED)

    Noah shakes his head, no.

                    PLOWMAN (cont.)

            Didn't think you would. Anybody

            from town'd ask to marry Hope,

            I'd say, 'Come up to the house—

            we've got turkey for dinner.'

They walk a few more steps in silence. They have taken the
last turn around the square and are now heading for the
drugstore.

                    PLOWMAN (cont.)

            I never knew a Jew before. . . .

            you go along all your life—

            thinking a certain way—someone

            jolts you and you have to look

            inside yourself.

                (a beat)

            That's what you've made me do

            and I'm not fond of you for it.

They continue to walk for a moment. Noah throws Plowman a
sidelong, hopeless glance.


17     CLOSE SHOT      HOPE                INT. DRUGSTORE

     She sees the two approaching, slides off her stool and exits.


18     CLOSE SHOT      HOPE        EXT. DOOR OF DRUGSTORE

     She enters the shot, stares down at the approaching men
     apprehensively.


19     TIGHT THREE SHOT      TOWARD PLOWMAN AND NOAH

     They enter the shot and stop, facing Hope. Noah can't look
     into her eyes, but stares at the ground disconsolately. Finally,
     Plowman speaks.

                                (CONTINUED)

19 (CONTINUED)

                          PLOWMAN
                I was just telling Mr. Ackerman—
                we've got turkey for dinner.


20      CLOSE O.S. SHOT        HOPE

        For a moment, she can't believe it—then her face breaks into
        a radiant smile as her eyes puddle up. With happy sobs she
        falls into her father's arms. Noah can only stare at the two in
        surprised disbelief, as we:

                                              DISSOLVE TO:


    This final version plays shorter than the earlier script version,
but occupies a half-page more because the directions are more detailed
and more set-ups are indicated.

    In the film, Noah's early 4-F status is irrelevant. His story starts
with his acceptance by the draft board. Hope's last line in the opening
scene with her father (scene 2) tells us that she and Noah have been
carrying on a romance. This is obligatory since, in the film, we have
seen neither of them after their first meeting. Without this brief and
indirect disclosure, the basis for the current scene would have been a
complete surprise to the audience, and not a helpful one.

    Changing the setting of the opening scene furnishes an unex-
pected technical bonus. In the first script, a dissolve was required to
carry Hope and Noah from the railway station to the drugstore. Such
a hiatus in the middle of a sequence, however brief, is never welcome.
The final version allows the sequence to flow smoothly and contin-
uously, with building interest, from start to surprising climax.

    It will be noted that the introduction of Mr. Plowman mentions
a New England accent, but no attempt has been made to write it. In
casting the part, however, great care was taken to select an actor,
Vaughn Taylor, who could "do" New England to a T. Though of far
less importance to the scene, the druggist, too, was picked for his
dialectal expertise as well as his acting ability.

    The question of anti-Semitism, though all-important in this se-
quence, is subtly treated. Noah is never placed in the position of
defending his faith, which, under the circumstances, would be self-
demeaning. The film deals with the subject again when Noah encounters a more violent form of the prejudice in the U.S. Army. But
these are relatively minor character conflicts in a story that deals with

themes of much greater general interest. Besides, films are not usually tracts, and even though a particular message may be of great importance to the filmmaker, it should be presented in the most palatable way; otherwise it misses its mark and its market.

# 5

# *Adaptation Continued. . . .*

There are a number of valid reasons for altering original material in adaptation. First is to improve it—at least so the adapter insists. I have rarely known a writer who didn't believe he could gild the lily— sometimes a little, often a good deal. (Every writer is an editor at heart.) As a matter of cold fact, this holds true even for the writer of the original material. I have been involved in the development of several screenplays written by the authors of the works from which they were adapted. In most instances the results were catastrophic. Sometimes the author chose to zero in on the least cinematic portions of his novel, but more often boredom, or what is currently called "burn-out," came into play.

The well-known author of one "classic" wrote a fine script: It was interesting, it was funny—and it was a completely different story. His explanation was that he was bored with the original material: He had already given it too much of his working life.* And there lies the greatest danger in any form of rewriting: the total loss of objectivity, an experience suffered by every artist. It has led to the curtailment of more than one career.

Leo McCarey's chief attributes as a director were a talent for writing and an unparalleled gift for comedy. He would create a scene, rehearse it, set it, then stew over it. The longer he stewed, the flatter it seemed and, as often as not, he would set about creating a new situation, whose immediate appeal lay only in its freshness. The hard-

*The producer assigned a writer who was faithful, in a Readers Digest sort of way, to the original novel.

est work a creative associate of McCarey's was called on to do was to convince him of the worth of his original concept.

Editing, compressing, or shortening are the integral operations of almost every adaptation. Dismissing those sequences which can easily be judged expendable, there are a few pertinent areas to examine. One is the cast of characters. A novel can have many, since it can devote time to describing and developing each character. (See any Joseph Conrad novel.) A film rarely affords such luxury. Three or four characters, at most, can be fully developed, while the rest must be painted with a very broad brush and, in the interests of economy, it is often advantageous to combine two or more characters into one.

In the sequence excerpted from *The Young Lions*, Shaw described Mr. Plowman in detail—physically and socially—in order to set up a challenging obstacle for Noah. In the film version, such detail was unnecessary. A properly cast actor supplies all the surface characteristics that the viewer requires, not only through his physical appearance but, as suggested earlier, through speech patterns, personal mannerisms, and choice of apparel. His *inner* character is disclosed through the dramatization of his reactions, both physical and mental, to the series of obstacles, conflicts, and crises he encounters over the course of the film. The need for one character to describe another in dialogue should never arise in a well-written screenplay.

The adapter must often rewrite a perfectly good sequence to develop its "playing" potential, a necessary component of every scene. Let us here examine a vitally important but rarely considered difference between the novel and its adaptation. The novel is meant to be read by *one* person, in a private environment. A film is intended for the many—en masse. Any behavioral psychologist will tell you that, given the same stimulus, an individual, alone, will often react differently than when he is a member of a group, even if that group's only common factor is that its members are in close proximity to each other. My own experiences in more than fifty years of editing and directing have borne this out over and over again. The phenomenon holds true for all types of films, but it is best illustrated, in its more simplistic aspect, in comedies.

A single viewer in a studio projection room will rarely laugh aloud at a funny line or a comedic turn, even though he appreciates the humor. But the same material, seen by a full house, will elicit a stream of spontaneous laughter. That which a single watcher finds quietly amusing fetches a chuckle from an audience: The single grin is a multiple laugh, a spontaneous but lonely chuckle becomes a belly laugh with a crowd.

*Group* reaction has a great deal to do with the reception of films. TV sit-coms always use "canned" laughter, often in addition to that of their live audiences, for the sole purpose of bringing the home viewer into the spirit of their offerings. A few aesthetic purists have tried to launch such entertainment on its own merits, without benefit of off-stage laughter, live or canned. They have always come up short.

In serious drama, that extreme contrast in behavioral patterns, the "lynch mob" in its various guises has long been exploited on the screen. It is one bit of behavioral psychology known to nearly every adult. But this reaction is often more than just a removal of inhibitions. Quite often the reverse is true. An individual will often tolerate moral concepts and social attitudes that the crowd, out of some sort of group convention, will refuse to support.

What this means, simply, is that it pays to analyze each original sequence, no matter how acceptably it reads. Alteration may be necessary to develop its "playing" potential. An elementary example is a portion of the "Strawberry incident" from *The Caine Mutiny*.

This sequence is an example of one of those rare occasions when at least a part of a written version has to be *expanded* when transferred to script form.

In the novel, the officers are called into the wardroom at 3 o'clock in the morning. There is a paragraph describing their sleepy entrances. Then:

> The door opened, and Whittaker, the chief officer's steward, came in, carrying a tin can. When he set it on the table Willie saw that it brimmed with sand. The Negro's eyes were rounded in fright; perspiration rolled down his long, narrow cheeks, and his tongue flickered across his lips.
>
> "You're sure that's a gallon can, now," spoke Queeg.
>
> "Yes, suh. Lard can, suh. Got it offen Ochiltree, suh, in de gally—"
>
> "Very well. Pencil and paper, please," said the captain to nobody. Jorgensen sprang up and offered Queeg his pen and pocket notebook. "Mr. Maryk, how many helpings of ice cream did you have this evening?"
>
> "Two, sir."
>
> "Mr. Keefer?"
>
> "Three, Captain."
>
> Queeg polled all the officers, noting down their answers. "Now, Whittaker, did your men have any strawberries?"
>
> "Yes, suh. One helpin' each, suh. Mr. Jorgensen, he said okay, suh."
>
> "I did, sir," said Jorgensen.

After some further questioning, Queeg asks Whittaker to bring in a tureen and a serving spoon, and the sequence continues.

As will be seen, some of this material was realigned, enabling us to eliminate excessive and needless exits and entrances, and the "waits" they would have engendered on the screen. The novel splits the sequence into two segments: first, the counting of the portions and, second, doling them out. In the film, these were combined into one continuous scene, allowing us to telescope the sequence considerably. Where in the novel, however, Wouk can say simply, *Queeg polled all the officers, noting down their answers,* the film finds it advantageous to show the entire procedure. To have shortened the scene by some sort of arbitrary time-lapse technique would have been a serious mistake. The *viewer* must savor the humor of the situation and take note of Queeg's erratic behavior, essential as part of the build-up to the future disclosure of his paranoid tendencies. Though dramatizing this section in detail increased its immediate length, the realignment of the scenes more than made up for the gain in time.

The script version followed the novel "faithfully"—in its fashion.

202    INT. WARDROOM                                    NIGHT

CLOSE SHOT        GALLON CAN SO THAT IT FILLS THE
SCREEN as it is set down on the wardroom table. CAMERA
PULLS BACK TAKING IN the full wardroom as Whittaker sets
the can down, his eyes wide with fright. Queeg sits at the head
of the wardroom table, staring straight ahead and rolling the
steel balls. The other officers are grouped around in various
stages of undress, their hair mussed, their faces creased with
sleepiness.

                         QUEEG
                  (in a distant voice)
            You're sure that's a gallon can
            now?

                       WHITTAKER
                  (perspiration rolling
                   down his cheeks)
            Yes, suh. It's a lard can. Just took
            it from the pantry, suh.

                         QUEEG
            You're probably wondering why I
            called this meeting.
                  (looks around)
            As you all know, we had an
            excellent dessert for dinner
            tonight—ice cream with frozen
            strawberries.
                  (clearing his throat)

                                        (CONTINUED)

202 (CONTINUED)

> About an hour ago, I sent
> Whittaker to the pantry to bring
> me another portion. He brought
> me the ice cream, all right, but he
> said, "Suh, they ain't no more
> strawberries." Gentlemen, I do
> not believe the officers of this
> ship finished a full gallon of
> strawberries at dinner. And I
> intend to prove it.

203     CLOSE SHOT   OFFICERS     FAVORING WILLIE AND KEEFER

There is a murmur in the wardroom. Willie and Keefer are
astounded.

204     MEDIUM SHOT        WARDROOM

> QUEEG
> (to no one in
> particular)
> Pencil and paper. . . .

Harding quickly volunteers his pen and pocket notebook.

> QUEEG (cont.)
> Mr. Maryk, how many portions of
> strawberries and ice cream did
> you have at dinner?

> MARYK
> (tight-lipped)
> Two, sir.

> QUEEG
> Mr. Keefer?

> KEEFER
> (feeling like a child)
> Three, Captain.

                                        (CONTINUED)

204 (CONTINUED)

> QUEEG
>
> Keith?
>
> WILLIE
>
> Two.
>
> QUEEG
>
> Jorgensen?
>
> JORGENSEN
>
> Two.

205     CLOSE SHOT   OFFICERS     FAVORING WILLIE AND KEEFER

They both look off toward Maryk. Maryk turns his head to avoid their glance. Over this we hear Queeg questioning the other officers, including Carmody, Harding, and Rabbit, as to the number of portions they had.

206     MEDIUM SHOT       WARDROOM

Queeg continues making notations on his pad.

> QUEEG
>
> . . . and the steward's mates had three. Am I right, Whittaker?
>
> WHITTAKER
>
> Yes, suh. One helping each, suh. Mr. Keith, he said it was okay.
>
> WILLIE
>
> I did, sir.
>
> QUEEG
>
> And I had four.
> (counting up)
> That makes twenty-four portions in all.
> (to Whittaker)
> Whittaker, I want you to dole into that tureen an amount of sand

(CONTINUED)

206 (CONTINUED)

> equal to the amount of
> strawberries you put on each dish
> of ice cream. Twenty-four times,
> to be exact.

                    WHITTAKER
                  (trembling)
            Yes, suh.

He begins ladling the sand into the tureen.


207     CLOSE SHOT        QUEEG

Sitting at the head of the wardroom table, the picture of
righteousness. He rolls the steel balls as he waits expectantly.


208     CLOSE PAN SHOT        OFFICERS

There is the faint clicking of the steel balls as they watch
Whittaker, o.s. Most of their faces are filled with resentment
and annoyance at the spectacle. Willie just shakes his head.
Keefer's gaze moves from Whittaker to the Captain.


209     MEDIUM SHOT        WARDROOM

Whittaker, the perspiration rolling down his forehead, finishes
ladling.

                    QUEEG
            Kay. Now, for good measure, do it
            three more times.

Whittaker does as he is ordered.

                    QUEEG (cont.)
            Mr. Maryk, take a look at the
            gallon can now, and tell me how
            much sand is left.

Maryk rises. Careful not to look at Keefer, he walks up to the
can.

                                        (CONTINUED)

209 (CONTINUED)

                          MARYK
                   (looking into the can)
               Maybe a quart, or a little less, sir.

                          QUEEG
                   (lighting a cigarette)
              Kay.

                       QUEEG (cont.)
                   (he looks around the
                    wardroom triumphantly)
                  Have any of you gentlemen an
                  explanation for the quart of
                  missing strawberries?

         There is absolute silence. No one speaks.


The final version of the scene, as it reached the screen, is similar
in most respects but shows one simple, though important, variation.
Instead of adding up the number of strawberry servings in a continuous
flow of questions and answers before measuring out the servings in
sand, the portions are ladled out immediately after each officer has
declared his share. The advantages of this re-alignment should be
obvious. First, we saved time. Second, in spite of the over-all decrease
in length, more time was available for establishing the ridiculousness
of the operation. Third, the opportunities to elicit audience laughter
were considerably increased.

Let us return to the novel. After totting up the total number of
portions, Queeg asks the steward, Whittaker, to pour out one ladle of
sand, which is passed around for the officers' inspection. They agree
that it approximates the amount of strawberries served with each
portion of ice cream. Then Queeg says:

"Very well, Whittaker, do that again, twenty-four times." Sand diminished in the can and piled in the tureen. Willie tried to rub the blinking
sleepiness out of his eyes. "Kay. Now, for good measure, do it three
more times. . . . Kay. Mr. Maryk, take that gallon can and tell me how
much sand is left."

That's it. After Queeg's command to transfer twenty-four ladles
of sand, there are exactly twenty-one words, which can easily be read
in four or five seconds. These twenty-one words cover the transfer of
twenty-four scoops of sand, a procedure which, if shown in its entirety,
would take fifty to sixty seconds. The pouring of the three additional

scoops are, in the novel, covered by four dots (. . . .) but would take an additional six or seven seconds on the screen. If played as the script indicates, these sixty-odd seconds would create a decided stall. True, part of the action is meant to be played over the reactions of the officers in the wardroom—scene 208—but this is too little, too late, and unworkable. The scene as described—CLOSE PAN SHOT—OFFICERS—cannot possibly be realized. No director would stage the scene in such a way that the officers could be lined up for the sort of pan shot that 208 calls for. But even if that were possible, the shot of the officers would run no more than about thirty seconds, if that, and would still leave us with an empty exercise. What can be done?

The answer is to run the questions and answers, the ladling of the sand, and the officers' reactions, in parallel. As the sequence was shot, the ladling starts after Maryk's "Two, sir." We watch two scoops of sand being transferred from the lard can to the tureen, and then Queeg questions Keefer. A cut to Keefer for his "Three, Captain," then back to show the three portions being doled out.

At this point we have nearly exhausted the surprise and humor of seeing the inane sand-scooping operation, so the pace picks up. Queeg's questions and the officers' answers run simultaneously with the transfer of the sand, until Queeg questions Whittaker. Here, a slow-down takes place in preparation for the pay-off. By the time Queeg, underplaying his own answer, says, "And I had four," the audience is ready for the big laugh—and it always comes. Integrating the ladling action with Queeg's interrogation permits pace, laughter, character development, and a tight hold on the viewer's attention. In other words, "it plays." The sequence runs as follows.


                          MARYK
                 Two, sir.



1       TIGHT SHOT       FAVORING QUEEG

                          QUEEG
                 Whittaker, dole out a scoop of
                 sand for each portion of
                 strawberries.

                          WHITTAKER
                 Yes, sir.

        As Whittaker picks up the ladle and starts to scoop up some
        sand, we cut to:

2     CLOSE SHOT          QUEEG

He watches closely as the steward ladles two scoops of sand
into the tureen.

                          QUEEG
                Mr. Keefer, how many for you?


3     CLOSE SHOT          KEEFER

He speaks with scarcely veiled disdain.

                          KEEFER
                Three, Captain.


4     CLOSE SHOT          QUEEG

Watching Whittaker dole out the sand. As the steward ladles
out the third portion:

                          QUEEG
                Keith?


5     CLOSE SHOT          WILLIE

                          WILLIE
                Two, sir.


6     CLOSE UP           QUEEG

Appearing to be fascinated by the procedure, he watches
closely as the steward starts to ladle out the sand. Here, the
pace quickens. Queeg speaks as the first scoop is being made.

                          QUEEG
                    (without looking up)
                Harding?

7    CLOSE SHOT    HARDING

> HARDING
>
> Two, sir.


8    CLOSE SHOT    QUEEG

His eyes remained glued to the ladle as it continues to transfer the sand.

> QUEEG
>
> Paynter?

Paynter speaks from his position behind Queeg in the C.U.

> PAYNTER
>
> Two, sir.

The ladling never stops.

> QUEEG
>
> Carmody?


9    CLOSE TWO SHOT    CARMODY AND PAYNTER

> CARMODY
>
> Two, sir.

> QUEEG'S VOICE (o.s.)
>
> Jorgensen?


10    TWO SHOT    JORGENSEN AND RABBIT

> JORGENSEN
>
> Two, sir.


11    INSERT    LARD CAN AND TUREEN

Whittaker's hand continues transferring sand from one to the other.

(CONTINUED)

11 (CONTINUED)

                              QUEEG'S VOICE (o.s.)
                Rabbit?


12     TWO SHOT      JORGENSEN AND RABBIT

                              RABBIT
                Two, sir.


13     CLOSE GROUP SHOT      FAVORING QUEEG

       As Whittaker ladles out the last two scoops:

                              QUEEG
                      And the steward's mates had
                      three. Right, Whittaker?


14     THREE SHOT      WHITTAKER, MARYK—WILLIE IN B.G.

                              WHITTAKER
                      Yes, sir. One helping each, sir. Mr.
                      Keith said it was okay.

                              WILLIE
                      Yes, I did, sir.


15     CLOSE SHOT      QUEEG

       As Whittaker finishes the last of the mates' three portions:

                              QUEEG
                      And I had four.

       For the first time he looks up—mumbles as he mentally adds
       up the portions.

                              QUEEG (cont.)
                      Twenty-four portions in all.

                                               (CONTINUED)

15 (CONTINUED)

Whittaker ladles out the Captain's four portions in a collective
silence.

QUEEG (cont.)
Now, gentlemen, this tureen holds
an amount of sand equal to the
amount of strawberries we had
for dinner tonight. Right,
Whittaker?


16    THREE SHOT    WHITTAKER, MARYK, AND WILLIE

WHITTAKER
Yes, sir.

QUEEG'S VOICE (o.s.)
Mr. Maryk. . . .


17    CLOSE SHOT    QUEEG

QUEEG (cont.)
Take a look at the gallon can—
tell me how much sand is left.


18    CLOSE SHOT    MARYK

MARYK
(looking into the can)
Maybe a quart—or a little less.


19    CLOSE SHOT    QUEEG

QUEEG
(pulling the can to him)
Kay. Now, have any of you
gentlemen an explanation for the
quart of missing strawberries?

(Note: The 19 cuts are derived from 10 set-ups.)

Three additional aspects of the scene are of collateral interest. First, scene 205 is lazy writing. If we are to *hear* questions and answers, they should be written into the script. Otherwise, as in this instance, the writer encourages set improvisation and a loss of time in shooting, which is many times more costly than the same amount of time spent at the typewriter.

Second and third, Whittaker was not asked to affect a "southern black" dialect, nor was he asked to play a frightened, perspiring stereotype. This characterization, somewhat to my surprise, came out of the book. It was not only ethnically undesirable, it was dramatically incorrect. To have played him that way would have made him obviously guilty, and the whole point of the scene was that Queeg was setting up a "straw man," at least in the eyes of all his junior officers. It was Queeg's *reaction* to the petty theft, not the theft itself, that was important.

The main purpose of this chapter, however, is to urge the budding screen writer to measure his characters and his situations not by how nicely they read, but by their power to inspire the desired reactions in a massed audience. If he can master this concept he will find himself writing a more cinematically effective script, and one less likely to suffer change and degradation as it moves down the assembly line.

# 6

# *The Image Is the Reality*

Imagery is a form of communication. In a novel it is frequently a communication (or communing) with one's self, as in thought, reverie, or the mental consideration of one's state of mind or physical condition. The verbal description of mental imagery is perhaps the most common aspect of the novel but, to use an apt cliche, it often loses something in the translation. *Pictorial* imagery, on the other hand, is an international language: It can communicate at a maximum level with everyone.

For the adapter, the translation of mental imagery to pictorial imagery can be a very difficult undertaking. For example, a novelist can describe the thoughts of a poker player who maintains a totally noncommunicating facade. The filmmaker must find a way of showing those thoughts pictorially—perhaps a slight, uncontrollable twitch at the corner of the eye, or an involuntary movement of the hand or foot (the Camera can get under the table). He can, if he is lazy, resort to "voice-over" narration, but here he must use words, and words are rarely as precise as cleverly conceived pictures nor, in the majority of instances, are they as interesting.

The technique of constructing a sequence through visual images, so important in the making of most *good* motion pictures, has been mastered by only a handful of writers in or out of Hollywood. The creative adapter will usually find it necessary to build an entirely new scene—a scene which will both aid and compel the actor to dramatize the desired information.

Here is an example of an essentially silent sequence which creates a compelling mood as it begins to develop both the story and its leading character.*

*Excerpts from *That Woman*, an unproduced script by Robert Alan Aurthur and Edward Dmytryk.

1        SMALLER POOL AREA                  (The locale is Las Vegas)

This pool is deserted. Beyond, a low line of connected
bungalows stretches out from the main hotel building. Water
from a dozen outlets sprays the area, causing everything to
gleam brightly in the sun. Bunched outside the entrance of
one of the bungalows are perhaps a dozen REPORTERS, soon
to be joined by their late-arriving confreres, now moving
swiftly toward them. From another angle comes an electrically
propelled maid's cart. As the two groups are joined, the MAID
directs her cart toward the bungalow entrance and tinkles a
bell to gain attention and be allowed to pass through. No one
pays her heed. Grim-faced, she thrusts her way through as the
crowd, noisily now, vies for position, all concentrated on the
nearest window. CAMERA PUSHES to the window and finds it
completely draped.

2        INT. MARCIA'S BEDROOM   CLOSE SHOT TO PULLBACK    DAY

MARCIA HOPKINS lies on her back in bed, entangled in
sheets, rolling on her shoulders in the height of a bad dream,
her hands covering her face. The room is dark, but the sudden
opening of the bedroom door throws a bright shaft of light
across a portion of the bed and night table.

3        MEDIUM SHOT        AT BEDROOM DOOR

The door has been opened by the MAID who stands holding
clean towels and bedding. Seeing Marcia, she retreats, quietly
closing the door behind her.

4        CLOSE SHOT        ACROSS NIGHT TABLE AND EDGE OF BED

In the center of the room in F.G. stands a half-filled glass of
water; next to it a pill bottle almost empty. Marcia moans,
turns, and her tousled head rolls FULL INTO FRAME. As she
awakens slowly, CAMERA WIDENS. In sudden panic, she
                                                    (CONTINUED)

4 (CONTINUED)

reaches for the lamp, snaps it on. Trying to focus, she fumbles
for a small, jeweled travel clock. Bringing the face of the clock
close to hers, she puzzles out the time: 11:20. All right, that's
one fact. Now she fumbles for a book of matches which lies on
the night table. Peering at it closely she ascertains she's at the
Sahara Hotel. That's two facts. She knows the time and she
knows where she is. Slowly she relaxes. Lying quietly for a
moment, she remembers what day this is, and suddenly panics
again. Another look at the clock, and relief. She still has time.
But she needs to be wide awake. From the drawer of the night
table she takes another bottle of pills and gulps down two
with a swallow of water. Sitting up, she reaches for a
cigarette. Lighting it, she hungrily draws in that first deep
morning drag and accepts as a matter of course the paroxysm
of coughing that follows. This is a morning look at Marcia—a
girl who takes pills to go to sleep and pills to wake up, who
dreams of being lost and panics in the half-awakened state
until she knows where and when, whose hair is a mess and
whose skin is drawn tightly across her face because the life
juices have not really begun to flow yet, and who calmly
accepts the fact that if she doesn't die from overdoses of pills,
she could go at any moment from smoking too much. The
coughing stops, and she sits staring across the darkened
room, accepting the fact that this day must be faced.

5      FULL SHOT      MARCIA'S BEDROOM

Rising, she crosses carefully to the windows and reaches for
the drape cords. As she pulls them the room becomes flooded
with hot sunlight. As the large windows are exposed we see,
with Marcia, the horde of reporters bunched outside. The
pulling back of the drapes catapults them into action.
Oblivious of the carefully tended plantings, even now under
heavy spray, in a body they charge toward the window.
Horrified, Marcia can, for just an instant, only stare at them.
Then she furiously draws the drapes again, plunging the room
back into darkness. Crossing back to the bed, she sits down,
eyes the phone balefully. She picks it up.

                                              (CONTINUED)

5 (CONTINUED)

>                    MARCIA
>                (very hoarsely)
>        This is Miss. . . .
>                (coughing, clearing
>                  her throat)
>        Excuse me. This is Miss Hopkins.
>        Please send up the biggest pot of
>        coffee you can find. . . . No,
>        nothing else. . . . Oh, yes, there
>        is one more thing. Get me Mr.
>        Reginald Shaw in Tucson,
>        Arizona. The number is 709-
>        6636. . . . No, I'll just hang on.

She gets up. The phone has a very long cord, and she carries it
into the bathroom.


6        ANGLE INTO BATHROOM

An inadvertent glance into the mirror, and her face twists
with distaste and an audible "Ugh!" A half-empty bottle of
whisky stands near the sink. She looks at it for a moment,
then slops some into the glass. Raising the glass, she's
nauseated by the smell and quickly lowers it again. Just then
her connection comes through, and she sits on the nearest
seat available.

>                    MARCIA
>        Sonny. . . . How are you. . . .
>        Me, I'm fine. I called. . . . well, I
>        called to ask you what time it is.
>        If nothing else, you always knew
>        the time, Sonny.
>                (laughs loudly,
>                  mirthlessly)
>        But seriously, folks, what I really
>        called for was to wish you a
>        happy divorce day and to thank
>        you for not asking for alimony. It

>                                      (CONTINUED)

6 (CONTINUED)

             was very sweet of you,
             Sonny. . . . No, I didn't call to
             give you hell, but if you'd been
             half a man, just half a damn
             man. . . .
                (fights back tears)
             . . . . No, I'm not crying. You
             always did enough crying for both
             of us. Sonny. . . .
                (tosses the whisky
                  down fast)
             . . . . if you had just been half a
             man. Sonny, listen to me. Sonny!
                (but it's obvious that
                Sonny has hung up)
           SONNY!!!

Every scene in this short sequence was specifically designed to be *visually* effective, to obtain emotional impact through pictorial treatment. It is no accident that the set-ups lend themselves to dramatic lighting. The shot in which a shaft of bright sunlight is suddenly thrown into the dark bedroom is in no way essential to the story: It is arbitrarily contrived to shock the viewer and to command his attention. When, a bit later, Marcia opens the drapes and floods the room with daylight, she also floods it with the outside world and all that it, with its horde of scavenging reporters, signifies on this particular day. Once more, Marcia is forced to take refuge in darkness.

*Camera treatment is especially important in a scene with little physical action.* The action can, and must, be supplied by the *visual* images, and here the writer gives the filmmaker a "leg up" on the scene. Only the most arbitrary director would fail to take advantage of such a running start. It is surprising and disappointing how often this aspect of filming is completely ignored.

As the sequence continues, the set-ups are designed, *in the writing,* to tell the viewer a good deal about Marcia: the bottle of pills, the half-filled water glass, her struggle to awaken—all these, when creatively staged and photographed, serve to involve the viewer in the film from the beginning.

Nothing is written here that cannot be accomplished by props, make-up, creative lighting, and solid acting. That's what good screen-writing is all about. It gives the cast, the crew, and the director a platform which can help them to extend their reach.

Just how much has the viewer learned about our leading woman in the first three or four minutes of the film? He knows that she must be an unusually important person to attract such hectic attention from the press. He sees something of her troubled state of mind, and understands that she is in the throes of an inner conflict. The off-beat, one-sided, telephone conversation tells him that at least part of that conflict is caused by her imminent divorce. This problem, Marcia's unsatisfactory relationships with men, becomes the subplot of the story.

As the script continues, Marcia's divorce proceedings are made even more traumatic by the rude and thoughtless behavior of the press. While seeking some friendly understanding, she encounters the man she will fall in love with and marry. In the next few scenes the writer takes advantage of the Las Vegas background and lifestyle to develop a sequence which, though its purpose is to further the plot, is of interest *in its own right*.

This is an extremely important factor in good screen writing. *Each* scene, *each* sequence, should have its own life, its own values. The viewer must be given the opportunity to absorb and react to each sequence as it stands, without being consciously aware that that scene is there only to further the plot or expose some facet of character.

| 1b | MED. SHOT | BAR | DOORS TO PATIO IN B.G. | DAY |

Marcia moves into f.g. and takes a bottle of whisky from a shelf. She weighs it thoughtfully for a moment. To hell with it; she's tired of drinking alone! She moves determinedly toward the patio, slides the door open, and steps outside.

| 2b | MEDIUM SHOT | EXT. PATIO | DAY |

Marcia crosses to the bushes that separate her patio from the one next door. Pushing through a jungle of bougainvillea, she disappears from view.

| 3b | FULL SHOT | EXT. ADJOINING PATIO |

Marcia steps through the shrubbery in the b.g., stops, a little perplexed. Lying on a chaise in the f.g. is BEN NICHOLS. That's

(CONTINUED)

3b (CONTINUED)

not his real name, but it bears a vague resemblance to its
European derivation. He is 43, dark and well-built. As a boy he
was a hell of a handball player and now excels in the more
gentlemanly game of tennis. Sitting on the lower part of the
chaise, gently rubbing oil into Ben's legs, is a beautiful
Oriental girl. That's all we need to know about her because she
won't be around very long.

It would be hard to tell that Ben is out of his element in Las
Vegas, because at the moment it might seem that all he needs
to make life perfect is a haircut—and he does need that. The
sight of Ben and the girl confuses Marcia.

                    MARCIA
          Oh, excuse me. . . .

She takes a moment to get her bearings.

4b      MED. SHOT      BEN      ACROSS MARCIA

He recognizes her, but in the moment that supplants the
excitement of recognition he, probably quite unconsciously,
decides to play it very cool. Like most every Broadway director
with three Pulitzer Prizes, Ben pretends to have a great
contempt for all that is Hollywood. Never noted in his Who's
Who biography is that he once tried to direct a film, and it was
terrible. Dropping his head back, he closes his eyes, holds out
a limp hand, and the perfectly trained Oriental immediately
hands him a tall, cool drink.

5b      CLOSE SHOT      MARCIA

It's been a long time since she was so obviously unrecognized,
and this confuses her even more. Then she looks around and
realizes that she is in the right place.

                    MARCIA (cont.)
          This is Milton King's, isn't it?

6b    RESUME BEN ACROSS MARCIA

MARCIA (cont.)
I mean, it was last night.

Without opening his eyes, Ben waves one hand toward the
double doors leading to the suite.

BEN
Inside.

Marcia starts toward the doors, unable to keep her eyes from
Ben. Is it possible that he doesn't recognize her? So engrossed
is she that she almost walks into the glass door.


7b    FULL SHOT    KING'S SUITE    TOWARD DOORS IN B.G.    DAY

MILTON is eating a late, late breakfast with his eyes glued to a
TV set that is still playing the Marcia Hopkins divorce tape.
The TV is angled so that we can see the screen as well as
Marcia's entrance through the glass door. On the screen
Marcia has just gotten into her car, accompanied by the
Lawyers as the Crowd gathers 'round. The Police try to clear a
way for the car. Two Cops on motorcyles start off slowly in
front of the car, their sirens whining.

COMMENTATOR'S VOICE
. . . . and as the car leaves we
can see Miss Hopkins in the back
seat. Her hat is off and the
famous Marcia Hopkins blond
hair drops down around her
shoulders. Is she lighting a
cigarette . . .?

MARCIA
(from b.g.)
No, but she could use one.

MILTON
(eyes still on set)
Over on the table.

(CONTINUED)

7b (CONTINUED)

>                    COMMENTATOR'S VOICE
> Yes, I think she is, folks.

>                    MARCIA
> Thanks.

>                    MILTON
> You're welcome.

Then he looks up as Marcia crosses for the cigarette. He
jumps up and almost chokes over his coffee.

>                    MILTON (cont.)
> Marcia!?!

She pats him on the back. Recovering, he crosses quickly to
the set and turns it off, suddenly embarrassed, as though
caught peeping into something terribly private.

>                    MILTON (cont.)
> But you're there!

>                    MARCIA
> That was an hour ago.

>                    MILTON
> How about that! The magic of
> video tape.

He laughs as though he's said something terribly clever and
funny, but Marcia isn't really with him. She sits suddenly,
terribly exhausted and sad, no longer interested in a
cigarette—or anything. After a pause:

>                    MILTON (cont.)
> Have some coffee?

No answer. He decides to give her some anyway. As he pours:

>                    MILTON (cont.)
> Did you meet Ben Nichols
> outside?
>                    (no answer—but
>                    nothing daunted)
> That's Ben Nichols—from the

                                        (CONTINUED)

7b (CONTINUED)

        theatuh, daahling. You take it
        black?
                (answering for her)
        Sure, you take it black. And no
        sugar.

As he extends the coffee to Marcia, he starts to sit on the
couch.

                MILTON (cont.)
        Ben's been out here casting the
        new. . . .

At this moment, her mind on her own pain, Marcia turns
abruptly toward him. Her arm hits his extended hand, and the
steaming coffee goes flying, mostly all over him. He yelps in
anguish.

                MARCIA
        Oh, Milton . . .!

                MILTON
                (overlapping)
        Oh, boy!

                MARCIA
        I'm sorry.

He gets up, staggers around the room on his ankles.

                MILTON
        I don't have to look for a new act
        anymore. I can now . . .
                (his voice rising
                  two octaves)
        . . . be the new Tiny Tim.

                MARCIA
                (starting to laugh)
        Milton, I am sorry.

                MILTON
        It's all right, really. You're a
        wonderful girl, only I'm surprised
        three husbands survived long
        enough for you to divorce them.

8b          CLOSE SHOT          MARCIA

She's not sure whether she should laugh or cry.


9b          CLOSE SHOT          MILTON

As always, he stops to think a little too late. Quickly, he tries
to cover up.

                        MILTON
                Hey, I'm sorry.
                    (he rushes ahead)
                Have you ever seen me do my
                Henny Youngman?


10b         MED. FULL SHOT          MILTON AND MARCIA

He switches to his Youngman delivery.

                        MILTON (cont.)
                My hotel room is so small even
                the mice are hunchbacked.
                Speaking of sports cars, they're
                getting so small I saw a man buy
                two today and roller-skate away
                from the store. Take my wife . . .
                please! My wife is so bow-legged
                that when she sits around the
                house, she really sits around the
                house.

Marcia laughs in spite of herself, and Milton is overjoyed.

                        MILTON (cont.)
                I've been in love with the same
                woman for thirty-five years. If my
                wife ever finds out, she'll kill me.

Now, out of her laughter, Marcia suddenly starts to cry, an
abrupt transition that takes them both by surprise. He's left
hanging hopelessly for a moment as Marcia fails to control

                                        (CONTINUED)

10b (CONTINUED)

    herself and gives way to heartbreaking sobs. Then, awkwardly,
he sits next to her as she goes into his arms.

                      MILTON (cont.)
        Ah, Marcia. . . .

                      MARCIA
        Milton, it's so rotten. . . . it's just
        all so rotten. . . .

                      MILTON
        Well, sure you feel lousy. It's not
        every day you get a divorce.
                (then, he can't help
                  saying it)
        It's every other day.

                      MARCIA
        I'm a three-time loser. Three
        strikes and out.

                      MILTON
        Marcia. . . . you can have any
        man in the world. . . .

                      MARCIA
        There are no more men in the
        world—only soft little boys and
        gay big boys.

                      MILTON
        Thanks a lot.

                      MARCIA
                (with a gesture
                saying she doesn't
                mean him)
        You know . . . my mother had
        four husbands and God knows
        how many other men. And not
        one ever stood up to her. Not one!
        And now I've had three husbands
        . . . and how many others . . .
                (a beat)

                              (CONTINUED)

10b (CONTINUED)

>How I hated her. And now I'm
>just like her. I can't ever be
>without a man, and it's always
>the wrong one.

                    MILTON
>Marcia, why? I mean, what's
>wrong? What do you want?

                    MARCIA
>If you won't laugh—it's a corny
>line I've had in every picture I've
>ever made. I want to be a woman.

                    MILTON
>You're kidding! Marcia, you're so
>much woman you make Sophia
>Loren look like a boy.
>         (it's hopeless)
>Know what you should do? Go
>back to work. Right away, now,
>tomorrow. Aren't you supposed to
>do the new Billy Diamond film?

                    MARCIA
>Milton, I can't. My last picture
>. . . I barely made it.

Unseen, Ben has entered and stands just inside the door. He
stares with fascination at Marcia.

                    MILTON
>But you were great in it.

                    MARCIA
>I looked like a fat, ugly cow.

                    MILTON
>You were the most beautiful thing
>ever. During the scene by the
>waterfall I fainted three times.

                    MARCIA
>And old. I looked a hundred and
>six.

                                        (CONTINUED)

10b (CONTINUED)

                              MILTON
                    Marcia, you're crazy.
                              (he looks up, sees Ben)
                    Right, Ben? You saw the picture.

                              BEN
                              (moving in)
                    I think I agree with Miss
                    Hopkins. She was shot all wrong.
                    The lighting and angles. . . .

He breaks as they both look at him in astonishment. A pause,
then Marcia stands, enraged.

                              MARCIA
                    <u>Who the hell asked you</u>!!!!

                              BEN
                    Sorry. I was just. . . .

                              MARCIA
                    But who <u>asked</u> you?! And who <u>are</u>
                    you??!!

                              MILTON
                    I told you. That's Ben. . . .

                              MARCIA
                              (starts to sweep out)
                    I don't want to know! How <u>dare</u>
                    you!

She flees from the room without a backward glance,
disappears across the patio. As Milton looks at him with
disgust, Ben indicates contriteness. He had obviously acted out
of a indefinable hostility.

                              MILTON
                    Ben. . . .

                              BEN
                    Well—you asked me.

                              MILTON
                    Ahh, Ben. . . . she's a decent girl,
                    and she's in real trouble. I mean

                                        (CONTINUED)

10b (CONTINUED)

> real trouble. She got divorced
> today. She's scared, miserable.
> Who needed you?!

                    BEN
> So—I'm sorry.

                    MILTON
> Don't tell me you're sorry.

11b     FULL SHOT     MARCIA     EXT. MARCIA'S PATIO     DAY

She has stopped just short of entering her room, trying to
control herself. A path at the rear of the patio leads to an alley
where cars are parked. Ben appears from the adjoining patio,
moves toward her.

                    BEN
> Listen, Miss Hopkins, I'm. . . .

Startled, she turns quickly. He gets between her and the door.

                    BEN (cont.)
> I just want to apologize. . . .

                    MARCIA
> Just let me alone!

                    BEN
>                (suddenly stubborn)
> No!

Since she can't escape into her room, and she doesn't want to
go back to Milton's, she turns and runs toward the rear of the
patio, flings open the gate and disappears into the alley.
Hesitating only a moment, Ben follows.

12b     FULL SHOT     ALLEY     ACROSS MARCIA'S CAR     DAY

Her car stands with the passenger side nearer the gate. She
climbs into the car, sliding to the driver's seat in f.g. She has
not completely closed the door on the passenger's side, and as

                                                  (CONTINUED)

12b (CONTINUED)

    she reaches to do so, Ben appears and grabs the door. The
    handle slips from her grasp, which only makes her more
    angry.

                         MARCIA
                Let me alone!

    Turning the key, she races the motor. Ben makes an
    instantaneous decision, jumps in as the car speeds off.

The preceding sequence illustrates a different aspect of screen
writing. Whereas the first section delivered character information for
the benefit of the viewer, the second section sets out to inform the
actor and the director. There are few opportunities here to characterize
the *real* Ben Nichols, since we see him in what is, for him, an unnatural milieu. His character, which will undergo more stress and
change than Marcia's, must necessarily be developed more slowly. But
at the first reading, the actor and the director should be given a preview. They must understand at once that what they see is not what
they are going to get. Both of them will eventually dig deeper into
Ben's character, but the writer's contribution gets them off to a flying
start.

Today, many filmmakers are afraid to deal with sentiment, dismissing it as sentimentality. But the ability to properly handle sentiment and its underlying emotion, to get the most out of it without
going over the line into mawkishness, is the mark of the true dram-
atist. The greatest dramas ever written or performed have been love
stories, concerned with the emotional contacts and conflicts of human
beings. If the characters in a film do not "touch" each other, how can
they possibly touch the viewer? Only if the writer can get *inside* his
characters will his stories become drama and not just narrations.

In this sequence, Marcia begins to unload her problem but, to
avoid a maudlin tone, her plaint is played against a counterpoint of
comedy. This enables the writer (near the start of scene 10) to take
advantage of a dramatic device, one which, when properly and honestly used, is *always* effective. The concept is deceptively simple; the
execution, both in writing and in acting, is very difficult. It involves
an off-balance emotional switch—laughter turns suddenly into tears,
or tears just as suddenly burst into laughter. Opportunities for using
this artifice are rare, and the reasons for the sudden break must be
carefully planted.

In this instance the reasons are strongly developed, but they are
purposely thrust aside during Milton's comedy routine. The break is

a sudden surprise, but the viewer will quickly recall the earlier emotion and accept its resurgence. However, the comedy interlude allows us to avoid an extended scene of self-pity, and its possible continuation is cut short by another variation of the same device, as self-pity suddenly turns into self-righteous anger.

The confrontation between Marcia and Ben is another version of the instant conflict with which so many dramatic romances begin. When ingeniously handled, nothing better has yet been created for this situation.

# 7

# *Point, Counterpoint*

The screen's dullest set-up is a knee-length profile shot of two players facing each other. The screen's dullest *scene* is recorded when those two players in that dull set-up tell each other in strictly utilitarian language what the scene is all about. Fortunately, quite a few directors have learned how to vary their set-ups; not many writers have learned how to flavor their scenes with the spice of variety.

Since *sound* and *picture* can be divorced at will, film presents an unequalled opportunity for unusual *composite* effects, or, as in music, the play of point and counterpoint. Think of the camera as one instrument, the sound recorder as another. As long as they stay in the same key, each can carry a different melodic line. The result can be far more absorbing than if they both carry the same tune.

The following excerpt will speak for itself. In the script it follows hard on the heels of the last sequence in Chapter 6.

1c    EXT. HIGHWAY  ANGLE TOWARD ALLEY ENTRANCE    LATE DAY

    There is little traffic, but even if there were it would make no difference to Marcia; without looking or slackening speed, she spins the car from the alley onto the highway, turning in a direction that leads out of town. A car, speeding in the opposite direction barely averts an immediate smashup by careening away from Marcia's car, brakes jammed, tires screeching.

2c    TWO SHOT    MARCIA AND BEN    OTHER CAR IN FAR B.G.

    Ben turns front, relieved that the accident has been averted. His relief is short lived, however, as he sees—

3c      INSERT        MARCIA'S RIGHT FOOT

Pressing the gas pedal to the floor


4c      RESUME TWO SHOT        BEN AND MARCIA

Her face is set determinedly. She looks straight ahead with no
sense of Ben's presence. Ben's eyes flick toward the
speedometer.


5c      CLOSE SHOT        DASHBOARD        INSERT SPEEDOMETER

The needle swings to and past 90 mph. The top of the
speedometer reads 140 mph. Actually, the car is capable of
doing between 115-120.

(NOTE: During this scene there will be a series of INTERCUTS
between Marcia and Ben, the speedometer, and the EXTERIOR,
this last to get a more objective sense of the car's speed from a
FIXED CAMERA POSITION.)


6c      RESUME TWO SHOT        MARCIA AND BEN

                        BEN
                  (very uneasily)
              I think it would be a good
              idea. . . .

                      MARCIA
                  (cuts in, sharply)
              Listen! I don't know who you are,
              and I certainly don't know what
              you're doing in my car.

                        BEN
              Then why don't you stop, call the
              cops and have me arrested?

If anything, the car goes faster. Ben tries to relax. The road is
free of traffic—they are in the desert now. Perhaps if he tries
another tack it will work.

                                        (CONTINUED)

6c (CONTINUED)

> BEN (cont.)
> Ever hear of Jason Powers?
> (no response)
> You know—the painter. He lived
> in East Hampton. I've got a place
> there. Ten years ago, when he
> was starving, I bought two of his
> paintings for a couple of hundred
> bucks each. I didn't even like
> them, but he was a friend. The
> same size pictures now go for
> fifty–sixty grand.

He stops suddenly—mouth wide open—stares ahead.


7c     BEN'S POV       APPROACHING TRUCK

Preceded by a car with a flashing yellow light, it is towing half
of a motor home which carries a large sign—"WIDE LOAD!"


8c     CLOSE TWO SHOT       BEN AND MARCIA

Ben closes his eyes, grits his teeth. Marcia looks angrily
straight ahead, oblivious to everything. Suddenly we hear the
sound of Marcia's car, echoing off the passing truck and motor
home, as it hurtles past. Ben takes a deep breath, opens his
eyes, continues doggedly without looking at her.

> BEN (cont.)
> Anyway . . . the minute he
> became wildly successful he quit
> painting. For the last four years
> of his life—nothing. Not one
> picture. He tried. Not a day went
> by that he didn't go into his
> studio. Then one night we were at
> the same party. Jason was in a
> rage about something. Cold sober,

                                        (CONTINUED)

8c (CONTINUED)

>but very hostile—somebody must
>have asked him why he wasn't
>painting any more—that always
>set him off. Everybody was going
>to another party, and we went out
>to our cars together. One of the
>two girls with him wanted to
>drive, and that just made him
>more angry. I said, 'Listen, Jase,
>my car's got something wrong
>with it; let me take yours, and
>you ride along.' He just stared at
>me like he didn't know me, and
>he said, 'You go to hell, too!'

His voice rises a couple of decibels and half an octave as he
glances quickly at Marcia, then back to the road ahead.

9c      BEN'S POV       FARM TRACTOR

A patient plodder, it is heading for home. Beyond, the second
half of the motor home is approaching at some speed. The
CAMERA (in Marcia's car) sweeps dizzily around the tractor
and back into its proper lane without an inch to spare. The
shot sways as Marcia fights the car back under control and on
a straight line.

10c     TWO SHOT        BEN AND MARCIA

Ben breathes again. Then—relentlessly . . .

>BEN (cont.)
>Anyway . . . a few minutes after
>I got to the other party somebody
>came in and said Jason was dead.
>He'd run off the highway on a
>straight stretch, just run off at
>about a hundred, hit a tree, and

(CONTINUED)

10c (CONTINUED)

killed himself and both girls. Two
girls he hardly knew who were
impressed with the fact that they
were with America's most famous
painter.
(pause)
What a bad thing he did.
(another pause)
The point is, Miss Hopkins, if
you're going to kill yourself do it
clean—and alone.

MARCIA
(tightly)
I didn't ask you in this car!!

She glances at him briefly, but in the moment her eyes are
averted she almost misses a bend in the road. Her foot hits the
brake, her hands whip the wheel; the car screeches into a
skid, then fish-tails back and forth as Marcia expertly regains
control. It takes all of Ben's nerve not to grab the wheel in
panic, and when the car maintains its equilibrium he sinks
back in a sweat, fully expecting Marcia to slow down now.
When he realizes that she has no intention of stopping, he sits
up, very angry. He's through coddling; finished cajoling.
Instinctively, his voice takes on the quality that has, when
ringing through an empty theater during rehearsal, turned
many an actor's blood cold.

BEN
Stop the car! Now!!

MARCIA
If you dare touch this wheel. . . .

BEN
I'm not going to touch anything.
But you are! You're going to stop
the car! Now! This second!!

The first bit of doubt shows on Marcia's face. He's getting to
her.

(CONTINUED)

10c (CONTINUED)

> BEN (cont.)
> I'm not about to end up dead from
> you, baby-doll, so cut the
> nonsense! Stop this car, right
> now!!

Almost imperceptibly, her foot lifts from the pedal—then completely off. The car loses speed as Marcia grips the wheel tighter and tighter, her face freezing into a mask of a chastened little girl, fighting back tears of guilt and anger. The car comes almost to rest, inching along until Ben reaches for the gear lever and snaps it from Drive to Neutral. The car stops. He switches the key to OFF.

It is dusk, soon to be night in that swift transition from light to dark that is characteristic of the desert. And it is very silent, the only sound being the quick breathing of Marcia and Ben. He lights a cigarette, his hand shaking slightly. Each stares straight ahead and then, slowly, Marcia lowers her head to the top of the steering wheel, her hands sliding up the wheel until they reach the side of her head. All at once she digs her hands deep in her hair as though to keep the top of her head from coming off. Still Ben doesn't look at her. It is very quiet.

This sequence is a director's and an editor's delight. The writer starts things moving with the first few cuts; then, simply indicating the obvious need for intercutting, he leaves the field to the director, the actors, and the editor. He knows the timing, the set-ups, the visual effects, and the stunts are out of his hands. These are technical aspects. Creatively, however, he has done the one thing that gives the scene real worth. By wedding a rather ordinary runaway scene to one which, if played in a bar or a living room would be merely a mildly interesting philosophical comment, he has contrived an exciting and absorbing sequence. The action gives Ben's story meaning, while the story underscores the danger of the action.

Although Ben's anecdote adds another order of drama and suspense to the scene, it really has nothing to do with the situation. It has no effect on Marcia—nor should it. Marcia is brought to her senses not by Ben's moralizing but by his talent for domination, and that is a direct statement of the plot.

Though Ben's effort at rational persuasion has no effect on Marcia—indeed, the scene would be trite and misleading if it did—it does tell us something about the real Ben. A simple battle of wills would have given us little more than a straight action montage. But here the writer has supplied action, philosophy, psychology, and character, all in one easy-to-take dose. By splitting the components of the film, he has given us not a fiddle solo, but a string quartet.

The next excerpt is an example of the sort of scene that can be realized only in films—the silent "montage" which speaks volumes. Here we have comedy, subliminal tragedy, irony, social contrast and comment, and an undercurrent of apprehension. Married life for Marcia and Ben will not be easy. Being a public idol is difficult—*living* with one may be impossible.

1d    LONG SHOT    EXT. FRANKLIN ROOSEVELT DRIVE    DAY

A limousine speeds south on the drive TOWARD CAMERA. On the left is the United Nations Building; to the right, the river. Weaving in and out of traffic, trying to keep up with the limo, are four smaller cars filled with newspaper people, their papers' logos stencilled on the car doors.

2d    LONG SHOT    EXT. RAMP TO MANHATTAN BRIDGE    DAY

The traffic is heavier and the pursuing cars find it difficult to keep up. In the right of frame is New York City Hall. As the cars pass BENEATH CAMERA:

3d    WHIP PAN TO FRAME

The speeding limousine, as it heads toward downtown Brooklyn.

4d    LONG SHOT    EXT. CRANBERRY STREET,
    ANGLE TOWARD HARBOR    BROOKLYN HEIGHTS

In this little backwash area of Brooklyn is a section with unique charm. There are rows of early Nineteenth Century houses, classic in design and well preserved. The most striking

(CONTINUED)

4d (CONTINUED)

feature of the area is its view. Directly opposite the tip of
Manhattan Island, it affords a panorama of the downtown
skyline. To the left, and clearly seen, is the Statue of Liberty. A
row of houses stretches down to a lower mall that runs for
several blocks along the waterfront. From the mall at the rear,
one sees that these homes are built on a steep incline and
drop three or four levels down from the street. Between the
houses and the mall is an area of trees and shrubs, or formal
gardens.

The limousine careens into sight around a corner and
CAMERA PANS it to the front of the corner house, where it
stops. A crowd of NEIGHBORHOOD PEOPLE has gathered for
the arrival.

5d     MEDIUM FULL SHOT          ACROSS LIMOUSINE TOWARD
                                  HOUSE

The car doors open; Alex and Wolfe emerge to run
interference. In the b.g. the bird-dogging newspaper cars pull
up. Ben and Marcia step out of the limo. This may be the only
time we will ever see Ben dressed up, and with sufficient
reason, for this is his wedding day. He helps Marcia, warding
off grasping arms and eager faces. CAMERAMEN are wildly
shooting stills in f.g. over the top of the limousine, while
others try to force their way through the crowd.

6d     REVERSE SHOT

As Marcia and Ben thrust their way toward the house. Marcia
is wearing a simple pastel chiffon dress and a tiny pill-box hat
and, of course, dark glasses.

7d     CLOSE SHOT       FRONT DOOR OF HOUSE

It is opened by a MAN in his middle thirties who looks
vaguely like Ben and is, in fact, Ben's younger BROTHER. He is

(CONTINUED)

7d (CONTINUED)

an accountant and he bought a new suit for the occasion and he couldn't be more uncomfortable or bewildered. Just behind the brother we glimpse an ELDERLY MAN and WOMAN, Ben's PARENTS. As Marcia and Ben enter the house, the parents' attitude toward their son is that of a total stranger and, if they dared look at their future daughter-in-law, they just couldn't believe it. The door is shut by the strenuous efforts of the Brother and Alex.

8d      FULL SHOT       EXT. PARENTS' HOUSE

As some people, caring not about the carefully trimmed hedges and window boxes, attempt to look through the lower front windows, others start to run around the corner of the house, trampling through the garden.

9d      FULL SHOT       THE MALL       ANGLE TOWARD SKYLINE

In right frame, part of the rear of the house; in left frame b.g., the striking view of downtown New York. Both curiosity-seekers and newsmen race around to the back, hoping to get a better vantage point. CAMERA SELECTS A STILL PHOTOGRAPHER more versatile than the others.

10d     FULL SHOT       REAR GARDEN       TOWARD HOUSE

The Photographer spots an apple tree whose branches spread close to the house. He scrambles up the tree and works his way along a branch to view through one of the lower windows. Delighted, he begins snapping shots.

11d     PHOTOGRAPHER'S POV       INTO INT. OF HOUSE

Through the window we see an old-fashioned living room. Aside from those people we have already seen, an additional

(CONTINUED)

11d (CONTINUED)

MAN plays a prominent part. He is probably a JUDGE, a man
in late middle-age, stout, balding, with the hearty demeanor of
a ward heeler who made good. Introductions are taking place.
The Judge is a big laugher, although we hear nothing from the
inside of the house.

From the attitudes of everyone inside, the whole idea is to get
to it and get it over with. Clearly, Ben is the director even at
his own wedding. Through it all he never really looks at his
family, and even from here they impress us as helpless losers.
The Judge would like to prolong his moment of glory, but Ben
simply wants to get to it. There is confusion as they line up in
the proper places—the Judge's back to us, Marcia and Ben
facing him. And then a moment of dissension develops as the
Brother and Father each urges the other to stand up with Ben.
Ben turns angrily to them, silencing them both. The Father
edges to Ben's side as the Judge opens his book

DISSOLVE TO:

12d    FULL SHOT        FRONT OF HOUSE        TOWARD DOOR  DAY

The crowd is much larger now. Two patrol cars have pulled up
and there are FOUR POLICEMEN ready to do their duty. A
LIEUTENANT of police stands head and shoulders over
everyone else in a position of command. The front door opens
and, as Wolfe and Alex precede the newly-weds, the Police
clear their path to the limousine. The Lieutenant makes his
way to Marcia's side where, with his arm linked with Ben's
around her back, he becomes her stalwart protector, not
unaware of the cameras as they click and grind.

13d    REVERSE SHOT        TOWARD CAR

A Patrolman opens the limo door and the wedding party
climbs in. Two of the cops run for their car, and with
screaming siren, they edge forward to lead the way back to
Manhattan. Both cars pick up speed as they break free,
disappearing around the corner.

14d    MED. FULL SHOT        FRONT OF HOUSE

> The crowd has surged away from the house. Hedges are
> trampled; rows of petunias crushed into the ground, and one
> of the window boxes sags from its place. The door opens
> tentatively, and finally completely, as Ben's brother realizes
> they are safe. The Mother and Father move to his side, and all
> three peer toward the corner where the car was last seen.
> They are silent; stunned; only fifteen minutes since the
> Arrival, and now it's all over. Their son brought a Love
> Goddess into their home, married her, and left; nobody really
> even bothered to say "hello." The Mother holds a home-made
> wedding cake completely untouched, which they forgot to take.

It is taken for granted that good literature has more than one
level of meaning, that each reader will absorb everything at his level,
and that he will be satisfied that that is exactly what the book has to
offer. He does not have the capacity to understand that deeper levels
may exist. *Alice in Wonderland* says one thing to a child, another to
the average adult, and something more profound to the intellectual
(or so I'm told).

Film has the same potential but, for obvious reasons, the filmmaker's first responsibility is to satisfy those viewers who are believed
to appreciate only the more "shallow" levels of meaning and, whatever
his pretensions, he works hard to perfect this important aspect of his
trade. With a little added effort, however, it is quite possible to throw
a bit of light into corners which are normally obscure.

The preceding sequence not only plays for the obvious humor of
the situation while hinting at problems that will confront Ben and
Marcia in the future; it also makes a valid, if ironic, comment on an
interesting aspect of that part of the "American Dream" of which we
are the most proud: the freedom of the descendants of immigrants to
escape their castes, to climb the ladder of success. The scene points
out to those who care to see it that the much admired and universally
desired escape is often achieved at the expense of another highly regarded ideal, a close and loving family life.

The point is, if you think you have something profound to say,
say it—but don't ever forget that "broad appeal" is the first requisite
for a long and successful film career. And if you can manage to make
that middle level entertaining enough, you may find that *every* level
is more than satisfied.

# 8

# *The Art of Weaving*

A screenplay is an intricately assembled body in which the plot (the skeleton) is far outweighed in interest and importance by the characters (the flesh). It can be compared to a symphony in which a variety of chords, tempos, and melodic lines are woven into a polyphonic ensemble, or a tapestry in which a number of monochromatic threads, of little aesthetic value in themselves, are interlaced to form a multicolored work of art, with all the richness that phrase implies.

A quantity of rules have been concocted to ease the labors of the screen writer; they also serve to curb his creativity. Happily, to quote the old saw, rules are made to be broken, and this seems especially true in filmmaking, perhaps because the art is so young. The newest sensation is often only the latest rule breaker. For example, one ancient stricture held that the leading man must always "play it straight," a practice which furnished steady employment for a host of comics who played the leading men's "best friends." However, William Powell, Cary Grant, and Jimmy Stewart proved that they could be romantic *and* funny, while acting up a storm. Another precept maintained that the story didn't really get under way until the "hero" encountered the "heroine"—or vice versa. As any bridge player can testify, strict adherance to even the most respected rules can sometimes lead to mediocre play, and occasionally to disaster. The above rule, for instance, may be valid for an ordinary film; in pictures of quality it is broken time and time again. But there is always a reason.

*The Caine Mutiny* does not suffer from the fact that Captain Queeg—the story's most important character, its reason for being— does not make his appearance for nearly half an hour after the start of the film and that he exits under a cloud with 20 minutes still to play. Strong collateral stories and characters keep the film alive before and after Queeg's tale is told. Similarly, in another classic, *Casa-*

*blanca*, Rick (Humphrey Bogart) appears eight minutes after the main title and Ilsa (Ingrid Bergman) walks into Rick's Cafe some 16 minutes later. These two do not face each other until 8 minutes after her entry into the film. Does that mean that the first half hour of *Casablanca* has little appeal for the viewer? By no means.

An examination of the structure and the make-up of this film may help us to understand how a number of threads, most of which, if handled with less finesse, would be considered quite hackneyed, can be woven into a superlative tapestry. First, the opening.

The film takes advantage of an old Hollywood device: making the viewer think he is about to see a film of world-shaking importance. A shot of a slowly spinning globe (and what could be more earth-shaking than that?) dissolves into a montage of stock shots and a map. The stock shots show groups of refugees fleeing the German invasion of France, while the map traces their flight from Paris through Marseilles across the Mediterranean and northern Africa to the unoccupied French city of Casablanca. Narration informs us that from here those few who can beg, buy, or steal exit visas for Lisbon can eventually reach the free West.

The first "straight" sequence immediately develops a dramatic situation—the obligatory *problem*, or *obstacle*. Two German couriers, carrying important letters of transit, have been killed, the papers stolen. A police dragnet rounds up the undocumented, and an underground fighter is killed as he attempts to escape the net. This action holds the viewer's interest while establishing the importance and value of the stolen documents and the peril involved in their possession. The sequence also creates a mood of suspense and imminent catastrophe that continues to underscore the entire film.

The opening also shows us the "stew" which was war-time Casablanca—less a refuge than an open prison for spies, revolutionaries, adventurers, and black-marketeers of every nationality, race, and color. Aside from the ever-simmering intrigue there is little for people to do, and those who can afford it spend their evenings dining, drinking, and gambling at Rick's Cafe Americain. Here, the latter half of the first eight minutes is spent in an assortment of vignettes of wheelers, dealers, and their "marks"—mere bits of colored threads, seen for a moment then disappearing into the neutral background until, at the needed time, they are once more displayed to lend their colors to the tapestry.

With the introduction of Rick (Humphrey Bogart) the main story gets under way. In short order we meet Ugarte (Peter Lorre), Captain Renault (Claude Raines), and the Gestapo Major Strasser (Conrad Veidt). But the next 13 minutes belong to Lorre. His story, though short, is a prime motivator. This extended vignette of a repellent but interesting trader in black market exit visas serves to deliver the stolen documents into Rick's unwilling hands while it develops, on a more specific and personal basis, the turmoil and peril of the times and the locale. It also establishes Rick as a man who refuses to take sides, even at the cost of another's life, and it sets up a perfect, though unpretentious, entrance for Ilsa (Ingrid Bergman)—24 minutes into the film. The third side of the triangle, Victor Laszlo (Paul Henreid), enters with her.

What raises this film well above the ordinary (and this is most important) is that the subsidiary characters are never treated as mere props to the leading players. Each has his own story and each such story is, *in its own right*, understandable, acceptable, believable, and intriguing. Bogart, Bergman, and Henreid are the main protagonists, but their story would be little more than a routine triangle without the obstacles and intercession of the other characters in the film as they attempt to manage *their own* destinies.

After Lorre's brief episode, there is Captain Renault, whose presence lends danger, humor, and opportunities for surprising character developments involving both him and Rick. Without him, a satisfactory denouement would be impossible. He is the "attractive scoundrel," a type that is always, when well done, a great addition to any adventure film. A man of easy loyalty, he acts as a tool for the Gestapo, but also as a genial buffer between it and Rick. His character requires no dredging of the past; he is what you see and hear, capable of any behavior, which proves of great value at the film's climax.

The same is true of Major Strasser. The single and sinister character and purpose of the Gestapo had already been delineated in so many films and novels that any digging in this ground would have been redundant. Still, a number of interesting scenes, plus the personality of Veidt himself suffice to make Major Strasser a complete character, who represents one of the chief *obstacles* that Rick must overcome.

An interesting minor thread is that of a young couple who are so representative of some of Casablanca's temporary inhabitants that they are not identified by name. They are seen at the film's opening purely as members of the general movement in shots of no greater length than those of any other background extra. Their story, carried essentially by the wife, illustrates the problems of the city's more needy refugees, and dramatizes the sacrifices that must be made to facilitate a flight to freedom. Starting as a small building block in the construction of Renault's character, they eventually serve a far more important purpose than their short "footage" would suggest. They are used to show us a side of Rick that he, and the film, have been at some pains to conceal.

It is essential that the beginning screen writer understand the technical importance of this kind of scene. To make Rick's trouble-

free existence in Casablanca legitimate and believable, it must be
established early in the film that he is completely neutral—refusing
to take sides, personal or political, he does not seem to care who wins
the war, nor does he interfere with local police action, no matter how
unjust it may be. But the plot demands that he must eventually take
a stand. Of course, the viewer doesn't know this, but we do, and so
the scene with the young couple whom he helps at no small financial
cost to himself. Although there is no story connection between this
sequence and the final scenes of the film, it conditions the viewer to
accept Rick's behavior in the climax, both emotionally and intellectually. It is always far better to contrive a *dramatization* of an unforeseen but necessary character transition than simply to verbalize it.

A most important secondary thread is Sam (Dooley Wilson) the
singer and piano player. He, too, has little to do with the plot directly,
but a great deal to do with bringing us closer to Rick and Ilsa, and to
the meat of their personal story. Here, a brilliant use of an old cliché,
the "our song" device, saves us miles of explanation and exposition.
Sam has only to start playing "As Time Goes By" and although, as
viewers, we know nothing yet of their past relationship, its *sense*
comes flooding back to us miraculously, even as it does to Rick and
Ilsa. We feel and believe that these two do indeed share a deep and
undying love. Sam's warm personality and loyalty help us to get un-
derneath Rick's apparently cold and selfish demeanor. This "reverse"
method of characterization—the "his dog loves him so he can't be
too bad" ploy—is a much used and abused device but, when woven
into a story with skill, it can seem fresh, and it can certainly be
effective.

Other minor threads weave in and out of the film, helping to
create a totally satisfactory tapestry. Sydney Greenstreet, as the de-
vious competitor, supplies a mixture of humor, suspense, and information. He, too, is a foil to bring out aspects of Rick's personality and
behavior. Sakall, the comic Germanic waiter, representing the softer
side of the Teutonic character, and Kinsky, the bartender, doing the
same for the Slavs, supply flashes of humor to alleviate the drama and
suspense.

A study of these and other threads of the fabric exposes, at first,
the mass of cliche characters and situations which contrive to make
this exceptional film. But a deeper analysis brings out a very important
point, one which the screen writer should constantly bear in mind:
He can avail himself of "outside" help of a kind that is rare in the
world of the creative artist. A writer who neglects to take advantage
of this help, whether through ignorance or willfullness, will always
fall short of his potential. For, beyond the help of the director and the
film editor (which can sometimes prove to be a hindrance) he can

count on the availability of the greatest pool of auxiliary talent to be found in the field of art—"acting" in all of its many categories.

Very few writers are able, in words, to create people as interesting or as compelling as Bogart, Bergman, Henreid, Raines, Veidt, Lorre, Wilson, Greenstreet, Sakall, and Kinsky. Each can contribute layers of personality and meaning that few authors could create; and, though a screen writer can hardly anticipate exactly who will play any particular role in his script, it will pay him to assume that he is going to get the best. He can then write each character with a built-in potential for acting creativity beyond that which can be gotten from even the most careful reading.

A study of the following schematic diagram (by minutes) of *Casablanca* may furnish some insight into the nature of the inter-weaving of the many subsidiary themes and characters which, when skillfully maneuvered, will manage to present the appearance of a monolithic whole.

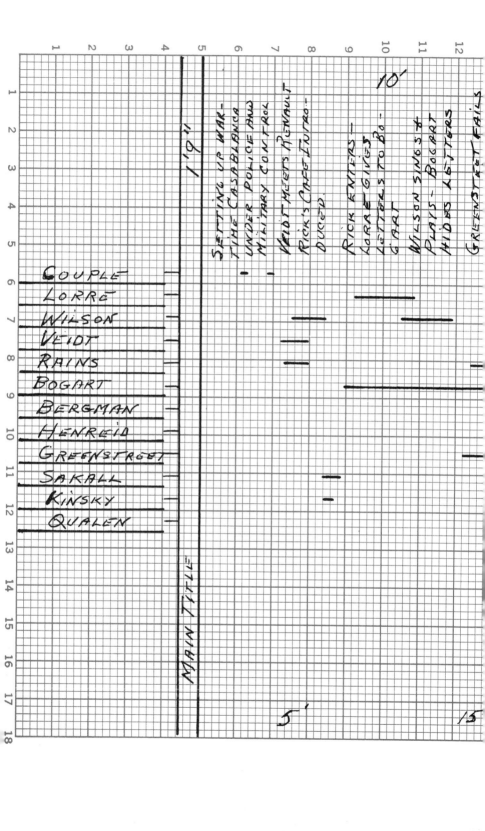

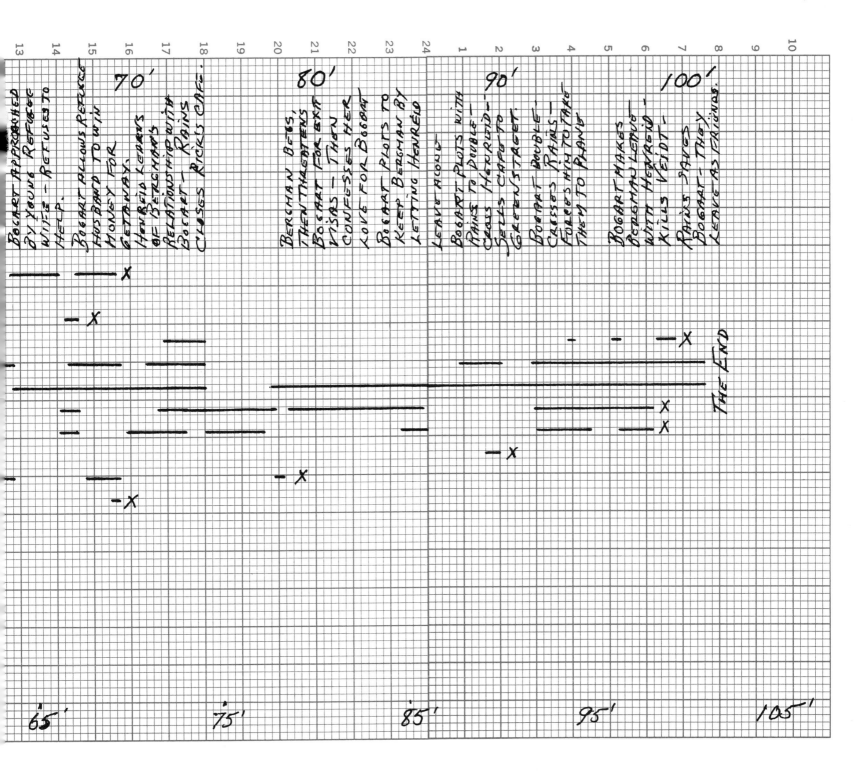

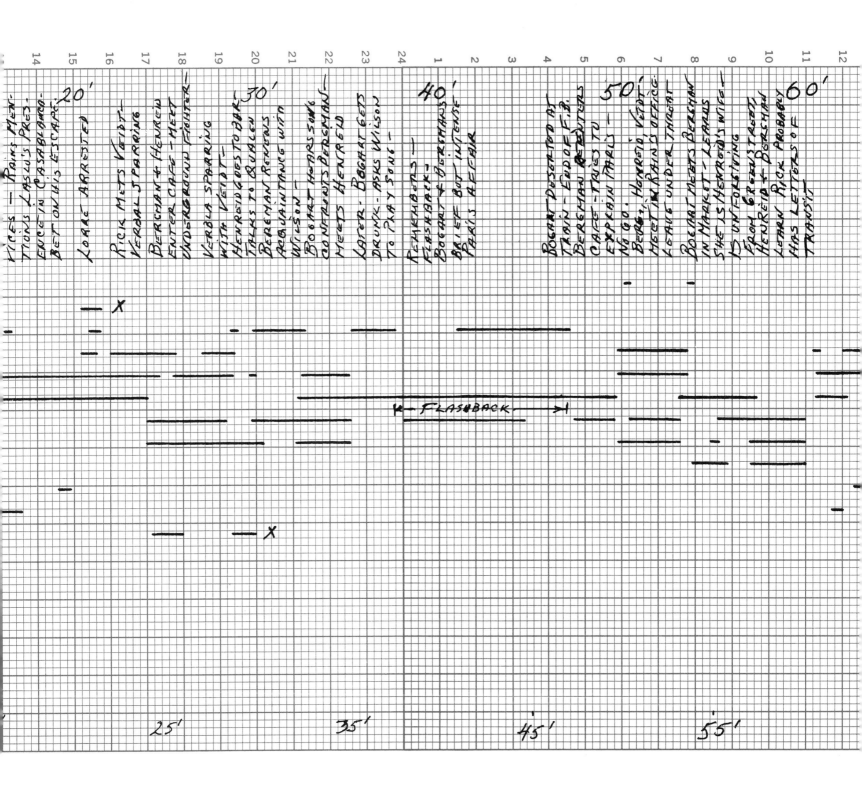

# 9

# *No Piece Without War*

One of literature's few unbreakable rules is simply this: Without conflict there is no drama. The degree of conflict can vary: It can be as earth-shaking as a world war, as futile as a religious massacre over a minor heresy, or as slight as an argument over an umpire's decision, but it had better be there. A scene without conflict is like oatmeal without salt or spaghetti without sauce—flat and inedible.

Conflict, however, does more than merely add spice or physical excitement to a situation. Its greatest contribution, and purpose, is to enable the viewer to catch a character *in reaction*. At any level, a conflict allows the writer to expose attitudes, beliefs, and emotions by confronting his character with a challenge, by placing him under stress. It is at such a time that a person's true nature emerges, resulting in defensive violence, a show of cowardice, a retreat into deception, or a decision to tell the truth. Without the stimulus of conflict a character will remain under control, unemotional, static—and very, very dull.

Conflict also serves to set up problems for the future, thus creating suspense (here used in its broader sense, not just as experienced in mystery or horror stories). It initiates intercharacter reactions, and the resulting attitudes can be expanded into dramatic transitions in later sequences. The following is an example from *The Caine Mutiny*.

34    FULL SHOT    INT. CAPTAIN'S CABIN    DAY

Willie and Maryk enter the cabin. CAPTAIN DeVRIESS,
Commanding Officer of the Caine, sits at a small desk in b.g.,
completely naked except for a small towel around his middle.
Willie is startled. The skipper is hardly his idea of what the

(CONTINUED)

**34** (CONTINUED)

>    captain of a U.S. battleship should look like, and his face
>    shows it. DeVriess takes it in stride, but misses nothing.

>                    MARYK
>           Captain DeVriess, this is Ensign
>           Keith.

>    DeVriess puts out his hand.

>                    DeVRIESS
>           Keith . . .

>    They shake hands. DeVriess settles back in his chair, waits a
>    moment. Then:

>                    DeVRIESS (cont.)
>           May I see your orders and
>           qualifications jacket? Or are they
>           a military secret?

>                    WILLIE
>              (coming to)
>           I'm sorry, sir . . .

>    He hands over the requested papers. DeVriess leafs through
>    them casually.

>                    DeVRIESS
>              (reading)
>           Princeton, '41—top five percent
>           in Midshipmans' School . . . uh,
>           huh . . . pretty good background,
>           pretty good record . . .
>              (looks up at Willie)
>           Disappointed they assigned you to
>           a minesweeper, Keith?

>                    WILLIE
>           Well, sir, to be honest, yes sir.

>                    DeVRIESS
>           You saw yourself in a carrier or a
>           battleship, no doubt.

>                    WILLIE
>           Yes, sir. I had hoped . . .

>                                              (CONTINUED)

34 (CONTINUED)

                    DeVRIESS
                  (cutting in)
              Well, I only hope you're good
              enough for the Caine.

                    WILLIE
                  (with just a trace
                  of sarcasm)
              I shall try to be worthy of this
              assignment, sir.

                    DeVRIESS
                  (keeping him on
                  the hook)
              She's not a battleship or a carrier.
              The Caine is a beaten-up tub.
              After 18 months of combat it
              takes 24 hours a day just to keep
              her in one piece.

                    WILLIE
                  (with little conviction)
              I understand, sir.

                    DeVRIESS
              I don't think you do. But whether
              you like it or not, Keith, you're in
              the junk-yard navy.
                  (he turns to Maryk)
              Steve, put him with Keefer in
              communications—and tell Tom to
              show this Princeton tiger and our
              other new Ensign around the
              ship.

                    MARYK
                  (with a slight smile)
              Yes, sir.

He and Keith head for the cabin door, but are stopped by
DeVriess' voice.

                    DeVRIESS
              And Keith . . . don't take it so
              hard. War is hell.

This could have been a simple narrative scene—a junior officer reporting for duty. But the immediate result of Keith's snide attitude is an atmosphere of conflict—a minor one, to be sure, but nevertheless a conflict which allows us to add a facet to DeVriess' character, his feeling for the ship, and the ship itself. It also reveals Keith's naivete, a trait that later makes him Queeg's only admirer. The reluctant, but inevitable change in that admiration dramatizes Queeg's alienation of the entire crew. This small conflict also enables us to contrive a legitimately up-beat "tag" for the film. As I analyze it now I find it truly remarkable how important the insertion of this minor conflict into a "minor" scene is to the dramatic evolution of the characters and the plot of the story.

Another sequence from the same film illustrates how a *contrived* conflict can give a scene body, interest, and character development. In this scene, DeVriess is leaving the Caine after transferring the command to Captain Queeg.

87      FULL SHOT      NEAR GANGWAY                    DAY

Willie is the O.O.D. as DeVriess walks briskly into the scene. Maryk and the other officers stand nearby, as do most of the members of the crew. In the b.g., Whittaker and the steward's mates finish loading the last of the Captain's bags into the gig. Willie steps forward.

WILLIE
Attention on deck!

All the men spring to attention. DeVriess snaps a salute at Willie.

DeVRIESS
Request permission to leave.

WILLIE
(saluting formally)
Permission granted, sir.

The Captain is about to start for the ladder when Meatball speaks O.S.

MEATBALL'S VOICE (O.S.)
Captain, sir. . . .

88      REVERSE SHOT      MEN OF THE CREW      OVER DeVRIESS'
                                                       SHOULDER

Meatball, Horrible, the Chiefs and the rest of the Caine's crew stand at attention.

(CONTINUED)

88 (CONTINUED)

> DeVRIESS
> What is it, Meatball?

> MEATBALL
> Nothing, sir. . . . a . . . a few of
> the guys chipped in and. . . .

He hauls out a square jewelry box, hands it to DeVriess.


89      OVER SHOULDER SHOT       ON DeVRIESS

He takes the box from Meatball's hand, opens it to disclose a
wristwatch. He looks up sharply at the men.

> DeVRIESS
> Whose idea was this?
>> (there is no
>> response)
> Well, I won't accept it. It's against
> Navy regulations.


90      OVER SHOULDER SHOT       MEATBALL, HORRIBLE AND MEN

Meatball glances at the others hopelessly.

> MEATBALL
> Well, that's what I told 'em sir,
> but . . .

> HORRIBLE
>> (cutting in)
> You don't always go by
> regulations, Captain.


91      MED. SHOT       FAVORING DeVRIESS

> DeVRIESS
> That's my trouble. I've been on
> the Caine too long.

                                    (CONTINUED)

91 (CONTINUED)

He places the case and the watch on a small temporary table
near the rail, then turns back to the crew.

>           DeVRIESS
>   Now you men take an even strain
>   with the new skipper and
>   everything will be all right.
>           (to Willie)
>   I am leaving the ship.

>           WILLIE
>   Yes, sir.

As DeVriess turns to the gangway, the bos'n starts piping.
DeVriess and the rest of the officers and men snap to
attention and salute. When the bos'n stops tootling, DeVriess
continues down the gangway, but stops almost at once. At eye
level in front of him is the watch case he had just put down.

>           DeVRIESS
>   Well, what do you know?
>   Somebody left his watch lying
>   around.

He takes off his own watch, puts it in his pocket, then
extracts the new one from its case. He slips it onto his wrist.

>           DeVRIESS (cont.)
>   Might as well have a souvenir of
>   this old bucket. Not a bad looking
>   watch at that. What time is it Mr.
>   Keith?

>           WILLIE
>   Eleven hundred, sir.

>           DeVRIESS
>           (adjusting the watch's
>           hands)
>   Make it ten-thirty.
>           (to sailors)
>   I'll always keep it a half hour
>   slow—to remind me of the fouled-
>   up crew of the Caine.

                                            (CONTINUED)

91 (CONTINUED)

He makes his way down the ladder and steps into the gig. It
pulls away into the open harbor.


92      MED. SHOT       OFFICER'S GROUP AT RAIL

The eyes of Maryk and the others glisten with restrained tears
as they watch the departing gig. As they start to wander away
disconsolately, Willie studies their faces in surprise.

                        WILLIE
                      (to Maryk)
              What's everybody so choked up
              for?

                        MARYK
              No matter what everybody says,
              Willie, I still think that some day
              you'll make an officer.

He walks away from the rail, leaving a puzzled Willie behind.


It should be quite obvious that the removal of the conflict arising
from DeVriess' reaction to the crew's gift would not only find us with
a pedestrian scene, it would also deprive the viewer of the opportunity
to enjoy a glimpse of a quirky character executing a humorous switch.
In this instance, the Captain's moment of conflict with the sailors,
followed by his 180 degree flip-flop in attitude, engenders laughter
which serves to mask the scene's sentimentality while allowing the
viewer to accept its sentiment. He can sympathize with the men in
their loss and find their reactions completely believable.

The depiction of a diametrically opposed personality is dramatized in the following sequence. Captain Queeg is holding his first
get-acquainted conference with the ship's officers. They are seated
around the mess table in the wardroom, drinking coffee. Queeg has
been giving the officers some personal history and is now winding up.

94      MEDIUM SHOT      FAVORING QUEEG

                        QUEEG
              I want you to remember one
              thing. Aboard my ship, excellent

                                              (CONTINUED)

94 (CONTINUED)

> performance is standard.
> Standard performance is sub-
> standard. Sub-standard
> performance is not permitted to
> exist. That I warn you.

95      CLOSE GROUP      WILLIE, MARYK AND KEEFER

Willie nods approvingly. Maryk's face becomes set. Keefer
slowly shreds his cigarette into his coffee cup.

96      MED. FULL SHOT      QUEEG AND OFFICERS

> QUEEG (cont.)
> (good-humoredly)
> Kay. Now that I've shot my face
> off, I'll give anyone that wants to
> a chance to do the same thing.

> MARYK
> (hesitantly)
> Captain—I don't want to seem
> out of line, but it's been a long
> time since this crew did things by
> the book.

> QUEEG
> Mr. Maryk, you may tell the crew
> for me there are four ways of
> doing things on board my ship—
> the right way, the wrong way, the
> Navy way, and my way. If they do
> things my way, we'll get along.

> MARYK
> (dryly)
> Aye, aye, sir.

(CONTINUED)

96 (CONTINUED)

> QUEEG
> (looking around)
> Kay. Anyone else?

A few of the officers clear their throats nervously, but no one speaks. There is a rap on the wardroom door. Queeg turns, annoyed.

> QUEEG (cont.)
> Come in.

The door is opened by a sailor named URBAN, whose dungaree shirt hangs outside his pants. He approaches Queeg with a dispatch.

> URBAN
> Beg pardon, Captain. Sorry to interrupt. Official message from ComServPac.

> QUEEG
> Thank you.

Queeg signs for the message, then sets it aside without looking at it. His eyes follow the sailor as he starts to leave, staring at his shirttail. As the man reaches the door, Queeg stops him.

> QUEEG (cont.)
> One moment, messenger.
> (Urban stops)
> What's your name and rating?

> URBAN
> Urban, sir. Seaman first. Signalman striker.

> QUEEG
> (never taking his eyes off the shirttail)
> Very well. You may go.

Urban exits quickly.

97    CLOSE SHOT        QUEEG

His face tense, he continues to look in the direction of Urban's
exit. His hand reaches into his pocket for what appears to be
another cigarette. Instead, he brings out a couple of steel balls,
which he proceeds to roll between his fingers and the palm of
his hand. They give off a faint clicking sound.

98    CLOSE GROUP SHOT        MARYK, KEEFER AND WILLIE

Uneasily, they wait for the Captain to speak. The faint clicking
of the steel balls comes over. Keefer stares at the Captain,
fascinated.

99    MED. SHOT      WARDROOM      FAVORING QUEEG

The clicking sound continues, as Queeg looks out at the men.
Then he breaks the silence.

                    QUEEG
          Gentlemen, anybody notice
          anything peculiar about Seaman
          First Class Urban?

The officers look at him blankly.

                    QUEEG (cont.)
          A shirttail hanging outside
          trousers is the regulation
          uniform, I believe, for bus boys,
          not however, for a sailor in the
          United States Navy. These are the
          things we're going to start
          noticing again. Mr. Maryk, who is
          the morale officer?

                    MARYK
          There is no morale officer, sir.

                    QUEEG
          Who's the junior Ensign?

                                              (CONTINUED)

99 (CONTINUED)

> MARYK

Keith, sir.

Queeg continues rolling the steel balls as he glances at Keith.

> QUEEG

Mr. Keith . . .

> WILLIE

Sir . . .

> QUEEG

You are now the morale officer.
In addition to your other duties,
you will see to it that every man
keeps his shirttail tucked inside
his trousers.

> WILLIE

Aye, aye, sir.

> QUEEG

Kay. If I see another shirttail
flapping while I'm Captain of this
ship, woe betide the sailor, woe
betide the O.O.D., and woe betide
the morale officer. I kid you not.

In the above sequence, conflict is the result of a difference of attitudes: Queeg's zealous regard for the rules versus the crew's casual disdain for them. The insertion of this apparently minor complication rescues the scene from what would otherwise be a routine exposition—a "talky" scene of Queeg laying down his policy for officer and crew behavior. But it does far more than that: It begins the development of what the viewer will come to know as the classic Queeg character. The Captain's behavior under stress, which is, of course, the spine of the story, is here first disclosed in almost comedic terms as Queeg takes refuge under his "security blanket," the two steel balls. Wouk's especially clever contrivance translates perfectly to the screen where, because of its essentially cinematic nature, it is even more at home than it is in the novel. Throughout the rest of the film, whenever Queeg reaches into his pocket, the viewer, like one of Pavlov's conditioned dogs reacting to a signal, immediately anticipates the onset of a problem.

It is very important for the beginning writer to understand that even such an apparently simple device can be of the greatest consequence in keeping the viewer's interest alive. Certainly, the story would have been less effective without it. And it all started with the small conflict created by a sailor's flapping shirttails.

As noted earlier, *Act of Anger* uses conflict extensively. Further examples will aid in the understanding of more of its uses.

Early in the script, Ben Kellogg, Counsel for the defense, meets the District Attorney, Frank Sayer, for a pretrial conference. Since this is Ben's first murder case, Sayer is somewhat patronizing—an attitude that frequently breeds conflict.

26      INT. SAYER'S OFFICE      CLOSE SHOT      SAYER      DAY

SAYER is a massive-bodied, big-headed man with that joviality especially useful to men seeking long careers in public office. He looks up at Ben and shoves out a big, soft hand in greeting.

>                    SAYER
>                (a bit tolerant)
>          Well, Ben . . . your brother told
>          me you might deign to appear
>          with us on this one.

CAMERA PULLS BACK to discover Ben, as he shakes hands with Sayer. By now we see two little plaques on Sayer's desk. One of them announces, "County Attorney—FRANK SAYER." The other submits respectfully that "IT IS BETTER TO LIGHT ONE CANDLE THAN CURSE THE DARKNESS."

>                    BEN
>          You look the same, Frank.

>                    SAYER
>          No, I don't—it's an election year.
>          Sit down—let's talk . . .
>                (as Ben sits)
>          Say, what do all you property
>          right land grant guys <u>do</u> on those
>          quiet, casual cases of yours?
>          Heard you just spent like five
>          months or something over in
>          Division Three. What takes five
>          months, for Crissakes?

(Author's note: This is a combative approach to begin with, de-signed to intimidate less experienced adversaries. Ben takes it calmly, but he will, of course, strike back.)

> BEN
> (refusing a cigar)
> Oh, history, mostly. Sit around in
> the judge's chambers—lie to each
> other a little about land rulings
> that were applicable a hundred
> years ago . . .
> (smiles)
> What do you fellas do?

27    CLOSE TWO SHOT    BEN AND SAYER

Neither man expects trouble here, but neither is unequipped to deal with a potential adversary. Their smiles are armored smiles.

> SAYER
> (grins now)
> Well, we don't take five months to
> bring punks like your Campeon
> boy to trial on Murder First, I'll
> tell you that.

(Author's note: The war is on, and not too politely. But it will heat up. The fencing, some subtle, some all too forceful, goes on.)

> BEN
> (nods)
> Well, assuming I don't have to
> ask . . .
> (a deferential bow)
> . . . The People for a continuance,
> so I can study the case . . .

> SAYER
> Continuance!

(CONTINUED)

27 (CONTINUED)

>           BEN
> Look, I haven't even <u>talked</u> to my
> client. . . .

>           SAYER
>           (chuckles; interrupts)
> Okay, Counselor . . . okay!
> Dedication duly noted. You can go
> out and search the soul of your
> client with a steely-eyed gaze, and
> do all you gotta do to satisfy both
> Constitution and conscience.

>           BEN
> Where is he? County jail?

>           SAYER
> County Hospital. Banged himself
> up pretty good, scooting off with
> his victim's Rolls-Royce yet.

>           BEN
> Mmmm . . .
>           (innocent aside)
> . . . still pretty well sedated, I
> suppose.

>           SAYER
>           (grins again)
> Ben, your selfless plunge into the
> front lines is a delight to
> behold . . .
>           (suddenly earnest;
>           leans forward)
> And the answer is <u>no</u>; he was not
> under sedation at the time of his
> confession. Your brother was
> there when they took it! Miss
> Latimer'll give you a copy on the
> way out.

Ben looks defeated, openly lost.

                                        (CONTINUED)

27 (CONTINUED)

> **BEN**
>
> Yeh. Well . . . let's see, then . . .

> **SAYER**
>
> Look, the April term opens
> tomorrow. Judge Groat will
> definitely list this matter first on
> the docket, so we can get started
> next Monday without fooling
> around . . . right?

> **BEN**
>
> (perplexed)
> What the hell is the rush for?


28      CLOSE SHOT      SAYER

Even for him this is an unpalatable situation.

> **SAYER**
>
> Your defendant happens to be a
> Mexican citizen. We got a large
> Mexican-American constituency
> in this county that gets nervous
> or sensitive about one thing or
> another every time you turn
> around.


29      CLOSE SHOT      BEN

> **BEN**
>
> (it dawns)
> And this is that good old election
> year, isn't it? So we do it all sort
> of neat and quick . . . hang the
> little bastard before the Mexican-
> Americans get off the dime, or get
> offended, or something . . .
> (nods in mock
> appreciation)
> . . . I think that's wise.

30        TWO SHOT        SAYER AND BEN

SAYER
(brought up tight)
Now look, Kellogg . . .

BEN
(quickly)
Then reduce the charge to a non-
hanging offense and you can have
your conviction. Right here, right
now. No trial, no publicity.

Sayer can't help but appreciate Ben's tactic. After a LONG
BEAT, he sits back relaxedly—and lets his usual smile return.
He chuckles.

SAYER
You might not have made too lazy
a criminal counsel at that,
Benson . . .
(shakes his head
slowly)
No, we got your boy and we got
his confession . . . and we have
got the evidence. Murder in the
first degree.

 

 

This scene has been reproduced in nearly its full length because
it illustrates several of the uses of conflict. It gives us some insight
into the minds of both Sayer and Kellogg, it discloses some of their
social and civil attitudes, it demonstrates their dexterity in combat,
and it delivers a good deal of story and plot information. Without the
conflict, which centers interest on the *two personalities*, the scene
would be an exercise in exposition, as a close analysis will show. But
the viewer must not be given the opportunity to analyze the scene:
Two skillful actors with strong personalities can keep the focus on
*character* rather than on plot, and the viewer will absorb the necessary
information with little awareness of its expository nature.

Conflict is frequently used when introducing two characters in
what might easily be a routine "meeting" scene. An example from
*Walk on the Wild Side* brings two characters, played by Laurence
Harvey and Jane Fonda, together for the first time.

19      FULL SHOT      EXT. HIGHWAY                    EVENING

Dove trudges along in the wind, the road behind him still
empty. At this spot repairs are in progress. One side of the
road is decorated with scattered conduits. Dove reaches a spot
where the conduits are stacked. Shivering, he inspects the lot.
Then he whacks one pipe with his stick, as if to scare out any
vermin that might be in it. A muffled voice calls out:

                         VOICE
              What's that? Who's that?

                         DOVE
          Who's what?

                         VOICE
              Go 'way! G'wan! Beat it!

Dove shrugs and starts to climb toward a higher conduit, but
stops as a figure emerges from the lower one. The figure is
gripping a splintered length of lumber, held like a club, and
raised threateningly. Although the figure wears overalls, we
can see that it is a girl.

                         GIRL
              I said g'wan—beat it!

Dove stares, surprised at seeing such a girl.

                         DOVE
              What are you doin' here?

                         GIRL
              My doctor recommended fresh
              air. What are you here for?

                         DOVE
              Lookin' for a place to sleep . . .

                         GIRL
              This floor's occupied. . . .

                         DOVE
                      (grinning)
              How about upstairs?

                         GIRL
              Ask the night clerk—and don't
              bother me!

                                    (CONTINUED)

19 (CONTINUED)

> She starts crawling back into her conduit.

>> DOVE
>> What are you so mad about?

> The girl turns with suppressed fury.

>> GIRL
>> I'm cold—and I'm hungry—and a
>> million miles from nowhere—and
>> in the middle of a heavenly
>> dream, you wake me up . . . !

>> DOVE
>> I'm sorry. . . .

> She turns, starts to crawl away, and then halts, turning to
> him with a sudden intensity.

>> GIRL
>> You got anything to eat?

> Dove looks at her, grins again, and reaches into his pocket.

>> DOVE
>> I got this . . .

> He takes out an apple and holds it out to her. The girl's eyes
> widen in mock amazement.

>> GIRL
>> For me?

> But in spite of the sarcasm, she drops her club, grabs the
> apple and starts eating like a starved animal. Dove watches
> her eat. She becomes aware of his look and stops angrily.

>> GIRL (cont.)
>> I can't help it if I slobber,
>> Mister—I ain't eaten all day.

The problem was to get Dove and the girl together out on the road. A casual meeting would lead to a casual scene. As it stands, the conflict starts immediately, supplying surprise, danger, and some mystery to the situation. From then, we're off and running.

The film, *Murder, My Sweet,* like most mystery and suspense stories, is based on a series of conflicts, one after another. Here is a meeting between two characters that set up the basis for the film, Phillip Marlowe and the Moose. We pick up the sequence in Marlowe's office.*

14     ANGLE WIDENS as he looks out of the window, tries to get comfortable. Something bothers him. He reaches inside his coat, pulls out a gun, puts it on the desk behind him. When he turns back to the window he freezes, swallows a mouthful of smoke, stares at the window pane. The sign across the street has just gone on. When it goes off again the glass reflects a stolid, brutish face, the massive features carved by the dim light.

       Marlowe turns slowly in his chair.

15     MARLOWE'S POV

       Standing quietly on the other side of the desk is a huge bulk of a man. From this angle he looks seven feet tall. Slowly, vaguely apologetic, he smiles. Then he speaks, his voice soft and straightforward.

THE BIG MAN<br>
I seen your name on the board<br>
downstairs.

16     TWO SHOT     MARLOWE AND THE BIG MAN

       Marlowe just stares at him.

THE BIG MAN (cont.)<br>
I come up to see you.

       Marlowe drops his eyes to his gun on the desk.

THE BIG MAN (cont.)<br>
(smiling again,<br>
looking around)<br>
You're a private eye, huh?

(CONTINUED)

*From John Paxton's script of R.K.O.'s *Murder, My Sweet.*

16 (CONTINUED)

He reaches down, pushes Marlowe's gun aside as if it were an
ashtray, sits on the desk.

> THE BIG MAN (cont.)
> I like you to look for somebody.

> MARLOWE
> (quietly)
> I'm closed up, pal.

He picks up his gun, returns it to his inside coat pocket.

> MARLOWE (cont.)
> Come around tomorrow and we'll
> talk about it.

> THE BIG MAN
> (undeterred)
> I looked for her where she
> worked, but I been out of touch.

> MARLOWE
> Okay, pal. Tomorrow.

He snaps on the light, glances impatiently at the phone. When
he looks back, the Big Man has taken out a roll of bills and is
peeling off a couple.

> THE BIG MAN
> I like to show you where she
> worked.

He shoves the bills across the desk toward Marlowe. At this
moment, the phone rings. Marlowe reaches for the phone,
hesitates, looks at the money. Putting the phone back in its
cradle, he picks up the bills, folds them carefully, puts them in
his watch pocket. He gets up, taps the Big Man on the
shoulder.

> MARLOWE
> Okay. You show me where she
> worked.

The Big Man smiles. Marlowe picks up his hat, snaps off the
light, and leads the way to the door.

In the average who-done-it, Moose might simply have walked into Marlowe's office and laid down his money. Logic says that Marlowe, whose "bank account was trying to crawl under a duck," would have been happy to pick up the job and the cash. But logic writes lousy drama, and the conflict shown in Marlowe's reluctance to talk with the Moose helps us to develop the big man's vulnerability, as well as Marlowe's. In addition, the scene supplies a mood of suspense that would otherwise have been absent, to the detriment of the film as a whole.

A short while later, these two enter the bar where Moose's lost girl friend once entertained. Again, a simple question and answer scene would have served to carry the story through to the more exciting meat of the film. But why wait? Here is the scene as played.

20    MED. FULL SHOT        INT. BAR                    NIGHT

Cozy, neighborhood stuff, uncordial to strangers. As Marlowe and The Big Man enter through door in b.g., the piano player stops in the middle of a phrase, glances uneasily toward a large man at the bar who looks as if he might be the boss, probably an ex-fighter settled down. The boss frowns slightly—The Big Man has obviously been in before.

The Big Man settles his bulk on a stool, with Marlowe sitting down beside him, slightly off center. The Big Man looks at the bartender.

                    THE BIG MAN
            Whiskey.
                (prodding Marlowe)
            Call yours.

                    MARLOWE
            Whiskey.

As the barman starts to comply without enthusiasm, The Big Man takes hold of his arm.

                    THE BIG MAN
            You never heard of Velma?

The barman looks toward the boss, who has circled behind The Big Man, and now puts his arm on The Big Man's shoulder in a soothing manner.

                                        (CONTINUED)

20 (CONTINUED)

>                    BOSS
>          Look, Joe, I'm sorry about your
>          girl. I know how you feel. But she
>          ain't here. No girls been here
>          since I had the place. No show, no
>          noise. I got a reputation for no
>          trouble.

The Big Man pays no attention to the boss, but continues to
talk to the bartender.

>                  THE BIG MAN
>          She used to work here.

The barman pulls away. The Big Man turns toward Marlowe.

>                  THE BIG MAN
>          You ask him about Velma.

>                    BOSS
>                (still patient)
>          We been over all that. Let's drink
>          up, Joe.

The Big Man is staring off toward a girl at the other end of the
bar. Brushing off the Boss, he gets up, crosses over to the girl.
She's fairly pretty, showy. He smiles.

>                  THE BIG MAN
>          You remember Velma?

A little frightened, she shakes her head "no." The Boss takes
hold of one of The Big Man's arms.

>                    BOSS
>          I'll have to request you don't
>          bother the customers.

The Big Man looks pleadingly at the girl.

>                  THE BIG MAN
>          So far you rate me polite, huh? I
>          don't bother you none?

Again, she shakes her head uneasily. Satisfied, The Big Man
thrusts out his arm effortlessly, but the Boss sails back

(CONTINUED)

20 (CONTINUED)

against the wall. Recovering, he steps up behind The Big Man, grabs his shoulder with his left hand and opens him up for his right. The Big Man just raises his left slightly, takes the punch on his forearm, grabs the Boss' wrist with his own right, and turns him around. Dropping a big paw into the middle of the Boss' back, he heaves, sending the man flailing and staggering across the room. He crashes through several tables, ends up against the baseboard, stirs, then lies quiet. The Big Man speaks to no one in particular.

> THE BIG MAN
> Some guys have the wrong ideas
> when to get fancy.

Marlowe has been watching the action with interest. Now he gets up and approaches The Big Man.

> MARLOWE
> Come on, pal. Eight years is a lot
> of gin. They don't know anything
> about Velma here.

The Big Man looks at Marlowe as if he had never seen him before.

> THE BIG MAN
> Who asked you to stick your face
> in?

> MARLOWE
> (tough)
> You did. Remember me? I'm the
> guy that came in with you,
> Chunky.

The Big Man considers that for a moment.

> THE BIG MAN
> (finally)
> Moose. The name's Moose.
> Account of I'm large. Moose
> Malloy. You heard of me maybe.

> MARLOWE
> (shrugging)
> Maybe.

                                        (CONTINUED)

20 (CONTINUED)

    Moose looks around vaguely. The customers have all sneaked
out. Against the wall across the room the Boss is slowly
getting to his feet. Moose's eyes grow soft and sad.

> MOOSE
>
> They changed it a lot. There used
> to be a stage where she worked—
> and some booths. . . .

> MARLOWE
>
> (anxious to go)
>
> You said that. . . .

> MOOSE
>
> (abruptly)
>
> I begin not to like it here.

    He reaches across the bar, grabs a bottle of whiskey, thrusts it
at Marlowe, takes another for himself, throws a bill on the
bar, and starts out, Marlowe at his heels.


    Again the conflict lends suspense to an otherwise routine scene
by showing Moose's potential for easy violence and the dangerous
unpredictability of his nature. It also allows us to disclose something
of Marlowe's character by giving him the opportunity to display his
smooth handling of a potentially explosive character and situation.

    Now, another sequence, another meeting, and an introduction of
another character. (The scene will be written in a master shot for the
sake of convenience.)


56     MED. SHOT     INT. MARLOWE'S OFFICE     DAY

    As Marlowe enters quietly, a tall, graceful young man whirls
away from the desk toward him with a startled, flustered
movement.

> YOUNG MAN
>
> Mr. Marlowe. . . .

    Marlowe was expecting Moose, of course. Now he looks the
guy over, nods slowly. The young man steps toward him with
a nervous rush of words. His voice is well modulated, effete.

(CONTINUED)

56 (CONTINUED)

                    YOUNG MAN (cont.)
          I took the liberty of waiting here,
          Mr. Marlowe . . .

He fumbles for a card, which he holds out to Marlowe.
Marlowe glances at it as he crosses over to sit at his desk.

                    YOUNG MAN (cont.)
          The elevator attendant gave me
          the impression I could expect you
          soon. I took the chance, as. . . .

                    MARLOWE
                    (interrupting)
          Who put in the pitch for me,
          Mr.. . . .
                    (he glances at the card)
          Mr. Marriott?

                    MARRIOTT
          I beg your pardon?

                    MARLOWE
          How did you get my name?

                    MARRIOTT
          Oh. As a matter of fact, I decided
          to employ a private investigator
          only today. Being Saturday
          afternoon, I failed to reach
          anyone by phone, and was
          somewhat at a loss. . . .

Marlowe is obviously not really paying attention. He pulls
Velma's photo out of his pocket, looks at it, then places it face
down on his desk. Marriott's voice goes up a couple of decibels.

                    MARRIOTT (cont.)
          . . . the directory listed several in
          this neighborhood. So I took, as I
          say, a rather long chance. . . .
                                        (CONTINUED)

56 (CONTINUED)

                        MARLOWE
                  (cutting in again)
        I'm in a clutch at the moment,
        Mr. Marriott.
                (Marriott looks blank)
        I'm pretty busy. I couldn't take on
        anything big. What's the job?

Marriott is upset by Marlowe's bluntness. He places his hands
on the desk.

                        MARRIOTT
        I'll require your services for only
        a few hours this evening. . . .

Marlowe says nothing, stares rudely. Nervously, Marriott
begins to rearrange the scattered objects on Marlowe's desk. It
could stand it.

                        MARRIOTT (cont.)
        I'm meeting some men shortly
        after midnight. I'm paying them
        some money. . . .

Marlowe takes his inkwell out of Marriott's hand, replaces it.

                        MARLOWE
        Better get your flaps down, or
        you'll take off.

A muscle flickers at the corner of Marriott's mouth.

                        MARLOWE (cont.)
        What's the deal—blackmail?

                        MARRIOTT
        I'm not in the habit of giving
        people grounds for blackmail . . .
        I have simply agreed to serve as
        the bearer of the money.

                        MARLOWE
        How much and what for?

                                      (CONTINUED)

56 (CONTINUED)

> MARRIOTT
>
> Well, really . . .
>> (his smile is still
>> fairly pleasant)
>
> . . . I can't go into that.

> MARLOWE
>
> You just want me to go along and
> hold your hand?

Marriott jerks back as if burnt. With a shaking hand he feels inside his topcoat for an expensive cigarette case.

> MARRIOTT
>> (acidly)
>
> I'm afraid I don't like your
> manner.

> MARLOWE
>
> I've had complaints about it, but
> it keeps getting worse. How much
> are you offering me for doing
> nothing?

> MARRIOTT
>
> I hadn't really gotten around to
> thinking about it. . . .

> MARLOWE
>
> Do you suppose you could get
> around to thinking about it now?

Marriott flushes, has trouble with his face again. He leans forward on the desk.

> MARRIOTT
>
> How would you like a swift punch
> on the nose?

Marlowe leans back in his chair, picks up Marriott's card, holds it out to him.

> MARLOWE
>
> I tremble at the thought of such
> violence.

(CONTINUED)

56 (CONTINUED)

>    Marriott snatches the card from Marlowe's outstretched hand,
>    turns and starts for the door. He stops and turns back
>    abruptly.

>                          MARRIOTT
>                I'm offering you a hundred
>                dollars for a few hours of your
>                time. If that isn't enough, say so.
>                There's no risk. Some jewels were
>                stolen from a friend of mine in a
>                holdup. I'm buying them back.

(There follows a page and a half of dialogue in which Marlowe
analyzes what he considers a most unfavorable situation. Then:)

57      TWO SHOT      MARLOWE AND MARRIOTT

>    Marlowe pauses, frowns at the fidgeting Marriott.

>                          MARLOW
>                        (with finality)
>                No, Mr. Marriott, I'm afraid I
>                can't do anything for you.

>    Marriott flinches, adjusts his scarf carefully, starts past
>    Marlowe for the door. As he passes him, Marlowe holds out
>    his hand.

>                          MARLOWE (cont.)
>                But I'll take your hundred bucks
>                and tag along for the ride.

>    Marriott stops, trying not to look relieved. He hands Marlowe
>    a bill, which Marlowe puts in his watch pocket. Then he
>    extends his hand again.

>                          MARLOWE (cont.)
>                And I carry the shopping money. . . .

Here, Marlowe's apparent intransigence and tough-guy attitude
supply the time needed to develop a subsidiary character into a person
rather than a symbol. Without the scene-long conflict, Marriott would
be merely a messenger, an agent, with no personality of his own. Since
he is killed in the next scene, it becomes necessary, in keeping with

the rule about developing three-dimensional characters, to take the
time to develop him here, and that time can be gained *only* by inserting
conflict into the scene. The conflict allows us to develop transitions,
and the transitions serve to keep the sequence alive.

One more short scene from *Murder, My Sweet:* Marlowe is in a
night club, awaiting Mrs. Grayle's return, when he is called out for a
word with Moose.

153    MED. SHOT                        EXT. TERRACE    NIGHT
       COCOANUT BEACH CLUB

       Moose is staring out to sea. Marlowe comes out from the
       cocktail lounge in the b.g.

                         MOOSE
                Ditch the babe.

                         MARLOWE
                What's the matter with you?
                Don't you want me to have any
                love life at all?

       Moose takes a firm grip on Marlowe's wrist.

                         MOOSE
                Ditch the babe.

                         MARLOWE
                Look. I'm a big boy now. I blow
                my own nose and everything. You
                hired me. Now stop following me
                or I'll get mad.

       Moose tightens his grip on Marlowe's wrist.

                         MOOSE
                Ditch the babe. I want you to
                meet a guy.

       Marlowe tries to remove Moose's paw from his wrist. No soap.

                         MARLOWE
                Take it easy. Another ten seconds
                and gangrene will set in . . .

                         MOOSE
                I want you to meet a guy.
                                       (CONTINUED)

153 (CONTINUED)

                          MARLOWE
                       (in intense pain)
                       Okay! Okay!

Moose lets go. Marlowe heads back toward the bar, wriggling
his fingers and rubbing his wrist. Moose follows him.


The scene and its conflict are self-explanatory. But conflict is
employed not only in scenes of violence. Romance, too, benefits from
its inclusion, and even a single love scene can profit from its magic
touch. Here is such a scene from *The Young Lions*.

Noah has just met Hope at a party given by his new and very
sophisticated friend, Michael (Dean Martin). As they leave Michael's
house for a walk in the rain, Noah tries to impress Hope with remarks
like, "You know, I'm told European women are more mature emotionally."

Hope accepts his offer to see her home, which is as far in Brooklyn
as you can go. After a ride on the subway, a bus, and a fair-sized hike,
they approach her apartment. (The sequence will be written here in
a master shot.)


65       MED. FULL SHOT   STREET OUTSIDE HOPE'S FLAT       NIGHT

         As they walk into the SHOT, Hope's pace slows.

                          NOAH
                       Are we getting warmer?

                          HOPE
                       You'll be glad to know that we're
                       here.

         She stops at the gate of an iron fence, starts to open it.

                          HOPE (cont.)
                       Goodnight.

         She closes the gate between them, and turns to face him. He
         draws a deep breath.

                          NOAH
                       Uh . . . I want to say . . . I'm
                       pleased . . . um . . . very pleased,
                       I mean . . . to have brought you
                       home.

                                                        (CONTINUED)

65 (CONTINUED)

                    HOPE
Thank you.

                    NOAH
I mean . . . I'm really
pleased . . .

He looks at her with the deepest longing. Then, probably for
the first time in his life, he cannot hold himself back. He leans
forward and kisses her. As he lets her go, she looks at him
steadily.

                    HOPE
Now, you do that with your other
girls—not with me.

                    NOAH
Yes—No! No, I don't. . . .

                    HOPE
             (cutting in)
Oh. Only with me.

                    NOAH
Uhh . . . you don't understand
what I mean. . . .

                    HOPE
I suppose you think you're such
an attractive young man that any
girl would just fall all over herself
to let you kiss her.

                    NOAH
             (groaning)
Oh, God!

                    HOPE
             (not through yet)
Never in all my days have I met
such an opinionated, self-centered
young man.
             (she turns to leave)
Goodnight, Mr. Ackerman.

She moves up the steps of the brownstone.

(CONTINUED)

65 (CONTINUED)

                          NOAH
            No, don't . . . uh . . . Hope . . .

The door closes behind her. For a long moment Noah looks
after her, hoping against hope (no pun intended). Finally, he
turns and starts down the street. After a few steps, he stops,
apparently confused. Reaching a decision, he walks back to the
brownstone, enters the gate, looks around, sees a window with
a light in it. Taking a coin out of his pocket, he climbs a step
up to the window and taps on it with the coin. After a second
series of taps, the front door opens and Hope appears in the
doorway.

                          HOPE
                      (whispering)
              Stop that! You'll wake everyone.

                          NOAH
                    (from his position
                      at the window)
              How do I get back to the city?

                          HOPE
              You're lost?

Noah climbs down from the window, approaches her.

                          NOAH
              No one will find me again—ever.

Hope comes down the steps to face him.

                          HOPE
              You're a terrible fool, aren't you?

                          NOAH
                    (a slight smile)
              Um-huh . . .

                          HOPE
              Well, you walk two blocks to your
              left—and you wait for the bus—
              the one that comes from your
              left—and you take it to Eastern
              Parkway. Now when . . .

                                          (CONTINUED)

65 (CONTINUED)

> (she stops, looks
> into his eyes)
> Are you listening to me?

                        NOAH

I want to say something to you.
I'm not opinionated—I—I don't
think I—I've a single opinion in
the whole world. I—I don't know
why I kissed you—I—I just
couldn't help it. I guess—
> (Hope tries to
> shush him)
I guess I wanted to impress you. I
was afraid that if I was myself
you wouldn't look at me
twice . . . .
> (he pauses a beat)
It's been a very confusing night—
I don't think I've ever been
through anything so confusing.

                        HOPE

You tell me tomorrow.

Noah takes a moment to assess this accurately. Then:

                        NOAH

The bus to Eastern Parkway . . .

But his eyes have nothing in common with his words. Hope
reads them sympathetically. She takes his face in her hands
and kisses him.

                        HOPE
> (still holding his face)
Don't get lost on the way home.

                        NOAH
> (a slight shake of
> his head)
Uh—the bus to Eastern
Parkway—and then—I love you—
I love you . . .

                                            (CONTINUED)

65 (CONTINUED)

>                    HOPE
>                   (smiles)
>         Goodnight—thanks for bringing
>         me home.

She turns and goes into the house, stopping at the doorway
for a final look back. Then she closes the door after her. Noah
looks at the closed door for a long moment, a faint expression
of wonder on his face, then he turns, walks through the gate,
and starts out for the Eastern Parkway.


The inclusion of a little conflict can make even love, at least on
the screen, more interesting.

This scene has been transcribed as played, not as originally written—or cut. It will be noted that, for a "love scene," there is remarkably little talk of love. Noah makes his declaration only at the end of
the sequence, long after the issue has been decided. But, to enable the
viewer to read the emotions properly, time must be provided for *looks*
and *reactions*. It may be a blow to the author's ego, but nobody can
write as much feeling into such a scene as can be supplied by the
actors. The author's obligation is to write a scene that gives the actors—and the editor—the opportunity to make the most out of the
*looks* and the *reactions* rather than the lines.

I cannot leave this scene without a comment on the *one* line that
really says it all: "You tell me tomorrow." It signifies understanding,
forgiveness, and promise. It is a perfect example of indirect story telling, and it renders unnecessary any courtship that might follow and
makes it possible to go directly to the scene with Hope's father (Book
I, Chapter 4).

# 10

## Clearing the Way

A near relative of *conflict*—the *obstacle*—is also an essential element of dramatic structure. Frequently, the obstacle is the source, or cause, of conflict, but ordinarily the term is reserved for inanimate opposition. Obstacles are often purely physical in nature: An alpine guide scales a mountain to rescue a stranded group of climbers, but the storm that has trapped them also hampers the guide. A racing car driver must claim the winner's purse in order to finance his daughter's liver transplant, but a damaged oil line endangers his chance for victory.

In McCarey's *Love Affair*, two lovers hurry toward a rendezvous at the top of the Empire State Building, but the woman is crippled while crossing Seventh Avenue. In *Murder, My Sweet*, Marlowe closes in on some valuable information only to be beaten, drugged, and imprisoned in a sanitarium. To get back on track he must shake off the drug's effects, overcome the strong-armed male nurse and an armed quack doctor, all formidable obstacles indeed.

Just as often the obstacles are attitudes—invisible, but as impenetrable as a stone wall. They can be disapproving attitudes of family, friends, or neighbors, or attitudes within the characters themselves. A "drinking problem" *(The Lost Weekend)* is an obstacle to a character's progress in his profession and a source of conflict with his family. Another character's conscience prevents him from enjoying the fruits of a shady business transaction engineered at the cost of his ethical principles.

Most *attitude* obstacles trigger conflict within the character, and these are among the most common sources of drama. Classic tragedy is *always* based on this premise; so is a type of film in which a character overcomes a *mental* obstacle in order to conquer a *physical* handicap resulting from fate or misfortune. For example, a swimmer loses her legs in a boating accident but fights back to the point of living a normal life, to the great delight of her friends, her family, and the audience. (There has been a spate of such films recently, most of them based on actual characters and real situations.)

In Noah's scene with Mr. Plowman (Book I, Chapter 4) we have not so much a conflict between the two men, but one man's battle against a most formidable obstacle within himself—religious and racial prejudice. In this instance, since it is a minor hurdle in a long race, the obstacle is disposed of quickly, cleverly, but arbitrarily. At other times such an obstacle would be the basis for an entire film (*Crossfire, Gentleman's Agreement,* or *Pinky*). But whether used as a minor or a major obstacle, differences in attitude are the bases of some of the most believable and acceptable situations in stories of substance.

Perhaps the easiest way to clarify this concept is in terms of folk myths and fairy tales. Hercules could not be his own man (or demigod) until he had surmounted the obstacles presented by a series of labors requiring superhuman effort. Ulysses, interested only in making the short journey home from Troy, sails more than a thousand miles and faces a hundred perils: Circe, the Sirens, Scylla, Charybdis and a host of other obstacles of all shapes, sizes, and natures. A modern film, dealing with present-day problems in an up-to-date drama, could be broken down into a similar pattern. Certainly, no soap opera could exist without its Circe and a full quota of sirens.

No discussion of obstacles is complete without a consideration of the obstacle that is *self-induced*. This is best exemplified in scenes of *suspense*, a dramatic device most obviously demonstrated and most easily recognized in mystery, horror, and adventure stories, but which also plays an important part in straight drama and in comedy. Virtually all great comedians have depended heavily on suspense in their efforts to command viewer sympathy, empathy, and emotional participation. Stills of Harold Lloyd, showing him hanging by his fingertips over bottomless canyons or car-crowded streets, are included in almost every pictorial history of motion pictures. Anyone who has seen *The Gold Rush* will vividly remember the sequence in which Chaplin's hunger-crazed and hallucinating companion (Mack Swain) stalks the fat chicken he assumes Charlie to be. These classic scenes are no less suspenseful because they are hilariously funny.

The comedy sequences just cited and the automobile scene in Chapter 7 are examples of a form of suspense in which imminent *real* danger threatens one or more of the film's characters. All disaster stories follow this pattern. A useful variation finds the film character completely unaware of the impending peril while the *alerted viewer* is on the edge of his seat, pulling for the hero to discover his danger in time to avoid its consequences.

However, the most effective and spine-chilling form of suspense is that in which the presence of danger and the resulting fear are *self-induced*. In such sequences, the *source* of the suspense is not seen, often not even present: It is merely suggested. Few things frighten us as thoroughly as our own imaginations, and one of the advantages of this construction is that it immediately involves the viewer, since some form of self-induced fear has been experienced by everyone.

For example, a character walks down a dimly lit street at midnight, the "witching hour." (You're already ahead of me.) Once the imagination has been triggered by some apparently unusual sound or sight, each new vibration, each sigh of the wind, each shifting of a moon-cast shadow, is magnified into a life-threatening peril, even though under normal circumstances each would have been a quite ordinary part of an everyday scene. In reality, nothing has changed—nothing, that is, except that the character's imagination, fueled by an instant surge of adrenaline, now shifts into high gear. And the viewer always reacts in sympathy.

This suspense pattern may be extremely common but, if handled with even moderate skill, it is never trite or dull, because we are working here with basic animal fears—fears that have been with us for no one knows how many millions of years. Such a sequence is often developed into a *continuing line* of *increasing tension*, during which all sophistication is stripped away and only a final scream or burst of relieving laughter can release the viewer from the clutch of self-induced terror. For instance, our character enters a house in which some danger lurks, or so he has been led to believe. As he hesitantly makes his way through its rooms, every darkened nook, every unopened (or open and creaking) door, every sound, including the heightened beating of his own heart, increases the original tension. When such elements are properly intercut with that character's cautious movements and his fearful reactions, the suspense sequence will hold the viewer's attention more completely than any other type of scene. And beyond the area of fear and suspense, this concept of self-induced emotion is worthy of consideration in most aspects of script construction.

The development and arrangement of conflict and obstacle furnishes the bare-bones skeleton of the plot. The effect they have on the story's characters—the pain suffered in conflict, the effort and strain expended in eliminating obstacles, the joy and sense of accomplishment derived from triumphing over these constraints—furnish the story's flesh.

Filmmaking is story telling, and an indispensable ingredient of story telling is the story teller *within* the story. Filmmakers usually speak of this aspect of the film as its *point of view*. There are only a few such formats available, and choosing the right one for any particular film can make a decided difference in its effectiveness.

In mystery melodrama, for instance, the point of view (POV) is often that of the central figure, the detective or the private eye. When the rules are strictly adhered to, no scene is shown in which the detective is not involved, either as an active participant or as a necessary observer. In this format, the story teller must play fair with the viewer, since a good mystery is a game in which he is invited to match wits with the detective. If the filmmaker shows scenes that do not include the detective and are, therefore, presumably outside his knowledge, the viewer has an advantage; on the other hand, if the detective displays possession of vital information not shown on the screen, the viewer is cheated. Balance is important. The only, but usually decisive, advantage enjoyed by the detective is the time allowed him to consider the evidence (off-screen, of course), which is usually much greater than the two hours or so at the viewer's disposal.

Raymond Chandler's stories always kept faith with the rule and the reader, who saw and heard as much as did Marlowe. His problem was to make the same deductions to arrive at the same conclusions—a possibility always within reach.

The preceding POV can be used for almost any film, but at the cost of mental and physical mobility, so its use outside of melodrama is relatively rare. Here, the problem is not to solve a crime but to investigate the mysteries of human nature, to explain its behavior and its reaction. This necessitates meeting it on its own grounds. The writer must invade each character, pry into his feelings, examine his behavior, both inside and outside the ken of his family and friends. Since *all* the characters must be so scrutinized, one character's POV is insufficient for the task.

For such films two techniques are available. First is the use of a narrator—a friend, a relative, a historian, or even the character himself—who has arrived at an omniscient or a historical point of view of the story's characters and events *after the fact*. In this format, the story and the incidents are things of the past, sometimes distant, often as recent as yesterday; but the facts and the feelings involved, including psychological insights into the characters' minds, are now known, at least to the narrator. An important aspect of this format is that the narrator is free to add his own judgments, make his own comments on the characters and the events he is reviewing.

The second POV is purely objective. The viewer sees the story as presented to him through the eye of the camera by a completely invisible, impartial, and disinterested entity which is in no way involved with the characters or the events of the film. This format is perhaps the most common of the three. Although the POV presented by the screen writer may be changed by the producer, the director, or even in the editing, he usually sets the pattern. It is obvious that careful thought must be exercised in choosing the format that best fits the material.

Another format, closely related to the narrator's POV is the *frame*. The *frame* is a special form of flashback. (A flashback, as the term implies, is recollection; it is used to deliver information from a time and/or a place which cannot be shown in a direct linear fashion.) The *frame* differs from the flashback in that it always contrives to make the *main body* of the film the subject of the recollection. There are specific reasons for using this format.

On infrequent occasions it is useful to alert the viewer to the *effect* before he knows the *cause*; to intrigue him so with what is obviously a *result* that he will want to know *how* such a result could have been effected. For instance, it is Christmas Eve. A gentle snow falls on bundled-up pedestrians who greet each other with a "Merry Christmas." The sound of distant carols is heard over the soft crunch of boots on the crisp, fresh snow. Into this cold/warm scene shambles a sorry figure, dressed in tattered overcoat and shabby hat, his hands thrust deep inside his pockets to protect them from the cold. As he nears the camera we see a drawn face, unshaven and unkempt. But a certain awareness in manner, a certain light in his eyes, tell us that he is something other than just another street tramp.

He stops at a store, still open for late shoppers, and stares through the window at an artfully displayed creche. The camera moves in on the biblical figures and we dissolve through to another creche in another time. Now the camera pulls back to reveal our "tramp," fashionably attired, celebrating a happy Christmas in the bosom of his family.

If the scenes are properly realized and we can avoid an impression of utter hopelessness (which would be an audience turn-off) the viewer will be curious to know what happened: *How* could a man of standing and substance be reduced to the state in which we first saw him? If the viewer can sit still long enough, we'll tell him—or rather, show him.

In *Murder, My Sweet* we start with an interrogation in progress, focusing only on the hot, bright light. As the main title ends, we pull back to find Marlowe, his eyes heavily bandaged, surrounded by a group of plainclothesmen. After a little urging from the lieutenant, Marlowe begins to tell his story, and we dissolve to the place where it all started, his office. At the climax, we find ourselves back at the interrogation once more as Marlowe finishes his narration. A short tag to tie off a few last loose ends and to furnish an up-beat ending, and the film is over.

An important requisite of the *frame* is that something be left unsaid or undone during the flashback, something which requires that we return to the frame to complete the story. Otherwise, the whole body of the film is merely an anticlimax. This is vital even if the film ends tragically.

For instance, the "tramp" of our first example, after reliving his story in memory, might pull away from the store window and fall down, dying, to the snow-covered sidewalk, only to be carried into the store and comforted by good samaritans imbued with the spirit of the season. Even as he dies he finds himself once more experiencing the warmth of Peace on Earth, Good Will to Men.

The *frame,* like all flashbacks, is a technique to be used sparingly, but when it fits, it is very effective.

Surprise is another important element but it, too, must be carefully assessed. Properly used, it can be an emotional experience for the viewer, and it can eliminate tedious and unnecessary story telling. An example from *Mirage,* starring Gregory Peck.* In the film, Walter Matthau plays Ted Cassel, a very unusual private eye. He is an ex–refrigerator repairman, and Peck is his first client, and neither one is comfortable with the situation. Cassel is naive, honest, ingenious, and helpful—an altogether likeable, even lovable fellow, but not to Peck's enemies. One morning Peck walks into Cassel's office to find him dead, strangled with the desk telephone cord.

This discovery is a surprise and a shock, both for Peck and for the audience. (Inside a theater an audible reaction of shock, grief, and disappointment is always forthcoming.) But, although the film loses a winning character, the drama gains a great deal. First, it was possible to elicit an unusual reaction from Peck. The ordinary responses to sudden death—screaming, violent crying, hysterics—are usually ineffective, frequently unbelievable. And rarely does the viewer share the actor's shock and pain: He merely observes it. In this instance Peck's shocking discovery leaves him dazed, immobile, expressionless, for a long, long beat. Then, as the reality of the senseless murder finally sinks in, Peck finds relief, not in screams or tears but in violent physical action. He tears up the office. And the viewer, *sharing* Peck's surprise and shock, also shares his rage and sympathizes completely with his violent response. Without this empathy the scene would have been excessively melodramatic.

Purely for the sake of violence, many of today's film-makers would have dramatized Cassel's murder, and the explicit violence might have pleased those who delight in sadism. But *personal identification* would have been lost, and Peck's reaction to finding Cassel's body would have sparked no resonant reaction in the viewer, since there would no longer have been any shock for him; and Peck's sub-

*Mirage,* Universal Pictures, 1965.

sequent venting of his rage and grief would have seemed an excessive reaction. As it stands, surprise makes a qualitative difference in the dramatization of this portion of the film by allowing us to look more deeply into Peck's mind during an unguarded moment. The increased understanding of our leading character necessarily affects the remainder of the film.

# 11

# *The End*

We have reached the end of the story, and if it looks familiar, don't be surprised. It is. It's where we started. Whatever by-ways are travelled during a story's development, its ending is usually implicit in its beginning. Let us spend a few minutes retracing our steps.

In the beginning, the leading character *needs* something, *wants* something, or is under a compulsion to *do* something (these are all facets of the same stone)—something usually out of the ordinary, at least for him. His needs may be physical, social, professional, or personal; they may be selfish or altruistic. To satisfy any one of these needs he sets a goal—to reach that goal he must make some decisions. Our beginning usually ends with his first decision, and its establishment may require a minute or two, or half an hour.

Regardless of the length of the beginning, the so-called "middle" follows hard on its heels. The protagonist sets out, literally or figuratively, to realize his goal, to effectuate his decision. This part of the story is its body. It takes up the greatest amount of time and covers the most ground because, along the way, the protagonist faces hazards, encounters obstacles and an assortment of positive and negative characters, all of which cause conflict and often force a change of plans. New decisions must be made to accommodate unfamiliar situations, and new directions must be taken to minimize the resistance of the obstacles.

So far, this is an outline for any action film. For a *good* film the new decisions and directions are important not so much in themselves but in the fact that *confrontations*, especially when they are forced by troublesome attitudes, generate changes within our protagonist. The decisions based on those changes tell us whether our character is growing or seeking refuge in retreat. This is the absolute minimum imperative of any drama. Without it a story becomes a mindless action film, an adolescent exercise.

When the conflicts have been settled and the obstacles surmounted or by-passed as the result of the protagonist's series of decisions, he has attained his goal—Ulysses has come home—and we
are back at the beginning—almost.

Only almost, because there is never a pot of gold at the end of
the rainbow; it's not whether you win, but how you play the game;
and the bluebird of happiness is back in your own back yard. Three
clichés, classic in their triteness, but how apropos to good writing.
For it is fairly safe to say that the complete attainment of a goal is
rarely the finale of a good film. It is the growth and development
within the protagonist's mind and *heart* that lead to a satisfying and
acceptable conclusion. In Dickens' *A Christmas Carol*, it is not the
Christmas dinner enjoyed by Tiny Tim and his family that brings joy
to our hearts or a satisfactory conclusion to the tale; it is the fact that
Scrooge has been transformed into a man who can now cheerfully
supply it.

That is the important point to remember. There *must* be some
resolution of the protagonist's problems, and there must be *growth*.
*The Lady or the Tiger* may be a literary curiosity, but it satisfies
no one. In Dickens' story, Scrooge is the only character who lives and
breathes, for he is the only one who changes, who grows. And growth
is life. I firmly believe that one of the reasons for television's flight
from New York to Hollywood was the New York filmmakers' tendencies to delight in "kitchen sink" episodes: "slice of life" segments
whose basic tenet seemed to be that in that dreary environment nothing really changes. There is movement, but no growth.

Most of us prefer a pleasant ending, but a film's resolution need
not be a happy one. It must, however, give the viewer food for thought;
the resolution may be negative but the lesson must be positive—a
vision that makes the film worth looking at. The viewer must feel
that something has been added to his life, not taken away; that even
if the battle is lost, something has been gained in the fighting.

In discussing the film more or less as a whole it is necessary to
make certain points, to draw certain distinctions. We have been considering *one* person's goal, the development of one person's character.
But though the protagonist's problems are our main concern, equal
care and thought should be given to every other character in the story.
They also have goals toward which they strive, and their paths cross,
ricochet from, or interfere with that of the protagonist. They, too,
must make decisions and those decisions are often the source of our
protagonist's problems. The more believable they are the stronger the
dramatic situations, and the compromises, the accommodations, and
the resolutions of these situations are what delineate our characters.
Those are the actions which stimulate the tell-tale reactions.

As a matter of fact, a perfectly valid story can be (and often is) conceived in which the leading character has no needs and wants to make no life-altering decisions. He is happy with the status quo. It is the needs and decisions of those around him which force him to take action, however unwillingly, and his character and its growth are revealed in the actions he takes. *Casablanca*, a film we have analyzed in some detail, is a perfect example of this genre, and a perfect example of the value of strong subsidiary characters.

Technically, two aspects of *pace* and *length* are interrelated. These concern the beginnings and the ends of scenes and sections.

Preparations to get into the scene, either physical, as when actors are required to move into certain positions, or oral, as with the verbal sparring that sometimes precedes the gist of a scene, are usually a waste of time. They are of use only if they are essential to character development. Scenes should appear to be segments pulled out of a continuous existence, not as a skit staged for the entertainment of an audience. In effect, the viewer looks in on a scene after it has started, and his attention is directed elsewhere before it completely subsides. A re-examination of the many examples given in this book will demonstrate the point. In every case, little time is wasted in getting to the meat of the scene, or in leaving it when it has had its say. "Clever" extensions at either end, if overlooked by the director in the shooting, will be quickly eliminated in the cutting room. "The face on the cutting room floor" is there because it had nothing to say.

However, the concept of "pace" is often misconstrued. Certain schools of writing teach that no scene should run more than three or four pages—which is fine if you've said it all in that time. But as a postulate it ranks with the cutting theory which holds that no cut should run more than 6 or 7 feet, regardless of the content or quality of the scene—which is sheer nonsense. A great deal of my reworking of scripts which contained such scenes was to *consolidate* them into fewer scenes of greater length. It is easier to develop pace, to achieve a flow, to fix character, or to show a transition, if one is given the time to do all that; and the result is better filmmaking and a more rewarding film. Quick cuts and jerkiness do not necessarily furnish speed,* but a properly paced *flow* of information does, whether it be action or dialogue. It is the viewer's *mind* that must be moved by the images on the screen, and that can be better accomplished if it is not jolted to a halt every two minutes or so. In fact, scenes that come and go too rapidly are difficult to follow and will often force a viewer to "tune out."

The best-made films stress the continuous development of plot and character. There may be lapses in time, occasionally covering

*See Book IV, *On Film Editing*.

months, or even years, but they are not lapses in the story's development, to which they are usually unrelated. Their elimination is accomplished smoothly and without the expenditure of time. The current tendency to avoid dissolves and eliminate fades completely is direct evidence of this conception.

Now, a few words of advice on method and procedure.

- Develop a second memory. Making notes is fine, but a notepad is difficult to manipulate while driving on a freeway, and ideas punch no time clock and disappear with frightening speed. A minirecorder which easily fits in your pocket or your purse is made to order for the job.
- Spend time on research—as much as you can afford. It will help you to create more valid characters, and it will often be the source of fresh ideas.
- In conjunction with the research, visit as many *locations* as possible, both interior and exterior. They, too, can inspire ideas and simplify many problems of staging. (Final staging is the director's prerogative, but if the writer has no basic staging in mind, how can he write a scene?) Beyond this, when the story goes into final screenplay form, the writer should always visit the selected locations. I have found this practice very beneficial for both the story and the budget. Scenes can be more accurately placed against their backgrounds, and previously ignored features of even familiar locations may provide improved settings for the eventual staging and playing of scenes. When cost or a mistaken sense of responsibility prevent the writer from seeing the location, adaptations must eventually be made by the director, who may or may not be equal to the task. In any case, there is always a loss of time and an increase in cost.
- All locations, including interiors, should be chosen for their aptness. Open space is *not necessarily* more dynamic than a closed room. It serves no purpose to play a scene in a beautiful mountain meadow if it belongs in a drawing room. The only added effect it may have on the viewer is to confuse him. If the characters are strong and the situation is true, the scene can be played against a concrete wall and the viewer will hardly note the difference. Only if the scene is weak (nothing is perfect) or the background adds some special and useful significance, should its consideration be of prime importance.

# 12

## *The Tag*

I would like to say that a close study of this book and strict adherence to its guidelines will make you a screen writer—but it wouldn't be true. No one can give you the secret of screen writing because no such secret exists. No one knows exactly how to write a superior screenplay. It is a matter of instinct and experience—or *talent, living, learning,* and *practice.*

The talent comes first. Almost everyone thinks he has an artist locked inside of him, but that isn't true, either. And although living, learning, and practice may make a good technician, they will not make an artist unless he also has the gift. That's the bad news.

The good news is that no person is born with the word "artist" stamped on his or her forehead. Many a gifted individual has lived and died without an inkling of his gift; others, through circumstance or fear of failure, have never given themselves the opportunity to release their creative potential. The bottom line is that you'll never know what kind of an artist you might be, or if you are an artist at all, unless you try.

This book alone cannot make you a screen writer, but it can make you aware of what screen writing is all about. Well, perhaps not all, but quite a good deal. I encourage you to read as many other books on the subject as you can tolerate; each will have at least some different slant on the art. Then, if you are one of the fortunate few with a gift for the craft, that awareness plus experience (both your own and that of others who have gone before you) and practice will increase your chances of writing something worthwhile.

So, read, and put to use, and go with God, or your teddy bear, or whatever talisman serves to strengthen your faith in yourself. That's what you need most to make your dreams come true.

# Book II

## ON SCREEN DIRECTING

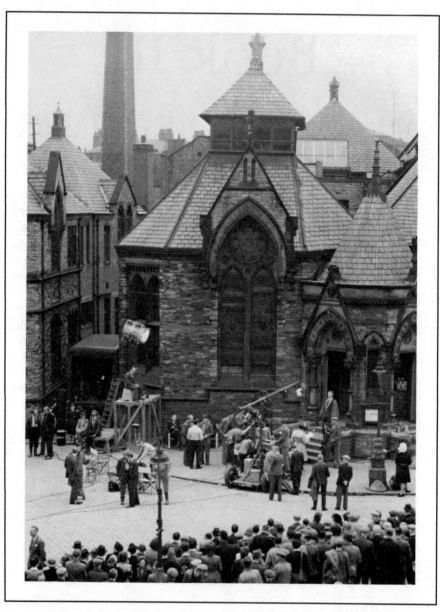

*Film as collective art—lighting, sound and camera crews prepare to film British actor John Mills for a scene in* So Well Remembered, *this scene taking place in front of the town hall of Macclesfield, England.*

# Introduction

Leo McCarey, the great comedy director of the thirties and the forties, two-time Academy Award winner, was pleading his case before a banker. He hoped to borrow a million or two for a prospective film. The financier was puzzled, trying to place McCarey in his scheme of things.

"I know what a cameraman does," he said. "He photographs the film. And I know that a scenarist writes the script. Actors, of course, act. But, tell me, Mr.—uh—McCarey?—what does a director do?"

Leo decided to try another bank.

That was long ago, of course. Since the French have decided to legitimatize that bastard of the arts, the "Cinema," classifying its varied aspects, genres, and occupations, as is their wont, and have pigeon-holed the director, or at least an occasional director, as "auteur," the screen director is a more familiar figure in the outside world. But, though 90 percent of all film students in hundreds of colleges and universities in the United States and abroad want to be directors, few of them really know what a director does.

A large percentage of the students I have worked and talked with have a vague notion that the director is a kind of artistic dictator who orders the actors to stand here, walk there, or "read" the lines this way. Very little could be further from the truth.

To begin with, the making of a film is both a business enterprise and a collective art. It is manufactured as well as created. Most arts, physically, are quite simple: a man, a chisel and a chunk of marble; a woman and a piece of stretched canvas plus a few tubes of paint; a musician and a piano; some sheets of lined paper and a pencil. Or, of course, an author, a typewriter, and reams of blank paper. But whether a film is a pot-boiler or a true work of art, it is necessary to collect a great deal of money, a group of artists from nearly all categories of art, plus an even larger group of technicians before a film can really happen.

The director is the person who blends all these various arts and techniques, stirring them in such a way that in the end he achieves a homogeneous piece of work called "The Film." He must know how to "use" the various members of the production company, how to play them as a concert pianist plays the keys of his Steinway. He must know how to cozen, to coddle, to flatter, to drive, to delegate authority without dropping the reins. He must be an expert in logistics, he must remain comfortable while making a thousand decisions a day, he must be willing, even eager, to think, to dream (though the dreams may degenerate into nightmares) twenty-four hours a day, and still retain his sanity.

A reader, scanning the table of contents, will note, probably with some surprise, that the first half of this book is concerned with script and with cast and crew relationships. That's about par for the course. On the average, at least half of a director's total working time will be taken up with preparation. Only then will he be ready to utter those magic words, "Roll 'em, Camera, Action!"

*One consideration in reviewing a script is the amount of expensive location shooting that will have to be done. Here Dmytryk directs Robert Ryan in his last film, Anzio. Needless to say, to get such backdrops as the Colisseum, you need to film in Italy, where this picture was made.*

# 1

# *In the Beginning . . .*

## *The Script*

"In the beginning was the word—and the word was God." Ignoring the sacrilegious use of this biblical phrase when applied to the average film script, writers of all faiths quote Christianity's favorite apostle when arguing the relative merits of their contributions to the collective art. Hyperbole aside, there is some justification for their claims. Without a screenplay there is no film. However, the real question is: Who writes the story which ultimately appears on the screen? And why must a director concern himself so deeply with the script?

For nearly half a century I have read dozens, sometimes hundreds of scripts each year; scripts written by professional writers. If I found one in a hundred worth making I considered myself fortunate. And one per thousand would probably be the ratio for a truly exceptional story. This is to be expected; there are only a few great creators in any field. Yet, almost every writer considers his work the top of the line. Again—normal. Giving birth to a script can be as painful as giving birth to a baby and is often much more prolonged. Find me a mother who thinks her newborn is ugly. What writer would spend hundreds of hours pounding a typewriter if he thought the final result would be claptrap? One of the key distinctions between "art" and most other professions is that the artist must believe in his work; he must "do his thing" whether or not it earns him a penny. A gas station attendant, on the other hand, would hardly pump gas for the sheer love of it. Unfortunately, belief in one's self does not alone an artist make.

Nor does total faith in the value of words make a good motion picture. It merely gives rise to the sort of film we see so often today—

173

what film scholars all over the world call "talking heads." What seems to have been forgotten by nearly all writers, producers, and even most filmmakers, is that the motion picture, *at its best*, is not truly a dialogue writer's medium. It is a medium for images rather than words, and after the original story is laid down, further creative steps can, indeed should, take place. These steps are usually taken by the director, with the help of a sensitive cameraman, an ingenious cutter, and, more often than is realized by the general public, creative actors.

The writer's point of view is necessarily largely subjective; the director must be objective, at all cost. (This need for objectivity will be mentioned time and again in the following pages; it is one of the chief attributes of a good director.) The filmmaker will certainly have a subjective preference for certain themes and styles, but he must take a very objective look at how best to present those themes and styles to the film public. Nothing can kill a career more quickly or certainly than self-indulgence.

No, a script is never "the word of God." Most producers will not consider a script "final" until the director has had his go at it. Unfortunately, that "go" doesn't always do the job: The average director is no better than the average writer. He can demean as many scripts as he can exalt—maybe more.

However, in this area the top directors have a few things in their favor. First, a really superior filmmaker usually has a greater sense of the visual, the "filmic" quality of a scenario, if only because his knowledge has been acquired on the field of battle, where his weapons are the camera and the scissors rather than the pen or the typewriter. His favorite quotation is not "In the beginning was the word," but "One picture is worth a thousand words." He can, at least he should, always try to change a sequence in which most of the information is relayed through dialogue into one in which the essential message is conveyed through action and reaction. In fact, the ability to make this transformation is what raises a particular director above most of his colleagues.

On a more common level the director can simplify dialogue through the intelligent use of his camera. The lens can frequently catch, in silence, what the writer presents in dialogue. Adolphe Menjou once testified that a clever actor can insinuate propaganda into a film with "the lift of an eyebrow, the shrug of a shoulder," and thus subvert a nation's government. The first part of his thesis, at least, is not too far from the truth. Even the character of a set can often dramatize the character of a character far better than words. And the expression in the eyes of an actor, especially when enhanced by appropriate music, can not only serve to eliminate a whole page of dialogue, but can intensify the film's hold on the sensibilities of the audience.

There are three basic sources for film material: the theatrical play, the novel, and the "original screenplay." The first of these presents few problems beyond "opening up" the setting. Inevitably, it remains a play, however good it may be, rather than a true motion picture. The novel and the original screenplay, i.e., a scenario written expressly for the screen, are the major sources of film material.

Most film stories are adaptations of novels, and these adaptations confront the writer with the most varied and difficult problems. The average novel is much longer than the average screenplay, necessitating extensive editing and careful selection. If *The Caine Mutiny*, for example, were to be dramatized in its entirety, the film would run 14 to 16 hours, obviously an impossible undertaking.* In actuality, the writer will analyze the theme, the plot, and the characters and select those segments of the book that best exemplify what the novelist has to say in these areas. (The novel's adapters may, of course, choose to modify, curtail, extend, or otherwise "improve" the author's point of view.) Once these selections are made they must be arranged in proper sequence (which is not necessarily the order of their appearance in the book), connecting links must be created that will blend the edited portions into a smooth and complete whole, and, most difficult of all, essential "stream of consciousness" passages must be dramatized into visual scenes.

The third source of film material, the original screenplay, may also present editing difficulties. Most scenes are overwritten, and the director must have a keen awareness of the limits of the viewer's attention span, or rather, the limits of his forbearance. A verbose scene can turn off the viewer/listener, not only from that particular scene, but from the entire film as well. Attention lost is difficult to recapture. Overstatement in the script implies lack of understanding in the viewer, and what viewer cares to be insulted by being "talked down to." I have yet to see an audience which fails to grasp the "profundities" of even the best film.

One world-famous filmmaker of the thirties and forties worked frequently with an equally acclaimed writer. Few people outside of their immediate associates knew the true nature of their collaboration, which went something like this: The writer would present ten or twelve pages of newly written material. The director would scan it, then pick up his blue pencil.

"The opening line is fine," he might say, then he would cross out the next half page. Continuing in this fashion through the rest of the sequence, he would edit it down to about four pages, then return it to the writer with instructions to "smooth out the breaks."

*The development of the miniseries in TV opens up distinct possibilities for full translation of novels to film.

The films they made together were among the best of their time. On the strength of these films the writer was permitted to direct a couple on his own. They were total disasters, choking to death on their own verbosity.

The example is not exceptional. Directors, too, become blinded by their rewriting "brilliance" and fall prey to their own arrogance. A prime and primary approach to any work of art is one based on humility. Fred Allen, in answer to an interviewer's question concerning the comedian's contribution to his comic material, said, "I write best on dirty paper." That, too, can be a great talent, one that every director should cultivate.

The original screenplay suffers from inadequately developed characterization much more frequently than the novel. The shorter form gives the writer less room for the development of both plot and character, and for some reason plot is favored over character by most film playwrights. In my opinion, the characters should always be the chief concern of any writer. If they are interesting and fully developed, the plot often comes quite easily. Confrontation between two vital human beings is drama, per se. They can be placed in any of a number of situations and the scenes will almost write themselves. It is commonly accepted that the number of plots is extremely limited, but variety of character is almost infinite. Few people objected to the fact that *The Westside Story* was merely a reworking of *Romeo and Juliet*, a stale plot indeed. Few were even aware of it. The plot gained new life because the audience was interested in the human beings involved in it.

The "plot first" writer usually winds up with a contrived sequence of situations, and most often creates two-dimensional beings whom he can squeeze into his arbitrary plot. It is revealing that the words "contrived screenplay" have become a cliché with those who make or evaluate motion pictures.

The plot writer is usually concerned with "action," which he takes to mean more or less violent movement on the screen. But a relatively placid scene played by charismatic actors can move the mind of the beholder much more than the violent maneuvering of players with whom the audience is not in touch. Like a woman in love, intent upon her sweetheart's every gesture, the viewer will be more involved with the way a well-developed, sympathetic character moves, sits, or lifts a cup of coffee, than he will with the violent antics of a character in whom he has no interest and for whom he feels no empathy.

Given equal development, it is preferable to have your actors *do* things rather than say them—at least whenever possible. "Actions speak louder than words." "Show me, I'm from Missouri." In this cynical era the viewer knows that people often cover up their real emotions with dialogue. But a person's reaction to a crisis, or sudden confrontation, however momentary, can immediately reveal more truth about that person's character than pages of after-the-fact verbalization.

From the practical and logistical point of view there are several aspects of a script that call for careful analysis, particularly if the film must be made expeditiously and at a reasonable cost.

Most important is the number of characters in the cast. Within a set time schedule, the greater the number of roles the less time is available to properly develop all of them. Many films give full coverage to a few leading roles and let the lesser parts fend for themselves. The result is flat, pasteboard characters which weaken the integrity of the whole. It is desirable that *all* characters, however briefly shown, be presented as complete human beings. Any character worth keeping is worth developing. A well-developed minor character can pique the viewer's interest, enliven an otherwise routine scene, and confirm the humanity of the film's inhabitants.

Hitchcock was a past master of this technique. The leading man confronts a loiterer to ask for directions. But the loiterer is such an unusual, albeit believeable, "type" and is presented in such an interesting fashion, before or after the personal contact, that we wonder about him and his place in the story's scheme of things. As a matter of fact, we will probably never see him again, but his momentary presence has activated movement in our minds and has served to increase our involvement in the film.

It is often possible and advisable to blend two or more characters into one, thereby furnishing room and time for more complete development of the remaining roles.

The number of locations (including sets) is also a factor that calls for careful examination. Moving a company from one location to another always takes time, even if the move is merely to another set on the same stage. The more hours spent in moving equipment, cast and crew from one location to another, the fewer the hours available for working with the actors on the scenes themselves. In the end, only those scenes, and not the location moves, are the concern of the viewer. As in everything to be discussed, there are exceptions, but the benefits of strict location analysis are many, not only in the area of expenditure, but also in the area of film quality. They should not be ignored.

There is one special technique most writers and filmmakers find difficult to deal with: manipulation of the audience. Every student of the screen knows that films manipulate time and space. So do all the narrative arts, though films make such transitions most easily and effectively. But audience manipulation is something else entirely.

Suppose we have two minutes of screen time to convince a viewer that character A will accede to a proposition presented by character B. Suppose, further, that the viewer knows that A is completely opposed to the proposition, or would normally take much time and thought to arrive at a decision. But we have only two minutes. How can we convince our viewer in such a brief time that A will agree? There are at least two ways to manipulate him into accepting that which we want him to accept.

First, and probably most common, is type casting: the use of an actor whose appearance and personality command our confidence. In Hollywood's golden era it was no trick to convince a viewer that Clark Gable, or any one of a dozen stars of either sex, could easily and quickly bend anyone to his or her desires. As a matter of fact, the filmmaker was hard put to keep the viewer from wondering why the leading lady didn't fall into Gable's arms on sight. But, cleverly manipulated, the viewer would swallow acceptance or rejection at the filmmaker's will until the final scene permitted the inevitable.

Second, and much more difficult as well as much more creative, is manipulation by situation. An example furnishes the best explanation. In a Russian film of 1931, *The Road to Life*, directed by Nicolai Ekk, a situation arises which demonstrates this technique most effectively. A gang of young hoodlums, wild boys of the streets, has been rounded up by the authorities, whose plan, this time around, is not to put them in jail, where most of them have served repeated sentences, but to rehabilitate them by installing them in a special school in the country. There they can learn to be shoemakers, carpenters, or mechanics. Naturally, none of these young thugs prefers the country to his familiar alleys, and most of them laugh at the thought of making shoes or building bird-houses. When the pleasant young official from the youth authority puts his proposition to the young hooligans all hell is about to break loose. But the official calmly pulls out a cigarette case, extracts a cigarette, then extends the open case to the toughs' leader. Russians are avid smokers, and none of the boys has had a puff since his incarceration. The leader hesitates, torn between animosity and desire. Desire wins. He reaches out and takes a cigarette, an action imitated by other members of the gang. Then comes the clincher.

The official has only one match. He lights his fag and then blows out the match. Now the burning tip of his cigarette, which he holds between his lips, is the only source of a light. Slowly the gang leader leans forward, then a smile creases his face, and he puffs a light from the official's cigarette. His action, of course, is followed by the others, which initiates a scene of general hilarity in which three or four boys simultaneously snatch their lights from the official. In the next scene the boys are on their way to the country and we, the audience, are perfectly satisfied that they have freely agreed to go.

Once it has been created the stratagem is obvious. The taking of a light from another person's cigarette, especially when, as in this case, the cigarettes never leave the holders' mouths, is an act of in-

*Location shooting is not the only thing that adds to the cost of the film. Another is the number and elaborateness of the sets required. This set was especially built on R.K.O.'s back lot for the film* Cornered. *Dmytryk discusses the scene to be shot on it with Dick Powell here.*

timacy which hardly suffers antagonism. And as antagonism dissi-
pates, so does recalcitrance. And so, in the space of a minute or two,
we rationally accept a decision that in reality might have taken much
time and very skillful pleading.

Techniques such as this one were highly developed by the early
Russian filmmakers, who lost the art when they, with the rest of the
world, decided to emphasize dialogue because of its novelty at the
time. It would pay us to retreat a couple of generations to recover,
and bring up to date, some of those aspects of the art of montage which
we could presently use to advantage.

But these examples deal more with creative techniques than with
script problems, and it behooves us to move on to other responsibilities of the director.

*Costume design begins early in the production process. Star Carol Baker here models part of her wardrobe for* The Carpetbaggers. *At top designer Edith Head presents her design sketches to, counterclockwise, Joe Levine, Marty Rackin and Edward Dmytryk (with cameraman Joe MacDonald behind him).*

# 2

# *To Make Ready*

## *Preproduction*

The director is a problem solver, and problems rarely march in single file. While he and the writer are putting the final touches to the script, which will probably never be quite finished, he will also be selecting a cast and assembling a crew.

The director of experience always has his "regulars"—men and women of proven worth who have won his confidence through past performances. If the preproduction sequence has progressed smoothly and the budget can afford it, these regulars are already on the roster, or standing by. The three persons on whom the director most deeply relies are the cinematographer, the film editor, and the assistant director, not necessarily in that order.

Photography can probably claim a greater percentage of fine artists than any other film craft, with the possible exception of set design. I'm not quite sure why this is so, but I do know I've never had a bad photographer on any of the nearly 60 films I have made. They came in different colors, races, nationalities: American, British, Japanese, Austrian, Hungarian, Turkish, South African and Italian. All were excellent. However, the rule still holds: The truly great artists are few, and when a director finds one he hangs on to him for dear life.

The exact nature of the cameraman's contributions will be discussed in a later chapter. Here it is only necessary to stress that compatibility is of the greatest importance. If an unfamiliar cinematographer is to be employed, it is wise to delve more deeply into his personality than his professional skills. It is relatively simple to judge the cameraman's lighting ability by viewing samples of his work; it is not easy to fathom his *working* personality.

In this situation most directors will seek recommendations from other filmmakers who have used the photographer in question. When doing so it is advisable to also keep in mind the working personalities of the directors being questioned. If problems are reported, it is equally probable that they arose from either side. Only when the enquiring director feels satisfied that he can work harmoniously with the cameraman should arrangements be made for his employment.

Besides supplying his lighting expertise, the cinematographer is often an important factor in the maintenance of good set morale. When you acquire a cameraman you acquire a family. Just as the director ties a string to his favorite cameraman, so the cameraman insists on keeping his proven aides: his camera operator, his gaffer, his camera grip. They, in turn, bring along their long-time assistants, and so a large part of the crew stems from the photographer's choice of his right-hand men, and he will generally keep a friendly but firm control over their on-set behavior.

The film editor (cutter) usually joins the company a couple of weeks before the start of active production. He is often considered the magician of the crew. Even persons with years of film experience will sometimes marvel at the cutter's skill as he wades through miles of "spaghetti" and emerges with a coherent film. Unfortunately, the editors' ratio of excellence is not nearly as high as that of cinematographers for obvious reasons: The best of them are frequently promoted out of their jobs. Most film experts consider editing to be the best all-around training for directing, and many of our filmmakers were once film editors. Unless the director has had a good deal of editing experience (and simply watching a cutter at work counts for nothing) he must depend heavily on his editor. When he finds a good one he rarely lets him leave his side.

The cameraman and the cutter are almost always "directors' men," that is, their loyalties are given to the director. It is sad, but too often true, that the relationship between the director and the producer is, to use the legal phrase, an adversary one. In this area, the problems most likely to develop on a film, especially one with a long schedule, have two basic causes. First is the conflict of interest that frequently arises between the concerns of business and the demands of art. The second, and certainly more troublesome cause, stems from the artistic pretensions of a producer who does not feel qualified to direct a film himself, but who can't help trying to inject his "creative ideas." It is axiomatic that two generals cannot successfully command one army, and when such a situation arises, the director needs all the help he can get. When push comes to shove numbers count, and the more artists on your side the greater your chance of victory.

I do not speak of winning in the competitive sense, but winning for the sake of artistic integrity. A confident director will listen to suggestions. Occasionally, he may even accept one in its entirety. More often he will discard them because they do not fit his over-all conception, with which the suggester is probably not familiar. A suggestion, even when not inappropriate in itself, may muddy values more important to the film. Usually even the accepted few will be reshaped, perhaps altered beyond recognition, to fit the director's total vision. The chief value of most suggestions is that they may disclose hitherto disguised scene weaknesses or suggest better approaches, thus forcing the director to explore new channels.

Under any circumstances, openness to suggestion must be carefully controlled, since it can present a number of pitfalls. Some overapproachable directors spend half their time dealing with unsolicited "help." The script clerk, the cameraman, the cutter, the prop man, and the coffee maker have ideas which they are eager to share if they see the director is floundering. However, none of them can possibly know the director's over-all concept, and the great majority of these suggestions are probably inapropos and time-wasting. A director with a mind that is too wide open usually has little mind of his own and is not a competent filmmaker.

And there's the rub. Every member of the crew recognizes indecision and insecurity. If the director exhibits signs of either one of these negative attributes the entire crew, from the cameraman on down, is immediately affected. Morale suffers, and so, obviously, does the film.

In truth, of course, the director *is* often unsure of himself or of the effects he *hopes* to achieve. As a cutter, I once worked with a director who, before stepping on the stage each morning, visited the men's room to vomit up his breakfast. Stage fright usually affects performers for a few hours, or even days, before their first appearance. But for this director stage fright was a daily visitor throughout the production.

Another example is less tragic and more amusing. After okaying a "print," Leo McCarey customarily looked back over his shoulder at members of his crew to read their faces for approval. On one film an electrician persisted in greeting McCarey's enquiring gaze with a deadpan wink. "I thought he was on to me," McCarey said. "I had to let him go."

To suffer from butterflies is no sin. Some psychologists suggest it may heighten an artist's performance. But it *is* a sin to show it to the world. Above all, a director is looked to for leadership, and leadership is what a director must demonstrate, even if he has to stage an act of his own.

As will be detailed later, the director should think a number of set-ups ahead for the sake of continuity. But it is also important that he think at least one set-up ahead in the interest of crew confidence.

When I have completed work on the current set-up with, "That's great! Print it," I move immediately, without a moment's hesitation, to my next camera position. Since the scene has already been rehearsed (see Book II, Chapter 7), I use a view-finder to fix the location and height of the camera and the scope of the shot. Then, while the crew is engaged in the routine activity that comes with every change of set-up, I collect my thoughts and concentrate on the work to follow.

The question of leadership is really the crux of the producer-director relationship. The best film executives have always understood the necessity for the director's on-set primacy and have done everything in their power to strengthen it. They have usually been complete delegators. If they have a suggestion to make they make it privately and quietly, understanding the director's need to protect his image both as a leader and as a creator.

Most intelligent people realize that an artist *must* do what he thinks best. He cannot execute another person's idea with a whole heart and mind unless he has first made it his own. A number of incidents illustrating this point have occurred over the years. An outstanding example (perhaps apocryphal) involved Howard Hawks and Harry Cohn.

During the period of script preparation Hawks and Cohn had apparently discussed a particular treatment of a particular sequence. Hawks eventually shot it, but not as originally agreed upon. Cohn viewed it the next day in his projection room, then stormed on the set to demand that Hawks restage the scene as originally conceived. Cool and suave, as always, Hawks assured Cohn that he would re-do the scene in question the following day. He did, and again Cohn viewed the rushes. It was the same scene, shot for shot, that Hawks had filmed the first time. Again Cohn stormed the set, again Hawks agreed to reshoot the scene, and again he shot it exactly as he had the first time and the second. But now Cohn decided to let well enough alone, and Hawks finished the film on his own terms.

If Hawks had been a lesser director Cohn might have fired him. If Cohn had been a better psychologist he would not have stormed the set, made a scene (no pun intended) before the whole crew, forcing Hawks to demonstrate his leadership in the only way open to him. Had Cohn discussed the issue in the privacy of his office it is quite possible that he and Hawks might at least have reached some acceptable compromise, and Hawks would have saved face by reshooting the sequence as a "second thought" effort.

The best executive and the best producer I have known rarely, if ever, visited the set. Many executives are not that considerate. Under sufficient provocation, directors have had producers removed from the stage. However, the best technique for handling such delicate situations is one that was used by that most capable practitioner of "cool,"

Howard Hawks. If a producer wandered on the set he was greeted by Hawks with the greatest civility. In his honor, all work ceased. A comfortable chair was quickly provided, and Hawks would engage the visitor in friendly conversation about anything except the work at hand. It usually took only a few minutes for the producer to realize that his presence was prolonging the schedule, and that only his prompt departure could trigger further activity. The prompt departure was always forthcoming.

None of this means that a producer loses all control over his production when the shooting starts. On the contrary, he can be helpful in many ways, and he almost always has an important, sometimes final say in the editing, and certainly in the marketing of the film. Beyond that, many directors can benefit from the tactful guidance of an intelligent producer. There have been a number of instances of directors "gone wild" when given total freedom. Even an "old hand" can become self-indulgent and occasionally run amok. But always, whether it be the producer's or the strong director's, the iron fist should wear a velvet glove.

Ideally, the relationship which the director enjoys with his cameraman and his cutter should extend to his assistant director—and it often does, but not always. Although the A.D. bears the title of assistant director and belongs to the Directors Guild, he is not always the director's man. Some independent producers as well as studio production departments succeed in making the assistant "their man" on the set. They can offer incentives and exert pressures to accomplish that end.

The possibility exists because the assistant director is an anomaly. He is *not* an assistant in the creative sense, but the set foreman. He sees that the set is efficiently organized, that everything the director needs is at hand, whether it be actors, extras, or special equipment, and he marshals the set for the director during rehearsals and shooting. Physically, he works harder and longer than any other member of the crew. He is (or should be) the first one on the set in the morning, oiling the machinery for a prompt start, and he will be the last one to "fold up" in the evening, since he must do his paper work after the shooting is finished and make sure that everything is in order for the next day's work. He should also be capable of handling minor crew problems and pacifying troubled actors. If he is exceptionally able he will leave the director free to do nothing but direct. On location his work and his hours are even harder and longer. The A.D. always has at least one assistant, called the second, to help him with his countless chores.

He also has the help of the production manager. In many areas their duties overlap. The P.M. has little to do with the daily running of the set, or with the handling of the cast but, since he is the main

*The producer-director relationship is vitally important to the film. Dmytryk meets with producer Buddy Adler on the 20th Century Fox back lot on the film* Warlock.

contact between the producer and the set, especially on the business front, he is the chief figure in budgeting, scheduling, and equipment procurement. He also makes all location deals and sets up the location apparatus. It is in this area that a top production manager can make the filming ordeal almost pleasant for the director, or a bad P.M. can bring it to near or total disaster.

Now that studio back lots have become real estate developments, shooting on location is a part, often a major part, of every film production. These locations may be found in any area of the world, including the North and South Poles. Filming distant locations involves the use of crews, actors, and extras of every race, creed, and nationality and, of course, company interpreters. Beyond that, these locations are owned or controlled by national, state, or city governments, by corporations or by private citizens. Representatives of one, or all, of these entities must be dealt with before a crew can work on any location, and the greatest part of the wheeling and dealing involved in this phase of the production is in the hands of the production manager. Since not all such persons are eager to cooperate with film companies, the P.M. has to have all the positive qualities of a diplomat, as well as a good head for business.

Many locations described in a script cannot be shot as indicated. Large parts of *Zhivago,* for instance, were shot in Spain. The storm in David Lean's *Ryan's Daughter* was filmed not in Ireland but in South Africa. The North African war scenes in *The Young Lions* were shot in the Borrego Desert in Southern California. Other examples could fill a book.

Selecting locations is customarily the prerogative of the director, although the producer, as guardian of the budget, may play an important part in the process. Once tentative locations have been picked, a small production team embarks on a tour of reconnaissance—one of the more pleasant aspects of filmmaking. The travelling group usually includes the director, the production manager, the cameraman, and the set designer. Interpreters are picked up along the way, as needed. Whenever possible, it is of value to include the screen writer, since script changes are frequently made to accommodate unforeseen differences in appearance and to utilize the full potential of the selected locations.

Actual filming always involves tremendous logistical problems, most of which are the production manager's responsibility. At least the key crew members and some equipment must be transported from home base to the location; and crews from the host country or, in the United States, the local unions, must be hired, as well as bit players and extras. Convenient housing must be located and provided for cast and crew. Breakfast and dinner are usually obtained at or near the housing, but lunch and on-set snacks must be catered on the set. Local trucking and personnel transport must also be supplied, as well as the fuel to feed the vehicular fleet.

Through all this there is the on-going effort to maintain good relations with the local officialdom and citizenry. An occasional dinner with the neighborhood's "wheels," a tour of the set, even a company dinner party, can work miracles of good will. A truly superior P.M. knows that a few dollars spent on such entertainment can save thousands of dollars in actual production. Good will is always more economical than a "good deal."

The duties of the set and the costume designers are obvious.

These artists are almost always competent, talented, and easy to get along with—if you don't compromise *their* creative integrity. They work in special fields with which the director is too often unfamiliar, yet they must have an understanding of his basic wishes in their areas. Neither a set nor a gown can be built without the director's signed approval, since he must be sure that the sets and the costumes will not only reinforce the film's character, but will also fill the needs of the scene's action. There should always be consultation and co-operation in these areas.

The remaining members of the crew have specific jobs, easily identified by their titles. The duties of the electricians, the set carpenter, painter, and plumber are obvious. As a rule, the last three are not permanent crew members, but report when needed. The set decorator always works with the set designer. He dresses the sets, supplies any needed signs, etc.

The property master, or prop man, for short, is in charge of all set dressing which can be easily moved by hand. He furnishes the ash trays, smoking materials (including an occasional cigar for the director), guns (for Westerns, or almost any film today) luggage, dinnerware, and even the food for scenes that require it. All these things are done only after consultation with the director and, possibly, the set decorator. As a matter of fact, the prop man's duties are quite extensive, since he also serves as general factotum for the director, handling the off-set chairs, seeing the director has his coffee or diet Coke, and acting as unofficial host to "friends" who may visit the set. He takes pride in anticipating the director's every filming demand, suffering when caught short in any way. That prop men have a decided upward mobility is attested to by the fact that John Wayne, the actor, and Henry Hathaway, the director (among others) both started their careers in the prop department. No where else in the film world do prop men come close to matching those in Hollywood. It is perhaps the only craft in which Hollywood is truly supreme.

Among the last, but certainly not the least, is the script supervisor. The title, like many others adopted by unions in the vain belief that they would impress employers at bargaining sessions, is misleading. A script supervisor does not supervise the script. She (the script clerk is usually a woman) follows all the action and dialogue shot, noting any deviation from the script, records the number and lengths of the takes, the camera lenses used, the size of the set-ups (whether close-up, medium shot, etc.), and the "prints" requested by the director. All this information is indispensable to the film editor. She must also keep track of the wardrobe worn by the members of the cast, their relative positions in any part of the scene, any unusual placing or change of props, and so on. She will often cue the actors at rehearsals and she will, on occasion, tactfully bring the harried director's attention to a missed line or a fouled-up piece of business. (It is surprising how often these things can pass unnoticed.) She is probably more aware of the film as a whole work than anyone on the set except the director. And she often mothers the entire crew.

Some special talents can be useful on a production. Two of these are the dialogue director and the sketch artist, though at least one of these titles is misleading. A dialogue director does *not* (or should not) direct dialogue. (The reasons for this will be explained in a later chapter.) Normally, he holds the script and cues actors who may be rehearsing off-stage. But I prefer to utilize a dialogue director as a creative assistant. As with the notorious captain of a ship, the director's position is a solitary one. While preparing one scene his mind is always occupied in part with the problems of scenes to be shot in the future. It is a permanent state of affairs, since one rarely anticipates a scene without problems. In this situation it sometimes helps to discuss one's doubts and insecurities, along with tentative solutions, with the dialogue director. If, during the course of the production, he can come up with one or two creative conceptions, even in part, he will certainly have paid his way.

The same holds true for the sketch artist. In my opinion it is a waste of time to have him sketch set-ups that the director already has in mind. But if he can conceive an original pictorial treatment for a future sequence that may be troubling the director he will earn both the director's gratitude and his salary.

A film's schedule is usually based on its budget, or vice versa. Very few budgets are unlimited. Once the below-the-line cost has been established (and if the director's work habits are known) the production manager and the assistant director can set about fixing the schedule. They do this with locations, set space, and actors' contract times in mind. In consequence, the film is rarely shot in script sequence, but in the order which will most economically utilize the production's funds.

An example: Recently an actor was hired for 12 days' work at a cost of three million dollars. Each additional day's work would have cost $250,000. Obviously, this actor's scenes were shot one after the other, regardless of where those scenes fit into the picture. In Hollywood, an actor is "carried," i.e., he is paid for days off between working days, so expensive actors will always be scheduled for continuous shooting. (With the exception, of course, of the leading players, who have run-of-the-film contracts.) Players who make a nominal salary need not be scheduled as tightly. It may be more efficient, therefore less costly, to carry them while shooting other sequences in which they do not appear.

A number of such factors are considered by the P.M. and the A.D. When their version of the schedule is completed and "on the board," they present it to the director. He will study it carefully, making whatever changes are necessary to accommodate plans his assistants were unaware of. Then he, the P.M., and the A.D. will make a final analysis of the board, and the schedule is considered set. The fact that the actual shooting almost always veers away from the original schedule is only one more indication of the vagaries of film-making.

The setting of the schedule is usually the final stage in preproduction. But one area has been purposely ignored, since it warrants a full discussion of its own. That is, of course, casting the film.

*Whether to cast well-known stars or unknown actors in a film is a recurring dilemma for the director. For Broken Lance, shot in 1954, director Dmytryk, second from left, opted for stars. On this lunch break near Nogales, Arizona he is surrounded (on his right) by Spencer Tracy and (on his left) Robert Wagner and Earl Holliman. Across the table is Jean Peters, Richard Widmark and, with his back to the camera, Hugh O'Brien. The film won an award for being the best Western of that year.*

# 3

# *Who's in the Show?*

## *Casting*

The cast. It sounds like a throw of the dice, and sometimes it is. But it shouldn't be. Everything so far discussed—the story, the crew, the director—works to one purpose: to bring a group of people onto the movie screen. In one sense, this group of people is the single most important element in any film. It must consist of persons who are empathetic, honest, and in most instances, attractive—well, in all instances, really, since even the brutes and the villains must *attract* the viewer's interest and attention. The selection of this group of people which we call "the cast" must be as much a work of art as any other activity involved in the making of a film. For a number of reasons it is of greater concern to the director than to any other person on the production. But let us approach the problems of casting in proper order. First, the stars.

In most productions the top two or three players are of interest not only to the director but to the producer or producing company, to the distributor, and to the exhibitor. Consequently, each seeks an input into their selection. In many instances a film can't be sold to an exhibitor unless, as he frequently puts it, he has some "names" to place on his marquee. The director may feel that a certain as-yet-undiscovered actor could play the leading role to perfection; but the producer, with the exhibitor in mind, will object that the actor has no "drawing power." Nine times out of ten he will be right. It takes time and money to sell a new actor to the public, both in terms of career and in terms of one film. The audience rarely cottons to a newcomer unless he or she has an especially winning part in an especially powerful story. There just aren't too many of these. But there are a few men and women who can "carry" even a mediocre film. These are the true and *only* stars.

They are stars for necessary and sufficient reasons; they have a combination of all the required qualities. They are usually physically attractive, they project strong personalities, they are "loved by the camera," and they can act. It is one of Hollywood's myths that many top stars are beautiful or handsome but not very talented. Obviously, that is sheer nonsense. Spencer Tracy was handsome—many critics also considered him to be the world's finest actor. The same can be said for Paul Newman or Robert Redford, for Jane Fonda or Vanessa Redgrave, as well as a number of others. Any director would accept one or more of these in almost any film. The producer and the exhibitor would be equally delighted.

The point here is that the casting of the top roles is almost always a collective decision in which the director may have to compromise his prediliction for "art" and integrity. Normally, the problem is not insurmountable and the compromise is painless.

Occasionally, however, a film of unusual quality requires "new faces."* Established actors undoubtedly bring their unique personalities to each part they play. A Bogart part is just that—however well acted, it is a Bogart part. (There are exceptions.) The "new" actors also bring their personalities into their screen characterizations, but since the viewer has no previously established image to refer to, he accepts the "new faces" as true representations of the people they play. These "new faces" often go on to highly successful careers. Their screen personalities then become as fixed as those of the established stars. There are a number of examples of such "overnight" discoveries: Dustin Hoffman in *The Graduate,* Richard Dreyfus in *American Graffiti,* and several of the young men in *Breaking Away.* The examples go on and on.

Discoveries of this kind are not equivalent to finding a beautiful face and a sexy body on a soda fountain stool. Those are *personalities,* discovered first, then inserted into what the discoverers hope will be successful debuts and, eventually, rewarding careers. Sometimes it turns out they can also act.

With a few exceptions, two or three star names are about all the marquees and the advertising media can accommodate with comfort. It is also just about all the film's dramatic needs can accommodate if good taste and the film's integrity is held in any regard. On occasion,

---

*I put "new faces" in quotation marks because most discoveries are not truly new. The majority of them have been learning and practicing their craft for years, and they have a world of experience when finally "discovered." Ben Kingsley, the star of *Ghandi,* is a case in point.

in an attempt to build a blockbuster out of a weak or uncertain script, a producer will pack his cast with stars, many playing "bits" which, in an effort to support their status and justify the added expense, are called "vignettes." Almost without exception this only serves to make the audience aware of the mechanics of entrepreneurship. Really good, appealing films need no such bolstering. On the contrary, over the years many fine and successful films have been stocked with good actors and no "names" at all.

Now back to the "average" film: The further one works down the roster of players the greater the director's freedom of choice, since the supporting cast, however important to the film, is no longer a major concern to the distributor. Though most producers continue to contribute to the casting process, as a rule their role becomes an advisory one.

The director who feels strongly about picking his own actors must know what constitutes good *screen* acting. Many actors, as well as most nonprofessionals, think the only difference between acting for the stage and acting for the screen is voice volume and intensity. This is demonstrably not so.

(For a complete analysis of screen acting from the director's and the actor's points of view, see Book III, *On Screen Acting.*)

The director casts his players on the basis of his familiarity with their work, the films he has seen, the recommendations of his colleagues or the players' representatives, and, occasionally, by personal interviews. He tries to find the actor who can "be" the character he originally visualized. However, the longer he "plays around" with the story's characters, the more he is inclined to take chances, to experiment, to look for new twists in his on-screen people. Often an interview with an actor will disclose interesting side characteristics, either in appearance or in attitude. Sometimes, the director purposely seeks to off-cast a part.

It is relatively safe to choose a player on the basis of past performance. It may also result in a "safe," routine characterization. Taking a chance, when successful, adds many a plus to the film's effectiveness. Dick Powell, the sweet-singing tenor in many Warner Brothers' musicals of the thirties, was an unexpected success as Phillip Marlowe in *Murder, My Sweet.* He turned out to be just the off-beat type the character needed; and many critics, as well as Raymond Chandler, the author of the Marlowe novels, considered him the best Marlowe on the screen, even though the character was subsequently played by better actors. Similarly, casting tough-guy Humphrey Bogart as the psychotic and vulnerable Captain Queeg in *The Caine Mutiny* was a stroke of near genius, for which the producer, Stanley Kramer, deserves full credit. As a matter of fact, most of the film's casting was off-beat, including former "pretty boy" Van Johnson as the earnest, not-too-bright executive officer and Fred MacMurray as the cowardly intellectual.

Occasionally, off-casting becomes a stunt, an "in" joke. Mike Mazurki as Don Juan may be worth a few laughs in the director's office, but it will bring only tears at the boxoffice. How the director casts his film should depend in part on what he feels the audience will accept, or what he thinks he can make them accept—or more than accept: take warmly to heart. Basically, that means they must love to love the protagonists and love to hate the antagonists. The viewer is just as much the key to good casting as he is to good story telling. Every good director tries to make the film he thinks is worthwhile; but if he can't make his viewers feel that the film is *worth* experiencing, he is only making home movies.

The director's techniques for working with actors will be discussed later, but here I must again bring up the question of compatibility. Getting the best performance is often a highly emotional experience, both for the actor and the director. The two do not always see eye to eye, either in the area of characterization or of technique. One actor's working habits may be antipathetic to those of his fellow artists. Conflict may sometimes give rise to great art; but in a process as complex as the making of a film, harmony can be a blessing.

Just as the director investigates his cameraman's working personality, so he must look into the characters and predilections of his players. There have been numerous instances of major strife caused by extreme differences in actors' working habits. An example: Glenn Ford is a professional. Like all true professionals, he prepares at home rather than on the set at the expense of the company's time. He is at his best and most spontaneous in the first few takes. Marlon Brando, a great actor, doesn't know what he wants to do until he has tried a variety of approaches. Before I cast him in *The Young Lions*, a director who had worked with him told me, "He can be quite dreadful for 70 takes, then there is take 71 and, suddenly, magic!" But by take 71 Ford was used up and dry. This difference in techniques led to an open battle on the set of *Teahouse of the August Moon*. The film suffered.

The cast of *The Young Lions* included Brando and Montgomery Clift. Clift presented problems of his own, but shooting numerous takes wasn't one of them. He was at his best in take one or two. Fortunately, he and Brando never shared a scene, so the differences that might easily have caused a shut-down never arose.* Vincent Sherman once made a film with Bette Davis and Miriam Hopkins, two of

---

* Let me say, however, that Brando grew to understand and appreciate the film. In consequence, his work habits improved tremendously, and for the greater part of the film he worked efficiently and with great dedication.

*Important considerations for the director in casting a film are the work habits of the actors—and how well he works with them. Here Dmytryk enjoys a light moment with stars Robert Mitchum and Peter Falk, along with an unidentified jeep driver, while filming* Anzio.

Hollywood's more headstrong actresses. I asked him whether he had enjoyed directing them. "I didn't direct them," he said. "I refereed."

A few actors of both sexes have an inclination to take over the production—to be King of the hill. This tendency, too, must be guarded against, but more of this later.

The casting of bits presents its own problems. This duty is left completely in the director's hands and it, too, will be enlarged on in a different context.

Unless special types are called for, the casting of extras is routine. They are supplied by Central Casting in the number required, and their disposition is usually left in the hands of the assistant director.

*Dmytryk here works with one of his favorite cameramen, Joe Mac-Donald, whose sense of humor often saved the day during troublesome times. The film is* **Alvarez Kelly**.

# 4

# *Working with the Crew*

Everyone wants credit—the neighborhood postman, the local butcher, the county coroner, the ambassador at large, and certainly every member of a film crew. I do not mean the quick flash of a name on the theater screen. I mean credit from his co-workers, his family, and, perhaps most of all, from his superiors, especially his "boss." The intelligent sharing and dispensing of credit can be one of the director's most rewarding investments.

The director should study every man and woman on his crew just as he will study each member of his cast. Since each individual reacts differently to outside stimuli, the director must subtly vary his approach to each person he works with if he is to get the maximum output from his crew. And just as one individual differs to some degree from every other individual, so does each crew, as a unit, differ from other crews. This is most evident when working with crews of different nationalities.

The members of an English film company, for instance, have a strong sense of dignity and personal rights. Woe to the director who violates those sensibilities. He can, and probably will, be sabotaged in the most subtle and ingenious ways. Like most Spaniards, the Spanish worker has his pride, which must be respected even if the director doesn't know what the man is proud of. The German crew respects a strong hand, while the Italian worker will feel you don't love him if you don't shout at him—his mother always did. (Incidentally, he will give you plenty to shout about.) But the Hollywood crew is unique. Over all, it is still probably the best in the world and, because its members are the most highly paid, they will suffer a great deal of nonsense.

Only under the most extraordinary circumstances will an English crew allow even a few minutes overtime; the American crew will work indefinitely long hours. It is only necessary that its members are adequately fed and paid (and the overtime rates can be staggering). The Hollywood crewman also has a high insult threshold: He will overlook snobbishness and sarcasm and smile tolerantly at the director's incompetence. As long as his union agreement is respected and he is paid well for his work, he will do his job competently. But if more than competence is desired, it must be earned.

From the start the director must inspire confidence. He must behave with assurance; he must make quick, positive and lasting decisions. And, most important of all, he must be secure enough to delegate duties and to allow each worker to complete those duties in his own fashion, even if it offends his own idea of efficiency. One of the most difficult things to learn is how to stand by while a subordinate performs some operation in his own, "different," way.

Henry Hathaway's "short fuse" was legendary. Once, seeing a laborer carrying a wooden plank in an unorthodox manner, he screamed, "Damn it! That's not the way to carry a piece of lumber!" Jumping up from his chair, he grabbed the plank from the surprised man's grasp and demonstrated his own method of portage. Hathaway had rough sledding when he started directing, but his crews learned to respect him for his talent, love him for his eccentricities, and to laugh at his screaming.

Only results count. If they are satisfactory, the ends justify the director's patience. Because "the ends" are increased crew morale, cooperation, and efficiency. If the director can so condition his crew that each member, no matter the size of his contribution, can go home at night and say to his wife (husband), "Honey, wait till you hear what happened on *my* picture today," the director will reap the benefit. If the film is successful, he will get most of the credit.

The "auteur" theory notwithstanding, no director makes a film on his own. He needs the help of every member of his crew—and in an important sense each member has equal standing. A Rolls Royce can't run efficiently if even one $1 spark plug is missing, and a production will not run smoothly if a single worker fails at his job. If there is one crewman whose work is not vital, he shouldn't be on the set. He is excess baggage, and that costs extra.

Most of a crew's work is routine, though the routine will vary depending on the director's work habits, his set-ups, and the type of lighting he opts for. In his choice of pictorial treatment the director deals primarily with one person, the cinematographer.

The lighting cameraman will have his own ideas concerning mood and style after he reads the script, and they will usually match those of the director. But the very richness of the English language makes it susceptible to ambiguity, and it is vital that the director discuss his conception with the cameraman. Sometimes this can be done simply, by citing examples from other films. However, if the director hopes to obtain original effects he must resort to other references. I prefer to show my cameraman a book of paintings by some artist who has captured at least a large part of the mood and style I hope to achieve. I may refer to Degas, or Renoir, or, for a medieval background, Caravaggio. For *Murder My Sweet,* which has become a prototype for the genre known as film noire, I chose Daumier.

The cameraman will quickly understand the director's intention and, if he is an artist, he will embellish, or simplify, or heighten the style with contributions of his own. As always, when working with a more-than-competent creator, the final result will be not so much what the director wanted, but what he *wishes* he had wanted. No one can ask for more.

It has been stated that the cameraman is always a member of the location selection crew. His presence is necessary not only because he must see the locations in order to estimate the type and amount of equipment needed for adequate lighting, but he must also note the position of the greatest light source of all, the sun. It is important that he learn when and *where* it rises, when and where it sets, and its course across the heavens between these two extremes. He must also extrapolate these factors to the actual date of shooting, since they vary with the time of year. A well-lit composition today may be in complete shadow a month from now. It pays to be aware.

The sun's position also dictates the number of day light hours. In the northern latitudes, say, New York, Rome, or Madrid, summer will add as much as six hours to each shooting day. London, Berlin, and Paris have an even greater time differential. It would seem to be the better part of commonsense to schedule location work for the summer months, but factors other than light are often more important. When film locations are shot in winter, either the cost of shooting goes up or the time spent in shooting, and quality, go down. Such "Alice in Wonderland" decisions are hard to debate, but the director should always keep seasons in mind.

Communication is another very important consideration, especially on foreign locations. In his own homeland, a director must only put up with the inconsistencies of his own tongue. On alien ground he must deal with the alien language and, unless he is completely fluent in it, he should have an interpreter. I do not mean a *local* interpreter, no matter how well he speaks the director's language. I mean an interpreter from the director's bailiwick, who will at all times be the director's man. Why? Let me cite an example.

For work in Hong Kong I took along a Chinese friend to be my ears. We employed Hong Kong interpreters (a standard procedure) who understood and spoke English perfectly. For the sake of protocol and

*The cameraman likes to choose his camera operator, who in turn likes to select his own crew. Here, on location in France for the filming of* The Mountain, *Dmytryk discusses a scene with cameraman Franz Planer while camera operator Til Gabani listens in from the ladder above.*

labor relations, I always relayed instructions to our Chinese crew and cast through one of these men. My friend always listened in, and in a surprisingly large number of instances he would report, "He (the interpreter) did not say what you asked him to say."

Blame it on the ambiguity of the language, or on the fact that almost everyone knows how to do it better than you do; whatever it is, this problem is universal. Whether the language was Italian, Hungarian, or Hebrew, local interpreters were frequently inexact; and I was always thankful for the presence of my own linguists, who would keep us all at it until understanding was complete.

Shooting on a distant location presents other special problems, not only in working and communicating with the crew, but in its selection. Here, the director, the production manager, and the assistant must exercise special care.

A crew away from home resembles soldiers in foreign climes or tourists abroad. Occasionally, the rules of decorum which prevail on home grounds will be abrogated, leading to production slow-ups and added expense. To many people outside of southern California, people from Hollywood are aliens from outer space. Though the citizens of a distant town may be very hospitable, they are constantly on watch, and the embers of suspicion can quickly be fanned into the fires of xenophobia. At all times, tact is of the greatest importance. So is proper, and legal, behavior. For years after the filming of *Around the World in Eighty Days*, Paris was virtually off-limits for Hollywood productions because Mike Todd had towed citizens' modern cars off the streets at night without first getting permission from the authorities. He "fought and ran away" successfully, but the visiting productions that followed him paid heavily for his transgressions.

Excessive drinking, drugs, or anything that diminishes or distorts rational behavior can be a serious problem, even if the company is isolated in the desert. An example: On one such location our wardrobe man proved to be a heavy drinker. During studio shooting, when he went home every night, he was harmless and a good worker. Away from home and mother it was a different story. The cast and crew stayed in the same motel. Every evening after dinner he became a holy terror, fighting with fellow crewmen, bothering actors, and letting me know where I had goofed during the day's shooting. There was no time for gentle, sympathetic treatment. After a few days he was replaced.

Malingering can also be a problem, even on a nearly perfect Hollywood crew. Another production of mine was scheduled for several weeks' work in the French Alps. A few days before our departure from Los Angeles, the crew was assembled and the difficulty of the work was laid out carefully and positively. That work would include shooting near the top of Mont Blanc, daily mountain climbing to locations well off the beaten paths, and filming on nearly vertical, snow-covered slopes. Each day's schedule would usually start with a hike up steep mountain sides, lasting from a half to two hours. Coming back down hill in the late afternoons would be hardly less arduous.

Each member of the crew was questioned individually. All felt eager, healthy, and challenged—or so it seemed until we were in the Alps and ready for our first climb. I had picked a young man as script clerk because I assumed he could more easily take the "heat." How wrong I was. On the day before shooting started he disclosed that he had lost the toes of one foot in Korea. My sympathy for his handicap was completely eclipsed by my anger at his cupidity. He had obviously tricked us into a free trip to Europe, Paris, and the Alps, knowing he could not make even the slightest effort at climbing.

Fortunately, the company included a female secretary who had considerable experience as a script clerk for David Lean. She took over immediately and made every climb with little difficulty and no complaints. Normally, we might have had a serious and costly delay before a replacement could arrive. So much for chauvinism.

*Although much of* The Mountain *was shot on location in the Alps, this scene is a close-up shot on a set at Paramount Studio which was later inserted into an outdoor sequence. Spencer Tracy is the mountaineer.*

# 5

# *It Ain't Necessarily So*

## *Set Design*

No examination of the problems of preproduction is complete without a discussion of set design. Sets, as distinct from locations, are an indispensable part of almost every film. In this area the director has many options, and therefore many decisions to make.

He can choose between "live" (real) sets and film sets constructed on the stage. He can opt for expansive and expensive sets or he can make do with the simplest possible construction. He can build complete, fully detailed sets, à la D.W. Griffith or C.B. DeMille; or he can ask for minimal sets fleshed out with matte shots, miniatures, forced perspective, or a combination of any or all of these.

He can also vary the size of any set required. If, for instance, the director has a short scene, say one of four or five pages, he can diminish the scope of the staging and shoot against two walls instead of three. The elimination of a single wall can save thousands of dollars. This is a small sample, in a limited area, of the law of diminishing returns. The question is this: Does one lose more in value by somewhat limiting the scope of the short scene than one gains in dollars by limiting the size of the set? The loss in dramatic value may be unnoticeable, while the dollars gained might be better spent in expanding a more important set or in affording more time for the shooting of a more crucial scene. To put it another way, is the building of a third wall merely an exercise in self-indulgence which adds nothing to the scene? If the director is conscientious he will resort to the law of diminishing returns many times during the course of production.

Of course, many other factors must be taken into account when choosing sets. Let us consider the simplest form of the problem—a

standard interior, say, a large living room. It would be quite possible
to find a satisfactory room of this sort in some private residence. But
what are the advantages or disadvantages of such a set as compared
to one built on the studio stage?

The chief, and perhaps only advantage, is cost. Such a room could
be leased for immeasurably less than the cost of constructing a similar
set on the stage. Some directors might consider the "realness" of the
live set another advantage. Against these are arrayed a long list of
disadvantages, of which I will enumerate a few.

- Great care must be exercised when working on a live set. It is
  usually private property, and any damage would be inconvenient
  to the owner and costly to the production. The extra care necessarily involves extra time.
- Lighting is much more difficult and probably not as effective,
  since the freedom of lamp positioning is decidedly limited and
  overhead lighting next to impossible.
- Space is severely restricted. There are no "wild" walls, and the
  camera, its tripod or crab dolly, the lights, and the personnel
  necessary to manipulate all this equipment must be accommodated within the room itself, leaving little space for the staging of the action.
- Movement and variety of set-ups is severely limited, as is the
  possibility for shooting in more than one direction.
- Heat and ventilation problems become acute, as does access to
  the working area.
- The expense of transporting cast, crew, and equipment to the
  room's location would decidedly diminish the savings in set
  cost.

Against these must be placed the following *advantages* of the
stage set:

- It can be planned and built *exactly* to the director's specifica-
  tions and, since it will be designed by an architect with a special
  talent for developing the set's visual and dramatic potentials, it
  can be at least as "real" as any live set. In fact, where special
  "character" is required, such as aging or dilapidation, the stage
  set can look more "real" than any live set in existence.
- There is much more freedom of crew action—nothing of special
  value has to be protected for a concerned owner.
- The cameraman has complete lighting freedom. Normally, there
  are no ceilings, and overhead lighting is standard. But ceilings
  can be quickly rigged for set-ups which demand them.
- All walls are "wild", i.e., they can be taken out when additional

room for set-ups is desired and replaced when needed. (This is common practice.)
- All equipment can be kept off the set. For a long shot, even the camera can be positioned outside an open end of the set.
- The director can take full advantage of the entire set in staging his scenes. Movement of actors is limited only by its four walls, not by lights, camera, or personnel.
- The absence of a ceiling and the presence of stage air-conditioning make working conditions more pleasant, and the work correspondingly more efficient.
- Time on the set is not limited by the needs and demands of private owners or their near neighbors.
- The power supply is unlimited. No special electrical sources or noisy generators are required.

Perhaps the greatest advantage of the stage set is that it can, and should, be designed to specifically enhance character, create mood, and further the over-all concept of the film. The odds against finding a live set that would perfectly satisfy all these requirements are staggering.

However, as the set grows larger the differences in advantage decrease. Strictures of space, lighting, and accessibility are diminished in the live set—say, a banquet hall, or a sports arena—and the greatly increased cost of building such a large set from scratch tips the balance against it. In the extreme, of course, if the director wants to shoot the Colosseum he must go to the Colosseum. Or must he?

Today's filmmakers are often spoiled. Unlimited funding can be a blessing, but it can also diminish the need for ingenuity and anesthetize the creative senses. Working with a skimpy budget can sometimes result in miracles of improvisation—yes, and art.

An example: I was making my third film as a director, a B movie called *Golden Gloves*. As the title suggests, many of the scenes had to be staged in a prize-fight arena. I hoped to get the Hollywood Legion Stadium and 3,000 extras; the B budget allowed me an empty stage and 300 bodies.

When I had absorbed the shock I started to study the real thing. I noticed that the arena house lights were on only between rounds; while the fighters were working, the ring was brightly lit from overhead, and the house lights were dimmed. This, along with clouds of cigar and cigarette smoke, made it impossible to see anything beyond the ring, except—and there lay the solution. We would use the long shot only when a round was in progress. Not only would the attention of the viewer be centered on the fighters, but the rear of the stadium would be in relative darkness.

Setting up the long shot, I placed the 300 extras, minus 20 or 30,

*Much of* The Caine Mutiny *was shot aboard a Navy destroyer, but this wardroom was built on a stage at Columbia Studio to match the real thing. Dmytryk and Stanley Kramer listen as the Navy chief technical advisor briefs Fred MacMurray, Van Johnson and Humphrey Bogart.*

in the shape of a triangle between the camera and the ring, with the apex of the triangle at the camera. The people at the sides of the triangle just overlapped the edges of the frame—no body was wasted. When we were ready to shoot, the lights over the ring brightly back-lit the spectators between the ring and the camera. Grips ran through the aisles with bee-smokers, filling the set with a smoky haze.

Then came the "except". At the back of the stage, far beyond the ring, black drapes had been hung from ceiling to floor and stretched from wall to wall. In front of the drapes, rostrums of varying heights had been placed at odd distances across the stage. On each rostrum sat two or three extras, taken from the small group we had set aside, each armed with a supply of flare matches. These extras could not be

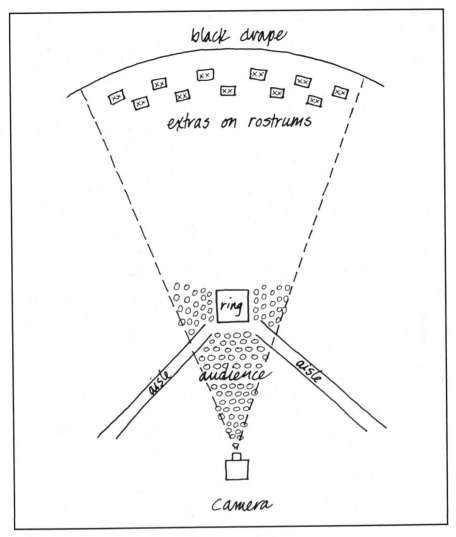

*Book II - Figure 1*

seen in the dark, but during the shooting of the scene they would, from time to time, at random, light their flare matches, which were bright enough to photograph. The effect on the screen was of a couple of thousand fight fans, invisible in the darkness, except when occasional smokers lit their cigarettes.* (Figure 1)

At any cost the scene would have been original and arresting. At

---

*This effect can be so spectacular that in recent years it has often been used in outdoor stadia as part of the half-time entertainment at night football games.

its actual cost it was exceptional. Effects of this sort can be frequently achieved through a wide assortment of means. Film affords the film-maker almost endless opportunities to create—to deceive the viewer, if you will, but to deceive him to his advantage. That is the essence of creativity, whether in filmmaking, writing, or, let us say, dancing. Did Nijinsky really pause in mid-flight? Of course not. But he moved in such a way that the viewer believed he did, and exulted. Through creative deception the artist distills the essence of life, situation, or character, and shows the viewer truth, free from extraneous or obfuscating detail. In an art that is also a business, he can also save a buck.

Another example of money-saving technique, borrowed from Murnau, involved the use of a set built in forced perspective.

In *So Well Remembered*, a film made in England, a scene called for staging on the crowded terrace of the House of Commons. But the terrace was not available for filming and, since it is extremely long, duplicating it would have busted the budget. I could, of course, have shot *across* the terrace, but it would have lost its inherent effectiveness.

The art director came up with a wonderful idea. His plan called for some 50 feet of the terrace, seen lengthwise, to be built at full scale. Beyond that the perspective would be so forced that the succeeding couple of hundred feet could be depicted in another 50 or so. It meant bringing the sides and the floor of the terrace together at decidedly sharp angles.

But there was a hitch: How could we populate the diminishing section of the terrace? The solution wasn't all that difficult. Furniture (tea tables and chairs) were built, also in perspective, in diminishing proportion. To occupy the chairs, I selected a number of extras, ranging in size from near average for the forepart of the perspective section of the set, through little people of progressively decreasing stature until, furthest from the camera, the smallest midgets were seated.

Shot from the only position possible for the desired effect, the terrace appeared to stretch away from the camera for hundreds of feet and, magically, the people occupying it were all of normal size.

No matter how it's done—with shadows, forced perspective, paper cut-outs, or mirrors (yes, that too, and quite often)—the more such techniques are understood and utilized, the more effective and engrossing films will become.

*Once the shooting starts, the director is the man in charge and must know what he wants. Here Dmytryk directs actor Gregory Peck in* **Mirage.**

# 6

# *The Shooting Starts*

The start of a film brings stage fright, insecurity, and some indecisiveness, which is to say it is no different from an opening night in the theater, the first round bell in a prize fight, the first charge of a fighting bull, or the first play in a football game. Everyone on the set feels it, although it probably affects the director and the actors more than members of the crew. I have never made a film without wishing I could reshoot the first few days' work. The problem, then, is how to counteract the weaknesses of the average beginning.

There are valid reasons for this state of affairs. The first is psychological, and the second is practical. Even if the director is familiar with most of his crew, there will always be a few individuals whom he knows only superficially, if at all. Many of the actors will be comparative strangers, in spite of the brief meetings at casting interviews. No matter how conscientiously the director has tried to get acquainted with the new members of both cast and crew, he has had no opportunity to know them "under fire." The differences between off-set and on-set behavior are often startling.

So, like a good boxer during the first round of a fight, the good director spends a measurable amount of time in "feeling out" his coworkers. This detracts from the necessary total application to the business at hand, and he may overlook a number of the little things that go to make up a day's work. The same can be said for the cast and the crew.

There are several ways to deal with this bothersome period. Perhaps the best is to schedule "walk-throughs" for at least the first two or three days of production. By walk-throughs I mean action scenes of no special dramatic content. For instance, an actor might drive up into the foreground of a shot, get out of his car, and, as the camera pans with him, walk into a building; or there might be shots of the

217

actor roaming city streets; or, as in most suspense films, a number of silent set-ups taking the hero through a series of dimly lit sets as he proceeds to a fateful rendezvous.

Such scenes, whether shot on location or on a stage, are not, as a rule, too demanding of the player and are relatively easy to stage. There are usually a number of them in a script, though logistical requirements might permit only a few of them to be placed at the head of the schedule board. This ploy also takes advantage of the fact that an audience is not nearly as critical of action scenes as it is of dramatic confrontations, in which the actors should be at their best.

Two or three days of such work will "shake down" the entire company. The director, the cast, and the crew can get rid of their butterflies and be ready to settle down to serious filmmaking.

If the schedule does not offer enough of such action to fill the necessary two or three days, another gambit may prove satisfactory. Holding full, though casual, rehearsals of the first few scenes on the schedule can easily occupy the required breaking-in period. And though the production department may scream at the apparent loss of time, that time will usually be recovered because of the increased confidence of those who make the film.

It must be remembered that the schedule is not a constitution— it is merely an estimate, a hope. It is safe to say that not one film in a hundred moves exactly to schedule. It can also be safely said that probably as many films come in under schedule as over schedule. Like most everything else in these days of computer science, the schedule is a statistical approximation, nothing more.

What isn't statistical is the desire to get the best possible scenes on film, and the secret of accomplishing that lies in the director's ability to get the best possible performances out of his cast.

"What does the director do?"

Many directors besides Leo McCarey have been asked that question. At the university I hear it nearly every day. A full answer would take a week. The simple answer is, "He makes the actors feel completely secure." That is the ideal, rarely reached. But the closer the director approaches that ideal, the nearer he is to making the perfect film. Instilling security, however, is not an easy matter.

Before shooting starts the director should meet his actors as often as necessary. The necessity in question is agreement on characterization. There will usually be little difference in opinion, for obvious reasons. Good actors are also intelligent persons. If the characters and the situations are written to be understood by the average viewer, as they should be, they will certainly be understood by the actors. After all, understanding character is their business.

As previously noted, however, meanings can be ambiguous,

equivocal, or even inconsistent. An actor may sometimes be puzzled by an apparent contradiction in his screen character as it is depicted in two different scenes of the script. A few words with the director will usually clear up the problem. The actor will realize that an alternative interpretation of one of the scenes will allow it to square with the other. As his confusion subsides, his grasp of the character grows and his insecurity diminishes. However, if this concern applies to a number of scenes in the script, a review of the story as a whole is in order. If what the director saw as a clean, straight-line story is confusing to the actor, it will undoubtedly be confusing to the viewer. The director should then set to work with the writer, or on his own, to clear up the ambiguities.

In the interests of economy, efficiency, and performance, such problems should be eliminated before the production goes on the floor. The actor must have time to immerse himself in his role long before he plays his first scene.* If he knows clearly what the director expects of the character and agrees with his conception, he will function at a higher level of awareness and security. The key word here is *security*.

The insecure actor will give a "safe" performance—and it will be just that, a performance. (Though I will use the word "performance" frequently in this book, it must be understood that I do so for lack of a better word to describe the end result of a screen actor's work. In a film, the actor must "be" a character rather than "perform" as such. (See Book III, *On Screen Acting.*) The actor knows that if he speaks his lines in a competent manner he will avoid trouble. Since the director may not be cognizant of the actor's full potential, he will accept the performance as the actor's best. But is it?

The good director always encourages his actors to take chances, to try for something new, something beyond the accepted interpretation; and most of the truly gifted actors will try to surpass themselves if they are confident the director will not allow them to look foolish. The director should observe the actor's creative flights with a discriminating and analytical (not critical) eye. He should separate the good from the bad and communicate his analysis to the actor, who will shade his efforts accordingly. The hoped-for result is that always-welcome comment from the critics: "The player lived the part—she *was* Jane Doe."

On location in Paris, Montgomery Clift would sometimes awaken me at two or three in the morning with, "Come on up! I've got something to show you." (Thank God we were staying at the same hotel.) When I arrived in his room, he would demonstrate an idea for some

---

*This suggestion also applies to the bit player who is cast after the production is well under way. He should always be given a few days before he reports on the set to "get into" his role, however small.

future day's work, sometimes (even when sober) literally climbing the walls. I knew him well enough to realize that that wouldn't be his on-set performance, so I would try to understand what he was getting at, and I usually did. If I said, "Monty, I'm not too sure," his immediate response was always, "O.K., let's forget it. We'll come up with something better." Although more often than not his idea wasn't what I wanted, when he did strike the right chord, it was a plus, an improvement on the original conception.

The point is that he felt secure enough with me to try anything, no matter how bizarre it might seem at the time. The bizarre, properly rescaled and rearranged, can become reality—an exciting, effective reality, the kind that surprises the viewer but leaves him thinking, "That's it! That's just the way it is!" It is the kind of audience reaction that distinguishes every fine film from the ordinary flick.

Of course, that kind of cooperation between actor and director requires mutual confidence, and mutual confidence is based on open communication.

There is always at least a little imp in paradise. People differ, communication isn't always easy, some insecurities are very deep-seated. They will have nothing to do with scenes, scripts, or roles, but lie deeply buried in the personalities of the people involved. They have commonly, and I think mistakenly, been lumped under the category of "temperament." These insecurities are sometimes exceedingly difficult to deal with.

Webster's unabridged defines "temperamental" as "having or showing a sensitive, easily excited temperament." And "temperament," in turn, is defined as "Constitution or frame of mind; esp. the character of mind or of mental reactions characteristic of an individual."

Straightforward and, except for the inclusion of the borderline words "easily excited," hardly pejorative. But the word "temperamental" as understood by the man in the street, has come to have a decidedly derogatory meaning. It is used primarily as a put-down of performers—musicians, opera stars, and actors. Even top athletes who dare to bridle at stupid questions are branded as "temperamental" by the sports-writing community. Since temperament does exist and must occasionally be accommodated or dealt with, it will pay us to analyze this highly misunderstood emotional phenomenon.

Fifty years ago, Thomas Wolfe wrote, "The effort of . . . creating something seems to start up a . . . bewildering conflict in the man who does it . . . so that he feels he is struggling not only with his own work but also with the whole world around him, and he is so beset with . . . bewilderment that he lashes out at everyone . . . even against . . . his true friends."

The question arises, *why* does the artist experience such conflicts? The chief cause is insecurity—not only concerning his creation, but concerning its acceptance by the critics and the audiences. The artist is always "before the bar." He is forever being judged and he never knows in advance whether the verdict will be a "thumbs up" or a "thumbs down."

Even success in one film gives him only temporary relief. While singing the creator's praises the critics will often hedge their bets with phrases like, "Now we must wait to see if the artist has more bullets in his gun, or if this is strictly a one-shot deal," leaving the creator to wonder if he will ever be able to live up to the things said about him and his work. And the better the work, the sharper the reaction if his next effort fails in the slightest. In the interest of trying new ways the artist cries, "Give me the right to fail!" But the critics and the people usually turn a deaf ear.

Actors are, as they should be, extremely sensitive, and suffer in varying degrees from this syndrome. The older, more experienced artists will have come to terms with it. The younger and/or less analytical will strike out at "the whole world around them"—and on the set that usually means the director, who is by no means immune from attacks of insecurity himself. If he is sympathetic and supportive, he will try to make the troubled actor understand that although creation is a battle, it is a battle that must be fought within oneself. If he can get *that* message across, he will find that the bouts of temperament will quickly diminish.

Another problem of temperament stems from insecurity of the ego rather than insecurity of the creative urge. On rare occasions the director will face a test of strength with an actor, not necessarily a star. He may just be trying the director to see if he has the strength to run the company. His own security and part of his career may depend on it. He is usually someone who has been around long enough to know that a weak director will probably produce a weak film. If his doubts are removed, and he is satisfied that the director can "cut the mustard," the rest is easy sailing, at least in the area of personality conflict.

Occasionally, however, for ego-oriented reasons, an actor wants to be king of the hill. His challenge comes early and unmistakably. If the director is to remain in charge of the film, this is a battle he *must* win.

The challenges vary, and so do the solutions, but it is vital that the director recognize the signs immediately and quickly arrive at the answer. Since this is a rather vague exposition, an example is in order. The following is a mild, almost amusing one, but it could have become quite serious. It occurred on one of my first films. I was young and inexperienced.

A middle-aged actor, a man of talent, and himself a "little theater" director of long standing, was playing an important role in the film. From the beginning, he would approach me early in the day. The dialogue would run something like this:

"Eddie, I have been going over today's scene, and I've got a few problems." (Of course, we had already worked out the scene the day before.)

"What bothers you?"

"Well, here where I say, 'Thank you,' I'd be more comfortable with 'Much obliged.' And here, where I have to say, 'Goodbye,' I'd rather say, 'So long.' "

The lines were usually more complex than that, but his changes were that inconsequential. That was the crux of the matter. He was simply putting me on the spot, forcing me to defend the scene exactly as written, or give in to his piddling demands. It was the transference of decision-making authority that mattered, not the dialogue.

I resisted, of course, feeling rather foolish and uncomfortable. For two or three days I was in a quandary. Then I arrived at a solution. As he walked onto the set one morning, I called him over to me. I had already asked the prop man to place his chair beside mine.

"Sit down, John," I said.

"What's up?"

"I went over your scene again last night, and I have a few suggestions." He raised an eyebrow at me. "Here," I said, "where you say, 'I'd rather not,' I felt you might be more comfortable with, 'I don't think I should.' " He looked at me for a long moment.

"No," he said. "I feel quite comfortable with the line as it is."

"Fine. But here, where you say, 'I'll be there tonight,' wouldn't you rather say, 'I'll be there this evening' "? Another long pause.

"Oh, I think 'I'll be there tonight' is satisfactory."

And so it went throughout the scene, but he was now the uncomfortable one. I wasn't sure whether it was because I was now putting *him* under the gun, or just that he realized I was on to his game, but he never challenged me again. From then on he listened cooperatively to any suggestion I had to make.

This brings us around to style—the director's style. Each director has his own, but they are simply variations of two basic directorial methods. The first, which is rapidly disappearing, is what was once called "teutonic," for obvious reasons. The early German directors who came to Hollywood were quite dictatorial. Dick Powell recounted an experience with one such director.

"You walk through that door," he told Powell, "take four steps into the room, stop, count three, then look to your right."

"Why?" asked Powell.

"Because I tell you to," was the answer. Throughout the rather uncomfortable film, it was the only answer he got.

This important scene from Crossfire was called daring by some because it ran for so long without dialogue. Dmytryk let the two actors, Gloria Graham and George Cooper, tell the story with their emotions and actions rather than words.

Today, it would be unthinkable for the director not to discuss a scene with his actors. Even if the director is quite adamant about a particular treatment which requires arbitrary positioning, there should be a complete understanding of *what* the moves are, and *why*. He might even explain his set-ups and the effects he hopes to achieve. Then he will encourage the actors to fit their established characterizations into the desired pattern, to integrate their concepts with his. If the director's treatment is valid, there will be no difficulty in giving him everything he is looking for, and more.

The teutonic method may still be useful, but only for a highly stylized film. Certain "art" films may depend on exact juxtaposition of set-up and scene, but even then there is probably more to be gained by making an actor aware of the desired result. Who knows? He may even be able to contribute a little.

It may relieve the reader to learn that almost everything I say in this book has its exceptions. Here, I must register an especially marked one, where the exception is, thankfully, the rule. On re-reading this chapter I have realized I may, to put it gently, be scaring the daylights out of the potential young director. To put his mind at ease, I hasten to say that the troublesome actor is rare. I have never had more than one or two in any film, and the casts of most of my films were 100 percent talented, pleasant, and a joy to work with. The true professionals like Tracy, Bogart, E.G. Marshal, Agnes Moorehead, Deborah Kerr, Van Johnson, and many, many others were magic; and working with them almost cancelled out the tribulations of producers, finances, and logistics. But even one carelessly tossed monkey wrench can create havoc in an otherwise smooth-running machine, and it behooves the aspiring director to recognize personality problems and to learn how to deal with them.

The questions of insecurity and the tender ego have been discussed at some length, as has the need for bolstering both of these personality traits. There are a number of ways of accomplishing this. For the sake of the uninitiated let us mention a few.

1.  Praise a job well done on every possible occasion. (This also applies to the crew.)
2.  Give full and open credit to anyone making a useful suggestion.
3.  Avoid any statement or action that is belittling, especially on an open set.

It can be stated as an axiom that the greater one's insecurity, the more vulnerable is one's sense of dignity. A world champion boxer will shrug off a drunken challenge to his manhood, but an insecure actor will react strongly to a tactless questioning of his talent. I have seen a good character actor destroyed by a cruel and thoughtless director who was engaged in his own "struggle with the world around him." Directors who openly criticize actors in the presence of the crew and their fellow artists are certain to make the actor withdraw into himself. How, then, can the director expect to get an out-going and natural performance? The director who neglects to treat an actor as an equal is doing himself a great disservice. If not for the sake of decency, then surely for the sake of the film and his own reputation, the director should behave in a manner which will guarantee the actor's whole-hearted support.

During the first rehearsal of any scene there will inevitably be mistakes—errors in timing, movement, or dialogue. It is counter-productive to enumerate, or even mention, such mistakes until more rehearsals have taken place, and then it will probably be unnecessary. The actor is surely aware of his miscues and, like most of us, he hates to have them brought to attention. Given time, he will "clean up his act" until he has the proper handle on it. Making him aware of his errors too early in the going not only violates his sense of dignity, but may create a "block" in his mind, which can cause difficulties in succeeding rehearsals or takes.

If, as sometimes happens, the actor is unaware of a mistake and persists in it, the wise course of action is to take him aside and clarify the problem quietly and privately. The actor will appreciate this, and his confidence in the director will increase accordingly.*

At other times an actor may misread a line, not out of ignorance, but because his conception of its meaning may not be the desired one—it happens to the best of them. A correction must be made, but how? Obviously, the actor can "read" a line better than I can, or he wouldn't be in my film. Laurence Olivier aside, how many directors can tell Paul Newman or Dustin Hoffman how to speak effectively? Certainly not I, even though I *should* know what's right or what's wrong when I hear it. Only in extreme cases will I give an actor what I consider a proper "reading." Instead, in casual conversation, I will recount an experience or tell a funny story which somehow illustrates the proper meaning of the misread line. No matter how subtle I try to be, I am always surprised how quickly the actor will say, "Gotcha!" The next time the scene is played the reading will be perfect.

Anything which makes the actor conscious of the set-world around him while shooting detracts from his concentration. Consequently, the camera crew and the script clerk should be instructed never to speak directly to an actor about "hitting his marks," or matching his

---

*Of course, not all corrections are made in so prudent a manner. In the give and take of an enthusiastic rehearsal, suggestions are sometimes broadcast for the entire set to hear.

action, unless he specifically asks for such information. The same holds true for the sound mixer; if he has trouble hearing a line he should, like the cameraman or the script clerk, check with the director, who will discuss the problem with the actor at the propitious time.

The player's "eye line," i.e., the area his eyes may look out on during the playing of a scene, should also be kept clear, both of visitors and of crew members; some movement, however far in the background, may catch his attention and distract him from the scene.

It is very important to keep one other stricture in mind: On the set the actor must rely on the director for correction, assistance, or approval. If he is in any doubt about whom he should look to when the director says, "Cut!" he, the director, and the film are in serious trouble.

Since the primary focus of this chapter has been on psychological traits and attitudes, one further bit of information is in order. Aside from, or possibly because of, all the miseries which accompany the making of a difficult film—the irritable stomach, the occupational nightmares, the nocturnal shakes—if the schedule runs more than forty days, paranoia is sure to raise its ugly head. The "creative" people start feeling sorry for themselves and suspicious of each other. Each is certain all the others are ganging up to do him in.

Only one thing can be done about it: recognize it for what it is, a temporary aberration of perception. The act of recognition serves to defuse the paranoia's more dangerous effects. Beyond that, I recommend that you pretend you are observing your little world of filmmaking from far beyond the stratosphere. You will be amazed how small your problems will look from that perspective.

*When actors are on camera for close-ups, Dmytryk insists that the other actors in the group be on stage, and not be represented by stand-ins. Here Robert Young is filmed close up for* Crossfire *with Robert Mitchum throwing his lines to Young.*

# 7

# *Shooting Techniques*

Critics and students of films often say, "Movies are a director's medium." That is hardly an arguable conclusion. But what is it, exactly, that makes the statement true?

The making of a motion picture can be roughly divided into four categories: story, interpretation (acting), editing, and shooting techniques. The director is the only person who has input in all of these areas, and his control over the last category is total. Unless he has a thorough knowledge of film staging and set-ups, his films will always be found wanting, regardless of the quality of the three other basic elements.

The director does not simply stage a scene, point the camera at it, and record it on film. Nor, if he wants to be regarded as a master of his craft, does he limit himself to routine long shots, group shots, two shots, and close-ups. There is an almost infinite number of variations of these primitive classifications, and the director should have such a close acquaintance with all of them that he can bring them into use instinctively. He should not have to labor, as I have seen some inexpert directors do, to solve a simple set-up problem.

However, experience can sometimes be a millstone around the director's neck. After years of using most of the set-ups in the book, the temptation to fall back on a dependable technique is very strong. If the director has a solid conception of his physical treatment, his positioning of the camera (the set-up) will be automatic—or almost. He should at all times search his mind for a variation which will enable him to present the scene at its best. Much will depend on the scene's place in the film and its intensity. A set-up that might work perfectly near the start of the film may fall short if it is used for a similar grouping at, or near, the climax. Although a thorough knowledge of the mechanics of set-ups is of prime concern, the director's creative instinct is his most important asset. Only on it can he build a reputation for style and filmmaking excellence.

Nuances are as important in a set-up as they are in a line of dialogue or in a performance, but if the viewer sees them as such the director has failed.Like properly used symbols, nuances should enrich the scene as a whole and not be seen as an exercise in theory or technique. A "director's touch" should only be recognized in post-viewing analysis.

Ordinarily, a set-up can't be selected until the director knows how the scene is going to play. Unless he is a disciple of the teutonic school, he won't know that precisely until he's had a run-through of the scene in question.

Ever since the invasion of sound there has been some argument about the relative merits of full preproduction rehearsals (theatrical style) versus prescene rehearsals, i.e., rehearsals held immediately prior to the shooting of the scene rehearsed. Both methods have been used, but the overwhelming percentage of filmmakers employ the latter. Full rehearsals were originally favored by directors who came to films by way of the theater. It was the technique with which they were familiar and, more important perhaps, it gave them the opportunity to see the eventual actuality in the embryo. The director who has been trained in filmmaking has learned to visualize the whole film while familiarizing himself with the script. Although his general conception is formed at that time, he has the added advantage of keeping himself loose for possible changes he will make as the shooting progresses and the film comes to life. The full rehearsal too often "sets" the form of the film; when actual production starts, the mind resists further changes, especially when filming falls behind schedule and the going gets tough.

An additional problem with preproduction rehearsals is that the full cast is rarely available. Since a player must be paid from the day he reports for work (and rehearsal is work) the expense of hiring actors who may not be used until late in the schedule becomes a factor which must be considered.

A marked advantage of the prescene rehearsal is that the actors need only memorize that scene's dialogue. For all but those few who have a photographic memory, this is a convenience which is greatly appreciated.

A method of working that has served me remarkably well is to rehearse a scene the day before it is to be shot. The current day's filming comes to a halt about 4:30 in the afternoon. The stage is cleared of all except the key personnel and, with the next day's cast on the set, a casual reading is held to get the "feel" of the scene. The next step is to work out the moves in conjunction with the dialogue.* The rehearsal may require as little as twenty minutes or as much as an hour and a half; and when it is finished the next morning's first set-up is laid out. Now cast and crew can leave the studio knowing what is expected of them on the following day. Dialogue and movement problems have been discussed and solved, every actor knows what to expect from the director and from the rest of the cast, the cameraman knows his lighting requirements, the gaffer and the prop man are aware of any new equipment or props which may be needed, and the assistant can place his calls with accuracy. All, including the director, can go home feeling that tomorrow's work is "in the bag."

The early "wrap" has many collateral advantages. The film's creative minds are still relatively fresh, and that is an important consideration. An eight-hour day is tiring, both physically and mentally, especially after the first few weeks. The "juices" dry up and ideas germinate reluctantly. Both cast and crew are more inclined to settle for the routine. Fatigue shows in the actors' eyes—even the make-up cracks, and a patch-up job is always a patch-up job.

Strange as it may seem, this "short day" method of working has always saved me much time. Every film made in this fashion was brought in under schedule and under budget. Benefits to the films were incalculable.

Early filmmakers customarily started each new sequence with an "establishing shot." As the name implies, this is a set-up that shows the characters in their milieu, whether it be an interior of a building or a spot on location. Before it is broken up into closer angles, the entire scene is often played in the establishing shot even though only a short portion of the take is intended for use in the edited film. It was also a rule that there be a progression from longer to closer set-ups in the cutting of the scene. Although a few of today's directors still follow this rule, it is usually ignored by the more creative filmmakers. If the achieved effect is dramatically sound, one can cut from a long shot into an extreme close-up, or vice versa. In one film I made a point of starting each new sequence with a close shot, disclosing the background only as the actors moved through it. Even though I made no effort to show the viewer the setting of any of the film's scenes, the review in *Time* commented particularly on the effective design and use of the film's sets.

I find the establishing shot a waste of time and money, except in one specific instance. If I am not quite sure of a scene or a planned set-up, I will shoot such a shot. It allows me to observe the scene as

---

*A more explicit exposition of the rehearsal routine is contained in Book II, Chapter 9.

*Sometimes there is no question that a scene will go unrehearsed, and that the first take will be the only one. In this scene from* The Mountain, *Robert Wagner runs down a virgin snowfield with a bag of loot.*

a whole, to pinpoint doubtful areas, and it gives me time to gather my thoughts and work out the necessary corrections or set-ups. On a more realistic level, the production report gives me credit for "shooting" rather than "thinking," which, at the daily production running, impresses those executives who believe that thinking is an unnecessary expenditure of time.

None of this is meant to imply that a "long shot" is a useless set-up. On the contrary, intelligent use of the long shot, as beautifully demonstrated in *The Black Stallion,* can be a tremendous asset. But too often, especially in TV films, it is resorted to solely as an establishing shot. As such, it is doing only half its job. Every shot, when properly used, should advance the dramatic thrust of the story.

If the director is filming a football game, for instance, he might choose to start his sequence with a long shot of the stadium rather than a close shot of the team huddle. The opening shot serves to "establish" that there is a football game in progress with a large crowd in attendance, nothing more. Now, think of the sequence as starting in a different way; a close shot of the quarterback barking signals then, in a series of cuts, the center hands him the ball, the play develops, the receiver streaks down the field, the quarterback evades a tackler and releases the ball, the receiver catches it in the end zone. Now, for the first time, a full shot of the stadium as the crowd rises to its feet in a screaming reaction. The long shot here is employed for dramatic emphasis, as well as an establishing shot. Even though, in the earlier shots, the background has been exposed incidentally, at no time would an audience be in doubt that the game was being played on the gridiron.

The positioning of the camera for any set-up is the prerogative of the director, not the cameraman. Only the director knows what he wants the camera to see, what he wants to include in the frame and, just as important, what he wants to exclude.

There are two methods for lining up a shot. The first is to establish the set-up, then stage the scene within the area the set-up covers. I call this "bringing the actors to the camera." The second is to work out the movements with the actors, then position the camera to pick up the rehearsed action in the most effective way. This I call "bringing the camera to the actors." Both methods are useful, though for most scenes the second is preferable. The actors have greater freedom for "being." There is no artificial constraint, although careless "wandering," which will occasionally occur, especially with some "method" actors, should be resisted.

The first procedure is useful when visual effects are of prime importance, or when the background plays a vital role. But, in general, the method which allows the actor the freedom he needs to help improve the development of his character is the most desirable. In truth, many of my set-ups are the result of the combination of the two methods: I allow the actors full freedom until they feel comfortable in the scene. Then, as rehearsals continue, I tighten the moves and particularize the positions until the staging is most camera-effective. When both the cast and I feel completely at home with the scene, I can set up my camera.

A set-up which lends the scene a dynamic quality is obviously to be preferred to a stodgy "snap-shot." Here, staging and set-up go hand in hand. But to confine ourselves strictly to the set-up at this point, there are a few important observations to be made.

The dullest possible shot is one made at eye level. It adds nothing new to the picture. Unless one is Wilt Chamberlain or a Munchkin, it is the everyday point of view of every person over the age of sixteen. It is preferable to position the lens either somewhat below or somewhat above eye level. The variations from the normal should not be too obvious, but they should be off-beat enough to give the viewer a subconscious nudge. The choice of above or below the level of the eye will depend on the nature of the shot. Normally, the low set-up is preferable for close group shots or close-ups. One advantage of this position is that it affords a better look into the actor's eyes: in a high-level shot the viewer would be looking down at the player's eyelids.

The high set-up is especially useful for long shots or full shots in cramped areas. In most long shots it is preferable to see the ground on which the actors stand rather than yards of empty space above their heads. The fuller the shot, the higher the lens can go. It must be re-emphasized that there are exceptions to these generalizations, even in respect to the eye-level shot, which can, of course, be useful. But when an exception is made it should be for a very positive reason.

What has been said for the eye-level shot can be repeated for the profile shot. Outside of a better view of the ears, little is gained from such a set-up. The eyes are not clearly visible, depriving the film of one of its great advantages; and the figures (usually two) are of similar size, depriving the viewer of the dynamic effect of size differential. *

As previously stated, the actor's eyes are unquestionably the most effective means for transmitting emotion. In *Wuthering Heights*, the eyes in any one of Laurence Olivier's close-ups expressed more love than all the writhing bodies in the films of the last decade. By the honest use of his eyes a fine actor can register almost any emotion without "making a face." It is worthwhile to repeat, "The eyes are the windows of the soul."

The shoddy way the close-up has been misused and overused by

---

*An obvious exception is a shot made against the setting sun. The resulting silhouettes project a beautiful effect of their own.

the great majority of TV directors has done this special shot a great disservice. Like any valuable technique, the close-up should not be used indiscriminately lest it lose its value. At its best the close-up is climactic, and it should be reserved for climactic moments. Every editor knows that the simple act of cutting from a general shot to a close shot adds an important dimension or significance to the scene. But the continual and continuous use of close-ups leaves him nothing to pull out of the bag when a dramatic accent is needed. Just as a skillful actor, when playing an argument scene, will save his full vocal power for the scene's peak, so a good director must recognize the emphasis value of his close-ups and husband them accordingly.

Incidentally, in speaking of close shots one speaks of a variety of set-ups. A close shot can be an "individual," i.e., a waist figure of one person; it can be so close that only the player's eyes are seen; or it can cover any number of close-up positions between these two extremes.

The lighting of a close-up can differ considerably from the lighting of the general scene. As with the choice of size, it is dictated by the dramatic emphasis and the immediate mood required. It can be beautifully shaded or shadowed, shot against the set background or a portrait flat. When it is properly integrated into the edited sequence, not a soul will notice the difference in treatment. But whatever the lighting style, one thing should be remembered—the eye light. This specially adjusted light source that appears as a small highlight in each of the actor's eyes makes them "come alive." The proper use of this technique is rapidly disappearing as "flat" TV lighting takes over; but it is most important and should always be used—unless, of course, an appearance of dullness is desired.

In staging a set-up for more than one person, grouping is a prime consideration. It is essential that the camera should record only what the viewer should see. At times, what is left out of the shot is as important as what is kept in. Many years ago I watched a director shoot a small group scene. The people involved were a young husband and wife and the wife's parents. The director was one of several theatrical directors remaining in Hollywood after the exodus of most of those who had invaded the town with the coming of sound. Quite naturally, his techniques had been learned in the theater, and he had never made a complete adjustment to the special demands of the screen.

In the scene, the parents started a somewhat bitter argument with the young couple. Shortly after the start of the scene the mother took over for both herself and her husband. At this point, the director had the father move off to the side of the room, where he proceeded to scan the titles on a shelf-full of books, leaving the other three to continue the argument in front of the camera. Later, I asked the director why he had moved the father out of the scene, since it was the least likely action a truly concerned parent would have taken.

"I wanted him out of the shot," he answered. "He was standing out like a sore thumb."

I didn't mention that a film director would simply have moved his camera up to a three shot, thus eliminating what he considered an awkward grouping. An individual shot of the father would then have served as a useful cut, either to show his reactions to pertinent parts of the conversation or as a "cut-away" if the master shot had to be shortened.

The scope of the set-up is determined by the amount of information the shot should deliver and the dramatic impact the director wants to make. In his Westerns, John Ford took advantage of his backgrounds. To do this he used the startling scenery of locations like Monument Valley and well-placed camera set-ups. The impact of the beauty, the starkness, and the loneliness of his long shots added greatly to the viewer's understanding and appreciation of the characters inhabiting those areas. At the opposite end of the scale, Hitchcock used extreme close-ups superbly to instill fear and terror as his characters reacted to startling or inhuman confrontations.

In short, each set-up should say exactly what the director wants it to say. If it discloses less than he desires, the hoped-for effect on the viewer is diminished. If it gives more information than necessary, it dirties up the scene and confuses the audience. No matter how "artistic" the set-up might be, if the audience is confused it is also bored.

Here we enter the area of *composition*, a touchy subject with many directors. Theorists have laid down certain rules for aesthetic composition that intrigue students of the art, but which most working directors ignore—not because they are cultural clods but because they know that most of the rules are based primarily on static groupings. What is valid in a fresco is frequently invalid on the screen. Screen images are dynamic: They change, and move in relation to each other, and dynamic composition won't sit still long enough to be adequately explored. Beyond that, the director can only rarely give the viewer the time he needs to *study* a particular composition. Usually, by cutting, he forces the viewer's instant attention to a particular part of the screen; and if aesthetic rules interfere with his intent, aesthetics surrender the field to the demands of dramatic flow and just plain old story telling. Yet, in spite of all this, directors like John Ford and David Lean have managed to flash more compositional gems on the screen in one film than could be housed in an average museum, if only they could be frozen. And almost all good directors spend a good deal of their creative efforts in this area.

There are exceptions. One tyro director rejoiced, "I've finally learned the secret of staging for the screen. I just visualize the action as though it were taking place under the proscenium." The few films he made looked it. The viewer was always looking *at* a scene, an illustration with a neat border around it, rather than being *in* the scene, participating with the people on the screen. Whenever possible, which is most of the time, I prefer to get in as "tight" as the grouping will allow. The shoulders of the characters on either side of the shot should be out of the frame, giving the viewer a participant's perception. This technique of having someone, or something, in the picture extend outside the edges of the frame is quite important. Even in extra-long shots, where the actors are clustered near the center of the frame, a "foreground piece" of some sort—a stick of furniture in an interior, a boulder or a shrub on a location, a trash can on a busy street—any of these, cutting in on the edge of the frame, will serve to enhance the impression of linear continuity between the viewer and the image on the screen. When properly lit and integrated into the rest of the picture, foreground pieces add significantly to the illusion of a third dimension.

There is a kindergarten fault in staging (and composition) that is inexcusable. I refer to "lining up" the actors. It may be acceptable in a "sitcom," but never in a film. Yet I have seen experienced directors align their people as if they were standing inspection. Except in rare instances, people in real life do not stand side by side to hold a conversation. They are usually face to face, whether there are two, three, or more participants.

Here I must reiterate: Film actors are *not* on the stage. There is *no* up-stage or down-stage on the film set. There is no fixed directional relationship to the audience, real or imaginary. Actors *do not* play within the confines of a narrow sector: Theirs is a 360-degree world, just as it is in real life. It should come as no surprise that the camera can move *anywhere* within the full circle. If an actor feels slighted because his back is to the camera in a group shot, a reverse close shot will quickly put his nose back in joint. (You are not under any obligation to use the set-up in the edited film.)

And that is the real secret of proper staging. No matter where or how an actor stands in one shot, he can be presented from a different perspective in another. If the director understands cutting even slightly, he can properly design set-ups to cover any grouping.

A useful consequence of the loose relationship between camera and cast is known simply as "cheating." A filmmaker cheats in many ways: with make-up, with lenses and lens filters, with lighting, etc., but the word "cheating" is reserved for a special technique that might be called "arbitrary positional variation." That means that as set-ups are changed, the positions of the actors, relative to each other or to their setting, can also be changed, not on the screen but in actuality. Before things get out of hand, however, I will again resort to two simple examples to clarify the concept for the beginner.

Example 1: A scene involving two people. The background is a desert location featuring cactus and Joshu trees. The scene is four or five pages long and will require a full day to shoot.

Location filming always starts as early in the morning as possible, the actual time depending on the season of the year. The light is good early in the morning or rather late in the afternoon. High noon brings "flat" light and an unattractive picture. In the morning, the sun lies to the east, casting, let us say, shadows on the left side of the leading actor's face. In the late afternoon, the sun lies to the west and, if the actors have maintained their original positions relative to the background, the shadows will be on the right side of the same actor's face. If we shoot a medium shot early in the morning, and a close shot covering the same action later in the afternoon, the shadows will jump from one side of the face to the other with every cut. They will, at least, if the actors retain their original positions because the scene demands it.

The solution: Reposition the actors at frequent intervals along an invisible half-circle on the ground even as the sun sails in its arc across the sky, thus keeping the facial shadows relatively consistent. At each new position the background may be somewhat different but, unless it is of more importance to the scene than the foreground action, no one will notice it, not even the next day at the rushes.

Example 2: A small group in a room, say a home library, lit in subdued fashion. A door in the distant background opens onto a brightly lit living room, where a party is in progress. In the full shot, the background as a whole is shadowed; but when the camera is moved in for a close shot of one of the members of the group, it is found that he is framed against the brightly lit door, which now looms large in the picture. To cut from the subdued scene to the brightly lit one would deliver an unwelcome shock.

Solution: Arbitrarily move the actor to a more suitable background. Again, if properly shot and cut, the changed position will be far less noticeable or disturbing than the actual one.

Such "cheating" is frequently resorted to, sometimes in an extremely sophisticated and complex manner. But for *that* the director needs a good deal of experience and an almost mathematical sense of positional relativity.

Whether the camera simply "pans" the actor across the set or moves with him on a "dolly" track, the moving shot has much the same requirements as the stationary shot, except for one thing— the start. An obvious start to a camera movement will often make the viewer conscious of the "mechanics" and pull him back into the theater. To circumvent this, many ploys are available. The simplest is to make sure the actor moves first. Once the viewer's eyes start to follow the actor across the screen, the panning of the camera will appear to be a natural extension of his movement. (See comments on eye movement in Book IV, *On Film Editing*.) To move away from a static composition is more difficult.

An example: The director wants to "pull back" from a pile of trash at the entrance to an alley, then pan to a full shot of the street. A simple stratagem would be to have a slight breeze (stirred up by a fan, if necessary) blow a piece of paper out of the trash pile in the direction of the camera pan. As the scrap of paper flies through the air, the camera moves with it, panning and pulling back simultaneously. Once the action is properly started, the rest of the movement is accepted on its own.

Another example: A close shot of an ashtray on a table, holding a burning cigarette. A hand reaches in and picks up the cigarette. As the hand withdraws, the camera moves with it, disclosing, first, the owner of the hand, and eventually, a room full of people behind him. The two examples, for easy understanding, are cliches. You can take it from there: All you need is a little imagination.

There is another kind of camera movement, even more commonly used. It is what might be called a "corrective move." Except for extreme long shots and tight close-ups, the camera should rarely be fixed throughout the scene. If one of the actors moves, a compositional adjustment will probably be required, and the camera must move to accommodate it. (I do not speak here of a simple correction made by moving the camera head, but one made by moving the entire camera on a dolly. For most shots, a "crab dolly" is a necessity.) The movement can be as short as a few inches or as long as several feet. It is the only way to maintain an attractive composition while keeping the scene fluid.

So far we have been discussing limited groupings, but crowds are also an element in many films. The "crowd shot" is the bete noir of many a director, since most of them are mild agoraphobes to begin with, and some filmmakers delegate the handling of background crowds to the assistant. This shifts the responsibility but doesn't always solve the problem.

The film crowd is difficult to deal with on a creative level because it has no entity of its own—too often it is just a crowd, a horde of nameless, featureless extras, muttering unintelligible phrases and engaged in meaningless activity. One solution is to turn the crowd into a *mob*; a mob always has a purpose. The earlier example of the football crowd is apropos. If we start with the crowd, we have only a large number of people gathered in a stadium. If we reserve the full shot of the stadium until the touchdown has been made, we show a large number of individuals, as one, in a mob reaction to the exciting play on the field. The crowd now has a common purpose and a common reaction.

When no common purpose is possible, as in a party sequence, it is wise to break the crowd up into its components—first, into manageable groups, then into individuals. Each individual is given a background and a purpose, then the process is reversed; the individuals become a part of a group, and the groups merge into a crowd. For the actual shooting it is preferable to follow one person whom we know, or want to know, through the crowd. Starting with a close shot of our actor, and always keeping him as the center of interest, we pull back as he moves through the room to discover the presence of the crowd.

In shooting an actor against a crowded background (say, at a race track) it is often useful to diminish the crowd concentration as the camera (in separate cuts) moves closer to the center of interest. In a tight close-up, the crowd can be eliminated entirely. The closer the set-up, the more distracting are the background people. In the close-up, the viewer's attention should be concentrated on the actor. As in all good "cheating," what is not on the screen will not be missed.

*Dmytryk, flanked by cameraman Gabor Pogany, sets up a scene for* Bluebeard.

# 8

# *Use of Lenses*

Recently, a master's candidate was reading his pre-thesis paper to a board of examiners. His subject was the genre known as film noire (which, incidentally, I consider a silly classification). In some detail, he mentioned social ramifications, lighting treatment, and a few other pertinent factors, but at no time did he speak of the selective use of lenses, without which film noire could hardly exist.

Most people have some knowledge of still cameras, and they know that lenses have different focal lengths, which they classify loosely as "wide angle," "normal," and "telescopic." The film student knows that the 35 mm film camera uses a number of lenses of specific focal lengths. They *should* know that each lens also has specific uses.

The normal lens complement for a 35 mm camera would be one of each of the following—25 mm, 35 mm, 50 mm, 75 mm, 100 mm, and possibly a zoom lens. Zoom lenses, although very popular in the 16 mm field, are little used in professional filmmaking, except for special "moving in" and telescopic shots. Zoom lenses have varying limits of magnification.*

The 50 mm is the standard, or "normal," lens in filmmaking. That means that a figure shot at a distance of 20 feet from the camera will appear to be 20 feet from the viewer when he sees it on the screen. The background will also appear to be quite normal, as will the lines of perspective.

Any lens with a focal length below 50 mm is called a "wide angle" lens. Like all lenses outside the 50, the wide angle lenses have special properties which are actually distortions from the normal. For example, a 25 mm will make a figure standing 20 feet from the camera

---

*For reasons having to do with background distortion, whenever possible a "moving in" shot is made with a dolly and a lens of fixed focal length. See further note on zoom lenses at end of present chapter.

243

appear to be 40 feet away when seen on the screen. Each succeeding plane behind the figure will also have doubled its apparent distance from the viewer. A fountain, say, which is actually 100 feet behind the figure, will now appear to be 200 behind it, or 240 feet from the camera. (A 35 mm lens will make the same figure appear to be about 32 feet from the camera and the background will recede to the apparent distance of about 160 feet.)* Such lenses not only artificially lengthen the distance between the object and the viewer, they also broaden the background proportionally—hence the term wide angle lenses. However, it is the first property which has the greatest application in films.

The "narrow angle," or telescopic lenses, as the term implies impart an opposite effect: They narrow down the width of the background and diminish the apparent distance between the object and the viewer. If shot with a 100 mm lens, a figure at 20 feet will now appear to be 10 feet from the camera. Longer focal length lenses are increasingly telescopic.

All this is basic knowledge to the camera buff and the cameraman, but what does it mean to the average director? Unfortunately, not much. But it *should* mean a great deal, as a few examples will show.

An actor, starting at a distance of 20 feet, will take 8 steps to reach the camera. When photographed with a 50, the action on the screen will appear to be quite normal—and quite ordinary. If the same action, from the same distance, is now shot with a 25, it will take the actor the same 8 steps to reach the camera. As seen on the screen, however, he will appear to be approaching from 40 feet away. In other words, taking the same number of steps, moving at the same pace, with the same effort, and using the same amount of time, he will apparently cover *twice* the distance of the first shot. Each stride will now appear to be 5 feet long instead of the normal 30 inches. Interesting, but what is its practical application?

Let us say we are filming a modern version of *Dr. Jekyll and Mr. Hyde.* Whenever Dr. Jekyll is before the camera we will use a 50 mm lens, showing him as an ordinary human being with average physical characteristics. On the other hand, when shooting the same actor as Mr. Hyde, we will use a 25. Immediately his movements will appear to be effortlessly greater, projecting a sense of superhuman power. Further distortion properties of the lens, which we will discuss shortly, will add to the appearance of menace.

A related effect can be obtained by moving the camera. Let us

---

*These distances are approximate (but close) and, on a two-dimensional screen, the viewer is rarely able to judge such perspectives with the accuracy suggested. But the different effects, however subliminal, can be dramatically very effective.

say we are shooting across a bed toward a door in the background, some 20 feet away. On the bed lies Mrs. Jekyll. In an early scene, the Doctor walks into the room to bid her goodnight. It takes him 8 steps to reach the bedside. Later in the film, Hyde repeats the entrance of the earlier scene. But now we move the bed up to within 10 feet of the door, with the camera moved in proportionately. Since we are now using the 25, the door will still *appear* to be 20 feet in the background, but Hyde, like a vampire swooping down on his victim, can reach the bed in 4 steps. Miraculous? No—clever use of the camera lens.

At the other end of the scale, if I wanted to show a man grow weak, I would shoot him with a 75, or a 100. Then, since he would *appear* to be starting from a distance much closer than the actual 20 feet, but would still need 8 steps to cover that *apparently* shorter interval, each of his steps would seem to be short, weak, and ineffectual.

The examples given have purposely been caricatures, but a truly fine demonstration of creative lens use appeared in a "short," made some years ago, of Bierce's *An Occurrence at Owl Creek Bridge*. Most of the film depicted a subconscious, hallucinating experience. Near the climax, the lead actor imagines he is running desperately toward the safety of his home, but something in the real world is holding him back. He runs with all his strength but, as in a nightmare, he seems to make almost no forward progress. The scene was shot with a telescopic lens, which foreshortened his stride to inches instead of feet, and although the *actor* was covering a normal amount of ground with each stride, the *character on the screen* seemed to be barely inching forward in spite of his strenuous efforts.

The same effect can be observed in scenes of racing horses shot from directly in front of the animals. Since the camera must be a great distance away to avoid collision, a telescopic lens is used. The straining thoroughbreds, which actually take strides some 20 feet in length, seem to be marking time. Because of the accompanying shallowness in depth, the horses also appear to be closely bunched, whereas a side angle would show them to be spread out over a considerable stretch of track.

This demonstrates another important property of the lens. The narrow angle lens constricts the background and pulls it toward the camera, like the closed bellows of an accordian. The wide angle, like the same bellows pulled out, expands the background. The degree of these effects is inversely proportional to the focal length of the lens used. The longer the focal length, the closer the image; the shorter the focal length, the deeper the background.

Used in conjunction with foreground pieces (see Book II, Chapter 7) and properly lit, the wide angle lens provides a much greater illusion of depth, or the third dimension, than the normal lens. It also allows for a much deeper field of focus, which is another property of the wide angle lens. It is a more efficient gatherer of light.

These properties offer opportunities for interesting effects. In *Christ in Concrete*, a woman lies in an old-fashioned brass bed, suffering the pangs of childbirth. The camera shoots over the back of her head toward her husband, who stands at the foot of the bed, sharing her agony. During one spasm of pain, the woman grasps the bedpost behind her, straining to stifle a scream. I wanted to show clearly the wedding ring on her clenched hand while focusing on her husband's face, some eight feet away. Since the camera was only a foot or two behind the bed, carrying this depth of focus was extremely difficult. To solve the problem we used a 25 mm lens, stopped down, and doubled the amount of light. With a "normal" lens the shot would have been impossible to realize.

Even though it may seem to be a contradiction, I believe that far too much fuss is made over depth of focus for its own sake, often to the detriment of the impression we want to project. In a two-dimensional medium such as film or TV, a *sense* of depth is more important than *focus* in depth, which is often countereffective. One of the necessary elements in depth perception is the *relative* sharpness of objects at different distances. A series of mountain ridges are optically separated from each other by subtle variations in color and increasing softness of outline, which gives the view not only depth, but beauty. In real life, if we zero in on a beer mug held at arm's length the background is seen only vaguely. On a flat, two-dimensional screen, sharp focus would allow us to see both mug and background equally well (or nearly so) resulting in a flatness of depth perspective and some sense disorientation.

We take advantage of this effect when photographing most women in close-up. Such shots are usually made with a narrow angle lens, generally the 75, which has the property of de-emphasizing sharpness of feature slightly by flattening the face. Also, since the depth of focus is shallow, this lens can be sharply focused on the eyes, leaving the area around the ears and the tip of the nose slightly softer. This serves to direct the viewer's attention more completely to the actor's eyes, which, as has been repeatedly pointed out, are of paramount importance. (Incidentally, the lens stop is also a factor in most of these techniques, but that, of course, is strictly the cameraman's business.)

Softness means beauty in more ways than one. An actor who must look younger than his years should obviously be photographed softly. Erasure of facial lines, however, can be more satisfactorily achieved through the use of filters, as well as the 75 mm lens. This is a common practice, especially with actresses whose fans demand eternal youth. However, when using a filter, the director must try to be consistent. The director of one film starring an aging actress used a filter on all of her close-ups. Since youthful beauty was not required of the leading man: His close-ups were unfiltered. The difference in camera treatment and, unfortunately, the reason behind it, were blatantly obvious when the close-ups were intercut. Due to the thoughtlessness of the director and the carelessness of the cameraman, the attempt to conceal wrinkles only brought them to the viewer's attention.

The proper lenses, lens filters, and lighting can be used to good effect in covering skin imperfections as well. Because of an unfortunate childhood bout with smallpox, one of the forties' leading stars had a pock-marked face, but no one suspected it from her film appearances.

Opposite effects can be obtained with side lighting and wide angle lenses. A flat, featureless face can be given lines, planes, and even an angularity which can enhance the appearance considerably. On occasion, even an apparent flaw can be revealed to good effect. Van Johnson bore a marked scar on his forehead which, for his romantic roles at M.G.M., had been disguised with make-up and filters. For the role of the mutinying officer of the U.S.S. Caine, the scar was made to order. Sharp focus and side lighting brought it out strongly, adding character to his usually rounded features.

The properties of the wide angle lens which give us interesting full shots have to be carefully controlled in close-ups. An actor's nose, when shot in close-up with a 25, appears longer than it really is. This can be quite effective when ugliness or a sense of menace is desired, as for a Mr. Hyde; but in most instances men's close-ups are shot with a 50. There will be occasions, however, when a 35, or even the 25, will be the lens of choice.

In *Crossfire*, for example, Robert Ryan played a psychotic killer. This aspect of his character was developed gradually during the course of the film. In the early scenes, his close-ups were shot with a 50, but as the story progressed, the focal length of his close-up lenses was diminished, first to a 40, then a 35, and finally to a 25. (Any lens below that would have produced a too-obvious distortion.) When the 25 was used, Ryan's face was also greased with cocoa butter. The shiny skin, with every pore clearly delineated, gave Ryan a truly menacing appearance. (Exceptional use of lenses, filters, and lighting should always be thoroughly discussed with the cameraman since these are also in his field of expertise.)

It should be apparent that most of the useful effects obtained from the wide angle lens require back to front movement, or vice versa, when movement is involved in the scene. There is little useful distortion if the actors move straight across the screen. This kind of movement joins the eye-level and profile shots as a technique to be

*Low key lighting was the important element in helping actor Robert Ryan play the bad guy in* Crossfire.

avoided. Let me try to describe an effective movement as compared to a "flat" one.

Many philosophers have pointed out that life is growth, and growth is movement. This is certainly true for life on the screen. A moving, changing image is alive; an unmoving image is, by definition, "without life." That is why a straight, cross-screen walk-through, where the image remains constant in size even though it moves laterally across the screen, is relatively dull. When the image moves from the background to the foreground, even as it moves from one side of the screen to the other, say, from left to right, it grows in size with each succeeding frame, and this makes a more marked impression on the observer's visual sense.

If, at the same time, we use a wide angle lens, say a 35, the apparent lengthening of the mover's steps gives him an added vitality and infuses the scene with more dynamism. Now we can, and should, go one step further by using an off-beat set-up. If we place the lens a foot or so *below* eye level, the camera will be forced to tilt up with the moving figure as it approaches until, just before it passes the camera, it seems to tower over the viewer. We now have an additional movement and a further accentuation of the figure itself to add to its growth and its impact on the screen.

In an extreme case, at the climactic moment in a chase, for example, when we want to obtain the most dynamic effect possible, we can add still one more movement as the actor walks, or runs, toward the camera. The camera can dolly, if only for a short distance, *across* the actor's line of movement. In this case, the camera should be dollying from right to left, panning right, and tilting up, all at the same time. If the camera is in the hands of a skillful operator, the only movement noticed by the viewer will be that of the actor; but, on the subconscious or subliminal level, the camera's contributions will have made the scene far more dynamic than if it had been shot with a 50 mm lens from a stationary, eye-level position.

The reader will have noticed the frequent use of the word "distortion" when referring to various properties of lenses. Distortions do exist; but, owing to certain negative characteristics of our two-dimensional medium and to human modes of perception, unless vulgar extremes are resorted to, they are never obvious to the viewer. Nor should they be. Their value lies in their ability to help emphasize character, appearance, and emotion. The director who knows how to use the set-up and the lens to maximum effect leaves the actor free to "be" the character rather than to try to "act" it.

Consider a villain—a heavy. Evil men and women are not too uncommon, yet those who think of themselves as evil are extremely rare. Almost without exception (if we exclude those decent people with overactive consciences) everyone rationalizes or justifies his actions. The thief who believes the world owes him a living, the embezzler who steals to bolster his unappreciated ego, the dope peddler who argues that he is dealing in vital services, the tycoon who behaves uncharitably toward his competitors and his employees on the ground that it is "only good business," or the killer who sees his action as "just retribution"—all consider themselves whole, nonvillainous human beings. And they should be played that way by the actor. But if he has to depend completely on his own resources to portray his character's less desirable qualities, he may have to "act" more than may be acceptable.

On the other hand, if the director can use all of the techniques at his disposal to *visually* impart the texture of evil to an arrant character, the actor will be free to play the part as a real human being rather than as a caricature. This applies to all the characters in a film. One of the great advantages of the medium is that there are so many techniques which, if properly and creatively used, can reach beyond the performers' own resources to make the film's inhabitants more dynamic and more dramatically effective, while still keeping them human and "real."

Those techniques have only been hinted at here, but if the reader sees the tip, he may become more readily aware of the iceberg.

At this point some reader will think, "Okay, I can vary the height of the camera, use abnormal lenses and lighting effects, etc. But how *far* should I raise or lower the camera, *how* do I select the proper lens for the proper shot, and *what* light effect do I ask for?"

Sorry. There are no specific answers. Rarely do situations repeat themselves exactly, and any answer would depend on the particular mood and action at a particular point in the film. Lowering the camera is a function of taste, not precept. The important thing is to take a crack at it, to risk the big gamble rather than to settle for the small sure thing. It is often better to be creatively wrong than to be technically right. Consider El Greco. Experts may criticize a purposely out-of-focus shot, or an "out-of-focus" line of dialogue, but what really counts in any work of art is the total effect, not technical perfection.

Note: The zoom lens is used to excess in TV production for the same reason that close-ups and dialogue are exploited: It saves time and money. However, no expert photographer will argue that the zoom can supply quality equal to that of a complement of first class fixed focal length lenses, although it is getting close.

*Director Dmytryk carefully outlines what he wants for a scene in* Murder, My Sweet. *Dick Powell and Claire Trevor listen intently.*

# 9

# *The Heart of the Matter*

## *Getting It on Film*

So far we have considered mainly organizational and technical aspects of filmmaking which, though very important in setting mood, enhancing dramatic impact, and creating an atmosphere of acceptance, are not really matters of life or death. To a considerable extent they are the packaging which makes the gift more exciting, and possibly more acceptable. But an empty box, no matter how attractively wrapped, will be a disappointment, whereas the gift itself has a value even if stripped of all extraneous ornamentation. Examples of this are seen on the screen every day: Stylishly packaged productions which have no content are financial and critical disasters, while crudely produced and executed films with strong dramatic or exploitational material become box-office bonanzas.*

My intention is not to diminish the value of the preceding chapters, but to stress a basic truth: What counts most is the "life" projected on the screen. That life will be rich and absorbing only when it is the result of honest writing, fine acting, and skillful staging; and the responsibility for extracting the maximum yields out of these requisites is in the hands and the mind of the director. Therefore, his approach to his work, the obstinacy with which he attacks his innumerable problems, becomes the single most important element in the making of a film.

Once the shooting starts the director gets little rest. His mind is

---

*Rossellini's masterpiece, *Rome, Open City*, was shot on raw stock discarded by the U.S. Army Signal Corps as unusable. The print was dreadful; the film was a classic.

on his scenes and their related problems throughout his waking hours—
he dreams about them during his sleep. As his work progresses and
his mind and body tire, his dreams become nightmares, and the temptation to say, "That's good enough, let's get on with it," grows stronger
with each passing day.

But when is anything "good enough"? The answer is, "Never."
"Good enough" implies there is something better, and if that's true,
it makes little sense to settle for less. But we are getting ahead of
ourselves. Let's begin while we are fresh, eager, and optimistic. Let's
start with the first rehearsal.

Whenever possible, rehearsals should be held on the day *before*
the rehearsed material is to be filmed. That material will usually
consist of an entire sequence, which may be scheduled for several
days' shooting, but the greatest concentration will be on the scenes
to be shot on the following day.

The first step is a casual reading of the scene.* By this time some
of the cast will have "learned," or memorized, their lines; others will
still be referring to their scripts. All will probably need some prompt-
ing. A few directors take on this duty themselves, but I recommend
that it be delegated to a dialogue director or the script clerk. The
director should be free to concentrate his entire attention on the actors
as they read their lines, and on the lines they read.

This reading—or readings, really, since there will usually be a
number of them—is indispensable for a number of reasons:

> Each actor learns how every other actor is developing his
> character. This may result in some modification of his own con-
> cept.

> The actors become aware of each other's work habits. It is
> at this point that danger signals arise, and here the director should
> start planning strategies to neutralize acting methods which might
> eventually cause serious friction. (See Ford vs. Brando, Book II,
> Chapter 3) Fortunately, this is not a common problem, but oc-
> casionally it does come up.

> The director, too, discovers his cast's work habits and fol-
> lows the development of the actors' concepts.

> Watching closely and listening carefully, the director catches
> dialogue redundancies (if any), becomes aware of areas which may
> need improvement or deeper development, makes mental notes
> of possible deletions or transpositions of phrases and, along with
> the actors, begins to get a real sense of those points in the scene
> which should be stressed and those to be "thrown away."

---

*The words "sequence" and "scene" do have particular meanings, but they are
often used interchangeably. When the meaning of either word is meant to be specific,
it can easily be so recognized from the context.

A rehearsal, in short, is the time for slogging, and much of the slogging takes place during the readings. It is at this time that the final writing, or rewriting, takes place. (And here let me repeat, it is as important to know when to leave well enough alone as it is to change it. Occasionally, a writer will give you a gem. Treasure it. Help your actors to give it their best, then stand back and enjoy it.)

However, although some scripts are better than others, few are perfect; and a director would be remiss if he made no attempt to correct a weakness exposed by the actors' efforts to bring a scene to life. Incidentally, such corrections are frequently made by referring the scene back to the original, or follow-up writer. Not all directors are competent script doctors.

Now to specifics. First, the dialogue: Each actor should make his dialogue his own, i.e., he should commit himself to a way of speaking that best fulfills his screen character. Such decisions are made in consultation with the director, who must do his best to be objective. Some shaping or modification of the actors' concepts may be desirable, but any attempt by the director to superimpose his own concept in this area leads to boring similarities in characterization.

Some directors ape the old vaudevillian who had performed a one-man act in which he played ten different characters by donning ten different hats. And that was exactly how, when given the opportunity, he directed, figuratively putting one of his hats on each actor in his films. Needless to say, it showed. The healthiest way to obtain variety of characterization is to permit each actor a good deal of freedom in establishing his screen persona.

As mentioned previously, one of the most difficult and least well-realized aspects of writing is "good" dialogue. It is essential that every line in a film (unless it is obviously a quote) should appear to be spontaneous. But most lines have been written, rewritten, honed, and polished until they sound anything but spontaneous. The most skillful actors have their own techniques for handling awkward or stilted lines, but such artists are as rare as great dialogue specialists. The following anecdote may serve as an example.

While preparing a scene for a film with Spencer Tracy, I found one speech, some half-page in length, to be altogether too "literary." I discussed the speech with Tracy and indicated that I was rewriting it in an attempt to bring it down to earth.

"I've already learned it," he told me. "Let's wait and see how it plays. If it proves awkward, we'll do your version."

We shot the scene the next day. While he played it, Tracy hemmed, hawed, hesitated, made slight repetitions. He broke it up so adroitly that it sounded completely extemporaneous. Perfect. But Tracy was probably the most skillful "phraser" in motion picture history. In normal situations the director must be prepared to help his actors as they search for effective spontaneity.

In trying to achieve "reality" some actors and directors resort to improvisation, and students often enquire as to its worth. In the hands of a director with great editing skills, improvisation has some value; but, unless one is to believe that actors are better writers than skilled dramatists, it is wiser to cast a wary eye on this particular technique. However, if a scene proves to be especialy stubborn, improvisation may furnish clues to the difficulties as well as suggestions for possible solutions. The final version of the scene is usually formalized by a writer or the director.

Another common source of trouble is the concept, held by many writers, directors, and actors, that every line of dialogue is important. It just isn't so. As a matter of fact I believe that half the lines in a well-written script are fillers or, in the language of the trade, "throwaways." Back to Tracy again. He had a reputation for underplaying. In reality, he was only giving his lines the importance he felt they deserved, tossing them away. As he once said, "When a line is worth shouting, I can yell with the loudest of them." And indeed he could. To give a casual line the same weight and consideration as a crucial one is to overact. Most "hamming" consists of just that: making an off-hand "Good evening" sound as earthshaking as a declaration of war.

In almost every film the most common problem is length—usually too much of it. Although overall length is given careful consideration from the moment of first writing, rehearsal readings will often reveal further redundancies in content, as well as in phrasing. Such redundancies must be conscientiously eliminated.

The problem is often intensified by the director's inability to see the forest for the trees. Let us suppose that a desired dramatic effect depends on spreading the delivery of a particular piece of information over a number of scenes. In such a case, too definitive an exposition in any one sequence would destroy the desired effect by making further reference unnecessary. Therefore, if staggered information is important, the amount delivered in each scene must be pared down to the absolute minimum.

At times there may be some doubt about such redundancies: Are they real or merely the result of being "too close" to the material. If such a doubt exists, it is relatively simple for the director to shoot the scene, with the questionable material included, in such a way that the final decision concerning possible deletions can be made in the cutting room. If a number of set-ups covering the questionable scene are available, deleting dialogue will present no problem for the editor. If, however, the scene is conceived as a master shot, some protection is necessary.

"Protection shots" are really a simple matter. A silent reaction close-up of one of the scene's participants, ambiguous enough to be

used over almost any speech, will usually furnish sufficient coverage.*
If, for some reason, this kind of cut is not feasible, a technique known
in the cutting rooms as "cutting to the kitchen stove" can be easily
applied. In plain words, a short cut of almost any object in the room,
or on the location, can serve as a cut-away from the scene, during the
course of which any desired deletion can be made. Such a cut may
also earn the director a reputation as a profound symbolist. Which
brings up an interesting psychological point, deserving of much more
investigation than can be given it here.

As long ago as 1920, Raymond Griffith, a leading comic of the
silents, was working his way out of a desperate situation.

"At this point in the fight," he said, "I reach under the bed, pull
out this fire axe, and start chasing. . . ."

"Whoa! Wait a minute!" cut in the director. "An axe under the
bed!? The audience won't believe it!"

"If they see me pull it out, they'll know it was there," was Griffith's answer. And, of course, he did, and they did. A viewer will accept
as pertinent almost anything he sees on the screen, even if it seems
to make little sense. If it's there, the viewer assumes it must be there
for a reason and, as often as not, he will ascribe any lack of clarity to
his own lack of understanding. Used sparingly, and with great care,
this principle can be of considerable service to a troublesome scene,
or to a director who doesn't know *what* to do.

But back to the rehearsal. When dialogue, speech mannerisms,
and length of scene have been put right, and the actors are feeling at
home in their roles and at ease with their lines, the pace of the scene
must be carefully adjusted. Usually this means a speeding up of tempo,
especially in relation to throw-aways and overlapping lines of dialogue.
It is an interesting aspect of film staging that the pace of an average
scene must be measurably faster than that of an equivalent theatrical
staging or, for that matter, real life. No one knows for sure why this
is so, though some filmmakers have plausible theories, but so it is.

Achieving an increased pace is a delicate operation. Overt pushing for greater speed leads only to scenes which appear rushed. The
needed acceleration must be induced in so subtle a manner that the
actors are not really aware that they have been coaxed into a faster pace.

An example from *The Young Lions:* In a "looping session," Monty
Clift listened to a tape of himself speaking some lines. He looked
puzzled, and turned to me.

---

*From an audience point of view, no reaction shot is truly ambiguous. As es-
tablished in Kuleshov's well-known experiment, the viewer's reading of a neutral
reaction depends, to a very great extent, on the nature of the shot which precedes the
reaction. In other words, if truly involved, the viewer will supply his own interpretation. Use it!

"That's not me," he said, ungrammatically and inaccurately.

"Of course it is," I assured him.

"It *can't* be," he protested. "I've never spoken that swiftly in my life."

I asked the projectionist to run the tape in sync with the matching picture. He did so, and Clift was finally convinced, though he continued to shake his head in disbelief throughout the looping session.

Bear in mind that a scene which appears to be normally paced on the set may be as dull as dishwater when seen at the rushes on the following day.

There are, of course, important exceptions to the general need for fast pacing, both in dialogue scenes and in scenes of action. In a dialogue scene one looks for the moment of transition—that confrontation with an idea or bit of information which carries enough novelty, importance, or shock value to make the receiver of the information stop to think. It is the pause for thought which makes the scene come alive, both on the screen and in the mind of the viewer. For even as the character on the screen is forced to stop to regroup his thoughts, his attitudes, under the impact of some unexpected or shocking statement or action, so the viewer is also marshalling his own reactions to the same information and forming new or stronger attitudes toward the film's characters. Thus it is often more important to properly gauge the length of time the viewer needs to digest the pertinent information than it is to be consistent within the scene itself. The exact timing for the actor's reactions can be achieved in the cutting room, but only if the director furnishes both himself and the editor the necessary material to play with.

Strange as it may seem, scenes of sharp or violent physical action frequently need to be slowed down. In a rather routine TV series, starring Hugh O'Brien as Wyatt Earp, made some years ago, the final episodes dealt with the legendary gunfight at the O.K. Corral. The scenes of the battle, which actually lasted only a few seconds, were filmed in slow motion. Each combatant, whether firing a gun, receiving a hit, or dodging one, was given full time on the screen. In other words, each of the many bits of action was separated from the whole, slowed down so it could be analyzed and understood, then rebuilt into the complete scene. The screen time involved was immeasurably greater than the real time of the original action, but for the first time in Western history the viewer could fully grasp the function and the fate of every gunman in that famous fight. "Time stood still" for the viewer, long enough to engage his full attention. I still consider it to be one of the most creative ideas ever to find its way into a very stodgy medium.

The time differential in the cited example was exceptional and anticipated the effectiveness of the now commonplace "instant replay" used in sports broadcasting; but similar, though less extreme techniques are often employed in filming action scenes. In shooting a prize fight, for instance, blows which are too quick for the eye to follow are slowed down to accommodate the viewer's ability to grasp the action fully.* The desired result is not necessarily accomplished through the use of slow motion (now a rather trite technique); it is more often achieved by extending and overlapping the cuts used to show the fight. The same method can be used in shooting battle scenes, accidents, etc. In other words, film gives us the freedom to be in a number of places at the same time: "In the meantime" is an easily realized point of view. It is most important for the director to remember that one of the chief advantages of film as an art is this freedom to manipulate *time*, as well as *space*, and it behooves him to learn how to use this special form of manipulation to maximum effect.

When the reading flows smoothly and the actors are at ease with their material and at one with their characters, movement rehearsals are in order. At this time it is customary for the director to initiate the players' starting positions and their preliminary moves. Although in this phase of the rehearsal the director may want to keep a somewhat tighter rein on the scene's development than he did at a similar stage in the reading, he will still find it fruitful to allow the actors a certain amount of creative freedom. As the rehearsals progress, and the players settle into the scene, it becomes easier to modify, even restrict, their moves, since changes will present fewer threats and will be more easily accommodated.

Moves should always appear to be the natural consequences of the emotions and attitudes expressed in the scene. They should never be made simply to furnish "action," nor should they be obviously choreographed. If a scene appears to be dull, the cause almost certainly lies deeper than mere lack of action. However, the dynamics of a good scene can be heightened by well-conceived movement.

As previously mentioned, even the direction in which a movement takes place can contribute to the scene's vitality. Bringing an actor toward the camera, for instance, can affect the viewer's reception in two ways: first, by bringing him closer to the center of expression, the actor's face and eyes; and second, by gradually eliminating his awareness of the background as it goes out of focus and the actor's face takes over the greatest part of the screen. A move away from the camera has the opposite effect, diminishing the presence of the actor

*One of the first victims of slow motion analyses was the "six inch" knock-out punch. Such fictional dramatization was the result of the fight commentator's attempt to rationalize his eyes' shortcomings.

while increasing that of the background and any action taking place in it. A move across camera does little beyond transporting the actor from one side of the screen to the other.

All this is extremely simplistic. It is mentioned only to give the student a starting point as his attention turns to set-ups. A number of these should have been visualized before the scene is rehearsed (a few possibly as early as the first reading of the script), and some may still be valid. But, except in the case of a highly stylized film, many camera positions may be modified because of the changes wrought during rehearsals.

Set-ups are a difficult area for the beginning director, and students often ask, "How do you determine where to put the camera?" That's easy. You put it where it will record what you want the viewer to see. *The director controls the viewer's attention.* It is largely a matter of instinct and experience. If your instinct is sound, your experience will be given the opportunity to grow; if not—well, there's always a place in the family business.

At this point let us consider two basic problems which, despite their apparent simplicity, cause beginners (and even a few old pros) a disproportionate amount of agony. The first involves the question of size (as in LONG SHOT, MEDIUM SHOT, etc.) especially in a cutting context.

Quite obviously, cutting from one full-figure shot to another, similar, full-figure shot will cause a "jump"—a distraction to the viewer—even though the set-ups are shot from different points of view. (Here, of course, I mean the *same* figure.) Just as obviously then, what is required is a *measurable* difference in the sizes of the two contiguous cuts. In other words, one can cut from a full-figure to a close shot, or from a close shot to a full-figure, but one should *not* cut from a full-figure to a calf-length shot—the size difference would not be marked enough to make the cut work smoothly. In this instance the cutting jump would not qualify as a desirable shock to the viewer: It would merely be undesirably disturbing. (The aforementioned stricture applies only to shots of the same person, or persons. Shots of two different people not only can, but often should, be of the same size—for example, the separate, but similar, close shots of two people in a dialogue scene.)

There are exceptions, occasions when two similarly sized set-ups of one person, shot from decidedly different camera positions, can be smoothly juxtaposed, but they must be carefully composed with the cut in mind, and the cut itself must be made with the greatest finesse. However, the overwhelming majority of cuts involve two set-ups of distinctly different sizes—one more reason why the director should not only understand editing, but also be able to keep the probable cutting sequence in mind as he shifts from set-up to set-up.

The second problem is one of "direction," i.e., the direction (screen right or screen left) in which an actor looks or moves. As an example, let us imagine a scene—a conversation between characters A and B. In the opening two shot (Figure 2), A is on the left of the screen looking at B, who is on the right side of the screen, looking at A to the left. In their respective close shots, whether over-shoulder (Figures 3a and 3b) or individual (Figures 3c and 3d) their looks must remain consistent, i.e., A should always look camera right and B should always look camera left, regardless of how sharply the camera diverges from its original two-shot position or how much the set-up varies in relation to the set or any of the set-pieces in it. (See "Cheating", Book II, Chapter 4.)

If more than two people are included in the master set-up, the "direction" problem becomes a great deal more complex. When filming a poker game, a board meeting, or a large family dinner, the question of consistent direction can tax the most mathematical mind.

"Direction" is also an important factor in exits and entrances, and in any cross-screen movement which carries over from one cut to the next. If an actor exits a shot to the left side of the screen (camera left, Figure 4a) and immediately walks into the next set-up, he must enter the new shot from the right side of the screen (camera right, Figure 4b). In other words, his movement must be consistently in one direction—in this case from right to left. A little thought will reveal why this requirement is of special importance in long, involved chases, "rides to the rescue," etc. It is needed to keep the action clean, consistent, and free of confusion. In effect, it shows our actors going from here to there, or vice versa, and not from here (or there) to God knows where. The actors should never meet themselves "coming back." It is sometimes permissible to mystify a viewer, or to surprise him, but to confuse him is completely unproductive and undesirable.

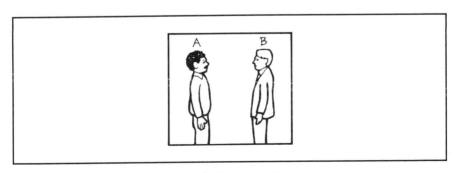

*Book II - Figure 2*

Figure 3a

Figure 3b

Figure 3c

Figure 3d

WRONG!
It appears that both are looking
off right - not at each other

Figure 3e

Figure 3f

*Book II - Figure 3*

There are other, more simple effects which benefit from consistency in "direction." Example: If the director wants a long shot of a plane flying from New York to London, (Figure 5a), he will usually show it moving from left to right. The reason is quite simple: Our maps show London to the right of New York, and the sight of a plane flying in the opposite direction would be at least temporarily confusing. By the same reasoning, if we now cut to our actors inside the plane (Figure 5b) their seats should face screen right in the direction

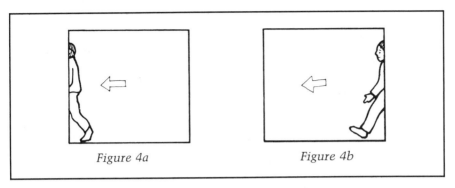

Figure 4a  Figure 4b

Book II - Figure 4

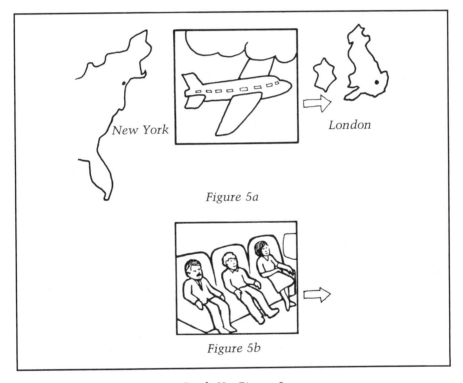

New York  London

Figure 5a

Figure 5b

Book II - Figure 5

of the plane's movement. This rule is frequently disregarded but, in general, unless there are pressing dramatic reasons for breaking it, it is wise to observe it faithfully.

And now a giant step backward. As the director watches the rehearsals in progress, he mentally re-affirms the scene's values, determines where he needs room, or space, where concentration, where high emotional intensity, and where emotional relief. If the scene is one of action, he must decide whether to stage it in comprehensive full shots, or in an integratable series of tight close shots.* Above all, he must keep in mind that the scene should *not* be looked at from a fixed position, as though seen on a stage. It is worth repeating that the camera can move in a 360-degree circle around the players, a fact which those who have been conditioned by TV sitcoms too easily forget.

By the time the scene is ready for filming the director should know exactly what, and how many, set-ups are necessary to thoroughly cover the scene, and exactly how the final set-up of the current shooting will lead into the first set-up of the sequence to follow. Even as a chess master must be able to think a number of moves ahead, so the director must be able to visualize his set-ups to the end of each sequence, and at least one set-up beyond.

Most films have at least one "problem" scene, a scene that fails to "come alive," which stubbornly resists any solution. Such scenes engender sleeplessness, gas pains, and prematurely gray hair. The causes of the problems vary and are difficult to discover—often, like Poe's *Purloined Letter*, because of their obviousness. I can only fall back on an example, a scene whose problem, a contradiction in character, was easy to recognize but whose solution was not.

In *The Young Lions*, Dean Martin played an admitted coward, a man reluctant to lose his life in what he considered a useless war, who even deserted a friend in need to take a "cushy" noncombat job well behind the front. But his conscience (and the plot) made it necessary to get him back to his outfit, now fighting the enemy in France. In the script, he quarrels with his girlfriend in a London pub and, egged on by his feelings of guilt, in a rash moment of pique he takes advantage of a general's presence to demand reassignment to his old unit.

The scene was well written, well rehearsed, and well played. But it didn't ring true. Martin's cowardly though likable character had been so well established that it was difficult to accept his sudden change of heart: It was completely illogical.

After repeated rehearsals, discussions, and coffee breaks, I was hit by a sudden inspiration which, like most inspirations, became instantly obvious. We were in a pub, so it was to be expected that Martin would have been drinking. The solution was something the script had not suggested, and I was slow in seeing—Martin was drunk! (If Martin had had his Las Vegas reputation in 1957 the solution might have been more easily arrived at.) Every viewer will accept the fact

---

*Note the shower murder scene in Hitchcock's *Psycho*, which consisted of nearly 100 close shots and inserts, none of which showed the knife entering the body.

*"A director has to know when to leave his stars alone—to play, to relax, to get acquainted," Dmytryk says. Here Dean Martin and Montgomery Clift get relaxed for their party scene in* The Young Lions.

that a person under the influence of alcohol can do extremely illogical things. (See Book I, Chapter 3.) Not a line was changed, but the moment Martin's elbow slipped off the edge of the table in an uncoordinated, tipsy move, and his words came out slightly blurred, the scene became alive and believable.

It may relieve the reader to learn that when the director has succeeded in eliciting a fully satisfactory rehearsal, the worst is over. The next hour or two belongs to the cameraman and his crew as they light the set, and to the sound mixer as he fixes his optimum mike positions. When these artists have completed their work, final rehearsals are in order. These are required to allow the sound and camera crews to make corrections, to practice their moves, and to apply their final touches—and to get the actors back into the swing of the scene. Now all that remains is to record their work for posterity. This may take some time if actors falter, or technical problems arise, but if the cast is truly professional it will often be perfect the first time around. On the other hand. . . .

Some years ago, when low budget films were a large part of every studio's output, many of them limited their B directors to a prescribed number of takes in any one set-up, usually four. This led to deception; after four unsatisfactory takes, the director would move his camera four or five inches, call it a new set-up, and continue shooting the scene until it was played to his satisfaction or until he ran out of time. In films made on a tight budget, takes and time are synonymous. Here, again, the law of diminishing returns is brought into play.

The director may have a satisfactory take "in the can," yet feel that continued effort might result in something more nearly perfect. But the actors may be tired, dried up, or just not functioning perfectly at this particular time, and the shooting can go on and on. At some point, the director must decide if the cost in time and money is worth what little improvement *might* be gained, and if that slight improvement will really add measurable quality to the total worth of the film in the first place.

Another wasteful practice is the continued effort to get one perfect master shot when the director intends to cut the scene using several set-ups. If the director knows cutting and has visualized the cuts in the scene, he need not, and should not, wait for a perfect *complete* take. If the first half, let us say, of take 2 is well played, and the second half of take 6 is just right, and the director knows that somewhere in the middle of the scene he will use at least one cut from another set-up, takes 2 and 6 will serve as one perfect take, even though neither is completely perfect in itself. Further shooting is clearly a waste of time.

The same holds true for close-ups, two shots, etc.; any angles which will be intercut. The director need only remember which parts of which takes were usable, then, via the script clerk's notes, pass the information on to his cutter.

Then there is a related problem: the preparation, lighting, and shooting of unnecessary set-ups, a "sin" more often committed than one would expect. Quite simply, if a director with a 60-day schedule shoots twice the number of set-ups needed to properly cut the film, he is cheating himself of 30 days of his schedule, days which might have been more productively used to improve those scenes eventually used in the film. I have known directors who have actually overshot to this extent, but they were few. Still, most directors, whether because of insecurity or lack of awareness or concern, are not as assiduous in this regard as they should be—completely in their own interests. Quite obviously, all of a film's material and artistic resources should be spent on the scenes which will wind up in the film, not on the cutting room floor.

While set preparation and lighting are in progress, or even while the shooting is under way and the director is concentrating on the scene's quality, or lack of it, part of his mind is concerned with the next set-up, and the many others to follow. Even while he is dealing with the special problems of this necessarily fragmentary stage of filming, the director must bear in mind several requirements of the film as a whole.

One, already mentioned, is staggered flow of information. Another is tempo, not just the pace which contributes to a scene's vitality, but the overall tempo of the film. This tempo may vary with the sequences even as tempo varies in the different movements of a symphony, but its general direction is up. Just as the range of an actor's physical movements should be modified as his image grows larger on the screen, to the point where his body is motionless in a close-up; so the tempo of a film should increase as the viewer grows in awareness of story situations and in understanding of the film's inhabitants. When the viewer knows the film's characters well enough to be able to anticipate their reactions, those reactions should be curtly handled. It is only the unexpected action or reaction that needs to be dwelt on.

A third item of considerable consequence is the link. A film is a collection of a number of sequences made up of a greater number of scenes which, in turn, are created out of an even greater number of set-ups. Once recorded on film, these set-ups are called "cuts." In most films it is imperative that one cut flows smoothly into another in a continuous array to form a scene; that each scene joins, apparently seamlessly, with those on either side of it to form a sequence; and that the sequences follow each other fluidly. The general idea is to keep the viewer's train of thought from jumping the track.

Necessary pacing and smooth linkage can be accomplished in the cutting room, but a better film will result if the director controls the pace and prepares the proper sequence springboards as he shoots. Naturally, this is difficult, since so much of the average film is shot out of sequence; but a cosmetic job done in the cutting room rarely approaches the perfection of proper timing achieved on the set. There just aren't that many great creative editors around.

*Dmytryk began his career as a film cutter, so he learned early what he wanted to see on film. Here he is with one of his favorite cameramen, Harry Wild, in 1945.*

# 10

## *Together at Last*

### *Editing*

Film editing or, as it is commonly called, "cutting," is unique. It is the one art or craft that is indigenous to motion pictures. All other film arts are borrowed or adapted. Stories and acting are as old as civilization, at least. So is music. Photography has its antecedents in pictorial art, and chemical means of recording images dates back to the early nineteenth century. Film editing, which owes little except nomenclature to literary editing, was brought to life by motion pictures and it, in turn, brought motion pictures to life.

Film editing can be roughly divided into three categories: cutting, editing, and "montage." Of these, only montage is truly an art, although editing does, at times, approach that plateau. As it is understood today, montage is a limited technique in which a number of cuts, usually silent, are arranged almost in collage form to indicate the passage of time or, occasionally, a manic or psychotic state of mind. But in the last decade of the silent era the Russian filmmakers developed the technique into a high art which has not since been equalled.

This distinctive technique was just beginning to blossom when it was nipped in the bud by the advent of sound. When films learned to talk, montage died, and Russian films became as verbose and as dull as those of their political and artistic competitors—perhaps duller, since most of the mandated propaganda was difficult to dramatize or digest.

Although the terms "film cutter" and "film editor" are commonly understood to be interchangeable, there is a definite, though informal, distinction. A "cutter" is a mechanic who learns a number of rather simple rules for cutting from one piece of film to another. He learns how to "cut in movement," how to bring people into a scene or out of it, how to avoid making cuts that "jump," i.e., are noticeable to the viewer. At best, he learns how to take the material given him and, following the director's scene selections and cutting instructions, how to build a smooth and properly paced film.

There was once a saying around the cutting rooms, "A good cutter cuts his own throat." The implication was that in a well-cut film, cuts were unnoticed and so was the cutter's contribution. The ideal was to splice together thousands of pieces of film, or "cuts,"* into a motion picture which the viewer would perceive as one continuous shot from beginning to end.

An unselfish ideal, surely—one not too frequently realized and not always respected. As a projectionist, I remember standing in the doorway of a cutting cubicle at Paramount in which Josef Von Sternberg was editing one of his films. At one point, Marlene Dietrich, looking over his shoulder into the moviola, tapped him for attention.

"That cut jumps," she said.

"I want it to jump," said Joe. "I want the audience to know there was a cutter on the picture—me."

Nevertheless, most cutters do their best to produce a fluid film, allowing cuts to jump only when some jolt to the viewer's sensibilities is called for. In which case, when properly executed, the jolt will register but the cut, or change of scene, will still pass unnoticed.

To assure a properly finished film, one of two conditions must be met: The director must be a good cutter himself, or he must employ a film editor who understands and shares the director's vision (gleaned largely from studying the script and watching the daily rushes with the director), and who is able to give the director what he "wishes he had wanted."

The cutter's first duty is to deliver a version of the film, usually called "the first cut," which the director *expects* to see. The assumption in that statement is that the director *knows* what he wants to see and, of course, good directors do, although only a few may have the necessary expertise to assemble such a version themselves. For this reason, the relationship between the director and his cutter is a very special one. The cutter is the director's right hand.

---

*In film parlance the word "cut" has several meanings, all easily understood in context. As a verb, "to cut", it signifies the act of cutting together a number of scenes into a finished film, or "work print." Beyond that it serves as a noun in several contexts: first, a "cut," meaning an unbroken strip of film recording all, or part, of a single set-up; second, the splice, or joint, between two cuts of the first kind; third, the total work print, especially when denoting the number of times the film has been reworked, as in "rough cut", first cut, director's cut, and final cut.

Ideally, the director should be an expert cutter or, better yet, a fine film editor. Only if the director knows how to put a film together himself can his vision be completely realized. To put it simply, no director can claim to be an "auteur" unless he knows how to cut.

An in-depth discussion of cutting techniques and editing concepts requires a book of its own (see Book IV for more detail). Here we can only consider a few of the problems the noncutting director may face. Perhaps the most difficult is one already mentioned in other contexts: objectivity.

At this stage of the filmmaking process, the director is often too close to the picture. After months of living with it, it is difficult to know if the lines are real, if the characters are truly developed, or if the film as a whole has the hoped-for impact on a viewer who is not only seeing it for the first time, but who has no prior acquaintance with any of its aspects. Since the director "knows it all," too subjective a point of view may influence him to eliminate portions of the film which he now finds all too familiar and stale, but which may be obligatory for audience understanding. The director must *always* place himself in the position of the viewer who is having his first look at the film. That's a difficult exercise. The process can be helped to a considerable degree if the director can manage to retain, and recall, the insights, understanding, and reaction he experienced on first being introduced to the story or the script.

More often, subjectivity brings a reverse effect. Pygmalion is not an empty fable. Many creators fall in love with their creations, whether they be poems, pastries, or pictures. For very personal reasons they may become so enchanted with some facet of their work that they are oblivious to the audience's point of view, which may differ widely from theirs. Probably no good director, living or dead, has been completely free from this failing. A couple of examples may help to clarify the point.

Erich von Stroheim made a silent film for Paramount called *The Wedding March*. I was a young projectionist at the time and had the privilege of showing him his first cut. It was 126 reels long—without titles—and took more than two working days to run. It was an exceptional exercise in montage and, from a technical point of view, an exceptional experience. But the average length of a film at that time was less than 90 minutes.

*The Wedding March* had to be chopped—drastically—so von Stroheim and his cutter went to work. Some six months later the film was down to 60 reels, still five or six times the allowable length for release. Exercising its contractual option, Paramount took the film away from von Stroheim and assigned it to another cutter, who succeeded in reducing it to 24 reels. These were split into two films. The first, under the original title, was a complete flop. The second was never released in the United States.

Obviously, von Stroheim's delight in his creation was not shared by the general public. The original version might have thrilled a connoisseur, but such thrills must be communicable to a sizable audience or the whole purpose of commercial films is vitiated.

The preceding example is extreme; the next one is closer to us in time and experience. It is Fred Zinneman's *High Noon*. Zinneman, too, found it impossible to get his film down to the length United Artists considered releasable, although in this instance the excess was nowhere near that of *The Wedding March*. He was reluctantly removed by Stanley Kramer, the producer, and the resulting shorter version of the film won a bagfull of Academy Awards, including one for Fred Zinneman.

In this case, the studio's decision was debatable. If released today, with longer films in vogue, Zinneman's version might be an even better film. Just maybe.

Many films are badly cut. Not all editing decisions are the result of constructive thinking. A common mistake is to assume that frequent cutting lends speed and vitality to a scene. That is by no means necessarily so. Such cutting more often results in a jerkiness of film line, which confuses the viewer and promotes the withdrawal of his attention, rather than increased involvement. "Action" is no more a function of the multiplicity of cuts than it is the function of physical movement.

A tight, exciting scene can be played in one set-up by people in fixed positions, and still move the viewer as effectively as if it were played in a series of cuts—sometimes more so. The ideal is to give any scene exactly the amount of movement and the number of cuts that particular scene needs and deserves or, as a mathematician might say, as are "necessary and sufficient." But then, that's the basic requirement of any good dramatic scene.

Occasionally, during final editing, the director may decide he wants an interchange of dialogue to proceed at a faster pace than originally played. If several set-ups have been shot and the material for such manipulation is available, the speed-up can be easily achieved. Each speaker's lines are placed on a separate tape and timed to overlap, as if in an interruption, the lines of the other speaker. The separate tapes are then re-recorded onto one master tape, and the close-up images are matched to the new recording. By using such a technique, the scene can be accelerated to break-neck speed, if so desired, or, on the other hand, slowed considerably if longer pauses for thought and/ or reactions are required. In either case, careful and objective analysis is called for. When carried to extremes these two versions demonstrate that mindless editing can, on the one hand, eliminate any sign of thought in the scene or, on the other hand, manufacture dull-witted characters with ridiculously long reaction times. Good performances *can* be destroyed in the cutting room.

Another important editing consideration is the eventual addition of musical background. By intensifying dramatic involvement, music will often make a scene "move" faster. To take full advantage of this effect, the director should have a good idea of where music is to be used. He can then afford to—indeed he must—give the sequence a somewhat slower tempo, relying on the musical score to bring the scene up to the optimum pace. If such a sequence is cut to move at its ultimate tempo without music, the addition of the score may impart an unwelcome hurried impression.

David Racksin, the composer, once said, "I have been told, 'We want to underscore this scene with a rendition of *The Marseillaise*,' but by the time the scene came out of the cutting room I could only play the anthem's first two bars—if I rushed them." Just one more thing for the director to consider while the cameraman lights the set.

These things, and much more, can be achieved through the cutter's magic, but like all legerdemain a lot of learning and much practice is required. No fledgeling director can consider himself an editor on the basis of a semester or two of cutting exercises at a school of the "cinema," and his demands for "cutting rights" only ask for trouble and a botched-up picture. In recent years this has repeatedly been illustrated by a string of costly "mistakes" which have spent a year or two in the studio's intensive care unit, the cutting room.

Good cutting and skillful editing are most essential to good film-making. They can be achieved in one of only two ways: Either the director finds, and keeps, an expert film editor as his alter ego for this stage of the filmmaking process; or he must determine to spend thousands of hours in the cutting room acquiring the mastery of this vital craft.

*In difficult locations, such as the windy heights of the Alps where much of* **The Mountain** *was shot, sound recording of any quality is virtually impossible to achieve. Therefore, sound looping often has to be done once the film has been cut.*

# 11

# Dressing It Up

## Dubbing

Postediting is the time for mental convalescence. Major cutting is completed and the director can once more view the world through unguarded eyes. He can repair relationships that have become strained during production, re-establish friendships with members of the crew, and become re-acquainted with his family. His job now consists of benign supervision, since the actual work is in the hands of experts whose contributions are largely dictated by the now-established form of the film. At this stage, many directors fade out of the scene, but the conscientious filmmaker will want to keep a measure of control to the bitter end.

It is at this stage that the producer comes back into the picture; and if the director slackens his hold on the reins, the producer is only too happy to pick them up. The knowledgeable executive may have some input at the editing stage, though that usually occurs after the first preview. He may also want to join in the discussions concerning sound effects and music, which is the next phase of the production process.

The "sound running" comes first. As the term implies, the film is shown to the composer, the sound editor, and their assistants. To help in establishing an objective audience feel, the first run-through should always be continuous. This first viewing is immediately followed by a sequence-by-sequence review, with frequent stops to discuss the sound effects needed to flesh out or correct the working sound track. These effects can be as simple as door-knocks, footsteps, sirens, and squealing tires, as complex as the thousands of effects needed for a battle sequence, or as original as the new sounds required for modern science fantasies like *Star Wars*. Unless the director has some very special ideas in mind, most films are taken in stride by the sound editors, although they will occasionally surprise everyone with an original and ingenious sound treatment.

Music is another matter. It is not nearly as cut and dried, and it offers further opportunities for creativity. Even a director with a tin ear will usually insist on an input into how much and where music is required. Normally, there is little disagreement concerning the amount or the placement of music; nor, if the director (usually in collaboration with the producer) selects a composer with an established body of work, will there be a difference of opinion concerning style.

A brief conference will quickly resolve such matters, including the question of instrumentation: Do you want a full symphony orchestra, or would you rather opt for a single instrument? (Example: *The Third Man*, with a full score played on a zither.) Or do you settle for something between these two extremes? A great deal depends on the content and style of the film, and some decisions may be crucial. Does a suspense sequence require dead silence, or eerie music; will a battle scene play better against the background of a martial score, or will the stark sounds of war supply a more effective mood?

How about a theme song? A number of films have ridden to success on the popularity of their musical themes—in a few instances, these have been more successful financially than the films which gave them birth.

Such decisions require serious thought, but they rarely present serious problems, even if some of them are arrived at tentatively. When the composer has created (or borrowed) his themes for the film and its leading characters, he will play them for the approval of the director and the producer. Final decisions are made, and the composer continues with his work, leading up to the recording of the music.

In the meantime, the cutter or the sound editor has been preparing tapes (and pictures, when used) for "looping." Looping is the process of recording clean dialogue to replace that which is indistinct or inaudible, usually because of the presence of excessive background noise. Almost every film will require some looping; a few which have been shot on noisy locations, such as busy streets, may have most of their dialogue replaced. Even night shooting in a remote desert may surprise the sound engineer with a deafening cricket chorus which will drown out the players' voices.

Some directors charge their cutters with the responsibility of looping. The practice is indefensible on any production of quality. The dialogue recorded in a looping session should be as good, dramatically, as the original; and if that required the director's guidance at the shooting stage, so it does when looping. Only the director can know if he is getting the quality which the film demands.

The most common looping technique employs both sound and picture. Duplicate prints of the scenes to be looped are cut into short segments, usually consisting of no more than a line or two of dialogue. The tape is cued with a rhythmically timed series of "beeps" before the start of the dialogue; and the picture usually carries a scribed line, or scratch, also zeroing in on the frame at which the player must start to speak. Each segment is reviewed for pace and intonation, until the actor feels ready to perform, at which time his words are recorded on clean tape. The selected takes of each line of dialogue are then used to replace the original "dirty" versions.

My preferred technique uses *only* the sound tape. It is much faster, easier on the actors, and a good deal more accurate and acceptable. For this method, the dialogue is cut into the shortest possible phrases—the shorter, the better—and separate loops are made of each phrase. When recording, the actor listens to the loop as often as necessary, depending on the complexity of the phrase. When he is ready to record, the recorder is thrown on the line. The actor hears the original words and then, in the few seconds of silence that follow on each loop, he repeats them—mimics them, really. He must capture the original rhythm, intonation, and emotion, which is not difficult if the phrase is short enough. The loop keeps repeating the phrase until the actor has given a satisfactory reading.

This technique achieves the best reproduction of the original dialogue, as well as the most accurate synchronization. The director must, however, shoot the original scene properly, regardless of background noise, to ensure a "cue track" that carries the proper intonations and emotions. Only then can the looping supply comparable quality to the dubbed scene.

More sophisticated electronic techniques for looping do exist but, due either to higher costs or greater studio inflexibility, these systems are rarely, if ever, used.

Film colonies in all countries include actors known as "looping specialists." These artists are especially useful when a film is dubbed into a foreign language or when, as frequently happens in "international" productions, some of the film's local actors cannot manage English satisfactorily. These specialists usually command a number of accents or dialects, often enabling them to dub a number of different roles in the same film. They are also very skillful at "lip synching." It pays to be aware of their existence and their talents.

During the preparation for the final "mix," occasional checks of sound effects and/or music will be called for, but they will not be a major concern to the director until the music is to be recorded. Normally, recording sessions flow smoothly, but problems can arise; and settling differences at this time is more useful, and certainly more economical, than calling additional recording sessions after the sneak preview.

The postediting activity, which may take from six weeks to several months (on rare occasions even longer), culminates in the "dubbing," or rerecording session. Depending on the quality and the difficulty of the sound effects, and the speed and skill of the sound engineers (or "mixers"), the session will last for a week or two on the average—though here, again, some "epics" manage to take much longer. This is concentrated, eight-hours-a-day work—sometimes longer— and the director should devote his full energy and attention to this phase of filmmaking.

Most artists harbor some bias in favor of their own fields and, with the best of intentions, self-interest can creep into the film at this point. Perhaps the composer would like to hear just a touch more of his music, which may just possibly cover, or dirty up, an important bit of dialogue. Or, in a scene demanding heavy and complex sound effects, the urge that motivates the composer may also affect the sound editor. These tendencies are normal, often desirable, and certainly not to be criticized, but they do have to be carefully controlled. For instance, I often diminish, or even eliminate, "busy" background sound effects once the scene has captured the attention of the viewer, even as I thin out crowd people from the background of a close-up. Unless the "noise" has an essential bearing on the scene's dialogue, the viewer's awareness of it diminishes as his emotional involvement in the scene increases. (See Book II, Chapter 7.)

As a rule, only the director can objectively maintain a sense of the proper balance of the values involved in the mix.* If he ignores this important phase of filmmaking, he risks having a final result not exactly to his taste.

Of course, corrections are usually in order after the "sneak," but if improvements are to be made, it is always better to move from "excellent" to "perfect" than from "fair" to "good."

---

*In my entire film experience I have known only one "mixer" whose creative vision was such that I would have trusted his judgment on the proper mix for any of my films. His feeling for dramatic balance bordered on genius. But, like many another genius, John Cope died at an early age.

*Sneak previews can be valuable indicators of how a film can be improved before commercial release—but beware. A blue collar town that loves Westerns and war movies might not provide the most objective reaction to such films as* Anzio.

# 12

# *Let's Get It Out!*

## *The Preview*

Objectivity! Objectivity! Objectivity!

The sneak preview demands it in its purest form. Even the term implies it. Why "sneak"? To minimize the possibility of an "in" audience, a studio claque. At its best, the sneak preview can provide valuable insights into the film's relative values; at its worst, it can be a trap of self-centered deceit. And the trap is set at the very beginning with the selection of a theater and its audience.

It is quite likely that every theater within a 500-mile radius of Hollywood has been "pegged," i.e., the smart producer or director knows what kind of an audience patronizes each house.* One will be considered friendly, another neutral, another tough. Each will be classified by the average age of its patrons, by the presence, or lack, of audible reaction to humor (and what kind of humor), by its drama absorption rate, by its philosophical or religious outlook, and by its level of sophistication.

Darryl Zanuck refused to preview dramatic films on the ground that "If I don't know more about drama than the average audience, I shouldn't be running a film studio." A classic example of "asking for it". But Zanuck was probably right.

Musicals, and comedy in most of its forms, are different kettles of fish. A gag that brings gales of laughter in a studio projection room may leave an audience cold. Since in their early stages most musicals

---

*The same can be said of filmmakers in London, Paris, Rome—or even in Bombay.

contain "numbers" in excess (creative uncertainty), an audience will quickly register its order of preference and indicate obvious deletions.

What is the director's purpose in choosing a particular preview audience? Does he want his film to "play well" to impress his producer and the executives? If so, he will choose a friendly theater, whose audience will spark at the mere sight of the title announcing A MAJOR STUDIO PREVIEW, will laugh easily and long, and will view the film without cynicism or hostility. This type of audience will turn in a large majority of favorable comments even if the film is an unpretentious B movie.

If the film's action or comedy is based on car crashes, unbridled destruction of property, and violence, the director will opt for an audience of high school and college students. If it carries a religious slant, he will sneak it in the nearest farm community; if it promotes a liberal message, it will be shown in a university setting or a minority community. If it is a heavy drama, a theater catering to an older audience will be selected.

If, on the other hand, the director seeks an honest, even a hard evaluation, he will choose a theater known for its tough or cold audience. After all, a truly humorous sequence will play well with *any* audience, young or old, though too much sophistication may misfire in the Bible belt. And a solid dramatic scene, containing no corn or soap, will get across to viewers of almost any age or background.

"Preview cards" are distributed to viewers at all sneaks. These cards ask the viewer to evaluate the film as poor, fair, good, very good, or excellent. As in all straw polls, there are pitfalls. At a well-attended showing in a moderate-sized neighborhood house, the studio can expect a harvest of from three hundred to four hundred cards. Of these, a few from ultragenerous viewers will rate it "the best I've ever seen!" Another five or ten, at the opposite pole on the generosity scale, will say, "It stinks!" Obviously, both extremes should be discarded. The rest can be considered more or less objective, and should be so analyzed. But are they? Not as a rule.

One of the more curious, but perfectly natural, postpreview phenomena is each craftsman's interpretation of the audience reaction. A good comedian could probably do a ten-minute routine on each person's remarks as the studio contingent seeps out into the theater lobby after the screening. The sound mixer will say, "It *sounded* great!" or, "The speakers need fixing!" The cameraman will comment on the quality of the print. The composer will like his music but wish for "a little more presence during the love scene." The cutter will be pleased that the cuts didn't jump, but he'll want to make a few more "snips." An actor, if present, will usually be somewhat self-critical. And the executives, though exuding optimism, will usually suggest

that the film could "lose fifteen minutes without hurting anything."*
If the film has played well, the director will be euphoric—a great load
has been lifted. If the film has not played well, he will call his agent
and urge him to "get me one to recoup on before this one gets out."

Another curious phenomenon is that 20 "fair" cards will out-
weigh 100 "very good" ones. Studio executives, especially, are always
more reactive to one adverse opinion than to ten which are favorable.
The very old-fashioned and palpably unrealistic attitude that a good
film should be unanimously loved still exists in the minds of many
distributors and exhibitors. That's not only improbable, it's impossible. I first learned that bitter lesson as a B director.

The film, a Karloff staple called *The Devil Commands*, was pre-
viewed at an exceptionally friendly theater in Inglewood. The house
was packed. The introductory title, THIS IS A MAJOR STUDIO PRE-
VIEW, elicited the usual anticipatory applause. Then came the first
main title card: BORIS KARLOFF in *The Devil Commands*. There
was a chorus of descending "Aahhs." Half the audience got up and
walked out. I was devastated. For a few moments I blacked out mentally. When I could think rationally again, I realized that if I had been
a disinterested viewer I, too, would have left the theater, since I never
went to see Karloff movies. It had nothing to do with the ability of
the actor or the quality of the film—not one of those leaving the
theater had seen a foot of it. It simply meant that those people did
not spark to Karloff as a primary star, or to that type of "horror film."
If they had walked out in the *middle* of the movie we would have
been in trouble. But such a film appealed only to Karloff fans, of which
there were enough in the world at large to make Columbia a neat
profit if it were produced at a controlled cost. It was and it did.

Another example of outside opinion: Some years ago, MGM produced one of Hollywood's greatest films, *Zhivago*. The nation's leading news weeklies, *Time* and *Newsweek*, reviewed it. One considered
*Zhivago* a truly great film; the other saw it as the decade's disaster.
If these intelligent, sophisticated, knowledgeable critics could have
such an extreme divergence of opinion, what can one expect from a
preview audience composed of average citizens?

In truth, the most useful preview results are those obtained by
observing the viewers *as they react* rather than by reading their "second thought" preview cards; and such reactions should be analyzed
piecemeal rather than as a whole. It is quite possible the audience
will pinpoint faults which those close to the film have overlooked

---

*It took me years to discover they weren't concerned so much with the film's
pace as with the shorter running time which would allow them to coax one more
audience per day into the theater. Some fine films have been weakened by this policy.

(sometimes due to wishful thinking). For instance, if it is a drama, does the viewer feel it is too long; is he bored? And is it *really* too long, or has it simply lost the viewer, making it seem so? This could be the result of one or more of a number of factors other than running time.

Is the film completely and continually understandable? If not, the shortcoming might be due to obscure writing, inept staging or, surprisingly often, lack of clarity in the dialogue spoken by a foreign star whose command of English is not too secure, or an English-speaking actor who equates slovenliness of speech with realism.

Is the pace too slow, allowing the viewer's attention to wander? That fault can probably be corrected in the cutting room.

Are the characters properly developed? There have been instances where, for the sake of an upbeat tempo, character development has been sacrificed in favor of action, resulting in the loss of audience interest. If the characters are not sufficiently developed, neither is the viewer's empathy.

Are some of the lines overly dramatic? Melodramatic dialogue is corny, and corn will usually elicit "horse laughs" rather than emotional reaction.

The question of laughter, or "laughs," applies to drama and melodrama as well as comedy. There should be some relief, or release, in the starkest of films. But laughs should be studied and understood. There is more than one kind of laughter, especially from a film audience. There are chuckles, chortles, snickers, the cozy laugh, the warm laugh, the hearty laugh, the belly laugh, the horse laugh, and an assortment of others less common. These are sometimes hard to distinguish or interpret. It is even harder, in the case of "bad" laughs, to analyze the cause and remove it. But it can be done. (See Book IV, Chapter 6.)

Comedy laughter is not too difficult to analyze. There is "good" and frequent laughter, there is "good" but infrequent laughter (you're in some trouble), there is no laughter (deep trouble), or there are horse laughs (put it on the shelf). The director should be aware, however, that laugh scenes in a film must be handled differently from such scenes in the theater. On the stage an actor can wait for the laugh, or continue quickly if none is forthcoming. In a film the actor and the director are in the dark, even after a preview, since not every subsequent audience will react in the same way—a fact of life which every comedian has learned. In films, the technique of choice was pioneered by the Marx Brothers, who piled laugh upon laugh in rapid-fire order. A viewer might miss a number of gags because they were covered by laughter carrying over from the previous lines, but he could come back for another showing, sit close to the screen, and catch the missed dialogue, which is exactly what a gratifyingly large number of viewers did.

Not to be overlooked is the mechanical preview, in which the audience reaction is recorded as a graph which is coordinated with the picture. If the audience is well chosen as to cross-section of the movie population, the graph will be remarkably similar for every running of the film, even though the make-up of the audience changes with each viewing. An obvious advantage of this technique is that low points of interest are objectively recorded, leaving little room for argument based on personal reaction or wishful thinking. Filmmakers who truly seek to eliminate subjective judgment, either by themselves or by others, will usually opt for the mechanical preview.

Some films, either because they are very good or hopelessly bad, require only one preview; others may need several, with changes being made between showings to correct revealed faults. At last, even these come to an end, and the director can let go—except for one final moment of agony, the press preview. The ultimate judge, of course, is the audience for whom the film is made, but the critics find that hard to accept. Based on their own individual reactions, they will rip your work to pieces or praise it to the skies. Either way, your ego is in great danger.

*Eddie Dmytryk rests a moment between takes while shooting Anzio.*

# Postscript

Beyond the immediate area of techniques necessary for intelligent filmmaking in general, there is much special, even unique, information which must be researched and acquired for each separate film. Perhaps one of the most attractive aspects of filmmaking is the opportunity it affords for seeking and gathering special knowledge in discrete fields.

During actual filming, the director will always have the assistance of one or more "technical experts," which is not necessarily an unmixed blessing. It has been my experience that *one* technical expert is not always right, as a second technical expert will be only too happy to testify. Since the director is the arbiter in any dispute, technical or otherwise, a certain amount of discreet double-checking may be needed. In any event, it behooves the director to acquire as much knowledge as he can tolerate in all the areas his film covers.

Unless the director chooses to limit himself to a single genre he will, in the course of a normal career, make films depicting characters living and working in a variety of historical periods and physical and social environments. For instance, if he is to make a serious Western, he must study the West and its inhabitants (natives, invaders, pioneers, etc.), as they *really* were, not as presented in western myth. (Although the myth will also reward serious consideration.) A Civil War film will require a careful study of the period, of northern and southern economic and social structures, armaments of the time, etc. A modern war film will, if it involves land fighting, necessitate learning a good deal about Army organization, personnel, and tactics, as well as the history of the particular war. The knowledge and information so gained will be of little use, however, if the director then makes a Navy film. The history, the education, the attitudes and philosophies, and the personalities of the men in the two services differ to such a great extent that a completely new study of the new Service would be required. Incidentally, the director will benefit immensely if he takes the time to view the hundreds of thousands of feet of "stock" material available at the respective service archives.

Oddly enough, the director not too infrequently fails to inform himself of a technique he rubs elbows with every working day: the technique of acting *for the screen.* Such acting should go hand in glove with the specific demands and advantages of the film medium, an art which has its own methods and its own results. Unless the actors can bend their special talents to the screen's requirements, no film can fulfill its ultimate promise.

# Book III

## ON SCREEN ACTING

### Written in collaboration with Jean Porter Dmytryk

*An actor must first feel the various human emotions—the reactions will follow naturally. Maximillian Schell, one of the world's finest actors, in* The Reluctant Saint.

# Introduction

Acting is almost certainly the oldest of the arts. Long before he painted the walls of his caves, primitive man staged initiation ceremonies and "counted coup," much as the American Indian did well into the nineteenth century. And "counting coup," the recital of one's courage and prowess in battle or at the hunt, often involved the most strenuous and hyperbolic (today we would call it "hammy") kind of acting.

Before the advent of the written word, the story teller was perhaps the tribe's most treasured asset; he was its geneologist, historian, and entertainer. He enjoyed protection and privileges far beyond those of most of his community. After all, even the chief was expendable, with a covey of ambitious citizens ready to take his place, but a good story teller was (and still is) hard to find. Quite obviously, the better the presentation the better the story, and the better the acting the better the presentation. The verbal story teller's art has persisted to the present era, surviving even in some relatively sophisticated modern societies.

The invention of the alphabet led to more formal and more artful techniques, all of which have been reported and described by a thousand critics, historians, and practitioners in thousands of books, which spares me the necessity of detailing them here.

Until recently, all acting performances, from the warrior singing his own praises, through the bard singing those of others, to the modern actor breathing life into some playwright's offering of suspense, action, or high drama, had two things in common—they told a story, and they had an immediate audience.

Then came the movies and the capability of recording performances for future viewing. For the first time in the long history of dramatic art the performer was divorced from his audience. To be sure, the audience was still indispensable, but it congregated somewhere down the line. In fact, the performer himself could also be a part of his own audience. But now he had to work alone, removed from the encouragement, the warm personal satisfaction he had once derived from his rapport with his auditors.

And that, in a nutshell, is the reason for a special work on acting for the screen. It is the *absence* of audience rapport, plus its corollary, the absence of the pressure imposed by its presence, as well as the freedom to place the actor at any arbitrary distance from the eventual viewer, that makes *screen* acting a different art, a more honest art, and an art that has its own premises and its own techniques. In the succeeding pages we will see what those premises are, and we will analyze the techniques that spring from them. We will do that not as teachers, but from the standpoints of the director and the performing artist.

*Actress Jean Porter talks to Jack Dawn.*

# 1

# *The Interview*

Interviews—what budding artist can avoid them? No director will risk using an untried actor without first interviewing him. Even if he has had some professional experience and/or can supply material for viewing—a test or a bit of previously shot film—a personal interview is desirable, if not mandatory.

The interview is probably the first contact between actor and director, and first impressions are important. Quite obviously, since the director is bestowing and the actor is receiving, it is the impression the actor makes on the director that is important, not vice versa.

Every director has his own prejudices, his own way of making judgments, but there are a number of factors with nearly universal application. Any young actor who neglects to consider such factors is not giving himself half a fair chance. For instance, if possible (and it usually is) he should get as much information as he can about the director in question. He should then be able, well short of obvious flattery or downright boot-licking, to present that side of his personality which will most positively impress his interlocutor. It's fine to be yourself, but don't let it all come out in a brief interview: The "self" you present may not be the "self" he will want to see on the screen or work with on the set. And for God's sake don't, in an effort at ego establishment, pontificate on the low quality of films in general. He may consider your remarks as youthful impertinence rather than mature and valid judgments of his profession.

Let us now get into specifics. Let us assume a young actress has stepped into my office for her first interview. I know that her knees are a bit wobbly and her palms are sweating, and I will do everything I can to make her feel at ease. This is not a purely unselfish exercise— I must judge her under the most nearly normal conditions possible, not as a person trying to behave naturally while suffering from considerable stress.

295

But, to repeat, first impressions *do* count, and I will waste no time, for example, on an actress who enters my office wearing "shades" and shows some reluctance to taking them off. If her eyes betray the results of a sleepless night, that is her misfortune. I will not be deprived of most of my basis for proper judgment; I must be able to see her eyes at all times. The eyes are probably the most important single feature of any actor's presence or personality (have you ever seen a dull-eyed movie star?), and unless I can see them as we talk I cannot properly judge whether or not they can bring life to a character on the screen.

I do have my prejudices, and one of them is sloppy dress. Sloppiness may be chic in your environment; it isn't in mine. An actress' manner of dressing gives me some sense of her consideration for others, as well as offering a healthy hint concerning her level of taste. Overdressing for the occasion is as bad as sloppiness. And though taste in clothing does not necessarily guarantee taste in character portrayal, more often than not it does help to make a decent impression.

The same, of course, can be said for make-up and hair styling. Punk hair-dos may be "in" in your set; I find them distasteful. Something attractive but not too startling is unquestionably safer, and probably better. Remember, at this point we are discussing impressions, not ability. You may get no opportunity to show your wares if my first impression discourages a favorable assessment of your personality.

As always, however, there is an exception. If some inside source (most probably your agent) has given you an accurate tip on the character up for grabs, by all means dress the part. If an accent is required, use it—but only if you are very, very good at accents. This can be a make-or-break situation, so be careful. If your information has been inaccurate, and you dress as a street-walker when the director is looking for a Bryn Mawr co-ed, you can blow the whole deal. So be quite sure of what you're doing, or play it safe and be yourself.

Given a positive first impression, I usually spend a few minutes in casual conversation—about anything but the purpose of the interview. Some lessening of tension is the first order of business, and it gives me the opportunity to gather at least a slight impression of the actress' character. For it is that character I must deal with before we can arrive at a character on the screen, and some knowledge of her personality is needed before I can assume that there will be a good working relationship on the set.

Unless the actress has a super-clever agent, she is probably in the dark about the nature of the part for which she is being considered. When it is time to get down to business I will disclose the role I have in mind—its purpose and its character. If my impression is positive up to this point, I will probably let her read (to herself) a scene from the script. But at this point I never ask for a "cold" reading. Some actors are quite adept at sight readings, while others find them difficult. Ability to sight-read is not an accurate measure of acting talent. Montgomery Clift read like a rank illiterate, yet few would question the brilliance of his final characterizations.

The interview draws to a close, and if I consider the actress a promising candidate I will ask if she has any film which she considers a good showcase for her ability. A film is always the easiest, and usually the best, source of information; and if the answer is positive I will make arrangements to view it, using it as a basis for my final decision. If, on the other hand, the actress has no film, or considers what she has to be inadequate or inappropriate, I will ask her to prepare a scene for a live reading.

Some actors already have such scenes in their repertoires, usually something they have worked on in an acting class, something in which they feel secure. But such scenes, as a rule, bear no relationship to the character in question, and the performance may be too practiced—so they do not always serve the director's purpose. In my experience, it does no good, and it can work active harm, to play Ophelia when the character the director wants to see is a hip kid in the 80s. That is why I usually ask the candidate to study a scene from my script as the best material for the test reading.

If the scene requires a second actor (and it usually does), I will ask her to bring him with her. This might be the actress' coach (if she attends acting classes) or it might be the most suitable member of her circle of acting friends.

In any case, no sensible director will ever take an active part in such a reading. One cannot be a competent participant and an honest observer at the same time, and here objective observation is all-important.

At such a reading I look for a number of things: How well has the actress learned her lines in the time available? Does she know them well enough to be able to be "with" her acting partner as she reads? Does she listen to him? Does she look directly at him to make her points? Can she throw away a casual line and still maintain her vitality? Does she *have* vitality? Are her reactions spontaneous or contrived? If the scene calls for laughter, does she laugh easily and well? If it calls for tears, can she manufacture her own? If the scene demands anger, does she maintain control of her voice? Can I see the "acting wheels" turning in her brain?

I do not expect perfection in any of these areas, but if the actress can get a B+ across most of the board she will probably get the job. Then the real work begins, for that series of questions relates to a good deal of what acting for the screen is all about. In the succeeding chapters we will proceed to discuss them in detail.

## THE ACTRESS SPEAKS:

When called for an interview, the first thing I do is ask my agent, or whoever, "What's the part, and what's the story like?" I will be given either very little or quite a bit of information. It's whatever he knows. It could be only, "They want a prostitute" but, on the other hand, he might say "They need a darling girl to play opposite John Travolta." And just hope he says, "They're looking for someone different." That's what you must keep in mind. With all the copying done today, too many people look alike, sound alike, and act alike. Be an individual. Believe me, it is someone different, with something new to flash, who will get the part.

If you're given a clue as to the kind of part you're going for, set that deep in your mind and start preparing to be just that. Dress for it, make up for it (or down), and actually take the character apart and build your own background for her. If you're fortunate enough to have been told what the whole story is about, that makes it easier. You know then how and why your character "is there," and what happens to her.

At this point let me say that rarely is an actor called for a part that doesn't suit. The casting office and/or the director have seen photos or perhaps your work, and what they have seen fits what they have in mind. Above all, don't ever go after a part you don't feel is right for you. But if you sincerely want it, and you're given the op- portunity to show what you can do—GO GET IT!

From the moment you are called you think of nothing else. You don't go out, you picture yourself as the character, and you live with it as much as you can until the actual interview. Then you walk into the director's office with as much self-assurance as you can muster.

You are introduced by the secretary, and you will usually find several people in the room: perhaps the producer, the writer, and sometimes a dialogue director to read lines with you. A first-class director never reads with you—he needs to watch every move you make—every expression, every reaction. He must watch you as you hear the dialogue being spoken as though you've never seen or heard it before. Often, it is what's in-between the lines that proves to be the most important.

The director is cordial and tries to make you feel at ease with a little small talk. Try your best to make him think you are at ease so you can get on with it.

The moment comes for the reading. If you have been sent the script, know it. Have it memorized. Know all the lines—his and hers and yours. Know the scene so perfectly that it seems a part of your life that you are allowing them to look in on. If you have been handed the scene in the outer office just a half hour before, do your best to learn it well enough to look up from the pages as often as possible, especially at crucial points, to show that you have a clear understanding and feel for the character.

When the reading is over, you are never sure whether they liked it or not. Even if you feel you have made a good presentation—even if the director says, "Very good!"—don't believe him. You are rarely told, "The part is yours," right there on the spot.

You thank them all, with charm and poise, and if you can remember their names (especially the director's), it's a point in your favor to say goodbye to each one personally.

As you close the door behind you, your hands trembling unnoticeably, you say goodbye cheerily to the secretary, take a quick count and account of the waiting actresses (if there are any), and out you go.

You can't think of anything else. You aren't hungry. You call your agent as soon as you get home to report your views on how it went. If you don't hear something before bedtime you try to eat a little and you try, unsuccessfully, to sleep. You imagine many things . . . your hair was wrong . . . you should have stood instead of sat . . . they didn't like you. Then you question it all. Are you right for the part? Is there someone better? You toss and turn and finally drop off just before you must get up. Every actress has a full day. As soon as you know your agent is in his office you call him, to let him know where you'll be throughout the day.

You barely make it through the aerobics class and stumble to the health bar for a snack. If you have an answering service you check that out. Nothing. You go for your voice lesson and have never felt less like singing; but you sing. The show must go on, and all that. After all, if you don't get this part there will be another one to audition for, and you must work to be at your best. But here's the secret. If you're going to get the part, you really feel it, deep down. Of course, this is where some of the greatest disappointments occur. A person knows she's done a good job, and she feels she's clinched the part. But what has happened during that endless time between the interview and the decision? It may have ended with the part being given to a better-known name, or to someone whose appearance fits more readily with the rest of the cast, or—God forbid, for this is hard to take—to the girlfriend of one of the executives.

You're home at last, still able to function, but barely. You make yourself a cup of herb tea, and the phone rings.

You've got the part!

You thought you were excited before, but now all hell breaks loose! You scream with delight, and the dog howls with you. You're on the phone to all your friends, and finally to your mother.

The agent has told you the script would be sent over by special messenger, so you don't dare go out. Pizza is delivered. The script hasn't arrived and it's bedtime. You call your agent. He calls you a pest, but you know he loves you. You've just made him a few bucks. He promises to check with the studio tomorrow.

The doorbell rings, and it's the script. "Hello, script! Oh, you marvelous thing, you!" You devour it. Up all night. Great. Great. Even though you're not the lead, you can make this part important. You turn off the phone and sleep late the next morning.

As you plug in the phone, it rings. Your agent is mad. He's been trying to reach you to tell you the script has been sent and that you are to report to the studio for wardrobe fittings in one hour.

You make it, of course. You find that the director has already okayed suggestions made by the wardrobe designer for the character you are playing. All she (or he) has to do is choose a color that suits you—one that will blend with colors worn by other actresses you will be playing scenes with. Wardrobe departments do a good job preparing far ahead of time for the whole film. By the time shooting starts you know what you'll be wearing in every scene.

If required at this time, you may be sent to the make-up and hair dressing department. The make-up man (or lady) likes to see, well ahead of time, the people who are to play key characters. He has read the script, knows the scenes and the characters, and has in mind what they should look like. Hair styles are suggested and agreed upon between you and the department heads, subject, of course, to the director's approval.

You go home after a very full and exciting day, chat with your friends on the phone, assure your mom that everything is perfect, play with the dog, do a few (neglected) exercises—then you pick up the script and get serious.

Your call is to be on the set, ready to shoot, at 9:00 A. M., Monday. This means a 7 o'clock make-up call, and that means getting up at 6:00. You will not go out all weekend. You will study the scene (or scenes) to be played on Monday. You will eat carefully and well, and you will be sure to get enough sleep. Your eyes must be clear and your mind must be alert.

During the weekend you will imagine how things will go. Reading the script, you can picture the set in your mind—you can even see yourself moving around in it. Once the film is under way you can usually count on visiting the other sets you will be working on. This helps in the preparation of the scenes involved. As you lie in bed and envision Monday's scene, you wonder if the director is seeing it as you are. What is he like? What do you know about him? What does he know about you? Have you heard that he is difficult? No. You don't really know anything. But you've had enough experience to know that he is boss. However, you mustn't be afraid to try things, *even if they're not written in the script.* Especially *if they're not writ-ten in the script. You've made notes on ideas to ask him about.*

*You wonder what the other actors will be like. You pride yourself on being able to work with all sorts of people, so you can certainly handle other actors. Your thoughts return to the director, and you call your agent to see if you can find out more about him. Your agent calls you a pest, but he fills you in on whatever he knows about the director and his way of working. You feel better. Above all, you want what the director wants. You crawl again into the character you are becoming, and you build her history. Where was she born? What were her parents like? What was her childhood like? What are her favorite foods? Colors? Does she like animals, or is she frightened of cats? Judging by her relationships with others in the script you will know how to play her. Now you wonder why the director chose you. Because you are perfect for the part. Knowing this, you are finally able to sleep.*

*The alarm goes off. It's 6 o'clock, and you're up like a shot. A tablespoon of honey and a glass of hot lemon water, steam the face with hot water, oil on the face, then cold water to close the pores. Into a pair of jeans and a top, and you're off. Total happiness. You rehearse your lines all the way to the studio.*

*Hollywood is a unique and wondrous place. As you pass other cars on the road, three out of four of the drivers will appear to be talking to themselves. Actually, they are rehearsing their lines while on their way to cut a record, do a commercial, or play a part in a film. It's a trick we have out here—driving unconsciously so that we can concentrate on something else.*

*You are on time for your make-up call. The make-up department of a studio is one of my favorite spots. It is warm and exciting, and it's fun. There's always coffee and doughnuts or danish. The first day is made easy by this wonderful group of experts. The studios hire only the best in this field, and they're well-seasoned, with mounds of experience. Each one is quick to figure you out. They know you instantly. Some will try you with little jokes and one-liners, and you watch them banter with each other. When you are alone with one, he (or she) will quickly tell you all about the others. By the time your hair has been shampooed and styled, and your make-up is finished, you feel you've known them all for ages.*

*To be "On Time" is your most important assignment in the routine end of the business. Every minute counts when shooting a film. Each minute literally costs thousands of dollars. The production department works hard to set up a schedule that will be most eco-nomically efficient for all concerned. When you are hired, the com-pany expects you to be where you are told to be at exactly the time you are told to be there. There are no excuses and no mistakes.*

If your part of the film is important enough, you will be assigned a dressing room on the lot, as well as a portable dressing room on the set. If you are this lucky, on the first day of production your wardrobe lady will meet you in the make-up department, take you to your dressing room, and help you into your costume. Your dressing room is your sanctuary and should be treated with reverence. Here you can rest, and study, and think—and be completely alone. And an actress never invites a man into her lot dressing room. She is watched, and this is a no-no. As silly as it may sound to many of you, I hope you will remember it, and consider it carefully. The film business is a serious business, and you do not want to get a reputation for playing around at work. Make dates for off the lot, and not during working hours.

After the wardrobe lady has checked your clothes, you touch up your make-up and your hair, then glance at your first scene again. You are ready. You head for the set.

*Serious discussions of character take place during the first reading, which usually precedes the scene to be shot. Here Dmytryk talks about a script with Gregory Peck and Diane Baker for* Mirage.

# 2

# *The Reading*

Few scripts are so profound that an intelligent actor will find it difficult to understand the background, the intent, or the characterizations involved. That, of course, is an exaggeration. *No* script is that profound. One that is will attract a small audience indeed. It makes no sense to assume that the script for a film made to appeal to an average audience, which means it must be understood by that audience, is so abstruse as to be beyond the grasp of the average actor.

I have never met a good actor who was unintelligent. On the contrary, the great majority of competent actors range the scale from quite to very bright. It is only the occasional writer's or director's ego, smarting at the sight of the public attention, even adulation, heaped on performers, that leads him to pretend that he possesses an esoteric knowledge of the script's characters and content denied to the actors. The director who is sometimes quoted as saying, "Actors are puppets," is probably pulling the interviewer's leg. In any case, his next film will belie his words by exhibiting the most creative cast he can buy.

There may be some casual exchange of information between actor and director during an office visit to discuss wardrobe, make-up, and so on, but understanding of character and content is usually taken for granted. Any discussion of them, if it takes place at all, usually will be left for the first rehearsal, and then it will probably concern itself with further developments and nuances rather than with basic understanding. That understanding has been there from the first reading of the script. If not—if the actors express some confusion about the screenplay and its inhabitants—it is not the artists but the script that needs overhauling.

No two directors work exactly alike, but in my experience the first serious discussion of character, in conception and realization, takes place during the readings which usually precede the first rehearsals of the first scenes to be shot. Many directors set this up for the first day of filming. Whenever possible, I prefer to arrange such a rehearsal for the day preceding the start of actual production. At this time, neither the cast, the crew, nor I are under any pressure. The butterflies have not yet started to flutter or, if they have, they do so feebly; bodies are relaxed and minds are clear and more willing to range afield. An atmosphere of exploration can now be established which will last throughout the greater part of the schedule.

In keeping with the more relaxed atmosphere, I ask my actors to read and rehearse in a casual manner, to make no effort to go all out emotionally this early in the proceedings. When the actors *do* go all out, I want it on film.

Readings come first. Before the camera is brought near the set or a single light is lit, everyone must know how the scene will go. (It will not necessarily *play* as well as it *reads*.) At this stage the director will have a good idea of how the scene will be staged, of how it will be played, but his early conceptions must not blind him to new, possibly superior avenues which may open up when the actors are allowed to offer their contributions.

The first sequence to be shot will be the subject of the reading. That sequence may be short, or scheduled for three or more days of filming. The reading should cover the entire sequence, regardless of its length.

A reading is the time for testing, for listening, for molding, and for editing. The reading, which is not really a reading, since most of the cast know their lines, allows the director to hear the actors, and the actors to hear each other, for the first time. It is a fresh, occasionally a startling, experience. Even though the performances are not full bore, the manner of playing and the range of vitality contained in the scene quickly become apparent. A line of dialogue spoken by an actor may differ considerably from the other actors' conceptualizations of that line. That, in turn, may result in an alteration in the reaction, both physical and vocal, of one or more of the other members of the cast.

One of the most important things for an actor to understand is that acting is rarely a solo performance. Other actors are involved, and if the scene is to be played at its best, their concepts and their manners of execution will inevitably affect his—as they should. A truly responsible and responsive actor will find that his own concepts and the understanding of his character and his dialogue will be broadened by the contact and interplay with the creative ideas of the other actors in the scene.

Regardless of the ideas an actor may have conceived in preparation for this moment, during the first reading he should follow the script. Many changes may eventually be made in the scene—or none— but at this point it is unreasonable to assume that changes are inevitable or necessary. And if changes are to be made it is almost always the director who will lead the way.

This must be mentioned here because scripts can be freely re-written, and they occasionally are, not always to the benefit of the film. Once in a great while an actor may propose changes solely to establish himself as a presence, not because he truly finds shortcomings in the script. Honest suggestions will be considered by most directors, but they should be based on an intelligent analysis of the character, the scene, and the effect the changes may have on the other characters in it, rather than on a desire to bolster one's own ego, or one's part.

As the readings progress and the actors become more comfortable with the scene and with each other, suggestions can be made without triggering any shock, and only a little suspicion. An actor may have found that a certain kind of shrug says, "I don't care," or "I don't know," far more effectively than does the spoken line. He should try it. If it fits, and the responding actors react naturally to the character and not just to the line, they will probably accept the meaning of the shrug without realizing that the line itself has been omitted. The director will probably note it with silent approval—he may even have had something of the sort in mind and doesn't resent being beaten to the punch. He will also realize that the actor's sense of security has reached a solid level: He is now ready to offer, and to accept, changes.

The readings may reveal further redundancies, not only in those instances where actions or attitudes can replace lines, but more commonly in lines that are too verbose. Rarely is there need at this stage for additional information through dialogue. Deletion is usually the order of the day.

There is an important, though often ignored, facet in this area of acting. A silent action such as the shrug or a subtle change in attitude allows, sometimes forces, the viewer to involve himself in the scene (and the film) by asking him to furnish his own "lyrics." The actor shrugs, and the viewer thinks, "Aha—he doesn't care." He is directly engaged. If the line is spoken he will simply sit back and listen; he has no incentive to do more. But the goal of a well-made film, or a well-turned performance, is to weave the viewer into the fabric of the film, to make him a participant in the action. The more effectively an actor can do this the more highly he will be regarded. Once upon a time actors counted their lines and evaluated their worth by their number. But Jane Wyman won an Academy Award for playing a mute, and Douglas Fairbanks, Sr. was wont to say, "Give most of the words to the other actors—just let me have the toppers."

The readings will also reveal the scene's viability, or lack of it. A scene may read well but refuse to come to life when played. This is not an infrequent occurrence. The perceptive director will immediately start looking for the fault and for the cure. Here is where an actor's instinct can be valuable. Occasionally the entire scene is sick—more often it is a dishonest line, an unbelievable bit of characterization, or the indication of an inappropriate mood. In most of these cases a correction can be found which does not require radical surgery, but once in a great while the whole sequence must be scrapped.

In order to survive the rocking of the boat, the actor must be adaptable. He must remain unthreatened even though his lines, and sometimes his concepts, are changed—"evolved" is a more positive word. There can be trouble in paradise, of course, if the actor is not convinced that such changes are an improvement on his original conception of the scene. Fortunately, however, conflicts in this area are few.

To be on solid ground during these proceedings, the actor should have done as much homework as time has allowed. A contemporary character is easy to accommodate; but in stories dealing with other times and places, books are usually the best source of information. They should be studied and absorbed until the pertinent knowledge has become second nature. For contemporary situations and characters that may be somewhat removed from the familiar, direct contact and communication is often possible. An actress may be playing an only daughter but she, herself, comes from a large family. She should find an only daughter (she probably already knows more than one), question her, grill her if necessary. She won't learn the whole story, but she will get a feel. Playing a woman cop? Talk to one. If possible, accompany her on her rounds. It can be done.

In extreme cases, prepare to sacrifice a good deal of time and a fat slice of your peace of mind. In *The Snake Pit*, Olivia DeHavilland played a woman forced to spend time in a mental institution. She committed herself to one for, I believe, a period of two weeks. Under the best of circumstances it must have been a heart- and mind-wrenching experience, but it resulted in an Oscar-winning performance. A more squeamish actress could hardly have done as well.

Readings are not usually too difficult or too long. Sometimes there is little, or nothing, to be improved. But when one does expose a problem, a successful solution will eliminate most of the questionable elements in the scene. It is now set, but it still remains to be fully realized. The next step in the procedure is the rehearsal.

### THE ACTRESS SPEAKS:

*Everyone loves the movies, and almost everyone who comes to Hollywood wants to visit a "movie studio." That means they hope to set foot on a real sound stage and get a glimpse of what filmmaking is all about.*

*The sound stage is huge. It must accommodate several sets with walls of normal height while leaving plenty of space aloft for the enormous lights that are needed. Above the imaginary walls are scaffolds on which electricians walk while tending their lights. Sometimes there is need for a crane on which the camera moves about. The stage is usually square, with doors on at least two sides, often three. Huge doors that roll open are for the big items. Beside each there is a normal, warehouse-type door, but it is double. The first door allows you in from the studio street, but at the top of the second door is a light, and if that light is glowing red it signifies that the company inside is shooting, and not a sound can be made. You must wait until the light goes off before entering through the second door. The entire stage is padded, sound-proofed. Unless the film is a comedy, a musical, or a musical comedy, most stages are very, very quiet. And very dark.*

*I walked into Stage 6 and found it very quiet and very dark. Carefully stepping over large cables, I made my way to one side. As my eyes adjusted, I saw a light up ahead and heard voices. A laugh lightened my step. I came upon the set, not yet lit, and I noticed the director and some of the crew chatting and having coffee. The assistant director came to me and offered to show me to my set dressing room. The director immediately spoke my name and said pleasantly, "Don't get too comfortable, we're going to have a reading as soon as everyone's here."*

*Trying to be very business-like, I went into my portable dressing room and placed a few things on the make-up table, calling it "mine." It's important to have a place of your own to withdraw to while in the middle of another world. That make-up table, with all the lights surrounding it, makes you feel like a star. You quickly remind yourself that you're not. Not yet. I picked up my script and returned to the set. The other actors were there.*

*The director was jovial and spoke of some humorous article in the morning's paper, which led the leading man into a story of his own. He was a name actor, so I had seen his work but I was not acquainted with him. This gave me the opportunity to look him over, to laugh at his joke, to make eye-to-eye contact to let him know I was friendly. The other actress seemed composed. I wondered what she was composed of. Beauty, for sure. But there was no jealousy here. Far from it. I wanted to appear professional, so I was hanging back until I was on.*

*The director took charge, told us where to sit and took his place in his own chair, which had been carefully placed where he could easily watch us. The leading lady opened her script to the scene. I did the same. The leading man said he didn't have his script with him—could he use someone else's? One was quickly handed to him.*

*(Was he going to be a problem?) We all knew our lines, but the scripts are always kept at hand in case there are any changes made for later study. The crew stood quietly by, and the director said, "Okay, let's have a listen."*

*The leading man started the scene, and I thought he was terrific. The other actress had a line, and she was okay. She was beautiful. My lines were coming up. I hadn't realized I was nervous, and I was late in speaking. I knew it, but the director didn't say a word. He let the scene finish with no interruptions.*

*"Now," he said, "I have just a few suggestions." I knew it. I bit my lip. "Since each of you knows the entire story," he continued, "you know what has happened prior to this scene, and you know what follows—let's see if we can't get more comfortable with the characters, get them to know each other."*

*He then cut out a few pauses that had been written in for the leading lady and suggested that she interrupt the leading man at one point, tightening the scene. And, of course, he wanted me on my toes—no dead air, shall we say? He spoke to us softly and kindly, but we were well aware of the importance behind what he was saying. He wanted something special from each of us.*

*An "on the set" reading can be different with each director. I had done a small part in a less important film not long before, and only enough time was spent on the reading to show that we knew our lines, after which we went quickly into the set for a rehearsal. Within half an hour we had our first set-up "in the can." (For those of you who don't know this expression, it means completed, in the tin, since rolls of finished film are placed in a flat, round tin can.) Naturally, this technique does not turn out the quality one might desire, but time is money, and sometimes there just isn't enough time or money for a director to get exactly what he wants on film. So he does the best he can. He expects the actors to know their lines perfectly and, more often than not, to stick to the script as it's written.*

*For live TV the readings are of prime importance. Contracted for two weeks to do a one-hour live show, I was called in for a full eight-hour session every day. The entire cast sat around a large table and read through the whole script—over and over. It was much like theater work, except that we could make dialogue changes. The director was good in his field, but the pressure of his job made him irritable and unsure of himself. By the time we were ready to shoot— live, in front of an audience—even Agnes Moorehead vowed never to do live TV again. And she didn't. This is the most difficult on-camera acting, because you can't be natural while worrying about tripping over cables as you change costume on the run, hoping to walk calmly through a doorway. Though many jokes are made after it's over, it is* deadly. *But you can see why the readings are so important.*

Back to the present situation; the director called for another reading. We were much more relaxed, and the timing was improved. He did break in here and there until we were close to what he wanted. He told us not to give our total emotion, to save it for the camera, so I was anxious to get going.

The scene we were preparing to shoot would come in the middle of the film, so my character was not only familiar with the other two—she had had a fight with the leading lady, gone on the make for the leading man, been rejected by him, and had lied to her father (a local gentleman of power) to get the leading man in trouble.

The director called for the cameraman and told us we would now move into the set for a rehearsal. Everyone listens when the director talks and tries to anticipate his plans. All of a sudden the set was lit by several large lights and it was daytime in a ranch house somewhere in the West.

*In this scene from Metro-Goldwyn-Meyer's humorous tale of teenage autograph seekers,* The Youngest Profession, *pert Jean Porter is surrounded by a cast that includes Edward Arnold, Marta Linden, and Agnes Moorehead.*

# 3

# *The Rehearsal*

The scene has been analyzed, the lines set, the characters developed and integrated, but there is more to be considered. How and where do players move? Or do they?

Most scenes do, of course, contain movement, but no law makes movement mandatory. Physical movement, though often advantageous, is not a "given" for all scenes.

Today, many students and young filmmakers appear to believe that physical, mechanical (i.e., movement of the camera) or editorial (cutting) movement is necessary to keep a scene interesting. This is a misconception: These are valid only as ameliorative techniques in the event a scene is badly written or inadequately realized. The movement which should concern the filmmaker is the movement which takes place in the viewer's mind, and the actors play a most important part in the process that makes such movement possible. A scene can be completely effective without the staging of a single move if that scene is well written, well played, and of real consequence.

A scene in one of Orson Welles' films showed several people discussing, at great length, an important family problem. They sat in a loose group, more or less immobile, for several minutes, yet the scene remained vital—moving and alive. On more than one occasion I have allowed a scene in which the actors were relatively quiescent to run, uncut, for nearly ten minutes because I felt that any arbitrary move or cut would have been simply gilding the lily, and just as artificial.

It is still true, however, that most scenes contain physical movement, movement whose purpose is to disclose "business," to reveal or conceal emotion, or to express physical nervousness or inner tension. For example, a character may walk over to a desk to pick up a relevant paper, or a pencil, or he may turn away from the other par-

313

ticipants in the scene and walk a few steps in order to hide an emotion or a tell-tale reaction, or simply to gather his thoughts before turning back to continue the conversation. He may stand up, or walk, to relieve some tension building up in his mind or body or, on an exterior location, he may be talking to a companion while walking toward his parked car or to the entrance to his apartment.

Movement is also used to accentuate dramatic timing. A pause while seated may appear to be simply a stall, but the same pause, or even a longer break in the conversation, can project a great deal more meaning if the actor is allowed to express the unuttered conflict, or change in attitude, through movement. Just as a vital reaction can be heightened if the reactor is looking away at the moment of thought impact and is forced to turn sharply toward the person speaking,* so more extensive moves can be used to accentuate those transitions which are the lifeblood of every well-written and well-realized scene.

It is important for the actor to realize that any such movement should be made for a reason, and made decisively. Nothing can deflate a scene as quickly as a weak, tentative move. If one player walks away from another in order to withdraw, say, from an embarrassment, a confrontation, or a verbal challenge, that move must be made purposefully. At such a moment, sauntering will completely undercut the desired effect. As a matter of fact, it is hard to conceive of a situation in which a casual or lethargic move is useful, except when such a move has a specific dramatic purpose.

In short, actors must consider their moves as thoroughly as they do their lines, and then proceed to incorporate them skillfully into their performances.

(A scene stands out vividly in my mind: I am staging a shot for *Raintree County* in which Monty Clift enters a bedroom where his wife (Elizabeth Taylor), pregnant, out of sorts, and restless, lies uncomfortably in bed. As he enters the room Clift's left hand swings the door shut behind him, but his right hand, also behind him, catches it before it can slam shut. Taking a short step backward, he closes the door softly. Only then does he move toward the bed and his wife.

After the rehearsal, while the cameraman is lighting the set, Clift spends at least twenty minutes in practice. He walks through the door, swings it behind him, catches it in motion, then closes it, all without any apparent attention to the action. He wants to make it look as though he has been through *this* door, in *his* bedroom, in *his* home, a thousand times, and that the whole procedure is strictly second nature, performed without the slightest conscious thought; his *conscious* attention is centered on his ailing wife. And that's exactly how it looks when we finally film the scene.)

---

*This acting trick, however, must be used sparingly—for obvious reasons.

The rehearsal which follows the reading takes all these aspects of movement into consideration. Indeed, that is its primary purpose. The movement rehearsal, or staging, is always initiated by the director. Most probably, he already has his basic set-ups in mind, and his staging, at least in the early rehearsals, will be determined by such plans. However, the creative director will always leave the door open for further development of movement and meaning as the rehearsals progress. As a rule, the original concepts will hold and few, if any, changes will be called for; but, as the actors work their way into the scene and begin to feel at home with it in all of its aspects, opportunities to improve the flow or the effectiveness of the scene may occasionally arise. An actor's suggestion in this regard will rarely be rejected out of hand.

However, the actor should always be aware of an important consideration. Some suggestions may be impractical because they do not suit the director's filming and cutting concepts. A movement may be too broad, for instance, to be easily accommodated by the most effective set-ups, or it may be conceived without due regard to the movements and/or the positions of the scene's other actors. Few directors are reluctant to treat such suggestions summarily, dismissing them quickly, with or without explanation, if they disrupt the homogeneity of the scene. On the other hand, only an insecure director would refuse to incorporate into his scheme of things a suggestion bringing improvement to the scene's content or effectiveness. In any event, the making of such a suggestion is worth the risk. Even one success in twenty attempts can serve to sweeten the pot.

Once the rehearsal has fixed movement and position, and the actors find themselves comfortable with the scene and with each other, the rest of the crew takes over. While the film machinery is moved into place and the cameraman starts to light the set and the stand-ins, the actors retire to their dressing rooms and their separate activities, whether they be rehearsing lines, dressing for the scene, or freshening make-up. At this time any lingering doubts or uncertainties should be discussed with the director. Because the next step is the real thing. The culmination of all the preparation, the studying, the reading, and the rehearsal will now be fixed on film and tape or, as they say on the set, "recorded for posterity."

## THE ACTRESS SPEAKS:

*The set was a large living room, with an entryway and staircase in the background. Two walls were movable to accommodate camera placement. The scene called for my character to come down the stairs, see the other two talking in the living room, and go to them. Their conversation is interrupted by my entrance.*

*My tendency is to move too fast. I had been told that more than once before on film jobs, so I planned to be more careful this time. But the young girl I was playing was bouncy, bright and, because of her youth, much too sure of herself.*

*While the crew watched, the director called for a rehearsal. The cameraman stood with the director. The other two actors and I had exchanged a few words and walked around the set, touching the furniture, getting acquainted with the props.*

*This was my home. The leading lady was my sister, and the leading man had been her beau. He had gone away to college and was back in town before taking a job somewhere up north. While he was away, studying, big sister had become involved with a new man around town and little sister (THAT'S ME!) had grown up. (You think you know the whole story already, don't you?)*

*I went to the top of the staircase, getting the feel of the stairs that I must treat as though I had been up and down them daily for eighteen years. I counted them, measured their width in comparison with my feet. In drama school I had learned a dozen ways to climb stairs and float, or clamber, down. This girl should be light on her feet but, most of all, completely unaware of the movement.*

*"All right, let's go," the director said. He had placed the two stars where he wanted them to stand and gave me an idea of where I should end up. "Just a run-through," he said.*

*I ran to the top of the stairs, then reminded myself to stop running.* Slow down! *This is what I had to keep in mind.*

*"Action!" the director said, and I was off. I scooted down the stairs, neatly nonchalant, paused near the bottom as I spotted the two people in the living room standing close to each other talking quietly. Then I moved toward them until I reached the point at which I had been told to stop.*

*The leading man—let's call him Ben—had his back to the stairway and had not seen me. My sister's reaction to my entry was to reach out and touch him to stop his talking, and her look to me drew his attention in my direction. This part of the scene was* mine.

*Here is a very important thing to be aware of and to remember. You find yourself realizing how important the scene is to the story, and how important your part is to the scene. If the scene is totally concerned with the information you are giving the viewer through dialogue and/or action, you can become awfully cocky. You are certain that you can't be cut out and that you can't be cut away from, either. The scene is yours. Watch out! This is the disease called Star Syndrome. Whether you are the star or not. All of a sudden a kind of euphoria sets in, and you can do no wrong. You have all kinds of ideas that are perfect.*

*Now is the time for all good men to come to the aid of this person. She is in trouble. Now is the time you must listen carefully to the director, and believe what you hear. Like a pilot, you'd better believe the instruments.*

*This is not meant to curb your enthusiasm or squelch your desire to incorporate some innovative ideas that have come to your mind, but if you're not careful at this point, you can annihilate your relationship with the director and the other actors. When you have everything, be generous.*

*The director gently moved me to one side and spoke quietly. I had come down the stairs too fast, had moved forward too quickly, not giving anyone else time to do anything. I apologized, and told him I would move very slowly. I went back up the stairs, he called "action" again, and I pulled in the reins. It even felt better. I had thought the previous rehearsal was okay, but when it's right, you know it's right. I came down the stairs lightly, paused at the sight of the two, and sauntered over to them. The timing was right for the other actors, giving them time to react.*

*My sister had the first line as I reached them, so it was suggested by the director that I pass her and plop down on the couch. Her eyes followed me as she spoke, which put her on camera. Now all three of us were in good camera view.*

*She wasted no time at all in chastising me for what I had done. As the rehearsals continued, I did a good job at listening. Then I had my turn. By this time I was on my feet, walking slowly around them. Suddenly I stopped for the big clincher line. I looked directly into my sister's eyes, spoke quietly, and soon the tears started to roll down my cheeks. Up to this point everyone in the audience found my character a naughty little smart-alec, and would have enjoyed seeing her done in. Now they had to weep for the poor darling.*

*This is what it's all about.*

*One must be technically skilled enough to fake any mood, yet make it believable. You must believe it.*

*Movement was as much a part of the scene as the dialogue. As we rehearsed, it all came together. With the director's guidance, the movements became so natural that a move would bring forth a line, or stop someone in the middle of a sentence. By the time we were ready to shoot the first set-up, we knew how the whole sequence would go, and we were comfortable with each other.*

*After being told to freshen our make-up and to get ready to shoot, the director came up beside me and walked with me toward my dressing room.*

*"You're really doing a good job," he said, "but I told you to hold back the emotion—the tears—during the rehearsal. I don't want you all cried out."*

*"Oh, that's all right. I can't help it," I answered.*

"Those were real tears. How come you can cry so easily?" he asked.

"Hey. In this world, the way it is, it's holding back the tears that's difficult. When given an open invitation to cry—that's easy."

It just so happened that my part was well written, and I understood the inside workings of this character from having known people like her. Getting to know and understand people in every walk of life, all situations, is the key. Of course, it can be heart-breaking. And you will cry.

*Actors and actresses must learn to limit their field of attention and block out the presence of the camera, the director, and the crew. Edward Dmytryk directs Guy Madison and Jean Porter in a scene from* Till the End of Time.

# 4

# *"Where Did Everyone Go?"*

The set is lit. Last-minute rehearsals for sound and camera have been held. Lighting retouches have been completed. The time for shooting has arrived. What does the director look for in the playing of a scene?

First of all, are the actors working with each other, or are they conscious of external distractions? The necessity to concentrate on the scene, on the one hand, and awareness of people and objects on the stage surrounding the immediate set, on the other, confront the actor with contradictory apprehensions.

Two technical, nonacting requirements are ever-present, and either can be a troublesome stumbling block. First is the need to "hit the marks" accurately—to stay within the range of the key lights. The director sets up his camera for the positions and movements which will most effectively capture the players' reactions and the mood of the scene. In turn, the cameraman sets his lights for those positions, and the actors must hit their marks with some accuracy if the lighting and the resulting recorded images are to be satisfactory. Yet they must never reveal, by attitude, reaction, or conscious bodily adjustment that they are searching for their marks—or reaching them.

Concentrating more on the marks than on the substance of the scene will produce a mechanical performance. An actor cannot possibly involve himself completely in the dramatic give-and-take of a scene while worrying about his position relative to the camera and his key light.

Experienced actors have learned to take these requirements in stride. Like heat-seeking missiles, they "feel" a key light instinctively, and if they are in it they are probably on their marks. Beyond that, they can reduce the problem by relating their moves to other actors

321

or to objects on the set: a table, a chair or sofa, or some other piece of set dressing which may be at hand.

Of course, a considerate director can make it somewhat easier for the actor by asking the cameraman to light more broadly (though well short of "flat" lighting), thus giving the player some leeway in his moves. Only in close shots is exact positioning of prime importance, and most such set-ups call for little movement from the actor.

This is one of the more difficult adjustments a screen actor must make; but once he has learned to accommodate it instinctively, he can become freely and completely involved in the scene itself—well, almost.

The second necessary adjustment may be even more difficult. The actor must learn to limit his field of attention. He must black out the presence of the camera, the director, and the crew. This is made somewhat easier for him by an obligatory convention: Off-the-set lights are usually extinguished, leaving everything except the set in darkness. Crew members retire to the back of the stage or behind the camera. The actors' "eye-lines," i.e., those directions in which they look during any part of the scene, are kept free of people or objects that might attract or distract the actors' attention. The director will place himself close to the camera, or even under it. This enables him to see the scene from the camera's point of view and serves to diminish his visibility.

All this is done to facilitate the actor's effort to "live" with his collaborators in the scene. He must listen to *them*, react to them, and speak to them, not for the camera, the director, or the crew. For the good screen actor there is no audience, only fellow beings involved in a happening of substance. It is the only way a scene can be made to come alive and include the viewer as a participant rather than as an onlooker.

Perhaps the best way for the actor to cut off the distractions of the real world is to *listen* to the people in his world of make-believe. Concentration on listening serves to tune out distractions, both audible and visual. Anyone who has held a quiet conversation in the midst of a babbling crowd can testify to that. So, the harder the actor listens the more effectively he is able to disregard the disturbances inherent in shooting on the set.

Of course, one must listen to the "character," not the player—rapt attention should not slop over into the area of self-hypnosis. During the shooting of *One-Eyed Jacks*, an on-camera actor was listening to off-camera Marlon Brando delivering his off-stage lines. The actor's cue came—and went. He stood there spellbound and speechless.

"Cut!" yelled actor-director Brando, as he advanced on the actor. "Where, in God's name, *were* you?"

"Mar," replied the actor, "you were so wonderful, so overpowering, I was lost in admiration."

By that time the light was getting yellow, and Brando called it a day.

Stopping short of idol worship (or clever alibi) the most important skill an actor must develop is the ability to listen, which is not exactly a universal aptitude. Yet listening, *really* listening, not just pretending to listen, is the necessary prerequisite for nearly every other facet of screen acting; most of the actor's other skills—reacting, speaking dialogue, even movement—are inspired by what he hears.

The greatest compliment one actor can pay another is to say, "He *gives* me something!" What he appreciates is that his fellow player is heeding his words and observing his behavior; that he is, quite literally, giving him *attention*. And in keeping with the well-known Biblical prescription, the giver derives more benefit from his gift than does the receiver.

The camera is a powerful telescope; just try to estimate the relative size of a normal close-up on a "wide" screen. If the actor is concentrating on his next line instead of listening to the speaker, it can easily be seen, especially in a close-up, but also, to somewhat less effect, in a medium shot as well. And by far the greater part of the average film consists of medium shots and close-ups. Only in the occasional long shot will the absence of listening escape the viewer's attention, and even then he may react subconsciously to the lack of a proper attitude.

Keen observation is a necessary concomitant of sharp listening. The good actor concerns himself not only with the proper delivery of a line of dialogue, but also with the physical manifestations that accompany it. In fuller shots these may include relatively broad gestures and body moves, but in large close-ups, where such gestures and moves are discouraged, there are still tiny displays of those facial movements which commonly accompany speech. (A "frozen" face becomes an object of humor or of pity.) Such movements, whether they are broad or delicate, are an essential part of communication, both in real life and on the screen. They underscore the meaning of the spoken words—or belie them—but always they are unavoidable reinforcements. They supply nuances and almost always serve to round out the total message delivered in any line of dialogue.

With all this in mind the actor must watch his fellow players intently (unless, of course, inattention or avoidance of visual contact is the point of the scene) and listen intently. When he does so, his responses, both in reaction and in dialogue, will be generated by what he receives from the speaker, not just what he remembers of the script, and it will be much easier for him to make those responses appear to be spontaneous rather than arbitrary. At best, they *will* be spontaneous, and real-life spontaneity is the goal of every well-played scene.*

Here I am reminded that a third semitechnical adjustment is required in the search for spontaneity. It concerns the *repetition* of a scene—more properly, a "take,"—while shooting. A few actors—Tracy, Bogart, and Clift come to mind—rarely needed more than one take to register their optimum performances. Obviously, they had a minimum amount of trouble in achieving spontaneity. Most actors, however, need several tries at reaching "perfection" (a few will climb to forty, fifty, or more) and such repetition makes achievement of spontaneity very difficult indeed, not only for the actor speaking the lines, but also for the actor listening to them.

Perhaps the best way to arrive at a freshness of approach with each succeeding take is to *listen afresh*: to look for possibly unnoticed nuances in the readings or the physical attitudes of the other player. Unless he is an extremely mechanical actor (in which case he shouldn't be working in films), the player will usually have some variation, however slight, in each take; and it is that variation the listening actor should be looking for.

Willie Wyler had a reputation for shooting innumerable takes of every scene, though he would rarely, if ever, tell the actors involved what nuance he was seeking. He was actually relying on their doing "something different" instinctively in every take; and when that something "different" was something "right," Wyler had his desired take.

Of course, the something different also brings out a different reaction, but even if the speaker *is* a "mechanic" and repeats his earlier performances exactly, the very effort of looking for something new will serve to divert the listener's attention from the problem of repetition and to direct it toward the possibilities of change rather than the deadliness of rote.

### THE ACTRESS SPEAKS:

*When our picture was finished and in the theaters, this is the way the audience saw that scene. As my sister starts her tirade against me, I'm seated on the couch (a group shot). The audience watches her face, but as I rise and start walking around, it also watches my movements. At one point I turn to her and break into her speech with a line. They cut to a close shot of me as I start speaking, then, halfway through, they cut to a matching close shot of my sister listening to*

*Every student of acting should study Jack Lemmon's performance in, Missing. One careful viewing is worth a month of exercises. Here is attention at its highest level. The intensity of his listening, and watching, is awesome. His bodily movements and attitudes are also something to study, but these aspects of acting will be discussed in a later chapter.

me. They stay on her while she starts her answer, letting the audience digest her words, then cut to a close shot of me—listening. The audience listens with me while watching me fall apart as my sister's words expose me for the child that I am and make me face the unattractive truth of what I have done. The tears collect in my eyes and start rolling down my cheeks. I start my last line, but I don't need to finish it—I have to turn and run out. Good scene. Excellently directed. Superbly cut.

On this particular film, with this director, I became aware more than ever before of the importance of listening—of keeping the audience aware of your feelings at all times. The "scene-stealer" is an actor who keeps the viewer's eyes on him every minute he is on the screen, no matter what else is being done or who is doing it. The expert scene-stealer does this without making enemies of the rest of the cast. It isn't necessary to do anything more than what comes naturally.

The point is, the director shoots a large part of the scene in several different set-ups—group shots, over-the-shoulder shots, and close shots—of exactly the same dialogue. And an actor can't be certain which shots will be used. Even the director probably doesn't know at this point. He will decide when he has seen them all. But you must never let yourself get out of character from the minute he calls "Action!" A professional, a really good actor, plays it all the way and gives the other actors someone to play to.

Making a film is a collective effort of the entire cast and crew. If one person fails in his job the film is in jeopardy. The crew—the electricians, the gaffers, the prop men, the make-up, hairdresser and wardrobe personnel—all are there to help you look good on the screen. This does not make you more important. They expect you to do your job well so they can be proud of their work. And if you behave in a professional manner (on time, know your lines, be ready, and don't hold anyone up) you will be well liked, joked with, and treated as one of them. This makes for a happy company when the cast and crew look forward to each day's working together.

Confinement to space and marks bothers some actors in the beginning, but you can get used to this during rehearsals. You can hit your marks without ever looking down, by becoming aware of the location of people and/or furniture close to your stopping points. You can help the cameraman by feeling your light and watching shadows during rehearsal, and the other actors will appreciate knowing you are aware of their lights.

To be comfortable with your part, your character, is number one. Number two is to feel at home on the set, with the crew—this gives you the added confidence and support you need. So that when all the stage lights go out and only you are lit for the scene, the transition is smooth. Not a worry in the world.

*The faces of Rhonda Fleming, Regis Toomey, Dick Powell and Richard Erdman are waiting for a reaction from Jean Porter caught pick-pocketing in* Cry Danger.

# 5

# *"Make a Face"*

Sometimes it pays to go back to basics, to define our terms.

REACT: To be moved to action in response to an influence or a particular stimulus.
STIMULUS: Something that incites to action or exertion.

Two of the world's leading actors, Laurence Olivier and Alec Guiness, have recently indulged in some loose talk, or they have been misquoted. Each has reportedly said that screen acting is, in effect, "doing nothing." Such a statement may be simply a display of excessive modesty, a caution against "acting," or overplaying, a comparison of the relative intensities of acting for the stage or the screen, or it may be meant to indicate the necessity to avoid theatrical pretense in film acting. I refuse to believe, however, that it was intended to be taken literally. Certainly, listening and observing are not "doing nothing." Nor is proper reacting.

It has often been said that *reacting* is the essence of acting for the screen—and, by definition, to "react" is to respond to a particular stimulus. The stimulus, whether it be an idea, an emotion (like anticipation, fear, or grief) or the brain's recognition of a physical sensation like hunger, thirst, or an itch, may be generated within the actor himself. More often, perhaps, the stimulus comes from the outside, from another character in the scene, or from some circumstance or combination of circumstances outside the actor's control. There may even be more than one stimulus, leading to contradictory reactions and eventual *in*action. But the stimulus is always a positive force, even when it results in an indecisive or a negative response.

It necessarily follows that responding to stimuli is a continuous—an on-going—activity. As long as consciousness is present, it never stops. And it must never be allowed to stop on the screen.

From a director's point of view the response to stimulus (commonly called a "reaction") is perhaps the most important element in a film.* Every competent director searches his script for those moments that make the film *move,* and movement is impossible without change, whether physical or mental. Each change, or transition, necessarily alters the course of the character's subsequent action, thus enriching the plot and keeping the film alive.

The viewer recognizes a transition only through the player's reaction. A response to some physical action is easily understood; but a reaction to a new idea or intention, as expressed in a line of dialogue, is much more difficult to realize. The line itself rarely shows a transition since it is usually the pronouncement of a change already made by the speaker: It merely states a position and is, therefore, static. The listener's *reaction* to the stated idea contained in the line shows us the change in *progress,* which is dynamic.

I must emphasize here that the physical manifestation of a reaction, no matter how important, should not be exaggerated. "Broad" reactions are occasionally called for but on the screen the subtle reaction is usually the best—even in comedy. Our greatest comedians, men like Chaplin, Keaton, and Langdon, contrived broad, sometimes wild situations, but their *reactions* were usually remarkably subtle.

In dialogue scenes the reaction is almost always triggered while listening. The trigger which stimulates the response rarely comes, like a word cue, at the end of a line. It comes at the moment the *sense* of the line becomes apparent; and if that is obvious early on, as is frequently the case, the response will come well *before* the triggering line is completed. Such a reaction is usually visual, but when it is accompanied by a vocal response, the result is a natural interruption.**

A brief aside. Some years ago, writers realized that an actor *could* step on another actor's lines; that, in fact, it was not only a more honest, a more realistic reaction, but it was often more dramatic. That realization led to an interesting script-writing convention: Most dialogue was designed as a series of open-end or unfinished lines which were meant to be stepped on. However, in order to protect the "integrity" of his dialogue, a writer would still write the complete line, then add a few sacrificial words—an incomplete phrase—which the responding actor could interrupt while leaving the original line in the clear. But, since the proper reaction was still inspired by the proper stimulus (somewhere in the original line), the responding actor was forced to delay his response artificially for an additional and unrea-

---

*The failure to understand this sinks many screen writers. They are satisfied to write lines which provide the stimulus, but take the reaction for granted. In fact, the *reaction* is much more important than the line which stimulates it.

**See Book IV, Chapter 9, for a more complete analysis.

sonable length of time. This was dishonest, destroying reality and the scene's pace and rhythm. I believe this convention is now used only sparingly, if at all. It is far better for an actor to find and fix his own timing when confronted by the need for an overlapping reaction, even if it cuts the written line short.

The best reactions are a *natural* result of paying attention; they should be inborn and simple. Except in broad comedy or when contriving a deception, there is *never* any need to pretend, to manufacture a visual response—to "make a face." On the screen the camera accentuates reaction by magnifying the source, and the closer the shot the greater the need for limiting the reaction to the eyes alone. The honest reaction in life is usually a controlled one: Broad reactions, unless gradually approached, immediately label the reactor an extreme neurotic or a fraud. Even reactions—or, I should say, especially reactions—to extreme stimuli such as an announcement of death or a sudden infliction of pain must be very carefully considered.

As a rule, the immediate broad reaction to the announcement, "He's dead!" is very artificial and is so perceived by the viewer. The human brain and body usually react to such a crisis with a traumatic shock that temporarily prevents understanding and acceptance of the situation. It diminishes, or stops altogether, any immediate emotional response. The same is true for extreme pain, as anyone who has suffered a severe accident can testify. The shock of such a trauma often prevents the victim from even being aware that an injury has occurred.

Of course, not all reactions are quick or overlapping. When the sense of a spoken line is purposely obscure or (rarely) profound, the reaction must be extended and the subsequent vocal response delayed. If the meaning of such a line is intended to be grasped by the *viewer*, he must be given time to riddle it out. He can get that required time only if the player's visual reaction is arbitrarily prolonged. This may pose a difficult acting problem.

Because of prolonged script study and rehearsal, the actor knows the line and its meaning thoroughly; and he will frequently shorten his reaction, responding vocally before the viewer, who is hearing the line for the first time, can fully grasp its significance. It must always be kept in mind that, in a film, there is no leafing back to refresh one's memory, to restudy a statement. If the meaning is meant to be understood it must be made clear the first time around: The viewer must be given the time to absorb and analyze the given information. Obviously, it is preferable that the actor (with the help of the director) should estimate the time needed for such understanding and supply it through an extended reaction.*

---

* As a film editor I have, on a number of occasions, found it necessary to lengthen over-quick reactions by the use of special techniques. (See Book IV, Chapter 10.)

However, if the actor exhibits conscious awareness of the timing requirement, such a reaction will appear to be contrived. Just as he must conquer the problem of repetition in the interest of spontaneity, so he must solve the problem of arbitrarily imposed timing for the sake of audience understanding. The best way to block out such pre-performance awareness is to listen to the line in question as if it were a puzzler whose meaning is more complex than anticipated. Even if the complexity is not present, the listener's *search* for it will require the addition of an extra beat to the reaction. That beat will allow the viewer to catch up with him in his understanding. (It must be noted that the average script contains relatively few lines whose meaning requires extended reaction time.)

## THE ACTRESS SPEAKS:

*Study the stars.*

*Yes, even look to the heavens for help. Many of our great screen actors and actresses are gone, but we can be thankful to the film people who have protected and preserved their works. Watch the old movies on TV; look for special programs at museums; in most cities you'll find at least one theater manager who realizes that many people enjoy the old movies, the big stars.*

*Ladies, study Marlene Dietrich, Joan Crawford, Bette Davis, Ingrid Bergman. Oh, there are more, but these greats come quickly to mind because each had a style of her own that made her a star. It's easy to impersonate any one of these women, and in doing just that you can see what kept them in the limelight for so long.*

*For instance, pretend you are Dietrich, standing in a courtroom, favoring camera right, and someone speaks to you from camera left. Have you noticed how her eyes always move in the direction she is going to turn before she ever moves her head or her body? This is an important effect for the screen. In fact, it's delicious! She ALWAYS does it. It gives her time before she starts her next line. With it she captures the audience, then holds it throughout the scene. Just with this effect. I've often wondered how she discovered it. Her eyes move as far as they can to the right (camera left), then her head slowly turns until she locks eyes with her opponent or lover. Get it? Practice it. Most often you will find that your mouth will open slightly as you turn your head, just as hers did.*

*And how about that Joan Crawford? She snapped her head in response most of the time. She was famous for her snappy retorts. Pretend you are Crawford, standing in a courtroom, favoring camera right, and someone speaks to you from camera left. The moment the line is finished she snaps her head and looks directly into the speaker's eyes, then starts her line. This, too, grabs the audience. With flashing eyes, she is on fire, and they are with her all the way. Bette Davis was also famous for this attack, even for love scenes.*

*Bergman. Study the way she looks into the eyes of her lover, pulling her eyes up from the floor; study her steadiness and her passion. Have you watched her nostrils during a love scene? YES! Her nostrils widen and close, widen and close, as she becomes more passionate. Acting? Yes, and only for the screen. Only the camera can pick up nostril action, and believe me, it's an emotional jolt.*

*Men, study Bogie, Gable, Bill Powell, Spencer Tracy, and Jack Lemmon. Here again, others come to mind, but these greats had/ have such style—each with his own personality, of course, but also a trick or two. Bogie seems always to be studying the face of whoever works opposite him. Whether playing a lover or a heavy, his eyes shift and sift for information from his co-actor. With this tenseness, he makes you so aware of his emotions that you know what he's going to do before he does it—a smack on the lips or a smack in the face. And isn't it marvelous when he fools you and turns his back and walks out on the woman to whom he has just said the most beautiful things?*

*Gable. What can you say about the King who became a fine actor after he was a star? His looks and personality made him famous, then he realized that to hold on to stardom he'd better really learn how to act. In an interview, he once credited Spencer Tracy with showing him the way to relaxed easiness and more naturalness.*

*Tracy was the master at that. I don't believe he ever realized how great he was on the screen. He was a writer's dream. Spence could take any line, sometimes exactly as written, or with just a slight change, and make it sound as though it had just come to mind. With pauses, thinking on camera, he could convince an audience of anything.*

*Bill Powell started out playing heavies and switched to comedy to become a star. His sophisticated, clean look (even while playing a drunk) was the key, so he set his timing to fit his character.*

*Jack Lemmon is an excellent actor to study. To me, he is the perfect screen actor, from his toes to the top of his head. He can make you weep as he walks away, his back to the camera—his shoulders slump and his walk slows. You pull for him to look back at you; he pauses briefly, but continues on. Yes. Study Jack Lemmon, especially in Missing and The China Syndrome. He listens on-camera better than anyone I've ever seen.*

*All of this is to help you understand what screen acting entails. What makes a good screen actor. What makes a star.*

*And it doesn't hurt to steal a little here and there if you see something you can use to help develop your own style. Be good, but be unique.*

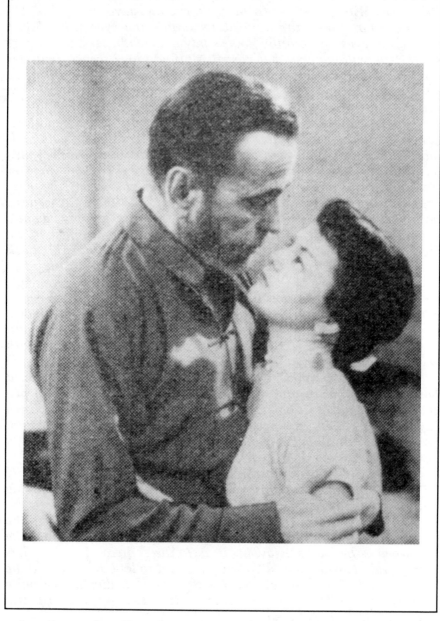

*Jean Porter plays Humphrey Bogart's Chinese girlfriend in* Left Hand of God.

# 6

# *"What Did He Say?"*

Film is an eclectic medium: There is nothing like it in the field of the arts. It can deliver a play, a ballet, a symphony, an opera, or a sermon; it can feature poetic dialogue or punk rock music, movement of various types and tempos, and even pictorial works of art.* It can present a classic tragedy or the broadest kind of comedy. In short, it can duplicate the works of any other field of art and often range beyond them. What other medium can give you *The Gold Rush, The Man of Arran, The Bridge on the River Kwai, The Wizard of Oz, Chariots of Fire, Mickey Mouse,* the action of *Bullit* or *The French Connection,* or the stark drama of the "Odessa Steps" sequence from *The Battleship Potemkin?*

This tiny selection, picked at random, exemplifies what many consider the best aspects of the medium: The films deliver their messages through the effective use of faces, reactions, attitudes, and movement rather than primarily through dialogue.

I mention this here because I (along with many others) believe that the modern film, especially as seen on the TV screen, has fallen on dull times. For a number of reasons, largely economic, most films today are merely a tiresome succession of "talking heads." In other words, with only rare exceptions, today's films are plays, and not very good plays at that.

There is nothing wicked in filming a good play. *Becket* and *A Man for All Seasons* come to mind as excellent and eminently watchable films. But to persist in filming plays is to continue using only a part of the screen's potential as art and entertainment. I think the film public deserves less talk and more movie.

The concentration on talking heads also does a disservice to stu-

*Regardless of the quality of its subject matter, a well-shot film will offer dozens of beautifully composed "pictures," though these may last for a few seconds only.

dents of acting—it tends to divert attention away from the kind of acting the best films require, the kind that has been discussed in the preceding chapters. Importance is centered on the reading of lines since that is by far the greatest concern of the average film. But the handling of dialogue is by no means the most important aspect of acting for the screen for several reasons.

To begin with, a truly objective reading of a good script will show that relatively few speeches are vitally important from a dramatic point of view. A large number of lines are "throw-aways"—that is, they do little to further the plot, they have no philosophic relevance, and generally no poetic beauty. Nor, as a rule, should they. Good plot construction is best accomplished through the proper development of the characters' reactions, and subsequent actions, to well-conceived crises (major or minor) and conflicts. Intellectual or philosophical relevance depends on the revealed depths of the characters and the dramatic presentation of their behavioral choices. And, for reasons to be discussed presently, most films have little use for vocal poetry, though there may be poetry in visual beauty and in human behavior.

An actor who uses an earth-shaking delivery when speaking a simple line is very pretentious indeed, yet I have known well-established players who have spoken a casual "Good evening" as if they were declaiming, " 'Tis the witching hour of night. . . ." The tendency toward this kind of elocution arises from the actor's inordinate respect for the written word. This not uncommon affliction is shared by a great many people who have no acting experience at all. But the actor, at least, should have an easygoing, casual relationship with words and lines, as he has with any good friends or old acquaintances.

Let us consider the sanctity of the written word. There is, of course, no such thing. These days even the King James version of the Holy Bible is being rewritten every month or so, and if you can rewrite God you can certainly rewrite any author who ever lived.

This should not be taken as a recommendation that every actor immediately start rewriting his current script, or that *any* actor should do so. What I do suggest is that the actor analyze his lines carefully, judging their relative values, their consistencies, and their dramatic legitimacy.

Is a particular line meant to be casual or does it carry a good deal of weight? If it is meant to be important, is it too obviously pretentious? If it is meant to be casual is it so written? A casual line can pose a number of problems. It may be overbearing, presuming more importance than it honestly possesses, it may be worded in a stilted manner, or it may be too "literary."

The casual line should not be lightly regarded, but studied as thoroughly as any other line in a film. If it belongs at all, it obviously serves a purpose; and though that purpose may be relatively unimportant, it is a necessary part of the whole and must be treated with respect. A throw-away that has a purpose is often more difficult to master than pretentious dialogue. Some rather good actors have had trouble delivering the casual line. (I am convinced that Spencer Tracy's much admired reputation as an under-player rested on his unbelievable mastery of the throw-away.)

Casualness does not imply indistinctness. Oddly, a line which cannot be understood gains in importance. The viewer hates to miss anything; and since he cannot know the indistinct line was of little real consequence, he will assume it is something he should have heard. A feeling of frustration or irritation inevitably follows. There are exceptions, of course. A well-known adage or a frequently repeated line can be sloughed off without damage since its meaning is immediately clear. In fact, it is often better to purposely slur such a line. For instance, an actor can say, "A butcher, a baker, a-da-da-da-da," and everyone in the audience over the age of three will be well ahead of the speaker. But in the great majority of instances it is the manner, the attitude, or the intonation that should distinguish the casual throwaway, not lack of intelligibility.

A study of the casual line brings out an important aspect of dialogue in general: *spoken* dialogue can, and usually does, differ considerably from *written* dialogue. A line, mentally absorbed off the page, may seem quite natural. Yet, when spoken aloud, that same line will sound awkward and unreal. This should come as no surprise. Until very recently the conventions of the written word differed widely from those of conversational usage.* Even today, in many languages, writing in the vernacular is unacceptable.

I have known very few authors who could write truly honest *speaking* dialogue. I do not mean this as a criticism, but as a statement of fact. I myself have written many a line of dialogue that I considered strikingly natural, but which, on being spoken, sounded more than a trifle starchy. For anyone brought up and educated in our society such difficulties are inevitable. The final test of a line's authenticity is always in the speaking, not the reading.

However—and this is a very important "however"—it is essential that the validity of the line be judged by its relationship to the character who says it, not the actor who speaks it. One of an actor's most baseless complaints is, "*I* wouldn't say it that way." Of course not. Even though an actor brings himself to every part he plays, the self he brings has most probably been reared differently, educated

---

*For this reason it is very difficult to guess how the language of, say, the eighteenth century was spoken, and patterning dialogue after the literature of the period invariably results in stilted and corny speech.

differently, has associated with different kinds of people in a different environment. It is the *character*, with his distinctive rearing and conditioning, who is speaking the line, not the actor. The only valid criticism would be, "I don't think the *character* would say it that way," and such a judgment would, of course, be debatable. Its final disposition would usually be decided by the film's director.

But back to dialogue. Written dialogue is a finished product—in real life most spoken dialogue is ad lib. The screenplay writer is often casual or off-hand with his scene descriptions, since he assumes that the director will construct and stage the scenes his (the director's) way. But he will slave over every spoken line since these, he fully expects, will be delivered more or less as written. He will edit, reconstruct, and polish most of his dialogue, and he is correct in doing so. As in most art, the scene is the *essence* of a happening, not the happening itself. Two buddies, planning a fishing trip, might spend hours, even days, discussing it; the writer must wrap it up in at most a page or two.

But too often the process of selecting and compressing dialogue succeeds in achieving a result identical to the dehydration of fruits and vegetables—a dessicated husk remains. The actor must find a way of giving that husk some appropriate flesh. (This is an exaggeration, but I hope it makes the point.) A line of dialogue in a script is usually properly constructed and polished; the thought is quite complete. Would it were so in real life.

Few people speak in polished, well-constructed, completely thought-out sentences—not when they ad lib. And the actor's job is to make the character real, to make his manner of behaving and speaking believable. To do this he must often take liberties with the written words. He might stutter a little (clod-kicking often makes speeches, as well as characters, appear to be more natural),* he may leave a portion of the line hanging, since rarely are one's thoughts positive and complete. He may repeat a word, even a phrase, in order to capture that uncertainty most speakers exhibit when vocally expressing an incompletely framed idea. He may decide (with the director's approval, or at his suggestion) to substitute a colloquial word or phrase for a more polite one, and always, unless he is playing a pedantic or a pompous personality, he will try to approach the vernacular.

It is inconceivable that an actor can become a *good* actor by simply learning to speak properly. He must necessarily develop a keen

---

*I once stopped Spencer Tracy in the middle of a take. "What's the matter?" he asked. "Spence," I said, "you're hemming and hawing a little too much." "Mr. Director," he shot back, seriocomically, "I am very highly paid for hemming and hawing." And even though we agreed that in this particular instance he was overdoing that bit, in general he was quite right. Nobody could bumble a line as effectively as the great Tracy.

ear for speech—*other* people's speech. He must be able to duplicate (not as imitation, but quite naturally) their speaking mannerisms, both oral and physical. He must learn their vocal graces and their vocal tics. He must be able to recognize the *sound* of truth and to detect the *sound* of deception, so he can incorporate these sounds into the speech of his character. He can do this only if he spends a good deal of his learning time in watching and listening to people—people from every walk of life. Just as the master impressionist studies the famous in order to caricature them effectively, so the actor must study the not-so-famous in order to portray them truthfully.

Such study and learning should lead not to imitation, but to creation. For example, a character may be patterned after a person who speaks in a slovenly fashion—so sloppily that only his close relatives and most intimate friends can understand him. Obviously, a faithful reproduction of such speaking habits would be gibberish to viewers unaccustomed to such speech. Above all, most of a film's dialogue is meant to be understood. So, a compromise is in order— one that is not truly a compromise but a reconstruction. Certain elements must be selected which project the essence of the character's sloppiness without rendering it unintelligible.

In *A Streetcar Named Desire*, Marlon Brando created such a speech pattern so effectively that many knowledgeable people wondered whether he could ever do a straight part without mumbling. Obviously, he could, and did. Mumbling was not, and is not, a part of Brando's normal speech pattern. It was an exceptional creative effort, made thoroughly real by an exceptional artist.

In short, an ear for the nature and the meaning of the "lyrics," and a facility for phrasing, is more important than the strict melody. The good actor must be able to "do something with it."

The quality of an actor's voice is obviously of great importance, as is his basic accent. A nasal whine can be repellent, but so can a vocal quality previously much admired in actors and orators—sonorousness. Resonance may be needed to reach the balcony; it can only be a problem for a microphone a few inches away. On the screen, the sonorous actor sounds pompous and ostentatious, and is effective only if he is playing Colonel Blimp or Senator Claghorn.

Voice quality and placement can usually be improved with practice and the aid of an inexpensive tape recorder. A marked regional accent can be lost and, indeed, it should be. The possession of, let us say, a strong Brooklyn accent may be useful when called for in a particular character, but it severely limits an actor's range and his acting opportunities if it remains a permanent feature.

Not too long after World War II, when English films were making a splash on the American market, I heard Olivier, John Mills, and a couple of other British actors discussing the question of the English accent, which many Americans found difficult to understand. They were able to agree that strong affectations were undesirable, for aesthetic as well as commercial reasons. Thus was born what has since been called the "Mid-Atlantic" accent—a reasonable (and pleasing) compromise between the American and the British treatments of the King's English.

In the United States, at present, television is undoubtedly affecting our speech patterns; and though regional purists may decry the "anchor man" manner of speech, it is really the only way for an actor to go. The use of the neutral, essentially unaffected accent now prevalent in certain parts of the midwest and most of the Pacific Coast makes it easier for the actor to superimpose any desired local accent over his normal one. Just imagine how difficult it would be to speak New England if your basic speech patterns came by way of West Texas.

A few actors still shout, or at least speak much too loudly. Most modern actors, however, have learned that the microphone can easily handle anything down to a soft sigh—stage whispers have no place on the screen except as a source of comedy. But by no means have all actors learned whom to talk to. Some, in a sense, talk to the mike: Even though they know they can talk as quietly as they wish, they still speak their lines for their effect on the audience. This is inexcusable because it is still declaiming, no matter how quietly. Conversations between human beings are only rarely declamatory.

Unless he is screaming at the wind, the actor should say what he has to say to the person, or persons, he is supposed to be talking to. Whether he is screaming, speaking in measured tones, or whispering, whether he is looking at them or avoiding their eyes, he should direct his words to his on-screen listeners. Only then will he be a real person and not a "performer." It is up to the director, the cameraman, the sound mixer, and the cutter to bring those words to an audience. It is not up to the actor.

Try an experiment. Speak any long monologue as you might speak it in a theater (if possible, record it on tape); then speak it confidentially to a person standing or sitting no more than four or five feet away from you. The difference will astound you and, I hope, convince you of the superiority, at least in films, of talking to your co-actors rather than to the audience.

THE ACTRESS SPEAKS:

*Motion picture scripts are rarely written exactly as they should be spoken. I've seen a few writers try it and it just doesn't work. A favorite writer of mine, Jimmy Clavell, once wrote a script with several different accents, plus the descriptions of how he saw the actors reacting, and it was the funniest thing I've ever read. I think it was his first try. He also laughed at it, all the way to the bank with the takings from his second try. He's never stopped laughing and writing and making money. But he did stop writing accents and directions.*

*Take the script given you and make the part yours. As you read and learn the lines, you may find you will have to change them just a bit to suit your own portrayal of the character. The director and the writer will appreciate this as long as your changes make it better. But don't go too far.*

*For instance, here is a scene as exactly written from Alfred Hayes'* script of The Left Hand of God, *in which I played Mary Yin, Humphrey Bogart's Chinese girlfriend. Bogie's character was called Jim Carmody.*

11    INT. CARMODY'S ROOM—FULL SHOT—LATE AFTERNOON

A big, square chamber, old, elegant, and warmly lit. Right, a single huge log burns in a stone fireplace. In the corners are four brass lanterns in soot-stained niches. Left, a modern desk with a green-shaded oil lamp whose light falls far enough to show Mary Yin, provocatively stretched out on Carmody's bed in f.g. Footsteps are heard, but Mary Yin continues to stare at the ceiling. Carmody, dust-worn, appears in the door in b.g. He stares and waits. Her not looking up is as deliberate as a pose before a mirror, for Mary Yin is as aware of Carmody as he is of her.

CARMODY
(finally, with a grin)
All right, Mary Yin—change the
pose. I forgot my camera.

She looks at him slowly, deliberately, then smiles.

MARY YIN
After so many days of hard
riding, I thought to see me this
way would be restful.

With a tantalizing movement of her body, she rises and saunters across the room, aware of his gaze trailing her slow passage. She is an exquisite half-caste. Little gold sandals glitter as she walks, dark blue silken trousers ripple provocatively. She arrives at the liquor cabinet.

(CONTINUED)

11 (CONTINUED)

>               CARMODY
>             (meanwhile)
>       You're a lot of things, but restful
>       isn't one of them.

Holding whiskey bottle and glass, she turns poutingly.

>               MARY YIN
>       It's been lonely without you, Kah-
>       ma-dee. There was nobody to play
>       the piano.

>               CARMODY
>       What's the matter with the radio?

Mary Yin brings the drink to Carmody.

>               MARY YIN
>             (with a shrug)
>       You know Yang. Nobody ever
>       turns off the radio here. All the
>       batteries are dead.
>             (hands him the drink)
>       Tell me what you did in the hills.

12      CLOSE TWO SHOT—CARMODY AND MARY YIN—LATE
        AFTERNOON

>               CARMODY
>       I spent six days collecting Yang's
>       taxes. . . .

He takes a long drink, then walks over to the desk, putting
down his cap, the Bible and his whip. Mary Yin stays in the
b.g.

>               MARY YIN
>             (somewhat eagerly)
>       Did you fight?

>               CARMODY
>       Dust—insects—the mountains . . .
>             (looking at her)
>       Disappointed?

                                              (CONTINUED)

12 (CONTINUED)

                    MARY YIN
                (crossing to him)
        A little.


As she reaches the desk she notices the priest's Bible. It is
dust-covered. She picks it up, curiously, as an object
completely alien to this room.


                    MARY YIN
        That's odd. A Bible. Where did you
        get this?


                    CARMODY
                (a slight shrug)
        A hotel room in Chicago.
                (takes the Bible,
                    puts it down again
                    on the table)
        Now beat it. Yang's waiting for
        me to check in.


                    MARY YIN
        You haven't kissed me.
                (her face close
                    to his)
        It's so dull here when you're
        gone.


He takes her somewhat roughly and kisses her hard.


                    CARMODY
                (breaking away and
                    crossing with empty
                    glass toward liquor
                    cabinet)
        You should have stayed in
        Chungking.


                    MARY YIN
        Why?

13    MED. SHOT AT LIQUOR CABINET—LATE AFTERNOON

. . . as he reaches for the bottle

> CARMODY
> It's not dull—and it's twenty days
> nearer the coast.

He fills the glass. Mary Yin comes into shot.

> MARY YIN
> Are you so tired of China?

> CARMODY
> (looking into his
> glass)
> For three years I've run Yang's
> tin army. You can get tired of
> anything in three years.

> MARY YIN
> (softly)
> Poor Kah-ma-dee.
> (as he looks at her)
> Other men would envy what you
> have.

> CARMODY
> This?
> (a gesture at the
> elaborate room)
> You buy stuff like this at auction.

> MARY YIN
> (caressing)
> Could I be bought at auction, too?

> CARMODY
> (a crooked grin)
> Sure—if they're selling calendars.

He breaks away. She catches his arm.

> MARY YIN
> Why did you come back to
> China—if you hate it so?

(CONTINUED)

13 (CONTINUED)

CARMODY

(a shrug)

Money.

MARY YIN

Yang pays you plenty. If it's
money you want—

CARMODY

Money, plus.

(as she frowns)

What does Jan Teng call it? The
illusion of freedom. Out
there's . . .

(a gesture toward
the window)

. . . the biggest prison in the
world. The accommodations are
fine—but every night I can hear
them turn the key in the lock.

(he swallows the
remainder of his drink)

Now beat it. Yang likes his boys
punctual.

He turns—and again she catches his arm.

MARY YIN

(sweetly)

So do I, Kah-ma-dee.

Camera holds on her as he strides out of shot.

*Reads okay, doesn't it! But can you see what I mean when I suggest a writer should not write accents, leaving it to the actor instead! I was playing a Chinese girl living in China, in wartime. I had Chinese friends to study but they were modern Californians, so I recalled some of the research I had done at M.G.M. While under contract there I was tested to play a part in Dragon Seed. The part was "Little Pearl," a young girl in Katherine Hepburn's family. Dickie Jones was to play my brother. While testing Bill Tuttle's fine make-up creations, I went through Metro's film library and looked at all the Chinese films I could get my hands on. I started thinking, walk-*

ing, and talking Chinese. I got the part, then it was cut out. How about that?! All of the preparatory work down the drain. Well, at Fox, on another film, I was able to make use of it all.

If the screen writer thought it was necessary to write the way he felt Mary Yin should pronounce Carmody's name . . . Kah-ma-dee . . . why not be consistent and write her complete lines with his idea of a Chinese accent?

What I did with all the lines was a "soft sell." It just so happened that "Kah-ma-dee" fit perfectly with the rest of my dialogue. Chinese shorten most of their words: When speaking English each word is cut almost like their chop-chop language. (Don't get me wrong, Chang. I love it.) But for the character I was playing, I had to make certain she was clearly understood, with all the mannerisms men like to think are Oriental. What they really are is feminine, with a capital F.

So for the dialogue I made sure my voice stayed sweet and soft, almost purring.

Speaking of purring, the scene did not begin as written. Instead of just lying on the bed staring at the ceiling, the director had me playing with a couple of Siamese kittens. Worked much better.

The director and Bogie and I worked well together, and the following changes were decided on, on the set.

Half of my second line was cut ("There was nobody to play the piano"), as was Bogie's next and half of my next. So it went. . .

MARY YIN

It's been lonely without you, Kah-
ma-dee. Tell me what you did in
the hills.

That was a relief to me because I had not been able to fathom the piano and radio and battery stuff in Chinese.

Further into the scene we cut out the action and the two lines relating to her finding the Bible on his desk. So it went from Mary Yin's line . . .

MARY YIN

A little.
(she moves into him
and continues)
You haven't kissed me.
(moves her face close)
It's so dull when you're gone.

He takes her somewhat roughly and kisses her hard.

*I repeated this descriptive action for a reason.*

*How many of you ladies have ever wished Humphrey Bogart would grab you somewhat roughly and kiss you hard?*

*Well, I was one of you! As a teenager sitting in the balcony of the Hollywood Boulevard Warner Bros. Theater, watching Humphrey Bogart in* The Maltese Falcon, *I nearly chewed up the upholstery wishing I could be up there on the screen, in his arms. I melted as he kissed Mary Astor. And let me tell you—and this came as a shock— I nearly melted when he kissed me as the Chinese girl.*

*By this time Bogie and his wife, Betty Bacall, and I were friends, and my husband was directing the film. But for one long moment (and it was a long moment because my darling husband, as a joke, decided to leave us in the clinch for as long as we could hold it), for that one moment I was able to forget Bacall and Eddie and the rest of the world.*

*So there you are. How funny life is. A dream comes true every once in a while. Especially in Hollywood.*

*The scene as rewritten ran as follows (cuts and descriptions are left out since a scene is rarely staged or cut according to script. And the director changed a couple of Bogart's lines):*

CARMODY

(finally, with a grin)

All right, Mary Yin—change the
pose, I forgot my camera.

She looks at him slowly, deliberately, then smiles.

MARY YIN

After so many days of hard
riding, I thought to see me this
way would be restful.

CARMODY

You're a lot of things, but restful
isn't one of them.

MARY YIN

It's been lonely without you, Kah-
ma-dee. Tell me what you did in
the hills.

CARMODY

I spent six days collecting Yang's
taxes—and a sore behind.

(CONTINUED)

> MARY YIN
> (somewhat eagerly)

Did you fight?

> CARMODY

Dust—insects—the moun-
tains . . .
> (looking at her)

Disappointed?

> MARY YIN

A little.
> (she moves into him
> and continues)

You haven't kissed me.
> (moves her face close)

It's so dull when you're gone.

He takes her somewhat roughly and kisses her.

> CARMODY
> (breaking away)

You should have stayed in
Chungking.

> MARY YIN

Why?

> CARMODY

It's not dull—and it's twenty days
nearer the coast.

> MARY YIN

Are you so tired of China?

> CARMODY

For three years I've run Yang's
tin army. You can get tired of
anything in three years.

> MARY YIN
> (softly)

Poor Kah-ma-dee.
> (as he looks at her)

Other men would envy what you have.

(CONTINUED)

                          CARMODY

This?

                    (a gesture at the
                     elaborate room)

You buy stuff like this at auction.

                          MARY YIN

                      (caressing)

Could I be bought at auction, too?

                          CARMODY

                    (a crooked smile)

Sure—if they're selling calendars.

                          MARY YIN

Why did you come back to
China—if you hate it so?

                          CARMODY

                      (a shrug)

Money.

                          MARY YIN

Yang pays you plenty. If it's
money you want. . .

                          CARMODY

I've found out there's something else.
                    (as she frowns)
What does Jan Teng call it? The
illusion of freedom. Out there's . . .
                    (a gesture toward
                     the window)
. . . the biggest prison in the
world. The accommodations are
fine—but every night I can hear
them turn the key in the lock.
            (he swallows the remainder of his drink)
Now beat it. Yang likes his boys
punctual.

                          MARY YIN

                      (sweetly)

So do I, Kah-ma-dee.

Camera holds on her as he strides out of shot.

*Today they would use Chinese actors for Chinese parts. And I think they should. I played Robert Walker's French girlfriend (living in a small French war-time village) in MGM's* **What Next, Corporal Hargrove.** *I had to study French for many weeks and watch* **The Big Parade** *over and over. Metro had a great film library, and all the contract players were encouraged to use it. I was very fortunate.*

*But you can be, too. Film is so popular today, and it is certainly recognized as the world's number one art form for reaching the greatest number of people. In any large city, if one cares to look, there are museums and libraries with old films for study.*

*Edward Dmytryk directs Jane Fonda in* Walk on the Wild Side.

# 7

# *Who Do You Think*
# *You Are?*

We were casting *Murder, My Sweet*. One actor, fresh from New York, frequently dropped into my office. He wanted—oh, so desperately—to play Moose Mulloy. The conversation always followed a pattern. Perhaps he thought he could wear me down.

"You're five feet nine," I would say. "The Moose is supposed to be six feet eight inches tall."

"I can *play* him big!" he would plead. But he didn't get the part. Mike Mazurki, the wrestler, at six feet four and a half inches the biggest man we could find who could act, got the role. Dick Powell, who played Marlowe, was six feet two, so even with Mazurki as the Moose I had to use every trick in the book to get an on-screen difference in height which was dramatically effective.

As Edward G. Robinson and James Cagney demonstrated so convincingly, *power* can be played regardless of size, but height cannot be acted. As for tricks, there's a limit to the build-up potential of a pair of men's shoes.

It is a mistake to assume that an actor can divorce himself completely from his screen character. To accomplish the divorce he would have to acquire new characteristics, adopt new habits. But the hallmark of a habit is that it is an unconscious or involuntary action or manner—a person does not *think* about how he picks up a fork at dinner, how he brushes his teeth or combs his hair. Such ingrained behavior is the result of a lifetime of conditioning, and it would be impossible to change one's exterior or interior patterns for coping with the routine demands of one's environment in the limited time available prior to actual performance. Even temporary changes in habit conditioning would require constant, long-term application of conscious effort. The *consciousness* would be bound to show.

A small number of actors who seem to value technique as an end in itself do attempt such transformations. (Introverted movements of this sort have cropped up at various times in all the arts.) But they attract only a minute audience with an extremely esoteric outlook: To most viewers their efforts appear to be self-conscious and self-indulgent.

With this in mind it would seem to be wise for the actor to bring as much of himself to his screen character as that character can accommodate, and to avoid most attempts at "creating" a person whose involuntary habits and attitudes are the reverse of his own. It would be sheer nonsense, for instance, for Robert Redford to play Scrooge, for James Garner to play the Godfather, or for Al Pacino to play a sweet-talking seminary student. In keeping with the old theater belief that comedians always want to be tragedians (and vice versa), such attempts might seem attractive to the artists, but they rarely, if ever, turn out to be attractive at the box office. A number of such extreme character reversals have been attempted,* and the results have been more tragic than the films.

Let us set up a specific example; let us imagine that Jack Nicholson is cast to play a blacksmith. How much of the character would be some hypothetical "blacksmith" and how much would be Jack Nicholson?

At this point I can hear some reader saying, "But Nicholson doesn't *look* like a blacksmith!" Well, he does and he doesn't. He isn't the blacksmith whose smithy stands under the spreading chestnut tree—but what blacksmith is? Not all smiths have brawny arms and muscles as strong as iron bands. Some who specialize in ornamental ironwork look as aesthetic as any other artist—even Jack Nicholson.

The point is that this particular blacksmith will look and act as he would if Jack Nicholson had chosen to be a blacksmith instead of an actor, and he would be no less real than would Longfellow's prototype. Nicholson would have to place himself in the time and the environment called for in the story. He would have to consider the smith's social status in that environment, his level of education, his racial and/or religious background, etc., just as he would in setting up any other character.

Physically, he would have to accustom himself to the use of

---

*e.g., by Cary Grant in Clifford Odets' film of Llewellyn's *None but The Lonely Heart*.

strange tools (just as Clift had to adjust to a strange bedroom door), which he would accomplish by practice; but he would manipulate those implements in his own way, depending on his own skeletal and muscular makeup rather than one belonging to an imaginary, stereotypical smith. Nicholson, for instance, might have to use more shoulder and body leverage in wielding a heavy hammer than would a weightlifter who could manipulate the same tool with arm strength alone. The difference would make Nicholson no less a blacksmith, only a less massive one.

However, learning to do something new is not as difficult as breaking and relearning a habit. For characteristics that have more to do with personality than with tricks of the trade, Nicholson would probably depend on the same mocking eyes, the same gently sneering grin, the same casual walk, the same general hand movements, whether scratching his head or his stomach, that he uses in all of his characterizations. And he would still create a legitimate blacksmith, unique but real as every blacksmith is, but, because he is Jack Nicholson, probably a good deal more interesting. Yet it is exactly because this particular blacksmith is someone unusual that we are telling his story. So here, too, Nicholson fills the bill without distortion.

Beyond all this another element is at work. Most people are basically xenophobic—every stranger is a threat—but because our blacksmith, even though a new and different character, has certain recognizable and familiar traits (courtesy of Jack Nicholson) he is more readily accepted by the viewer. The elimination of distrust permits quicker self-identification and deeper involvement in the film.

An in-depth study of the role will occasionally expose an invalid contradiction or a dramatically unprofitable character. A change will be in order. An apt example is the character of Christian Diestl, as played by Marlon Brando in *The Young Lions*. At the time the film was made there was a deal of controversy and debate about the reason, the incentive, and the result of the change in character—all of it based on rumor and unfounded statements. Only the screen-writer Edward Anhalt, Marlon Brando, and I were responsible for character alteration, and only we three know exactly what happened, and why.

Irwin Shaw's exceptional novel was written immediately after World War II, at a time when people's emotions concerning that holocaust were still at high tide. Nazis were the brutal enemy and many people assumed that all Germans were Nazis and therefore brutal. One of the novel's leading characters was Christian, a young German caught up in the ferment of his time. He starts out as an honest patriot searching, as many Germans were, for international respect. He believes in Hitler not as a Nazi but as a political messiah, and he discounts reported atrocities as temporary aberrations which will soon be eliminated. With the start of the war he becomes a soldier and, as the war progresses, his personality is brutalized until, at the end, he is transformed into a completely amoral and brutal human being. In short, he demonstrates that Nazism is a debasing philosophy.

But when the film was made, some twelve years after the war, every one knew that. And to say it again from the point of view of one of Germany's enemies served no new purpose. Besides, by that time we also knew that millions of decent Germans had opposed Hitler, and many had been executed for their beliefs.

In translating the novel to the screen we found no problems with the two American roles, but we felt that Christian's character left us nowhere to go but down and, in light of the public's current (1957) attitudes, gave us no opportunity to make fresh comments about Nazism or the effects of the war. In a truly collaborative effort we decided that such comments could be made more forcefully if we started out with a patriot who believes in the German effort to regain its national pride and its pre–World War I status, but who learns, as the war progresses, that the ends do not justify the means. (This is not a new idea but it can certainly bear frequent repeating.) Through Christian's eyes we see how the Nazi leadership brutalizes those who follow it blindly. As he becomes gradually more aware of the true state of things he realizes that all of his early hopes have been denied, and he grows to abhor the whole Nazi concept. At the end, he smashes his weapon to bits and deliberately walks into an American soldier's bullet.

The evils of the Nazi movement were not overlooked—only against such a background could Christian's disillusionment be dramatized. But we felt that showing a *German's* realization of the corruption of the philosophy he once believed in would expose its weaknesses more effectively than if we saw it through the eyes of one of its enemies, which would, in a way, be begging the question.

Shaw, of course, disapproved of the change. However, at least three out of four critics and viewers agreed with our point of view. Incidentally, the film was a tremendous success.

Those who objected to the change charged that Brando, unwilling to play an evil character, was responsible for it—a charge that was completely baseless. Brando was a cocontributor, nothing more. He has proved, both before and since our film, that playing "bad" characters is not one of his hang-ups.

The point here is that characters can be, and often are, changed to the benefit of the film. But they must always be real and, particularly in tragic drama, they must show growth, or evolution. Otherwise, both the character and the story are, literally, flat. Whether the character is "good" or "bad," the viewer must find him interesting and, whether or not he agrees with his outlook or behavior, he must understand him.

Every student of human behavior knows that no man, however wicked he appears to society, thinks of himself as evil. He rationalizes his covert thoughts and his overt actions. He has a "good" reason for his behavior. For instance, I once asked a prisoner who was serving time for drug dealing if he had learned his lesson. I hoped, I said naively, that he would not continue in such a despicable trade when he was back in the streets.

"Despicable!" he said, with a show of astonishment. "Have you ever *seen* an addict who badly needs a fix? He suffers terrible pain. I am a benefactor—a doctor—I ease his pain and make his life more bearable."

The point was also made, less dramatically but with wider application, in *The Godfather*. One of the mobsters (it may have been the godfather himself) justifies his participation in bootlegging with, "I deal in services. If people didn't want what I sell I wouldn't be in business."

The creative actor must keep this concept in mind. In order to keep his character honest and not just an illustration, he must be able to rationalize all of that character's behavior. He can also make the character more understandable, more appealing, let us say, by exhibiting some of the traits shared by most human beings. Again, in *The Godfather*, the title character is a strong family man: he loves his wife, his children, his grandchildren. He is faithful to his friends. He has an affinity for flowers. He loves dogs. He even loves his country, though he rationalizes the breaking of some of its laws, *as do we all.* (A prison warden once commented that if every citizen was held responsible for his legal transgressions practically every American would be in jail.)

An actor who understands this will rarely say, "I can't play this man that way—I wouldn't do what he does." Of course he can, if he can find the proper rationalization. If it can't be found, either the actor is at fault or the character is dishonest, in which case it should be reconstructed.

It often becomes necessary for an actor to portray personally distasteful behavior, but the bases for nearly all behavior are present in most of us, and a simple extension of those bases can help the actor to make the necessary adjustments. For instance, an actor might say, "I can't play a murderer—I could never kill." Nonsense. Has he ever swatted a fly, squashed a spider, or stepped on an ant? They are all forms of life, and if he can take it at that level he can kill—period. The adjustment is simple; he need only think of his victim as a gnat or (if he is a gardener) as a gopher or a snail. The substitution will furnish the motive for his behavior and will serve to settle him into any possible character, as long as that character is a valid example of humankind.

## THE ACTRESS SPEAKS:

*Putting yourself into a part you are given is what is expected. In* About Face, *one of the leading characters was written as a scatter-brained, giggly girl who liked and went after the leading man. As if those characteristics weren't bad enough, she also had been given a lisp. The lines were written in this fashion.*

GIRL

Come on, thweetie. Leths have
thom fun. Leths danth!

*Can you decipher, "Come on, sweetie. Let's have some fun. Let's dance!"?*

*When I was tested for the part I had been given just one scene and thought it a challenge. After getting the part, which ran all through the picture, I had a lot of work to do. After translating the lines, I practiced my own lisping night and day. I had to make this character easy and likeable instead of obnoxious. When she popped up unexpectedly in the most unlikely places (like Bugs Bunny), I wanted the audience happy to see her, even if the character played by the leading man was not. The audience had to sympathize with her desire to be with this guy and with her efforts to get him. I was able to master the lisp to the point where I could ignore it mythelf, and all of my expressions and actions took over. She ended up being a very pleasant and likable character, and the director, Kurt Neuman, was very pleased. Hal Roach studio signed me to a long-term contract because of the response to this part.*

*When I heard that MGM was looking for a teen-age comedienne to play opposite Virginia Weidler in* The Youngest Profession, *I wanted the part. The story was about two moviestar–crazy kids living in New York who would go to any and all lengths to get autographs of stars who come to the city.*

*My agent arranged an appointment with the director, and somehow he was able to get a script to me before the interview. The part was described as "a roly-poly comic, always falling down." Well, what could I do with that? It was a very good part—second lead—ran all the way through the film, and had scenes (cameos) with many of the top MGM stars: William Powell, Greer Garson, Walter Pidgeon, Lana Turner, Hedy Lamarr. I had to have it.*

*After going over and over her scenes, I went in to the interview prepared to change the director's mind, convinced that I could make it better. My suggestion was that this character be played as a soft little girl with a southern accent, absolutely overwhelmed whenever she is near a star. Instead of falling all over herself, she becomes almost immobile, mesmerized with awe. I read for him, sold him on my ideas, and got the job. The director, Eddie Buzzel, encouraged me constantly and called me his protege. After the film was finished I was awarded a long-term contract with Metro.*

*In* Cry Danger, *I again played the second lead, a prostitute-pickpocket. I loved doing that part. We were able to make her so loved that the audience felt broken-hearted when she was killed.*

*I've played myself many times in college musicals, singing and dancing and having a good time. No challenge there. It's easy for you when you're cast in a straight part. But even then, do everything you can to give some depth to the scenes. The main thing is to keep the audience's attention and make each person out there feel* something *for your character.*

*Richard Widmark's characterization in* Night and the City *was one of the most frightening neurotics I've ever seen. No one else could have played the part as he played it.*

*You can look at a bunch of lines, and read the story, and understand it, but—taking* your *character and bringing it to life—literally giving it life, that has to be you.*

*Imagine a character at the bottom of some stairs, looking up, then starting to climb. Is he a menacing villain? Or is she frightened of what's up there? Or is she being followed? Is it a character bringing home bad news, dreading the next few minutes? Or is this a girl filled with joy, having just left her lover, and is the audience aware that some kind of evil awaits her? See how many characters we can play! And each of us would play it differently. As we should.*

*Picture Debra Winger in the role Cissy Spacek played in* Missing. *They are both called "natural" actresses, and sometimes each comes off a little too natural. In trying to act natural, one has to be careful not to kick the dust.*

*And try to imagine Tom Courtney's version of* Tootsie *as compared to Dustin Hoffman's—or Hoffman's interpretation of Paul Newman's role in* Verdict. *They're all fine actors, and each brings his own character and personality into a role.*

*Let me repeat here: Don't ever go after a part unless you know you're right for it. I've heard actors say, "A good actor, a really* fine *actor, can play* any *part." Not true. Certainly not on the screen. In the theater, as a performance, possibly. For the screen you must look the part. A cutie-pie, sexy actress would never be considered for the roles given to Ingrid Bergman or Faye Dunaway or Meryl Streep. Even if she were capable as an actress. Neither would the director cast any of those three names in a cutie-pie, sexy role. You see what I mean.*

*Try not to get yourself typed. You can't change certain physical things about yourself, but you can give them dimension and meaning. You will eventually find one certain thing about yourself that gets you the jobs. Latch onto it and use it.*

*Comedy is always a magic formula.* Abbott and Costello in Hollywood with *Jean Porter* and *Frances Rafferty.*

# 8

# *The Magic Formula*

Every filmmaker who has talked with groups of students has heard the questions, "How do you do what you do? What is the formula?" So far as the questions concern the *creative* aspect of an enterprise, whether it be filmmaking or real-estate development, the honest answer is, "I don't know." A good deal can be taught, more can be learned, but you can't teach or learn talent, and creativity is a function of talent.

Thomas A. Edison once wrote that genius is 1 percent inspiration and 99 percent perspiration. Using a common mathematical technique, let us substitute the word "talent" for the word "genius." Then 99 percent perspiration plus 1 percent inspiration equals talent. But that still leaves us short of a definitive formula since without inspiration, which cannot be formulated, all the perspiration is nothing but water. At a more down-to-earth level, however, we can say that 99 precent preparation plus 1 percent implementation equals competence.

Good acting calls for a good deal of preparation, not only for each separate performance but for an over-all mastery of the craft. Every student of acting knows that career preparation involves thousands of hours, dozens of months, and many years of exercises. But acting exercises do not make the actor any more than writing exercises make the novelist, or practice in brush techniques makes a painter. If they did, we would have thousands of great writers, painters, athletes, and Oliviers. However, exercise and practice—particularly practice—do help an artist to perfect his craft and to hone his talent, if he has any. For talent is inborn and it comes in different sizes. The word "gift" is a synonym for "talent," and a most appropriate one, since talent *is* a gift, whether genetic or God-given. Without it all the exercise and practice in the world will produce only a technician, a journeyman practitioner of any art.

A person possessing a gift is not always aware of it, and often it is never given an opportunity to surface. But when it does it is, as a rule, recognized at once. For instance, it has long been known that mathematical genius shows itself at an early age, usually long before the start of any advanced training. The same is true for prodigies in music, painting, dancing, and so on. As for actors, one has only to note the number of startlingly good performances by children who have had no training at all. On the other side of the ledger are thousands of men and women who, driven by an irrepressible desire, have studied, exercised, and practiced all their working lives without developing anything beyond the most routine acting abilities. More than a few of these have polished their technical skills to the point where they can convince an uncritical viewer, but when their work is compared to that of a born actor the difference is as obvious as that between rhinestones and a diamond.

Whether one is gifted or a plodder, what are the exercises that can effectively perfect an actor's ability? In my opinion, the most important exercise by far is observation. An actor must be able to create a wide variety of characters, with an accompanying variety of intelligence and personality. For instance, Maximillian Schell, one of the very best of contemporary actors, played a Nazi officer in one film and a guilt-ridden Jew in another—the role of a musical genius in a third was immediately followed by that of a mentally retarded saint. These four extremely divergent types, each possessing a unique personality and a different level of intelligence, were squeezed out of one intellect—his. But if he had not carefully observed these differing types as he had known them through his own experiences (with the possible exception of the saint), he could not have portrayed them so brilliantly on the screen.

An anecdote may help to drive home the concept: Schell was introduced to English-speaking audiences in my film, *The Young Lions*, in which he played a captain in Hitler's army. In his next film, *Judgment at Nuremberg*, he won the Oscar for playing a German lawyer defending Nazi officers against war-crime charges. On coming into a studio theater to see a preview of *The Reluctant Saint*, the wife of our publicity director remarked to her husband, "I'm not going to like this film. Schell is completely miscast. He can only play himself— an arrogant Teutonic type." After the showing, in which Max, as previously mentioned, played an "idiot" saint, she came up to me and apologized. "Schell is not only an actor," she said, "but a great actor. I am now completely convinced that he can play *anything*."

Of course, Schell did not play a saint. He played an apparently retarded young man whose basic goodness and simplicity enabled him to perform miracles which, more than a hundred years later, resulted in his canonization. (Saints are almost never recognized as such in their lifetimes, at least not by the church.) And Schell learned how such a character might behave through observation of similar "real" human beings in their own environment, observation which he sharpened and dramatized through his own great talent.

Observation is preparation. One hour spent in observing people (or animals) in *their* environments is worth a month of technical exercises. And the key to productive observation is the ability to penetrate those environments, no matter how alien they may be, without disturbing them unduly.

Nearly fifty years ago I read a book written by a well-known British biologist.* It concerned the study of the wild life in a West African jungle. In keeping with the principle of indeterminacy, such a study is made difficult by the intrusion of the observer, since his presence immediately alters the environment. Sanderson's problem was to insert himself into the habitat without excessively upsetting it. He eventually realized that in the jungle "Everything drifts slowly hither and thither as if wafted forward by currents and cross-currents. To stand still is to arouse suspicion. . . . I drifted and eddied with the animals themselves. . . ." (He comes upon a herd of wild river hogs.) "Having drifted right in among them . . . I soon found myself right in the centre of the herd, noticed but unfeared by them."

Moving with the flow is not always easy. Some environments are difficult to penetrate, others are unfeasible. Walking into a truck stop in a three-piece suit will get you no answers, nor will barging into a D.A.R. convention in a punk rock outfit. Psychologists have long known that questioning a criminal, for instance, or a psychotic will elicit only the behavior and the answers that person believes you want to see and hear. To understand how a criminal really functions you have to infiltrate his way of life and, short of incurring a six-month prison sentence, that takes some doing. Even the great majority of criminal psychologists admit to only minimal success.

Lack of thorough understanding, whether of criminals or of any of a number of off-beat types, leads to stereotyping. The chief reason that so many dramatic portrayals are cliche is that the portrayer (and the writer) know *only* the stereotype. Once in a great while we see a character which is not stereotypical because the actor has taken the time and the trouble to get into his character's life. Such a portrayal is always highly effective: The truth is immediately apparent.

There is a world of difference between what *seems* true and what *is* true. As a boy of six in British Columbia I had a revelatory experience. We lived in a wild, mountainous region—rattlesnake country. While walking across a field one day I was startled by a sharp rattling sound. I stopped in my tracks and listened carefully. I thought I had

*Animal Treasure, Ivan T. Sanderson, The Viking Press (1937).

heard a snake's rattle, but I wasn't quite sure. (Later, I determined that the sound was caused by a moving chain in an abandoned well.) Much more alert now, I moved on. A few minutes later I was again startled by a sharp rattle, but this time there was no doubt, no need to stop and listen. The hair on the back of my neck told me it was indeed the warning of a rattlesnake.

An honest portrayal is like that: You just drink in the truth. There is no need—indeed, no desire—for critical evaluation. You simply "live" the vicarious experience.

But back to nuts and bolts. If you want to understand truck drivers put yourself into their milieu. You need not try to *be* a truck driver (they would probably spot the deception at once); you need only to be accepted by them. You can dress like them, try to use their language or, better yet, just listen. A few visits to truck stop cafes will shatter the stereotype and set you on the way to a more honest characterization.

Some such exercises are easy, some very difficult. But you must learn to take advantage of every opportunity. Are you going in for a flu shot, a cold treatment, or a physical? Study your doctor during every visit—you may some day have to play one. If you attend classes, study your instructor more closely than you do your lessons: Your grades may drop but you will learn more. And go to gatherings, all kinds of gatherings. Watch how people behave in church, at an evangelical meeting, a political rally, or a sports spectacle.

Shortly after World War II, I had occasion for the first time in my adult life to visit and work in England. I am an avid sports fan, and I attended every athletic contest that was conveniently available. I was immediately struck by an unanticipated phenomenon; English hockey fans very closely resembled American hockey fans. Their reactions to the various facets of the sport were identical. The behavior of British boxing aficionados was the same as that of their American cousins—the same hat-wearing, cigar-chewing, bet-making types peopled both nations' fight arenas. The same was true for wrestling, tennis, track and field, and even soccer, which, as far as crowd reactions were concerned, could be paired off against our baseball.* But what shook me was that the British boxing fan resembled the British hockey fan far less than he resembled his American counterpart.**

The same sort of observation is made by every filmmaker who visits a foreign studio, whether in London, Rome or Bombay. Once on a sound stage, the filmmaker is at home. Even though the workers

---

*The only sport for which I could find no parallel was cricket, which is like no other sport on earth.

**I later found the same similarities and differences existing in France, Italy, and other countries.

speak a different tongue, their movements, attitudes, even their surface appearances are strikingly similar.

The theory that members of a similar class from a variety of countries are much more akin than are members of different classes of the same nationality was not new to me, but the startling testimony to its validity was a revelation. So here, too, is another source of character delineation: class distinction. (See Book I, Chapter 3.)

There are a number of ways to get the feel of an unfamiliar class. One is to surround yourself with some of its accoutrements during your period of preparation. In a novel written a century ago by J. K. Huysmans, the chief character is an avidly curious but spiritually depleted Frenchman who finds it difficult to stray from his familiar surroundings. Wishing to visit the London of Dickens, he satisfies his desire in a most unusual way.

He packs his trunk and starts off for the railroad station, but stops at a book mart to buy an English travel guide. He browses through a number of them, reading about the London Museum with its paintings by familiar artists. Taking a Baedecker with him, he visits an English wine shop where he savors a glass of port and observes the convivial Britishers at play. His next stop is an English restaurant. Here he finds himself in the midst of more British types. Ordering oxtail soup, smoked haddock, roast beef and boiled potatoes, and some Stilton cheese, he dines with relish—washing it all down with a couple of pints of ale. Leaving the restaurant, he retrieves his trunk and returns home, satisfied that he has experienced the best of London without ever leaving his beloved Paris.[*]

A touch bizarre, perhaps, or just plain crazy, but it does carry the seed of an idea. You, too, can surround yourself with the trappings of your character's class and craft. Small furnishings, books, magazines, selected sports paraphernalia, etc., should not be too expensive or difficult to acquire. Visit his special haunts and eat his special foods, and try to enjoy them. Such an immersion into your character's life will bring more than a touch of reality into your characterization.

Maurice Chevalier once described another technique for thinking himself into a role, one he practiced as a young man. Standing before a mirror, he thought of himself as alienated from society, homeless, starving—a street beggar looked back at him from the glass. In this manner he ran successfully through a number of sharply differentiated characters, then found himself in trouble: He essayed the role of a churchman. He thought of himself as adoring God, full of holiness, selflessness, faith and charity. The face staring back at him was completely unfamiliar. So, taking a different tack, he thought of himself as ambitious, greedy, self-indulgent, full of cupidity, and with a lust

[*]From *Against the Grain* (A Rebours) by J. K. Huysmans.

for power. Voila! The mirror reflected the face of a classic career bishop. (This is Chevalier's story, not mine.)

Another area that will repay serious study is the field of aptitude testing, which relies more on a person's habits, inclinations, fancies and tastes than it does on innate skills or I.Q.'s. If you are about to undertake the role of a surgeon, for instance, aptitude criteria will tell you what inclinations the best surgeons have in common. Knowing and resorting to such data whenever possible can help to bring about the realization of a desired character.

Books are an ubiquitous source of information. Any actor attempting to learn about a variety of personalities through experience alone will find himself still woefully unprepared at the end of his life. A great deal of what we know must be learned vicariously, and the experiences of those who are skilled at communicating their insights are certainly among the best and most prolific sources of human observation. The odds are that no actress about to play a prostitute would care to get the necessary experience at first hand. But a careful reading of Kuprin's "Yama" *(The Pit)* will give her as much information as would a year spent in a brothel.

However, when using second-hand experience there is a caveat. Since even the most impartial of observers often make subjective judgments, it is wise to get at least a second opinion. Fortunately, a host of such opinions are as close as your nearest library.

Whether first-hand or vicarious, all these sources must be double-checked, tested, and weighed against each other, and finally sifted through your own ever-growing understanding of the human condition. Only then can you consider yourself a professional. And, whatever the level of excellence your talent allows you, if you are a true student of the art you will become a *better* actor with each passing day.


## THE ACTRESS SPEAKS:

*Observation will make you a comedian, if you don't watch out. And what could be better! Knowing how to play comedy will get you anywhere.*

*Comedy is our most popular form of entertainment. Everyone likes to laugh. And, more important, everyone likes to identify. Mr. and Mrs. Average love to see something happening on the screen that has happened to them—where they have been laughed at or where they have laughed at themselves. Or, better yet, something they might have thought of but didn't dare do.*

*You don't have to be a clown to be funny. The best comedy comes out of natural, everyday living and concerns things with which all persons can identify, simple things.*

*Observe a woman in a supermarket, standing at some distance, watching a man who is troubled with the tedious job of choosing which prepared dinners to take home from the frozen food counter. Aha! Obviously, he's a bachelor, and you can check her basket contents and see that she is single. This is a comedy situation that any actor would like to play. If you've never experienced it, rush to your nearest supermarket, take a basket, pick out a few things, and park near the frozen dinners. Watch the men, then watch the women who watch the men. Most rewarding.*

*There are other places for encountering natural comedy situations. In a large, busy drug store there is usually a seat near the pharmaceutical center where the elderly wait for their prescriptions. Here you can pick up an abundance of material by watching and listening.*

*Another place to study human behavior is the Social Security welfare office. Here you can sit among the people in the waiting room and pick up conversations, then wander closer to where you can overhear interviews. This will enlighten you and show you parts of life that can only be called tragicomedy. The Department of Developmental Resources: Most of the people coming in here cannot read those words or, if they can, they don't understand their meaning. They have been given directions, but they don't know what it's all about, and most of them are frightened. Study them. And study Skid Row in L.A., or the downtrodden area of any big city.*

*And the inside of a mental institution, often called a Health and Rehabilitation Center. Please check these out for important and sensitive human behavior. Queasy about this, are you? Don't be. In today's world of the "I'm one of you . . ." methods of treatment, you find yourself asking directions from a patient, believing him to be a staff member, or walking quickly by a doctor, feeling certain that he is a patient. Even in a locked facility, where the patients range from the elderly senile to chronic schizophrenics, you are safe, and there is so much to learn—about the characters on the staff and the patients. I know! We have a close family member locked up, and I'm there every week. Review* One Flew over the Cuckoo's Nest. *Excellent! And you'd better believe it.*

*You may be saying, "But this is writing material, creating stuff. . . ." True, it can be. But what it is is studying people in their natural environments. Make notes, mental and written, and file them away for future reference. One day you may need to recall these experiences as a suggestion, or an accompaniment to a part you're given. All this helps you to be prepared when called for the different categories and variations of roles. To be creative, especially in comedy, you have to have seen, if not experienced, the humor behind all this seriousness. Real humor most often comes from trying to resolve a serious situation (see any Laurel and Hardy comedy).*

*To study situation comedy, watch Cary Grant and Irene Dunne in* The Awful Truth *and* My Favorite Wife, *and William Powell and Myrna Loy in* The Thin Man. *Sure, they were given great material, excellent direction and editing, but these actors pulled it off. They are given credit for some of the best comedies ever put on film.*

*Blatant and over-obvious comedy may be good for a chuckle, but it certainly doesn't touch the heart. And, more often than not, it's called crude and vulgar, especially if blended with foul language, which offends many people and ruins many an intended effect.*

*Good, natural, funny situations with actors who understand timing and reaction: This is what it's all about.*

*Final touch-ups are given to Jean Porter before shooting a musical number in* Little Miss Broadway.

# 9

# *Help Is on the Way!*

On the sound stage an actor is never on his own. Whether he likes it or not, he is always surrounded by "helpers." These helpers exercise certain controls that he occasionally resents, but they also make available certain opportunities which make it possible for him to give a performance of greater depth and impact than he could in any other medium.

The controls, of course, are the fly in the actor's soup. Most actors, at one time or another, have complained that the director and the cutter are *really* responsible for their performances since it is they who control the editing process. A partial motivation for this complaint is the actor's fear that he may wind up as "the face on the cutting room floor." But the true intent of any director or cutter I have ever known has been to present each actor's efforts in the best interest of the film; and if the removal of a particular scene results in overall improvement, the actor benefits by virtue of his participation in a better film. Such operations involve questions of judgment and are subject to error. However, an actor's performance is not often damaged in the editing process: It is more frequently enhanced. But long before postproduction comes into play, the total impact of an actor's work can be expanded in a number of ways.

An actor entering the film field should acquire the best possible understanding of who his helpers are, and of the nature of their assistance. But first, let us examine how actors with an inclination toward self-indulgence can be circumvented.

Do you insist on doing it "your way"?

Many years ago a budding actress (who later became one of the screen's great stars) disagreed with her director (later equally renowned) about the way a certain scene should be played. Discussion failed to bring agreement, persuasion had no power: The actress insisted on doing her thing. Without further argument the director proceeded to shoot her version, take after take after take, hour after hour after hour. Finally, about midnight, the actress decided to try the director's version. "Cut," said the director, after the shot. "Print it, and let's all go home!"

Do you insist on having the topper?

The on-set confrontations of two well-known sophisticated comedy stars were well known. Each would try to "top" the other, and each had his/her own gag writer on the set. When Charlie Ruggles surprised Mary Boland with a punch line in the first take (which he often did) she, after a quick conference with her gag man, would top him in the second. The seesawing could go on for hours, and frequently did. I was cutting one of their films and remarked upon the amusing but frustrating situation to the director, Leo McCarey, more in sympathy than in any hope of solution. "Oh, I don't let it bother me," he said. "It keeps them on their toes. And I know you have a very sharp pair of scissors." Scissors are the answer to a number of selfish tricks.

Do you insist on dominating the scene?

In one of my films a method actor was externalizing an "internalization." As staged, he is seated in a chair with his back to the camera. Immediately after the start of the scene he rises, turns, and walks toward the camera, which pans him into a two shot for the continuation of the take. The actor insisted on remaining seated for an interminable length of time (probably more than a minute) while he internalized his emotions before rising and continuing with the scene. He thought it would play. Without any argument, I prepared to roll. The cameraman thought I was losing control. Somewhat startled, he whispered, "Eddie, you can't use that pause! It's a dreadful stall!" I nodded, then moved the index and middle fingers of my hand in imitation of snipping scissors. He suddenly smiled. For the moment he had forgotten that I was in control of the only control that really counted: the control afforded by a small pair of scissors.

Do you insist on hogging the camera?

Directors also control the set-ups. Actors are human beings and a few of them, as such, may be selfish. Some will make stabs at upstaging their fellow actors before they learn the futility of such attempts, and slow learners must occasionally be taught a lesson. A bright, talented, but self-centered young actress in one of my films illustrated the point. She had not been around long enough to realize that upstaging in a properly made film is impossible, since there is no *up* or *down* stage on a film set. Through the courtesy of a mobile camera, the viewer has a 360-degree point of view. When the actress, pleading inexperience in hitting her marks, persisted in trying to hog the camera, I shot an added set-up—a close-up of her co-actor. When I did not shoot a complementary close-up of her, she realized that her attempts at hogging the camera would only present her fellow artist with a large close-up every time she tried to upstage her. Being, in reality, a quick study, she never tried it again.

It is a mistake for the actor to try to maneuver himself into what he sees as the most advantageous position in respect to the camera. That is one of the functions of the director, and a good director will use his camera more to enhance the actor's performance than as a means of chastisement. His set-ups will be contrived to most effectively present the actor's reactions and movements in any particular part of the scene, subject always, however, *to the relative importance of every other actor in the scene.* When more than one performer occupies the frame, the actor must realize that *he* may not always be the essential center of interest—and that the purposes of the scene may best be served only by what he may consider preferential treatment of another player. But if the film benefits, so does he. It is far better to be a solid contributor in a fine film than a big star in a stinker. And always remember, the actor who consistently has his back to the camera in the full shots may wind up with the majority of close-ups in the edited film.

Besides helping the actor by presenting him to the viewer in the most effective shots at the most effective times, the director also carefully selects the lenses with which those shots are made. (A thorough analysis of the use of lenses as they relate to actors and acting will be found in Chapter 8 of Book II.)

The role of an expert boxer in a classic film was played by an exceptionally good actor, but there was a problem. The exceptionally good actor couldn't throw a good straight punch. In the long shots, a fighting double could, and did, fit the bill. But a large number of close shots are always needed, especially when, as in this instance, the fight is a vital part of the climax. How can you make an actor who throws a punch like a girl look like a champion? Don't try to guess. In this case it was managed by *reversing* the action. In other words, the actor extended his arm, his shoulder, and his body as far as he could toward the camera. Then, with all the speed and energy at his command (aided by an undercranked camera) he drew his arm and shoulder back as far as he could. When the film was printed in reverse the effect was that of a beautiful straight jab, delivered with speed and power—another prime example of the screen's "magic," a magic available in no other medium.

The manipulation of camera speed, as used to facilitate the shooting of fight scenes, is applicable in many other situations. Added speed is supplied by wide-angle lenses and/or underspeeding the camera. An interesting series of diverse effects can be manufactured through the use of *slow* motion (now often a cliche, but still effective when creatively used). Slow motion can add grace and ease to an actor's movements, or it can make them appear to be labored and difficult to effect. A wide-angle lens, head on, can make an actor, walking normally, seem to be taking giant strides; while a telescopic lens, shooting the same action, will show him to be struggling to take steps, which appear to be only a few inches long.

The final aid comes in the cutting room, where the selection of the best portions of the various shots are made for the final assembly. Given enough time and "takes" on the set, an actor can always deliver a "perfect" performance, at least as far as his talents allow perfection. Here, too, pace can be corrected or altered to any desired degree, inadequate performances ameliorated, and dramatic action, or reaction, highlighted. (See Book IV.)

In the final stages of postproduction sound manipulation can, when necessary, work small wonders with the actors' voices, and the addition of musical underscoring can add mood and emphasis to their performances. (This is most effectively demonstrated in sequences of suspense.)

All this may cause the budding actor to say, "But where is the fun or the creative satisfaction in all this? Everything is being done for me!" Well, not quite. The more experienced actors have learned that they can more easily concentrate on portraying real, honest human beings when they are freed from the necessity of creating excessively dramatic performances. (Spencer Tracy could play "Mr. Hyde" with an absolute minimum of the gruesome make-up traditionally used and, in the process, come much closer to a believable interpretation of Stevenson's tale.)

The actor can still shout when shouting is called for, gesticulate wildly when the occasion demands, or "make a face" when it is justified by the situation. But he need go no further in any of these directions than would his character in real life. Any excesses in appearance or activity needed for dramatic emphasis can and will be supplied by his helpers. (Though, for his own good, he'd better not call them that!)

## THE ACTRESS SPEAKS:

*Once you have been given a part you have the whole company, the whole studio, behind you—rooting for you, so to speak. They are all there to help you look and sound your best. All you have to do is be as good as they believe you are.*

*Do you practice acting for the screen? Do you attend special screen-acting classes?*

*When I taught film acting in Austin, Texas, I wrote some special "one person" scenes for some of my actors. With video equipment,* we recorded them on tape. *The tapes were invaluable in analyzing the exercises and, later, helped them in getting jobs.*

*I'm going to give you some of these scenes right here, for you to use as exercises if you care to. The camera is on you at all times, and there are no other voices. You must assume the other person is opposite you, just off camera, or on the other end of the phone, and you listen to his (or her) words. Please remember all that has been said about the importance of* listening *on camera. The camera (audience) is taking in all the other person is saying—by watching* you *and your reactions. Keep the pace, but don't rush it.* Get it just right.

## SCENE I—THE OBSCENE TELEPHONE CALL

The scene opens with SANDY, a young girl in her early
twenties, looking through a public telephone book. She can be
in bed or lounging on a couch. Flipping the pages, she sees a
name she likes, puts her finger on it, then runs it across the
page to the number. She looks at it carefully; then, on the
push-button phone near her, she punches out the seven digits
and waits for an answer. (While the phone is ringing on the
other end, show your anticipation—mildly, don't overdo it—
for what's ahead.) As a voice comes into your ear, you react
. . . then speak.

                    SANDY
          Hello . . . this is an obscene
          telephone call.
              (pause)
          You like it?

She pauses while a man speaks.

                  SANDY (cont.)
          Well . . . I mean . . . do you like
          . . . do you like the obscene
          telephone call?
              (pause, listening)
          Well, it's gonna get better.
              (pause)
          Ah . . . well, ah . . . don't go
          away. Are you interested?
              (pause, listening)
          You're interested. . . . Ah . . .
          how would you like it? . . . I
          mean, ah, how obscene would you
          like it?
              (pauses, listening)
          You'd like it very obscene. Uh . . .
          have you ever received an obscene
          telephone call before?
              (pause)

                  SANDY (cont.)
          You haven't? . . . But you've
          always wanted to? . . . Hm. . . .
          Right!

                           (CONTINUED)

I (CONTINUED)

>           (pause)
> Yes—<u>No</u>! . . . no, no. No, I'm not
> going to give you my name.
>           (rattled)
> Of course I'm not going to give
> you my name. This is an obscene
> phone call. . . . You think I'm
> going to give you my name?!
>           (pause)
> You're right! I haven't done this
> before. No, I haven't.
>           (pause)
> No. I'm not going to give you my
> name. . . . You want to give me
> <u>your</u> name? Oh, I <u>know</u> your
> name. I got it from the phone
> book.
>           (laughs)
> <u>Sidney</u>. <u>Sidney</u> likes obscene
> phone calls.
>           (pause)
> No . . . No, you don't know
> me. . . .
>           (pause)
> I just decided to do this.
>           (pause)
> Yeah . . . this is really kind of
> interesting, because you don't
> know who you're talking to. . . .
> You'll never know me. I can say
> anything I want to you.
>           (pause)
> I will. I. . . . I made up my mind
> that I was. . . . <u>WHAT</u>?!
>           (pause)
> What did you say?

There is a long pause while Sandy actually turns red in the
face.

>           SANDY (cont.)
> WWHAAT?!. . . . How dare you!

                                        (CONTINUED)

I (CONTINUED)

    She pauses in shock and embarrassment.

                    SANDY (cont.)
           How dare you say such a thing to
           me, because I know who _you_ are.
           You are a _terrible_ person. . . .
           And don't you ever speak to me
           that way again! Don't you ever
           call me again!

    Sandy abruptly hangs up the phone and looks directly into the
camera, realizing what she has done.

*Played for comedy, of course, this scene can end in at least two
ways. I had Sandy look into the camera, dead-pan, a little surprised,
still digesting the outcome of something she had planned entirely
differently.*

*Eddie directed this scene and had her finish it by looking into
the camera with a mischievous smile, as though she had baited the
guy into saying things to her she had wanted to hear. (And, if you
want to milk the laughs, you can finish* that *off by having her look
back into the phone book again for Sidney's number. E.D.)*

*Take your choice, kids.*

## SCENE II—GOODBYE, DARLING

> The scene opens on VIRGINIA, a middle-aged lady (sixtyish),
> greying hair, beautifully styled, dressed in the best of taste.
> She leans against the wall, just outside the hospital room. She
> has been sniffling into a handkerchief and we see the grief in
> her face as she looks toward a nurse who has just walked up
> and who now speaks from OFF-SCREEN. (VOICE OVER).

*(Note: This is the only line that will be VOICE OVER. It introduces
the scene.)*

> NURSE'S VOICE (O.S.)
> Mrs. Kershaw, we've done
> everything possible to save your
> husband, but he won't make it
> through the night. The doctor
> says you may have a few
> moments alone with him, if you
> wish.

> VIRGINIA
> (speaking to the nurse)
> Is he aware? Will he know I am
> there?

> No answer from the nurse is necessary. Virginia gives a weak
> and kindly nod of understanding. She then dabs her nose,
> pulls herself together, and goes through the door.

*(Note: This is easy video camera work. Simply pan her through an
imaginary door into the hospital room and go with her a very short
distance as she approaches what is supposed to be a hospital bed.
You can use a long table, with white sheets simulating a body. In
camera view, show barely the top of the sheet, thus enabling us to
believe the actress is speaking to her dying husband.)*

> Inside the hospital room Virginia closes the door behind her
> and walks up to the single bed in the room. She appears to be
> looking directly into her husband's face, and the audience is
> allowed to wonder about her thoughts. She speaks softly to
> him, and reaches out to touch him.
>
> (CONTINUED)

II (CONTINUED)

> VIRGINIA
>
> Howard. . .? Howard, can you
> hear me?

A pause, then she reacts to his opening eyes . . . his look to
her. She speaks softly and sweetly.

> VIRGINIA (cont.)
>
> Yes . . . yes, it is I. Your beloved
> wife of so many years. . . . Oh,
> Howard . . . I think back to our
> first years together . . . our
> young years. The joy! The respect!
> The pure unadulterated adoration
> I felt for you . . . the
> naivete. . . . Oh, how young I
> was! Then I grew up, didn't I? But
> you continued to treat me as that
> same child . . . how sweet. . . .
> But, Howard, during those years I
> became wise and inquisitive. . . .
> I guess you thought I was as
> simple as ever, or that I didn't
> care. . . . You never guessed that
> I watched everything you
> did. . . . I watched as your
> business grew from the losses of
> others. I watched as you took on
> strength as others failed. . . .
> You never trusted those who
> should not have trusted you. . . .
> And our children . . . you've
> never been able to tolerate
> Elizabeth and Martin . . . and
> those two idiots are yours! But
> Howard . . . Howard, can you
> hear me. . . ?
>> (she looks carefully
>> and deeply into his eyes)
> . . . Yes . . .
>> (a brief pause)

(CONTINUED)

II (CONTINUED)

>                    Howard . . . our son Robert, our
>                    brilliant son, Robert, your adored
>                    son, Robert . . . is not your son.
>                         (a brief pause)
>                    Oh, yes, you've left everything to
>                    him. . . .
>                         (a brief pause)
>                    He's mine, but he is not yours.
>                         (she pauses briefly,
>                         watching his face)
>                    Why, Howard . . . I haven't seen
>                    your eyes open that wide in years.
>                         (a brief pause)
>                    Yes.
>                         (changes tone, quietly)
>                    Our son Robert is not your son.
>                    Take that to your grave, you son-
>                    of-a-bitch!

She pauses, watches his face carefully as he expires.

>                    VIRGINIA (cont.)
>          Howard. . . ?

She reaches to feel his pulse, her eyes still watching his face
carefully. When she is satisfied that he is gone, she puts
herself back into the character of the bereaved widow, lifts her
kerchief to her nose, and CALLS OUT as she starts for the
door.

>                    VIRGINIA (cont.)
>          Nurse!

She exits.

## SCENE III—LATE

The scene opens as PAM, a beautiful young girl in her mid-
twenties, rushes breathlessly through a door, closes it behind
her, and leans against it. She looks straight ahead (just off
camera left) to an unseen man whom the audience will get to
know through her dialogue. (He will say just two words off
camera to start the scene. No more.) PAM has been running
and is breathing heavily as we hear his VOICE OVER.

                         MAN (O.S.)
            You're late.

Still breathing hard, Pam continues looking directly at him.
She moves forward just an inch or two. With a rather smug
look, she reaches into her bag, takes out a scarf and displays
within it—a gun. After a couple of seconds she tosses it onto
his desk (which has been placed directly in front of where she
is to stand, but not necessarily showing on camera.)

                         PAM
                   (still breathing hard)
              That was hardly an easy job you
              sent me on. I could have been a
              lot later. In fact . . . a hell of a
              lot later. . . .

She pauses, listens to him intently.

                         PAM (cont.)
              Trouble. . . ? Oh, just enough to
              make it interesting.
                   (pauses, listening)
              Mike . . . when he finds the gun
              missing, he'll know I took it.
                   (pauses, listening)
              No, I don't think I was followed.
                   (pauses, listening)
              I said think because I don't know!
              How does one know? It's dark out
              there. I changed cabs twice, and
              I've been running.
                   (listens, watches him)

                                              (CONTINUED)

III (CONTINUED)

>           Of course I was running. I was
>           rushing to get here like you said.
>           Look . . . I'm sure I wasn't
>           followed, and you've got the gun.
>           What do I get?

From off-camera Mike pitches her a key, which she grabs. She
looks at the metal tag on the key and laughs a sarcastic laugh.

>                    PAM (cont.)
>           Bonanza King?! . . . What is
>           this? A key to a hidden treasure?
>           A free hamburger . . . ? What
>           kind of detective are you . . . ? I
>           want to be paid!
>                    (pauses, listening)
>           The key to your . . . ??? Mike,
>           I'm new in this business, but I'm
>           good. I know it's a short-lived
>           business, but I also know that it
>           pays well. I wanna be paid now
>           . . . C.O.D., as promised.
>                    (pause)
>           Your place . . . ? Michael, I felt I
>           was lucky enough to get here . . .
>           and I just might make it to the
>           airport.

During this last line she has opened her bag, pulled out her
neat little black gloves, and has put them on as she speaks. As
she finishes putting them on, she pauses.

>                    PAM (cont.)
>           Once more. Pay now??

Pam looks steadily at Michael, then starts to shake her head
as though he has just said, "No."

>                    PAM (cont.)
>           I've heard of the old double-cross.
>           How do you like this one?

>                                        (CONTINUED)

III (CONTINUED)

    She reaches quickly into her bag and draws out another gun,
which she points directly at Michael.

PAM (cont.)

Your friend had a wad of dough

on him, and two guns. . . . Now

you'll have them both. . . .

(aiming carefully,

ready to shoot)

No, no, Mike . . . Too late.

    BANG!!! she shoots. Then she tosses the second gun onto his
desk, gives the body a cool glance, turns and walks out.

*There are several important things to remember about this scene.
Pace is important. She has been running, and though her heavy
breathing can lessen as the scene progresses, she is still UP. Secondly,
when it is decided (by whoever is directing this) where Michael is to
sit, be certain that you look directly at him, into his eyes. If you have
to use your imagination to conjure up this character, put him in one
place and keep him there. The viewer must see your eyes, so the
camera (if any) should be set low, shooting up slightly, and Michael's
chair should be raised a bit so that your eyes look directly at him.
The audience* must *see your eyes, and through them your feelings.*

## SCENE IV—NOT GUILTY

The placement of two off-camera characters is important to this scene. One is the judge to whom most of the scene is played. He should be very close on camera left, and a little above eye level, as though he were up on the bench. The other is BARBARA'S husband, seated some distance to the judge's left, and below eye level. BARBARA looks to the judge as she speaks to him, then glances occasionally at, or to, her husband. This girl is neurotic.

The scene opens as BARBARA approaches the bench. (She will take one step into center camera, medium close, and look directly at the judge.)

BARBARA

Please, Judge, let me speak for my
husband. He isn't telling you the
truth. I take the oath. He is not
guilty.
> (she pauses, listening)

No, he was not at home with me
. . . but I know he couldn't
possibly be the person you're
looking for. . . .
> (a pause)

He's an honest man. . . .
> (she looks at Jim,
> her husband)

Look at him . . . you can see it.
> (back to judge)

He has no record of any previous
violations. . . .
> (pause, listening)

Statement? His statement
admitting guilt is thoroughly and
completely false. . . . That's why
I'm here.
> (pause, listening)

Yes . . . yes, I believe he is
protecting someone.
> (pause, listens)

(CONTINUED)

IV (CONTINUED)

>                I can't tell you that.
>                     (pause)
>                Cannot? Will not? . . . What
>                difference? I will not if I cannot.
>                     (pause)
>                I don't know.

Barbara looks to her husband for a couple of seconds, then back to the Judge, and we see a change of pace.

>                BARBARA (cont.)
>                Yes, I <u>do</u> know. . . . Her name is
>                Franceska Borro. . . . She lives
>                at twenty-two eleven Oakridge
>                Drive.

Another glance to her husband, then quickly back to the Judge.

>                BARBARA (cont.)
>                You will find some of my
>                husband's things there, but I'm
>                sure you will also find proof that
>                it was <u>she</u> who killed Mr.
>                Lockhart.
>                     (pause)
>                Why didn't I tell you this before?
>                Because I expected my husband to
>                tell you . . . but of course . . .
>                no . . .
>                     (a short glance to
>                      her husband and back)
>                He is the martyr. . . .
>                     (nasty)
>                The hero. He would die to protect
>                his love.

She looks long at her husband and we see her start to break. Tears start to form.

>                BARBARA (cont.)
>                Oh, my God!
>                     (tears)
>                Oh, Jim, what have I done?

                                         (CONTINUED)

IV (CONTINUED)

    She snaps back to the Judge.

                    BARBARA (cont.)

          No! What I've told you is a lie. It
          was I! . . . Yes. Please believe me.
          I am the guilty one. He's
          protecting me!

    She looks again to her husband.

                    BARBARA (cont.)

          Oh, Jim. . . .
              (questioning)
          You did know. . . ?
              (back to the Judge)
          You see? He loves me. He is
          protecting me.

    She glances at her husband, then back to the Judge.

                    BARBARA (cont.)
              (breathing hard)
          Oh, my God. . . .!

*I've been asked time and again to explain how to cry real tears. All it takes is experience and living. Caring. Heart. The feeling must be real, then the tears come easily. If you are playing a scene where you have just been told your best friend has been killed in an accident, the tears are not immediate. At first, the shock is one of disbelief. Then you have to think about it. Here is where the heart comes forth. You think of the last time you saw him, that you will never see him again, that you didn't know you would never see him again, the things unsaid—dozens of thoughts such as these flash through your mind and if you really feel it, the tears will be there before you realize it.*

*You cannot manufacture tears. Oh, yes, if an actor simply cannot cry, the director will kindly suggest that he turn his head and pretend to weep, shoulders trembling, perhaps. Or you can cry into your hands. But you have to look up sometime! Directors and editors are masters at putting together a crying scene. They can always "cut to the kitchen stove" while a make-up person puts a liquid into the eyes of the heroine, then cut quickly into a close shot of her and, voila! Boohoo. But when you really* feel *a sad scene it isn't* only *the tears, it's everything that goes with it. Not long ago I watched a top actor in an Academy Award film do a crying scene and never saw a tear nor felt the sadness. He screamed his lines and grimaced to show his pain— but I felt nothing. 'Tis said he gave a good performance.*

*Laughter? How does one laugh on the screen? Well, for one thing, you certainly can't be in a sour mood. The scene, as written, must give you cause to laugh, but like a very tired, too-often-repeated joke (after you've studied the script at length), it probably no longer seems funny to you. So—you laugh anyway. If you have studied singing and breath control you can manufacture a laugh. If you don't sing, take a deep breath and let it out as you make laughing sounds (even ha, ha, ha works). Keep this going until you feel so silly you will actually be laughing at yourself. You can do it. Keep it up. Do the scale. Up and down. Start down and go up. Then start up and go down. It's fun! And don't worry about the neighbors as you practice. This is Hollywood.*

## SCENE V—BEST COFFEE IN TOWN

A young man quickly steps into CENTER CAMERA (CLOSE) as though he has just darted out of the rain. (He is in the alcove of a store front.) He has been sheltering his head with a folded newspaper and he begins to shake the water from it and to brush himself off. Suddenly he looks directly at someone CAMERA RIGHT. A young woman has spoken to him (OFF CAMERA). We have not heard a word.

> JEFF
> Oh, yeah . . . wet . . .

Jeff looks around at the street action but is again attracted by her voice.

> JEFF (cont.)
> New here in L.A.? . . . Yeah. . . .
> (wondering)
> How could you tell?
> (pause, listening)
> My <u>clothes</u>? . . . They're just
> ordinary clothes. . . .
> (pause, while
> she speaks)
> Raincoat! Oh . . . don't the people
> here wear raincoats?
> (a pause)
> Better things to spend their
> money on. . . . I suppose so. . . .
> (looks at her
> carefully)
> You look cold.
> (pause—then
> a statement)
> You're not.
> (pause)
> What? . . . A cup of coffee? . . .
> No, thanks.
> (pause)
> You'll pay? . . . That makes no
> difference to me. . . . <u>You'll</u> <u>pay</u>!

(CONTINUED)

V (CONTINUED)

> That would be absurd, as a matter
> of fact.
>> (listening)
> Vermillion. I'm from Vermillion,
> South Dakota.
>> (a pause)
> I am. . . . I <u>am</u> proud of it. A
> sweet place it is.
>> (thinking of it)
> Small and sweet.
>> (pauses, listening)
> What did you say? So my?. . . .
> Oh . . . <u>so</u> <u>are</u> <u>you</u>.
>> (looking her
>>   up and down)
> So <u>you</u> are.
>> (a pause)
> No, I <u>don't</u> want to go for a cup of
> coffee. And listen, young lady,
> where I come from the man asks
> the woman.
>> (listens, frowns)
> It's <u>not</u> old fashioned! . . . It's
> . . . it's just the right way to do
> things.

Jeff watches her carefully. He feels he may have hurt her
feelings.

>                        JEFF (cont.)
> You're shivering. You <u>are</u>
> cold. . . . I'll give you my coat
> and take you for a cup of coffee.
>> (pause)
> No!! . . . Why not?
>> (pause)
> You'll . . . make me some coffee
> at <u>your</u> place? . . .
>> (thinks about it,
>>   listening)

(CONTINUED)

V (CONTINUED)

>Best coffee in town?
>>(pause)
>You know . . . I've heard of
>things like this happening. You're
>crazy. How do you know I'm not a
>dangerous criminal?
>>(watching her laugh)
>Well, you don't have to get hysterical. . . .

He stares at her (and here you have a choice of attitudes—a chance to swing it in one of several directions).

>JEFF (cont.)
>Let's go.

They exit.

## SCENE VI—CAUGHT

The scene opens with a young man standing with his back to
the CAMERA (which should be angled). He is going through a
file drawer in an office filing cabinet. We feel his anxiety by
his movements. He searches rather frantically. Suddenly, there
is the SOUND of a door opening. Startled, he turns towards us,
looking off just CAMERA LEFT. (Focus on a spot!)

                    CHARLES
          Mark!

He is a bit relieved, but still tense. We hear the SOUND of a
door closing. Charles' look is steady, fixed on Mark as Mark
moves closer.

                    CHARLES
          What are you doing here at this
          hour? I thought. . . .
                    (pause)
          Yes, well. . . . I was looking for
          the Clayborn file. . . .
                    (a pause)
          Key? . . .
                    (a nervous laugh)
          I never returned my key when I
          changed jobs. . . .
                    (adding quickly)
          Not intentionally. . . . I simply
          forgot. . . .
                    (he interrupts himself)
          Mark, why are you looking at me
          like that? We've always been
          friends. I'm not a criminal.
                    (listening)
          Yes, yes, I know this seems
          wrong . . . but it's for a good
          purpose. . . . You'll see, if I can
          find what I'm looking for. . . .

Charles turns again to the filing cabinet and digs deeper and
deeper into the crowded files. He speaks while he searches:
                                        (CONTINUED)

VI (CONTINUED)

                    CHARLES
            There's something very
            wrong. . . .

Suddenly, he pulls out a file and turns into the CAMERA as if
to get more light on the file. He is becoming more and more
pleased with his findings.

                    CHARLES (cont.)
            Yes! Yes! . . . Here it is. . . .
                    (looking through it)
            The Osgood contracts to Mr.
            Clayborn. . . .

Charles turns to Mark with the good news and finds a gun
pointed in his direction. His expression changes immediately
from elation to confusion.

                    CHARLES (cont.)
            Mark. . . .

The confusion turns to fright as Charles looks into Mark's
eyes, then down at the gun (waist high), then directly into
Mark's eyes again.

                    CHARLES (cont.)
            Mark . . . I can't believe
            this. . . . a gun? . . . What do
            you want? The files? . . . We're
            on the same side, aren't we? . . .
            Well, aren't we?
                    (panic grows)
            If this information is so
            important . . . so dangerous . . .
            that it brings us to this. . . .
                    (panic builds)
            I'll give you the files and forget I
            ever saw them. . . . Don't look at
            me like that. . . . Mark . . . I'll
            put the files back. . . .

As Charles turns to put the file back in its place in the drawer,
we hear a gun shot.

*You have a choice of endings.*
*(1)  Charles gets shot in the back and falls.*
*(2)  Charles freezes, then turns in Mark's direction and sees someone*
      *else at some distance away and realizes that Mark has been shot.*
*(3)  Or create your own.*

*Jean Porter during film workshop in Munich.*

# 10

# *Keep It Alive!*

Rarely does a modern young actor discuss his craft without a disser-
tation on "energy." In the context of acting I find the word misleading,
if not distasteful. Many young actors assume that energy entails an
expenditure of power, which, in its properly used sense, it does. But
operating power is not what screen acting demands; accurately speaking, it demands more. It demands vitality.

My dictionary defines vitality as "the principle of life; animation;
the ability to live or capacity for lasting; continuance." It is impossible
to find a better definition for the essence of screen acting.

I have learned never to ask an actor for "energy"; the results can
be devastating. He will spit out the words, like a neophyte fresh out
of *Rada*, breathe loudly, indulge—and this is quite common—in violent gestures or movements. But quite often, just before I say "action," I will repeat the words, "vitality, vitality." And the actor will
know I am looking for *life* in the scene, not a volcanic explosion.

Vitality is an essential part of *every* performance, regardless of
the mood, the pace, or the state of movement or of rest. If Camille
had been lethargic as she lay dying, we would have been relieved to
see her go.

A well-known pianist once remarked that it was when playing
the softest notes that the greatest hand strength was required—to hold
back the fingers while they depressed the keys just hard enough to
make the soft sounds. So it is with vitality. Contradictory as it may
seem, a state of repose, of quiescence, even the act of quiet dying,
must have life, and these two apparent opposites are quite difficult to
harmonize. (Unless you have a deep understanding of oriental philosophy.)

The ability to produce a superabundance of vitality is probably
the secret of "camera presence." I have seen actors in a state of such

lethargy that they seemed incapable of functioning but, once before the camera, their bodies and their eyes would radiate vitality in its purest form.

Granted the indispensability of vitality, how is it acquired and how is it best exhibited or projected? As for acquisition, much of it is inborn. We all know people who are "bursting with life," some from the moment they first breathe it in. Most of us are impressed by the presence of vigor in people of all ages, and we are surprised to find that such vigor is usually accompanied by a wide, open outlook on life. Vitality is partly an expression of such elasticity and quickness of mind, and partly an expression of physical health.

Most people who approach an acting career possess awareness and alertness—many, however, pay little attention to their physical conditions. It is now a cliche to call an actor's body his "instrument," but it is a very apt metaphor. It is through the use of the entire body that most interpersonal communication is expressed, and communication is essential in acting.*

No violinist neglects his violin. He protects it from excessive dryness, humidity, dirt, or anything else that might prevent it from producing the best possible tones. The same is true for any instrumentalist, even a harmonica player or a virtuoso on the ocharina.

All this applies to persons in other walks of life—a hunter and his instrument of death, a schusser and his skis, a baseball player and his bat and glove, a bowler and his ball—on and on and on. So why do some actors treat their bodies so carelessly? Indolence, alcohol, and drugs are hardly the means of keeping their instruments in tune.

For obvious reasons, actresses have always been more aware of the necessity for maintaining their physical appearances than have their male counterparts, but the imbalance seems to be correcting itself of late. Most actors are now quite aware of the need to shape up, but two sets of tennis on Sunday will hardly suffice. A well-planned regimen that includes exercises for stamina, for strength, and for agility should be high on every young actor's priority list.

Acting academies have long taught fencing for agility and grace, and fencing is an excellent exercise. Like dancing and many pure sports, however, it requires many hours of work to do the job. (Most professional athletes now work out with weights in addition to their sports activities.)

I have always been partial to weight lifting because of its unmatched potential for overall development, and the fact that it produces maximum results rather quickly. (I am not referring to com-

---

*Dogs watch their masters intently; they get more information from their owners' bodily attitudes and movements than they do from their voice commands. No actor should be less observant than his dog.

petitive lifting or body beautiful building.) Extensive daily calisthenics, aerobics, and swimming will also do the job if they are allotted sufficient time. It is important that you choose a form of exercise that will develop *all* the muscles of your body. You never know when you may be called on to perform some unusual physical activity—stunt men do not always fill the bill.

Keeping your instrument in mint condition is one thing; playing it with skill is something else. A Stradivarius in the hands of an amateur will produce more pain than melody. For the actor, as for the virtuoso, the playing is the thing. Once your body is finely tuned and you have vitality to spare, how do you get it into your performance?

By showing concern, by concentrating, by paying attention. All of these words have a very positive connotation, and they all carry the secret of vitality in acting. Like a magnifying glass which focuses scattered rays of sunlight into one bright, shining spot, concentration, by definition and by practice, brings your vitality to a common center in a greatly increased state. So pay attention, concentrate, show concern—all for the person or persons you are involved with in the scene. If you do that with honesty, without pretense, you are well on your way to becoming an actor.

### THE ACTRESS SPEAKS:

*An actress may proudly consider herself full of energy and stamina and run through the day's work at bonkers speed. She may show impatience when mechanical foul-ups slow the shooting of a scene, or if a fellow actor stalls or has trouble remembering a line. This kind of nervous energy is just as bad as having no vitality at all. It is nerve-wracking to the rest of the cast and the crew. This type of person usually clowns around a lot, which is okay for starting off the morning but wears badly through the day.*

*If you have natural vitality it shows in all your movements, controlled and disciplined. Your inner energy is present in your eyes.*

*It is exciting to take on another character—to become another person for a while—but it takes a lot out of you. Even a small part which works for several consecutive days can leave you drained. Acting for the screen is much more difficult than acting in the theater, for many reasons not the least of which is waiting. You prepare for a scene, get yourself completely worked up for whatever is expected, then you wait until everything and everyone else is ready. Usually it is best to go to your portable dressing room, keep your mind locked in on the scene to be done, and wait patiently. If the scene is easy, you might find relief in reading, crocheting, knitting, or in any time-consuming activity that demands little attention. Whatever, it is better to be alone at this point.*

*The first time you will feel* all *of your lights is when you step in front of the camera for the final rehearsal. Get to know them. Your key light will be the hottest one you will feel. For close-ups, your eye light will be very small, very close, and usually just below the camera.*

During this final rehearsal you will become overly warm and probably perspire. Just before the first take, the director will signal the crew that he is satisfied and ready to shoot. At this point the make-up person and the hairdresser (who have been watching every move) will dash into the set, dab your face carefully with a make-up sponge, and rearrange a few strands of hair. Don't let this throw you. Ignore them and realize that they are there to help you. Perspiration reflects the lights, and a strand of hair can throw a shadow in the wrong place. I saw an actress throw a tantrum once, claiming this activity broke her concentration. But remember these are artists, like yourself, doing their jobs, helping your photographic image. They know you are concentrating. They won't speak to you.

Some preceding chapters contain what may appear to be a rather contradictory statement, one which I feel must be clarified to make you more comfortable. We keep saying, ". . . forget the camera is there." This is meant to remind you to put yourself so completely into the character you are playing and into the setting around you that you won't think about the camera.

But, of course you know the camera is there. During this final rehearsal make certain you know where the camera is at all times. If it is to "dolly" (to move) keep in mind exactly where it will be at the moment you will be doing, or saying, a particular thing. Rehearse the scene enough to fix these points firmly in your mind; then you can forget about the camera—maybe.

If you are in a close or medium-close shot and your eyes are to follow a person, or a car, across the camera—let's say from camera left across to camera right—be aware of the camera or there will be a jump. Simply imagine the object you are following goes in a straight line, right across the camera and on. Look through the camera as though it were invisible.

There may come a time when you are directed to look into the lens. This often occurs in TV sit-coms. If you are new at the game it might be a good idea to quietly ask the cameraman which part of his camera is the lens. It may not be where you think it is.

"Lights! Camera! Action!" What a beautiful phrase. If everyone loved screen acting as much as I do, we'd have little else happening.

Acting for the screen may one day be given its due credit. Because of all the careless, trite, slot-filling nonsense found on the "box" these days, I don't know. But there again, it has its place. There are some marvelous shows on television. Perhaps one day the networks and the advertising agencies will get together and set aside larger budgets for longer schedules, and shoot more films for TV. There is no doubt that, as a rule, the more time and money spent, the better the quality. And audiences are proving that quality counts.

But, even as things are today, do your best. Get whatever roles you can, in cinema or TV, and make them noticeable. Make people remember you for what you did with a particular role.

*Marlon Brando, shown here in* The Young Lions, *is a perfect example of a fine actor who can put himself into any role.*

# 11

## *Don't Be With It*

Acting styles change with the years. Every era has its "in" techniques. One such fashion, which started three or four decades ago, is still with us: "naturalism." Offhand, one would think that naturalism would be a fairly simple, realistic style, but some actors won't have it that way. If it isn't "put on," overdone, it isn't acting. So naturalism, at least in many instances, has become a display of eye twitching, nose picking, and fanny scratching.

Formal definitions indicate that as far as art is concerned, "naturalism" and "realism" mean much the same thing—but not quite. "Naturalism" is the depiction of what is natural, or instinctive; "realism" is the depiction of the natural world around us. Succinctly put, "realism" is showing a person in an environment where bed bugs abound; "naturalism" is showing that person absentmindedly (and that's important) scratching the resultant bites.

When such natural or instinctive activity is strictly in keeping with the character's milieu, it is also real; when it is arbitrarily engaged in without regard to the environment, it is an affectation and, as such, it destroys the honesty and the reality of the performance.

Stylistic, or affected, acting has another great drawback: Like any fad of the moment it doesn't age well. In clothes, an extreme style from any particular period becomes, in later years, a laughing matter or an object of curiosity. The same is true for stylistic acting.

The late twenties and the early thirties saw an influx of theater actors into Hollywood films, actors who brought with them the techniques then in vogue on Broadway. Today, many of the films they made demonstrate affectation in its most obvious form. One film features two actresses, one an acclaimed Broadway star, the other a product of Hollywood silent films. The difference in styles is striking. The theater actress' speech utilizes the broad A's then considered proper in her medium. Even though she is playing a middle-class midwestern woman, her training demanded that she speak with an accent William Wellman once described as "Kansas City British." It was neither real nor natural, but the style was "in."

The film actress, on the other hand, spoke clean-cut midwestern "American," a manner of speech with few affectations. From today's point of view, the theater actress' performance looks false, while that of the film actress is true, and will probably remain so for some time to come. The scenes in which they appear are colored by their acting styles—those of one seem cleverly contrived, while those of the other still carry the feeling of reality.

Most artists would like to believe that, contrary to Marc Antony's pronouncement, the *good* that they do will live after them. For all artists that means presenting, whether in painting, in literature, or in films, the essence of human thought and behavior. As every student of history knows, this has changed little over hundreds of years. We still find truth and enjoyment in Oliver Twist and Huckleberry Finn.

When acting is founded on the basic ethical and moral attitudes of mankind (and their typical imperfections), the film's characters remain dramatically effective through generations of time. Changing tastes in dress or behavior become purely surface phenomena laid over the solid base of long-lasting, essential human nature.

Errors in these areas are most often seen in the perpetuation of the stereotype and in the use of archaic or exotic language. As mentioned earlier, we have no working knowledge of common speech of the past since we have only the literary presentation of pre-twentieth century speech. The poetry of Chaucer or of Shakespeare mirrors the conversational speech of the men in their streets no more accurately than the poems of Dylan Thomas mirror the idiom of today. One of King Arthur's knights might have said, "Gadzooks!" or "Ho, varlet!" but, unless you're looking for laughs, you should no more use such expressions in depicting a man of the Middle Ages than you would pepper the speech of a grandfather type with "twenty-three skiddoo" or "you're the bee's knees." On the other hand, asking an actor who is playing Marco Polo to use modern colloquialisms (which has been done) is as unforgivable as asking a modern hipster to declaim with the rhetoric of a Winston Churchill.

The safe approach is to avoid linguistic excesses, whether you are using the jargon of a truck driver or a college professor (though either one can, at times, speak like the other). The same guidelines will serve in the presentation of any character, except in broad comedy where exaggeration is in the nature of things. But for relatively straight characterization, it is wise to remember a line from Robert Burns: "A man is a man for a'that." No matter what the cultural coating of a character, whether it be as extreme as the eighteenth-century simpering of a member of the royal court, or the sour demeanor of a nineteenth-century moralist, we are all brothers under the skin. Remembering that will give your characterizations "legs" and longevity.

## THE ACTRESS SPEAKS:

*Why is acting one of our most desired careers? Escape? Acting allows you to get out of yourself, to become another person. Power? While acting you can hold an entire audience and manipulate them as you please. Money? I do hope it isn't for the money, but as of late, screen actors' salaries are astronomical. You want to be loved? If you're not loved by someone already, acting won't help you.*

*To every beginner who dreams of becoming a movie star I just want to tell you—it can be done. It takes time, a long time. It takes patience, a great deal of patience. It takes persistence and hard work, lots of both. If you don't have the kind of character and personality to put forth, and put up with, all of these things, you probably won't make it. But if you believe you have the talent, the heart, and the strength to pursue—pursue! The rewards are worth the effort.*

*Look in the mirror. Are you beautiful? Gorgeous? Handsome? Pretty? Pretty good looking? Attractive? Which? Gotta be in there somewhere.*

*You must be photogenic for the screen. You must have good facial bone structure and your eyes, nose and mouth must be interesting, if not appealing. To be luscious is perfect, but we can't have it all. If you know you have an abundance of sex appeal, that helps. Your eyes are your most important asset, so take care of them. Your skin should be kept clear of all blemishes, so keep it clean and watch your diet.*

*To be of lasting importance on the screen you must have a healthy and attractive body. The camera adds ten pounds, so a woman must always keep her weight down. While you're young, that's easy, so start now and keep the good habits. One of the easiest ways to decrease in weight and inches is to simply eat half portions of what you have been eating. If you get hungry between meals, have a tablespoon of honey or a small piece of jack cheese and a cracker (just ONE). If you keep to this you'll be proud of yourself and you will enjoy being asked, "How do you do it?"*

*Exercise is a must, but in today's world everyone is so aware of this that I probably don't need to carry on about it. I would like to say that for a woman's body dancing is the most important exercise. It gives you rhythm, grace, charm, and style. Dancing helps you to develop easy, subtle, sexy body movements, with or without music.*

*Once you make up your mind that cinema/TV is the career you are choosing, write down your goals. Put them right there in front of*

you. Plan your work and work your plan. Prepare yourself in every
way you can, then go to it. Once you start, don't give up. You may
need to change course several times during your training, your amateur try-outs, and your planning, but remember that's as it should
be. You may start out playing comedy and discover you can do other
things, etc. Changes mean you are growing. But if you make a change
and don't like it, go back to what you are comfortable with. No matter
what, always be honest with yourself.

Most of us start out in school plays. Encouraged by audience
response, we believe we have a future in acting. It's easy to go on to
the next step and get into local community little theater groups. Every
town has at least one. Again, encouraged by good audience reaction
and backed by a belief in yourself, you move on. By this time you
should move to where the real action is. If you choose theater, your
move will probably be to the nearest city with a good, nationally
recognized theater, your ultimate aim being Broadway, of course.

If you choose screen acting, you will head for Hollywood. Hollywood is still the center for filmmaking, and it always will be. New
York has some television production, but Hollywood/L.A. has it all.
Sure, films are shot all across the nation, but basically, the center is
here. Tinseltown, the Filmworld, takes the brunt of all the sad jokes
made by those who fail and leave. They find fault with the place if
they're unsuccessful. No need to do that. It will survive, and you
may be back.

The first thing you have to do after arriving in L.A. is to get some
attention. (Don't rob a bank!) This may take some time, so you should
bring enough bread to carry you through four seasons, or you will
have to get an earthling job of some sort to sustain you. There are
always waiter and waitress jobs available.

Get acquainted. From a newsstand, pick up the trade papers
(Hollywood Reporter and Variety) to find out what's going on in all
the studios. Here you can also take note of which agents are getting
jobs for what actors. Study these. Learn to remember the names of
agents and casting directors.

Find out where fellow actors and actresses hang out and go there.
Listen to everybody and get to know them. Let them know you are
a likable person and no threat. Make friends.

Get an agent. If you have guts, and you do have guts or you
wouldn't be here, you will GET an agent. As an unknown, you won't
expect the top agents in town to be waiting for your call, but there
are all kinds of agents. And there are all kinds of legitimate ways of
getting an agent. You must sift through all the information you will
pick up here and there and choose for yourself the best way to go
about it.

Prove your ability to your agent. If you've only done school plays and little theater he will probably suggest that you get into some screen-acting classes and do some showcases where casting directors go to view scenes played by promising newcomers. These showcases are advertised in the trade papers and in Drama-Logue. Also watch for announcements from local universities or the American Film Institute. They advertise coming film production, and interviews are set up to choose actors and actresses for key roles. These student films are good experience and will give you film to show in future job hunting.

If you see in the Hollywood Reporter production chart that Gem-Stone Productions Co. is preparing "Do It My Way," and you happened to have seen it on the stage and consider yourself perfect for the supporting role of Marcia Mae, look to see who the casting director is, phone the company and ask for an appointment. (That is, if you have no agent.) Don't be bashful. Don't be rude, either. Just give it a try. Who knows? You might get an appointment. If you can't get an appointment by phone, go over to the production company and leave your photo and resumé with a note asking for an interview. Be clever. Make them want to see you. If that part is taken, maybe you'll get something else. Don't settle for nothing.

Remember all the while, and this covers a lot of time, you will be meeting people and becoming known. If people like you they will help you. You can't get anywhere in this town if you are disliked. Let people know, graciously, that you need help, and when given it, be grateful. Show-biz people like to give a hand, but they also like to know it's been appreciated; not by the buck, but by sincere warmth and continued friendship. When you get your first break, you'll want to give a party.

# Postscript

## To Whom It May Concern

One of the world's greatest dancers, Mikhail Baryshnikov, speaks about the absence of strong personalities among performing artists today: "It's a sociological problem for all of us, not just dancers but actors and musicians too. We are a lost generation, a lot of people who are aggressive and virtuosic but who have little inside. Some ask, 'Where's the beef?' I ask, 'Where's the soul?'

"Today's young performers have to get more cultural language, more exposure and education. They must learn how to project real feelings, to be real people. Being an artist in the biggest sense comes down to being a *mensch*."*

Baryshnikov's prescription is deceptively simple: Filling it seems to be very difficult indeed. Observation, listening, reading are essential but hardly enough. The key is "*real* feelings . . . *real* people." That means getting beneath the beauty (or the ugliness) of the skin to the person below. Surface manifestations will give us a picture, they will not give us art. A brief flash of truth will touch us infinitely more deeply than an hour of virtuosity. Jean and I recently saw a film in which two well-known actors ranted, raved, gesticulated—all quite skillfully—and we felt we were watching contortionists at work, virtuosic and interesting to look at but hardly worth taking to one's heart. A short while before we had seen a film clip—three short close-ups from *Casablanca*—in which Bogart and Bergman look at each other. That's it—no words, no gestures, *no tricks*—they just *look* at each other. But Jean and I both sobbed involuntarily at the sheer beauty of the scene. Because, in the entire art of acting, nothing is more beautiful than honesty and truth—presented with utter simplicity.

---

*Los Angeles Times, March 22, 1984; interview with Donna Perlmutter.

407

# Book IV

## ON FILM EDITING

# Prologue

It was early in the 1930s. A very important guest, Baron Rothschild, was being given Paramount's version of the Grand Tour. One of his stops was my cutting room, where I was asked to say a few words by way of defining my craft.

I was young and enthusiastic. Some twenty minutes later, as I paused for breath, the Baron smiled.

"It would appear," he said, "that film editing *is* the art of film-making."

I agreed, trying to ignore the twinkle in his eyes. Of course, I was then a film editor. A few years later, when I became a director, I would probably have changed my pitch—but not too much.

# Introduction

Today few people will deny that "the film," as it is commonly called, is the most dynamic of all the arts, and none can argue with the statistics which show it to be, by long odds, the most popular art form in the world at large. However, many who try to analyze its power and appeal are brought up short by the collective nature of its creation. They can study, criticize, and debate the "art," but they find it very difficult to define the "artist."

One accepted judgment of today is that the film is created solely by the director—the "auteur"—and in a few instances, a very few, that may be true. Putting aside for the moment the claims of the screen writer, the cinematographer, the actors, and a number of other workers, to at least some portions of creative credit, there is another craftsman without whom a film could hardly come into being—an artist who has it in his power to mold, to improve, even to recreate a motion picture. That artist is the film editor.

"Once more I repeat," said Pudovkin, "that editing is the creative force of filmic reality."* And Ernest Lindgren agreed. "The development of film technique," he said, "has been primarily the development of editing."**

These statements are as true today as they were 55 and 35 years ago. Not too long after Edwin S. Porter started experimenting with the intercutting of related and simultaneous action, and D.W. Griffith decided to shoot a "close-up" to increase the dramatic impact of a player's reaction, filmmakers found that by means of a "cut" they could manipulate space, time, emotions, and emotional intensity to an extent limited only by their individual instincts and creative abil-

---

* V.I. Pudovkin, *Film Technique*, Newnes, 1929.
** Ernest Lindgren, *The Art of the Film*, Allen and Unwin, 1948.

ities. Film editing thus became the essence of "motion pictures." Without it the best movie would be only a photographed stage play and the "art of the cinema" would have remained an unarticulated phrase.

While graciously giving credit to Griffith for initiating the technique, Russians like Eisenstein, Pudovkin, Kuleshov, and a few others developed montage into a special art form, although in this case necessity was certainly the mother of invention. The Germans, French, British, and Americans could tell their stories and make dramatic points with the help of printed "titles"; the inhabitants of the Western world boasted a high degree of literacy. But 90% of the Russian people could not read, and titles were useless. Images had to say it all, and they did so most effectively. Eisenstein's *Battleship Potemkin* is still rated by many experts as the finest film ever made.

However, the "art" of montage was almost eliminated by the advent of sound, with its "fixative" tendencies. It made a partial comeback in the forties, its resurgence brought about largely by Orson Welles and his *Citizen Kane*, but now it is once again suffering through a period of banality which is the inevitable result of the peculiar economic and "artistic" demands of corporate television. To put it bluntly, the art of editing has all but expired as a vital development; and, if Lindgren's thesis is correct, the development of film technique as a whole has all but expired with it.

So—this book is written with the hope of helping the beginning director as well as the embryonic film editor. It is just possible that a reawakening of the filmmakers' interest in the still unexplored potential of film editing may bring about the long overdue renaissance of the filmmakers' art. For that interest to arise it is necessary that the primary filmmaker, the director, must understand the importance of editing, and that he learn how to incorporate it fully into his filmmaking technique. Certainly, the extent to which his films approach the full potential of excellence will depend as much on his mastery of the editing craft as on his knowledge and practice of story and staging techniques.

# 1

# *Titles and Definitions*

There are as many levels in the practice of this craft as there are practicing craftsmen. They range from the "mechanical" to the truly creative and, when modified by the skill and ingenuity which any particular cutter may possess, as well as the input of directors and producers, they present us with the possibility of a nearly infinite number of styles and techniques, and an almost equal number of results.

The use of the word "cutter" in the previous sentence was intentional. In the twenties and early thirties, a cutter who called himself a film editor would have been considered a snob. Then came the Wagner Labor Relations Act and unionization. In an attempt to raise the status of the craft, which was considered by the less knowledgeable executives of Hollywood to be five or six rungs from the top of the filmmakers' ladder, it was decided that "film editor" had a more imposing sound than "film cutter," and henceforth that became the official terminology.* However, most film editors, at least in each other's company, still use the down-to-earth term "cutter" to define themselves and their profession.

It is probably safe to say that no two cutters will cut a film or even a moderately lengthy sequence in exactly the same way. So let us consider some of the varieties of workers in the field. First, one of that number who populate the fat part of the bell-shaped curve: the

---

* For the same reason a cameraman became a "Director of Photography," script clerks became "Script Supervisors," even though absolutely no script supervision was involved in their work, a set designer became an "Art Director," and so on to a ridiculous degree. Eventually, the Screen Directors Guild was forced to demand (and get) in contract bargaining, that no further craftsmen be gratuitously awarded the title of "director" of anything.

"mechanic." Working as an apprentice, he (or she)* learns a few basic techniques, follows the script and/or the director's instructions, and delivers a film to which his cutting has added not one whit of anything ingenious or original. On the contrary, his lackluster efforts may diminish the film's potential impact considerably. It is his good fortune that so few directors, producers, or studio executives have the expertise with which to judge his contributions, though I have rarely encountered a member of any of these categories who didn't consider himself to be one of the world's great editors.

At the top of the scale is the creative editor, the person with an understanding of dramatic structure, a keen sense of timing, a compulsion to seek out the scene's hidden values—values which even the writer and the director may not have clearly grasped (believe me, it happens!)—and a mastery of the technical skills needed to bring all these talents to bear on the film he edits. Unfortunately, there are very few creative cutters in the field, at least among those who edit other people's work. The reasons are clear, and a little sad.

On the average film, a cutter's status is usually beneath that of the director, the writer, the top actors, the producer, the photographer, the composer, and sometimes the set designer.** And his salary is proportionate to his status. This state of affairs often induces a potentially brilliant cutter to seek a career offering greater rewards, even though his talents may not lie along those other lines. Add to that the extremely long apprenticeship which assistant cutters are forced to serve, no matter how great their talents, and it is clear why so many quick, bright, and ambitious young men and women opt for alternative careers. I have known several promising young men who have abandoned the cutting rooms because they were unwilling to spend seven or eight years at menial labor before getting permission to put scissors to film.

At the top of the scale lies another trap. Really fine, creative cutters quickly earn a "miracle man" reputation. Promotion, difficult to resist because of increases in salary and status, inevitably follows—usually to the rank of director or, less frequently, producer. But these

---

* In the silent days a large proportion of cutters were women. At Famous Players Lasky, where I started my career, *all* the cutters were women. The advent of sound, with its technical complexities, led many executives to conclude that women could not handle sound-related problems, and many of them were discharged, some never to return. However, the best of them survived, and within a few years younger women joined them at the benches. For most of the life of motion pictures, a singularly male-oriented business, cutting has been the only craft, aside from the traditionally female occupations such as hairdressing, costuming, etc., which has fully utilized the talents of women.

**I understand that, at present, the *average* cutter rates less appreciation than ever before.

crafts demand their own special talents, and success is by no means assured. Indeed, the result is often tragic. For obvious reasons, a backward step is hard to take; and many cutters, in classic adherence to the "Peter principle," persist in hanging on as second or third-rate directors or producers rather than return to a first-rate cutter's status. Only a handful of exceptional men and women have been content to spend their working lives exercising their rare talents in the relative obscurity of the cutter's cubicle.

To appreciate the role of editing in the filmmaking process one must have some understanding of how a film is made. Working backwards from the completed work, we find that the film is divided into a number of *sequences*, each sequence corresponding, let us say, to a chapter in a book or a scene in a play. Broadly speaking, a sequence has its own beginning, middle, and end, although these are not as clearly marked as they are in the film as a whole.

Each sequence, in turn is divided into *scenes*, the number of such scenes varying from one to many. Example: in *Raiders of the Lost Ark*, the chase through the marketplace in the Arab town is one *sequence*, from the start of the chase to its conclusion. The *scenes* are those parts of the sequence which take place in any one location, whether they are as simple as a single shot taking the actors through the narrow alley, or as complex as the hero's confrontation with the assassin in black, a scene of considerable length, requiring a large number of set-ups.

Just as the sequence may consist of one or more scenes, so a scene may consist of one or more *cuts* derived from one or more set-ups. There is no one-to-one correspondence between set-ups and cuts, since one set-up may furnish a number of cuts, as usually occurs in the intercutting of matching close-ups in dialogue scenes.

The truth, then, is that in spite of the time, talent, and effort spent in writing, preparing, and shooting the film, it has no shape or substance until the hundreds, even thousands of bits and pieces which go to make it are assembled. And it is here that the editor puts *his* stamp on the film. Every artist, if he *is* an artist, puts his own imprint on anything he does. Gilbert Stuart's portrait of Washington is not the same as Charles Peale's. Cortes, Picasso, and Kandinsky would each have painted the same Paris street in his own individual, widely different style. Three directors would make quite different films from the same script. All that is quite commonly accepted. But what is not so commonly known is that, given a free hand, three different cutters will create three different versions out of the same material, and the results of their labors will depend not only on the quality of the filmed scenes but, to a considerable degree, on the talents and the skills of the editors themselves.

Needless to say, these skills come in different sizes, as do their effects on films. The glib phrase, "Saved in the cutting room," is heard not too infrequently in film circles. It sounds clever, but it hardly conforms to the facts. At the least, it is an exaggeration. The editor may improve a film by eliminating excessive and/or redundant dialogue, by selective editing of inadequate acting, by creative manipulation of the film's pace and the timing of reactions, by mitigating weaknesses of badly directed scenes and, on rare occasions, by more unusual editorial maneuvers. Any or all of this activity presupposes a clever editor working on a more or less incompetently directed film. However, as often as not, a more or less incompetent editor is working on a cleverly directed film, and not doing it justice. And, in any case, the editor works only with the material handed him by the director. Even if he creates a "miracle," the fact remains that the film he has been given carries *all* the ingredients of that miracle except, of course, for the creative ability brought to the cutting process by the editor. Finally, it must be borne in mind that although the editing magic is created in the cutting room, its creator is quite often *not* the cutter.

# 2

# *Who Cuts the Film?*

Who, exactly, does edit the film? Usually no single person, exactly. Although there have been a few notable exceptions, a good director always has the leading influence on the editing of his film, the value of that influence being proportional to his instinct for and knowledge of editing. An experienced producer can also have a marked editorial input at this stage of the production. And a cutter of established reputation and proven ability can have the greatest influence of all, if only because he sets the editorial "tone" by making the first complete assembly.

In 1953, Karel Reisz, in his excellent book *The Technique of Film Editing*, wrote, "In Hollywood . . . writers normally prepare their scripts in much greater detail and leave the director with the comparatively minor role of following the written instructions." If Hollywood writers, then or now, prepare their scripts in much greater detail, it is to aid the production staff in scheduling the film, not for shooting or editorial purposes. Quite to the contrary, no Hollywood director worth his salt would tailor his set-ups or his editing concepts to the script's measure. In more than 50 years as a cutter and director I have not known a single nonhyphenated writer with more than an amateur's knowledge of cutting, and few Hollywood writers make any claim to editorial expertise. Most write master scenes and make no effort to indicate other than routine scene subdivisions. So, the script writer, unless he also happens to be the director or producer of the film, can be eliminated as a contributor to its editing. And most writer-directors depend more on their cutters for editorial advice than they do on the "instructions" in their scripts, even if the scripts happen to be their own.

Editorial responsibility, then, narrows down to the director, the producer, and the film editor (with an occasional stray suggestion from a studio executive). Which one of these carries the main burden on any particular picture depends mostly on the director involved. It works something like this.

Most directors have had no hands-on cutting experience. Members of this group exhibit a broad spectrum of behavior. A few may take little, or no, interest in the cutting. The wise ones will "glom onto" a good editor, when and if they find one; then they will adopt a supervisorial stance, making known their dramatic desires while leaving the execution of those desires in the editor's hands. And a few will attempt precise cutting instructions.

For the conscientious cutter these last are often a source of great trouble. Not knowing the patois of the cutting room,* they are usually unable to verbalize their concepts with accuracy. Their "specific" cutting instructions almost always amount to editorial double-talk, which the cutter must then translate into workable and effective ideas. Now the question arises: Should he make the cuts exactly as the director spelled them out, or should he cut it *his* way to arrive at the results which he *thinks* the director wanted, basing his judgment on his interpretation of the director's expressed instructions?

The wise cutter will, of course, follow the second procedure, making the cuts in question *his* way to arrive at the desired result. And if he is a very good cutter that result will be, in the director's words, "exactly what I was looking for."

The less secure, or more restricted cutter will try to follow the director's precise instructions and usually find himself with a mess on his hands. Let me cite an experience of my own as an example.

On one of my first editorial assignments, I presented a first cut which was perhaps twenty minutes longer than optimum length, a running time by no means unusually excessive. It called for only a routine trimming to bring it down to size. Over a period of two or three days the producer and the director reviewed the film, running and rerunning a sequence at a time. Instead of eliminating whole scenes, or even sequences, as is customary and generally desirable, they called for the elimination of a phrase here, a modifying clause there—even, occasionally, a single word—necessitating what is called a "hemstitching job." So many cuts of this kind were demanded that

---

*Every craft has its own language or terminology, most of which is unintelligible to the layman. The special idioms of the sciences are generally acknowledged. But the languages of even those professions which deal with the general population, such as teaching or politics, and which should be completely understandable, are often arcane or esoteric. (See?) Many of the film terms as used in schools of the cinema, especially those dealing with genre or theory, have never been heard on a studio lot, a condition which will probably change as more film school graduates take their places in the "real" film world. But even here, since the cutting rooms are far removed from the sound stages, few crew members understand the cutters' special jargon.

a smooth, understandable cut was impossible, but the supervising editor advised me to make the cuts exactly as asked for even though he, too, considered them incompetent.

The cuts were made; the director and producer viewed the recut version in silence, then marched down to the executive offices to demand my removal from the film and dismissal from the studio. My career hung by a thread. Fortunately, the supervising editor, Roy Stone (may his courage be ever remembered) gave his version of the episode. I was permitted to recut the film properly, and all turned out well.

I was 22, and I had learned one of the most important lessons of my life: In any creative effort one must do one's own thing, even if that thing is being done to another's order. To do otherwise is to seriously risk a result which will please neither the requestor nor the executor.

On the great majority of films, then, all the actual hands-on cutting is done by the film editor, with the director and/or the producer supplying most, if not all, of the creative ideas involving changes in continuity, the editing or elimination of scenes or sequences, the manipulation of acting emphasis and audience attention. The part the cutter plays in these proceedings depends on the director's faith in the cutter's talent and on his willingness to allow the cutter to participate in the creative process.

But, whatever the degree of that participation, the cutter still has almost complete control of the tempo and the pacing of the film, and here he can do great damage or perform small miracles. Since tempo and pace are largely the result of technical manipulation of cuts, a technique outside the average director's sphere of expertise, lack of finesse in these areas, though frequently quite apparent, often remains uncorrected. Even an expert critic will rarely know where to place the blame.

Naturally, those few directors with a great deal of practical cutting experience are fully aware of this important aspect of editing and, unless they are fortunate enough to have editors who match or surpass them in editing intuition and technical ability, they will insist on cutting their own films. Some will allow the editor to make the "rough cut," to their instructions, while a few will undertake even that burdensome task. But all will make the final cut with their own hands, fine-tuning the films to their own satisfaction. This operation is as important to a film as it is to a racing car engine or a symphony orchestra, and *only* the person actually handling the film can properly make these desirable and necessary adjustments.

# 3

## *Keep It Smooth*

Film is a deceptive art—in many ways. Its collaborative nature is axiomatic, yet more than in most art forms, that collaboration is hidden from the audience. In a good film, the whole will always be greater than the sum of its parts. Every honest filmmaker strives to make a film which so enthralls the viewer that he lives and breathes only with the beings on the screen. If that viewer, during his first look at the film, is critically conscious of the sets, the photography, the acting, the director's "touches," the "brilliance" of the dialogue, or the musical score, the good director knows he has come up short of perfection. A film's first viewing should evoke emotional, not critical, response. Nothing so warms the heart of the director of a dramatic film as an audience which sits quietly for minutes after the end title, digesting lingering thoughts and emotions, gathering itself for the return to reality.

This absence of eclectic awareness or of technical appreciation is especially true of editing. The finer the cutter's technique the less noticeable his contribution. And this oversight persists. No non-professional viewer will remember the cutting, even in postviewing analysis, since most cuts are specifically contrived to pass unnoticed. If the film is well shot and well cut, the viewer will perceive it as a motion picture which seems to flow in *unbroken* movement on a continuous strip of film. And even if the film is *not* well shot, an extremely clever cutter can, at times, still shape it into a smoothly flowing narrative.

So, the good cutter finds his satisfaction in the appreciation and applause of those of his peers, associates, and superiors who are aware of the travail and brain beating he undergoes to arrive at a result which few will notice. Humility is necessarily one of his strongest characteristics.

The conditions which make "smooth" cutting possible do not all arise spontaneously in the cutting room. The ideal of invisibility is achieved through a series of steps: The first, and one of the most important, can be taken only by the film's director.

Strange to say, many directors have little understanding of the editor's needs; some of the best have exhibited shortcomings in this area. Even stranger is the fact that such shortcomings have not noticeably diminished the quality of their films, at least not to the average viewer. On careful analysis, even a good many of our "classics" display tortuous transitions, improper "screen direction," and unimaginative composition. Does that prove that expertise in any, or all, of these areas is nonessential? By no means.

What it does prove, or at least indicate, is that there are many facets to a film, and all of them need not be first-rate for that film to have audience appeal. A good film can be badly photographed on inferior stock (e.g., *Open City*) and still be a hit. A film can survive a mediocre score or even sloppy editing if the indispensable major elements are present in strength. The only sure stiflers of appreciation and enjoyment are badly written stories, careless dramatic structuring, inadequately developed characters, and funereal pacing.

None of this is meant to imply that a director may lightly ignore the "minor" essentials. But if he does, someone will have to cover for him, and that someone is usually the film editor. Cosmetic applications, however, rarely equal competence at the source, and a film made by a director with limited cinematic knowledge will always fall short of its true potential, even though its faults may be cleverly concealed.

As the director plans his set-ups for a scene, or sequence, he should anticipate where key cuts will be made, at least in cutting from one master shot to another. This means, for instance, that at the point of the cut there should be a marked difference in size, or angle, or number of characters, (or all three) between the two set-ups. If the first set-up shows, let us say, four players at full height, the next set-up should *not* show the same four actors at the same full height from the same point of view. A close similarity in the two contiguous cuts will guarantee a cut that "jumps", i.e., is noticeable to the viewer as a change of scene. (See definitions of various "cuts" in Book II, Chapter 10.)

It may seem illogical, but a decided change in size, e.g., cutting from the four shot to a close shot of one of the group, will make a smooth, unnoticeable transition, especially if the close shot shows a reaction or response to something said or done by another member of the group. However, the incoming cut should not present a point of view which will interrupt the flow of the scene, thus distracting the viewer and losing his attention.

Perhaps the greatest sinner of all is the "clever" director who "cuts in the camera." The phrase, which can be used in several contexts, usually signifies that the director, in any particular "take", shoots *only* that portion of the scene which he expects to use as one complete cut, whether it be an action in a full shot, or a reaction or *single* line of dialogue in a close-up. This technique is used in the false belief that it saves film, time, and money, or because the director fears the cutter will play fast and loose with the material if given too many options. The technique is self-defeating for two reasons:

1. It depends on sticking to strict "story-boarding," or cutting to script, thus "setting" the film prematurely and depriving both the cutter and the director of any opportunity for later improvement or enhancement.
2. It is clearly bad directorial technique, since it affords the actors little or no opportunity to "get into the scene" and results in superficial, often stiff, performances.

A close relative of the director who cuts in the camera is the director who ignores cutting altogether and shoots long master shots, "theater style," with little or no coverage. Though this kind of shot can be advantageous on rare occasions, most extended scenes need proper coverage for dramatic emphasis or constructive deletion.

Ernst Lubitsch, certainly one of the great directors in Hollywood history, once made this fatal mistake. He shot a dramatic scene in a single master shot, allowing no cut-aways, considering it completely satisfactory as it played. The preview audience failed to see it his way. Severe pruning was called for, but no protection set-ups had been shot. The entire scene had to be re-filmed in a number of set-ups at considerable labor and expense.

Even if the director feels that a particular scene plays at its best in a single set-up—and almost every director has resorted to this kind of shot at one time or another—basic wisdom demands that he protect himself against the occasional misjudgment. Such "protection" (the actual word used in this context) is cheap insurance and is obtained by a simple procedure, one known and used for more than half a century. (See "Cutting to the kitchen stove," Book II, Chapter 9.) A protection shot made on the spot will take relatively little time and will disturb the schedule and the budget far less than if it has to be made at some future date.

The truth is that every good director who has risen from the cutting ranks, and who feels secure in his cutting concepts, still "protects" himself liberally. He knows better than anyone how often additional cinematic values can be supplied through the cutting process.

# 4

# *The Cutter Begins*

At a purely technical level each editor develops his own approach to his work, although that approach will most likely be a variation of one of those few which time and trial have proven to be the most efficient. Here I will concentrate on the method that works best for me and which, naturally, I can support wholeheartedly. However, the beginning cutter can modify this procedure to suit his own needs and, what is more important, his special talents.

Quite possibly the cutter's first chores will be in the area of preproduction. This usually means a search for needed stock material. For instance, before starting production on *The Caine Mutiny*, I visited the Naval Archives in Washington, D.C., and reviewed many thousands of feet of film which had been shot by a host of photographers during naval preparation and action in the Pacific.

I had hoped to find usable footage of the great typhoon which scattered our huge invasion fleet in the latter days of World War II, but I had been naive. Cameramen can hardly be expected to stand on a heaving ship's deck during the height of such a storm, and the speed of color film in the early forties was wholly inadequate for filming under the prevailing light conditions. Eventually, of course, the whole of the typhoon sequence had to be shot in production. However, a number of shots of battleships firing practice salvos and bombarding island installations in preparation for marine landings were selected for use in the film.

"Stock shots" are used in many films, especially those involving sports, such as football games, automobile or horse racing, etc. On occasion, selection of such material may be delayed until postproduction editing, but it is better done before the start of shooting so that film shot in production may more accurately match the stock selected.

The cutter's work on the film itself starts on the day the first

427

rushes are viewed. The takes of the previous day's shooting are customarily assembled in the lab, or by the assistant cutter, most often in the order in which they were shot. At the company running the editor, and usually his assistant, sit at the director's side for two reasons: (1) The cutter records the director's take selections, where more than one has been printed, and (2) he makes notes of the particular takes, or portions of takes, which the director selects for his first cut. Some directors offer little advice at this stage, trusting the editor to make the best use of the filmed material; others give precise, detailed instructions for the use of specific takes, angles, or portions thereof. (See Book IV, Chapter 9.)

One day's shooting on even a moderately liberal schedule will hardly supply enough material for actual cutting. It may take the director two, three, or more days to complete a scripted scene or sequence. As the film is released to the cutter, his assistant will usually reassemble the takes "in sequence," i.e., in script order, with the close shots and close-ups placed immediately after the master shots which cover the same material. An exact assembly is rarely possible, since portions of a single take may be used as cuts at different places in the finished sequence; but the more closely the reassembly can approach the eventual rough-cut alignment, the easier it will be for the editor to organize his cutting routine.

Now, an item of great importance: When the assembly is ready it should be viewed on the "big screen." One viewing may be sufficient, but more often, especially if the demands of the sequence, technically or dramatically, are appraised as severe, the material should be reviewed time and again, until the cutter is quite sure which portions of which takes he wants to use, and where he anticipates making his cuts.

Many editors shape their editing concepts on the moviola, a technique I consider decidedly inferior. One does not see the same things on a small moviola screen, or even on the somewhat larger, though fuzzier, flat-bed screen, that one sees in a theater. The audience sees its film only on the big screen; and since every cut should be made with the audience in mind, the cutter must try to see each bit of film as a viewer will eventually see it in the theater. Even a moderate-sized TV screen offers far more scope than a moviola; therefore it, too, presents a somewhat different "picture" for the viewer's inspection.

Excluding art films, "film verite," etc., the usual theatrical film is meant to appeal to the largest possible audience, and sound theories of filmmaking, including cutting, are based on that fact. Staging, setups, and cutting should always be conceived to show the viewer what he should see at every point in the film. Sometimes it is what the viewer, whether or not he is aware of it, *wants* to see; sometimes it is what the viewer, whether or not he likes it at the moment, *should* see; and sometimes (quite often, really) it is what the director and/or cutter manipulate him into *thinking* he wants to see. But a cut, or even a short portion of a cut, which the viewer cares nothing about is a waste of time. All this may seem obvious, yet the verges of the road to film success are strewn with the bodies of hopefuls who ignored this principle and brought in films which, wholly or in part, audiences found flat and unentertaining.

This, then, is why the cutter should make his choices on the big screen. "Holding" a cut because of the beauty of a composition or the clever "bit" of a secondary character is of no value if the cut under consideration has delivered its full message. Lingering on a scene for some subjectively esoteric reason is one of the pitfalls of editing. The viewer, engrossed in the film, may not be seeing the cutter's "vision" at all. In cutting, as in directing, objectivity is of the utmost importance—self-indulgence leads only to disaster.

When the cutter feels he has his cutting concept well in mind, the next step is the cutter's bench. Here, too, routines differ. In preparation for the actual cutting some editors like to have the assembled rushes broken down into individual takes. These are arranged on the bench in sequence order and then selected by the cutter as he proceeds to stitch the scenes together.

Others prefer to cut directly off the assembled reels, pulling the takes down into a film bin as they select their cuts. Though some takes may have to be pulled out and set aside for later use, I find this method creates the least disorder. But, whichever technique is used, pieces of film will always be scattered helter-skelter, in the bin, on film hooks, and around the cutter's neck. Here is where a good assistant is invaluable. Keeping "trims" (i.e., unused portions of takes) instantly locateable is a requisite for smooth operation and efficient use of time: The "trim" of the first rough assembly may be the inspired cut in a later version.

Two distinct "machines," or pieces of equipment, are used in the cutting procedure. The first, the "moviola," dates from the early days of film; it is preferred by most Hollywood editors. The second, called the "flat-bed" and used by European editors, is of comparatively recent origin.

Having worked with both, my preference is decidedly the moviola. Frequent removal and replacement of film and sound tape is essential to the style of cutting discussed in this book; it is more easily and quickly accomplished on the Hollywood machine. Except for the beginnings and ends of most sequences, a cut should rarely be made "straight across," i.e., the picture and the tape should *not* be cut at their matching points. No matter how small, the overlapping of cuts requires careful manipulation if synchronization is to be maintained.

Cutters who use the flat-bed are more inclined to cut straight across, which leads to a "stop and start" technique and sloppiness. In addition, a film should be cut primarily for the picture, since that is what is seen on the screen, and this kind of film handling is more accurately accomplished on the moviola.

However, in the final stages of editing, especially when A and B tracks are used for sound overlaps, as well as for sound and music editing, the flat-bed is unbeatable. Every cutting facility should have one or more at hand.

Now, an important step: when the sequence is finally assembled it should be laid aside. Cutters who are not quite sure of themselves choose to review their efforts immediately. They risk a frustrating experience. Since all the cuts made are fresh in mind the cutter is sure to anticipate each one rather than go with the flow of the sequence. Consequently, each cut is almost sure to jump, and the cutter will be inclined to assume the jumps are caused by inadequate matching rather than by his anticipation. He will then attempt immediate corrections. The result can be pretty messy.

If the newly cut sequence is put aside for a number of days—even weeks—while another sequence or two is cut in the interim, the original cuts will have been forgotten and will pass on the screen without anticipation. All properly made cuts should now be unnoticeable. Only if the cuts jump at this stage will there be need for technical correction. As for the more demanding *editorial* corrections, that is a whole different story, which will be addressed in its proper turn. For immediate consideration, we will take up the problems of *cutting* technique.

Note: Film computers which store copies of selected takes on tape or disc are now available in many editing facilities. However, they are far too costly to be used in student situations, and are not discussed in this book. Since they are essentially storage and retrieval machines, they do not affect the principles of film editing in the slightest degree.

# 5

# *You've Got To Have a Reason*

The first two basic rules of cutting are*

Rule #1.  Never make a cut without a positive reason.
Rule #2.  When undecided about the exact frame to cut on, cut *long* rather than short.

Cuts should be conceived on the big screen, but they can be made only on the moviola (or the flat-bed). To put it more simply: Based on his viewing of the assembled material, the cutter decides where he wants to change angles, where to move into a close shot or cut back to a long shot, and where to cut to a reaction or a response. But on the big screen the film flashes by at 24 frames a second—a cut takes only 1 frame**—and a cutter can hardly spot the exact frame to cut on in this infinitesimal space of time. Therefore the cutter must view his film on the moviola, where he can start, stop, run forward or backward as quickly, as slowly, or as often as he wishes. He must be able to stop on the proverbial dime, and often needs to. In short, it is on the moviola that he finds the *exact* frame to leave one scene and the *exact* frame to enter the next.

*The rules of cutting, as stated, are mine. Some of those which I lay down in this book have been observed for many years, a few before my time, but they have never, to my knowledge, been codified. Experienced editors will probably agree with most of my rules. But if you want to question one now and then—have fun.
**Technically speaking, a cut, or splice, is made on the "frame line" between two frames of picture. It occupies the space between two sprocket holes, or one-quarter of a frame. Also, since its movement across the projection aperture is blocked from view by a synchronized shutter, it is never seen at all. What is seen is the change from one cut to the next.

The word "exact" is stressed because I believe that the proper cut can be made only at a single point. Obviously, cutting three or four frames to either side of the hypothetical "perfect" cut will make a difference of only three twenty-fourths or four twenty-fourths of a second—hardly enough to bother a viewer who takes five twenty-fourths of a second to blink an eye. But why be one-eighth of a second off target if you can be perfect? Beyond this purely philosophic consideration, when making an "action cut", three frames too much or too little on one side or the other can effectively spoil the match.

But first, to expand on Rule #1: This rule may seem obvious, but it is often ignored. The key here is *positive reason*. I have known cutters who felt that if they allowed a scene to run more than a certain arbitrary number of feet without cutting away they were not doing their job. But the act of *making* a cut should, in itself, deliver a message: "Here, I am presenting an addition, something beyond—not just something different." A cut should never be made only because the cutter feels the prevailing cut runs "too long." "Long" is a very elastic measurement. Aesthetically, a cut can be too long at one foot and not long enough at 500.

In *Broken Lance,* I shot two scenes which ran about ten minutes, or 900 feet each. One scene was played by Spencer Tracy and Richard Widmark, the other by Tracy and E.G. Marshall. These three were great actors who could hold an audience as well as anyone in films. Also, in both instances, I used a moving camera and moving actors, i.e., the camera could move from a long shot into a close shot and back again as the scene progressed; and the actors could move from a full shot into a close-up when greater intensity was called for.

In the finished film both scenes played at full length, without a cut. The scenes were so tight and so dramatic that intercutting would not have improved them in the least. I had, of course, made a "protection" shot for each scene (see Book IV, Chapter 3), but neither one was needed.

I have also, in certain action or montage sequences, used cuts as short as six frames, or one-quarter of a second. It took just that long, and no longer, for the cuts to deliver their total messages.

As a sequence is being cut the cutter should know where a particular set-up most effectively presents the information that is needed for that particular part of the scene. In other words, he will stay with the shot as long as that shot is the one which best delivers the required information, and cut to another shot only when the new cut will better serve the purposes of the scene, whether because the size is more effective, the composition is more suitable, or the interpretation is superior. One cuts to a close-up, for instance, to enhance a response or intensify a reaction. Deep feeling—emotion—is usually best expressed through the eyes; and the closer the shot the more clearly the emotion can be seen, and felt, by the viewer. However, cutting to a close-up when *no* such enhancement is called for is not only wasteful but it will tend to diminish the value of subsequent close-ups when they are legitimately needed. The overuse of *any* effect diminishes its true worth.

There are other, though infrequent, occasions when similar emotional intensity will play better in longer shots. In *Mirage,* Gregory Peck enters Walter Matthau's office and finds him strangled to death. After a brief moment of shocked inaction, Peck gives vent to his grief and rage through violence, smashing furniture and throwing a chair through a window. Obviously, this scene played best in a series of wide shots where the full range of his righteous anger could be given full play.

In short, as long as the sequence is playing at its best in the selected angle—leave it alone! The only reason for using another cut is to *improve* the scene.

Rule #2 may also seem obvious, yet how often have I seen it violated! Every cut is the result of a conscious decision, hard or easy, and as any psychologist can testify, making a decision can be a traumatic experience. The more options available, the more difficult the decision. I have often seen an inexperienced cutter agonize for hours over a single cut, and regret it instantly when the cut was finally made, feeling sure that one of his other options was preferable.

The rule that applies in school examinations also applies, logically enough, in cutting: The first immediate and instinctive choice is more likely than not to be the right one. Experience will eventually teach a cutter exactly where to make his cut the first time around, and the decision will scarcely register a blip on his mind; but if there is any doubt as to how many frames should precede or follow a reaction, let us say, it is wiser to leave the cut a little long. Trimming it down to proper size at a later run-through will prove to be simple— and much, much more neat. Splicing a few frames back onto a scene which has been lopped short makes "jumpy" viewing, and a cut full of such amendments makes proper visualization difficult and perceptive judgment impossible.

# 6

# *Cutting in Action*

Rule #3.   Whenever possible, cut "in movement."

The "action cut" is the first bit of cutting lore learned by every apprentice. Excluding cuts made at the beginnings and ends of sequences and self-contained scenes, cuts to reactions or responses, and cuts involving exchanges of dialogue, the cutter should look for some movement by the actor who holds the viewer's attention, and he should use that movement to trigger his cut from one scene to the next. A broad action will offer the easier cut, but even a slight movement of some part of the player's body can serve to initiate a cut which will be "smooth," or invisible.

As an example, let us take a very common sequence of cuts. In a full shot a player enters an office, approaches a desk, and sits down in the desk chair. The full shot has established the scene's setting and it is now necessary to zero in on the character as he proceeds about his business, so a close shot of him at the desk is in order.

The best place to cut to the close shot is as the actor sits, and here we have three options: We can leave the full shot early, as the actor reaches his chair, and show the complete action of sitting in a close shot which centers on the chair; we can allow the actor to sit in the full shot, cutting to the close shot only after that action is completed; or we can cut somewhere between the cutting points of the first two options. For most good editors that would be the automatic choice.

The exact cutting point would depend on the cutter's sense of proper timing. All exceptional editors have it to an exceptional degree. In our hypothetical example, the cut would probably be made at just the point where the seat of the chair and that of the player are about to collide. Even if that point is hidden by the desk it can be deduced from the movement of the body, a type of deduction often required in cutting. (See Book IV, Chapter 6.)

Cutting early would present us with some footage of the player's midsection, not exactly an inspiring sight. The late cut would carry the long shot past the viewer's point of tolerance, however slightly. The cut at the midpoint avoids these two faults, as well as some others to be discussed later, while enabling us to take advantage of the magic of the "action cut." If there are problems with differences of position in the two cuts (commonly called "mismatching"), or variation in speed of movement (which sometimes occurs as the result of sloppy staging), the timing might have to be modified; but the modification would be a forced compromise, and not the cut of choice.

In the reverse action, also seen in virtually every film, the player rises from his chair in the close shot, and the fuller shot continues his movement.* Here the cut would probably come some six to ten frames *after* the start of the action in the close shot. The longer shot would pick up his movement at nearly the same spot. Exact matching of position, however, might not result in the smoothest cut, for reasons to be explained shortly. Often an action overlap of three to five frames is desirable.

Contrary to common belief, the action cut does not *necessarily* require a measurable difference in image size. It is possible to cut from, let us say, a close-up of a player turning to his right, then have him complete his turn in another close-up, of similar size, shot from the new direction. It is even possible to move straight in, with no change in view line, from a close shot to a close-up, where the differences in size and range of movement are minimal. But this kind of cutting requires the most exquisite timing and relatively few cutters can execute it properly.

Often a cut must be made at a point where, unlike our previous examples, no broad movement is available. An actor may already be seated, for instance, and the demands of the scene call for a cut to a closer shot. In such a case, any matching movement—the turn of the head, or the raising of an arm as the actor lifts a cup of coffee or a cigarette to his mouth—will, when precisely timed, serve to camouflage the cut. The important consideration here is that there be just enough movement to catch the viewer's attention.

Some cutters prefer to cut just before the start of a movement, or immediately after its completion; but few, if any, of the top editors follow this practice. In situations of this kind the "static" cut cannot

---

* The experienced camera operator will maintain a fixed camera position, allowing the actor to rise out of the close shot. He will also set his composition at full height in the long shot. He knows the cut will probably be made during the rise, and that a tilting camera movement at that point would spoil it.

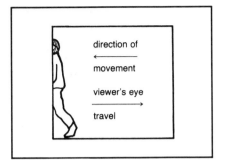

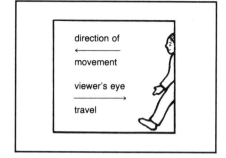

*Book IV-Figure 1*                              *Book IV - Figure 2*

be intelligently rationalized, and it is excusable only if the cutter is eliminating waste footage, and then he is merely making the best of an imperfect situation. If the timing of the action, as shot, is satisfactory, the action cut will always make a smoother transition.

However, most of the cuts in a modern film, with its emphasis on dialogue, cannot be made so conveniently. A player looks off screen at something or somebody, and a cut to that something or somebody is in order. But, at the moment of looking, the player is usually quite still, as in that well-worn phrase, "his gaze was fixed upon. . . ." Although in the absence of movement no action cut is possible, a smooth cut can still be made. But how?

Or consider a dialogue scene: Two people seated on a couch or at a table, riding in a car, or strolling down the lane, talking to each other for minutes at a time, often without apparent movement, especially in their close-ups. Still, frequent cuts must be made to the speaker, or to his listener's reaction. Here, too, smooth cutting is quite possible. But how?

By creating a "diversion" of a sort, which is also the principle at work in the action cut. But before we can discuss the principle we must build a hypothesis;* and to do that we will examine a close relative of the action cut, one that deals with exits and entrances.

An actor exits a scene by walking out of the *left* side of the screen, and we follow him as he enters the next scene *from the right*. This is proper "screen direction," so-called, and it is always shot that way (see Figures 1 and 2). Good editing practice rules that the cut *away* from the first scene should occur at the point where the actor's eyes exit the frame. The cut to the second scene should be made from three

---

* The building of this hypothesis took years of careful analysis and one moment of inspiration. Like the popular representations of the structure of the atom, it is purely a "construction," and it may have no relation to the actual truth. But it does what all good hypotheses should do: It works. Properly applied to any cut, or to the cutting concept as a whole, it will deliver a smooth, steadily flowing film.

to five frames ahead of the point at which his eyes reenter the frame at the opposite side of the screen. (The cadence of his step also comes into play, but it has no bearing at this point.)

But why, when the actor in the incoming cut appears at the opposite side of the screen from his point of exit (which, on the wide screen, can be quite a separation), is such a cut, when properly made, completely acceptable to the viewer as a smooth, continuous action? Because his vision has been clouded, or "diverted", by the apparently awkward movement of his eyes across the screen.

At the point of the cut, two things happen: (1) the exiting actor's eyes or face—usually the viewer's center of interest—leave the screen and, as a result, (2) the *viewer's* eyes, which have been following the actor's movement, encounter the darkness at the edge of the screen. These two actions cause a reaction: The viewer's eyes swing back toward the center of the screen, then continue to its right edge where they find the continuation of the actor's movement. All this has happened in a fraction of a second, not nearly long enough for the viewer to be aware of the passage of time, to be conscious of his eye movement, or to *notice the cut* that has slipped by in the interim. For, and this is the important factor in this process, the viewer's eyes have been unfocused during their forced move, and he has seen nothing with clarity.

Experiments in reading long ago established that a reader's eyes cannot focus while moving, and short pauses to focus on words, or small groups of words, are an essential part of the reading process. The same holds true for someone looking at the screen. As his eyes move, sharp focus is impossible. Therefore, if a cut, lasting one twenty-fourth of a second, can be made while the viewer consumes one-fifth of a second in moving his eyes, the cut will pass unnoticed. The trick is to get the viewer, or an audience of viewers, to move their eyes, en masse, at the desired instant.

Hints have been around for some time. Some cutters have long been aware of one such trick—cutting on a sharp sound—a door slam, for instance, or a gun shot—to disguise a cut. Sharp noises cause the viewer to blink, which, as noted earlier, will take approximately one-fifth of a second. The blink is the equivalent of the eye movement in the exit-entrance cut, or in the action cut. The "operator" in all of these cuts is the distraction which causes movement or closure of the eyes. The cutter makes his cut as the viewer's eyes blink, or are defocused by a movement on the screen, much as a magician masks a move requiring camouflage by distracting the eyes of his audience with the broad sweep of his cape, or a sharp movement of his "decoying" arm.

(An interesting sidelight is that these devices cause *automatic* reactions which are, for our practical purposes, the same for all viewers, young or old, sharp or dull, and are therefore easy to accomplish. The smooth "dialogue" cut, also based on eye movement, is a different kettle of fish.)

Filmmakers have often resorted to "deception" in order to deliver the "truth." The three- to five-frame overlap mentioned in discussing the action cut is one example of such deception. It is best analyzed in an examination of the exit-entrance cut. The overlapping (or repeated) three to five frames at the beginning of the second cut are redundant, and meant to be so. The viewer will, in a sense, miss them, since they flash by on the screen during the fraction of a second when his eyes are moving from left to right. When his eyes are refocused, the viewer sees the proper continuation of the actor's cross, not the short redundant overlap (see Figure 3a).

If the cut were made to match the action exactly, what the viewer would miss during the eye movement would be frames essential to smooth continuation of the cross. The short hiatus would now register on the viewer's mind as a tiny jump forward in the action (see Figure 3b).

An overlap made to accommodate the viewer's "blind spot" is useful in most action cuts. But it is quite a subtle technique practiced by relatively few editors. Its absence from a film will hardly destroy it for the viewer. However, in "static" cuts, the subject of the next chapter, the "blind spot" overlap is absolutely essential for good cutting. No cutter should be ignorant of its proper use.

Oh, yes, the cadence of the step, which was by-passed on page

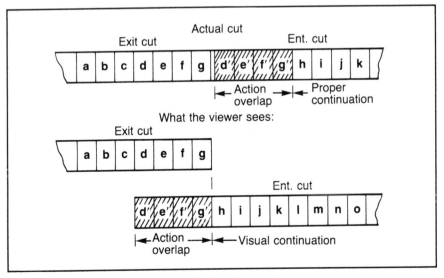

*Book IV - Figure 3a*

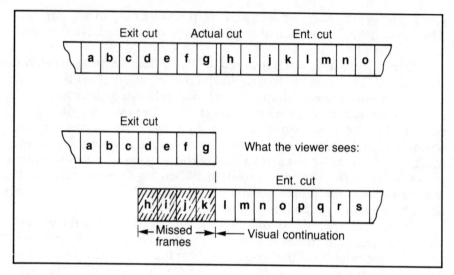

*Book IV - Figure 3b*

438: Most people have a strong sense of rhythm, as expressed in marching, dancing, chanting, and many other rhythmic activities. If this rhythm is needlessly disturbed, so is the viewer. Therefore, when cutting from one shot of a person walking to another in which the walking continues (as in an exit-entrance cut), care must be taken to make sure the walker's foot hits the ground (or floor) in proper cadence. If possible, it should be the same foot, but failure to match feet will not often be noticed and is not nearly as disruptive as breaking the walking cadence. Cutting at the instant the foot hits the floor also helps to accomplish a smoother transition.

If the shots are too close to show the legs or feet, the proper cadence can be deduced from a careful examination of the movement of the actor's body. The rhythm of the movement must be maintained even if the cut has to be shortened or lengthened by a few frames. In this case, maintaining proper rhythm is less disturbing than a slightly imperfect cut.

# 7

# *Keep It Fresh*

Cutters, on the whole, are a conscientious lot, but inevitably some are ignorant, some are careless, and some are lazy. The first condition is curable, the second correctable, but the third is unforgivable. The lazy cutter cheats not only his director, his producer, and his employer, he also cheats the viewer. A cutter who cuts "straight across" because overlapping takes more time and greater effort (which it certainly does) puts out a film which falls short of its potential.

Let us take a simple example, our old acquaintance, the exit-entrance cut. Quite a few working editors and almost all amateurs will allow the actor to make a full exit in the first cut, then hold the scene a number of frames more before cutting away. This kind of cutting is wrong on every count, whether technical or aesthetic.

1. It violates the rule concerning the viewer's eye movement.
2. It extends a scene which no longer has any meaning or interest to the viewer.
3. It increases the length of the film to no useful purpose.

Point 1 has been discussed in depth in the preceding chapter, except for one aspect. If the viewer looks toward an incoming cut, and no cut appears, he will search the scene which lingers on the screen for what he assumes the filmmaker wants him to see. (Unless he is deceived too often, the viewer will *always* believe the filmmaker has some reason for everything he puts on the screen.) When his search is rewarded with footage of an empty set he will be confused or disappointed, neither of which reactions recommends the cut.

Point 2. If the viewer is not confused or disappointed, he will simply be bored. It has been many years since a mere picture projected on the screen was considered amazing or amusing. Every part of a film must deliver its message, but the only message delivered by empty frames of film is that the cutter was inept, or too lazy to cut them out.

Point 3. This is an important consideration, and often a factor in a film's appeal. A few extra frames may seem to give little cause for concern, and if they appeared only once or twice in a film that might be true. But there are many cuts which lend themselves to this special kind of carelessness; and when such a fault is often repeated, the total amount of unprofitable film can be considerable.

The most serious aspect of this miscut, however, is its immediate effect on the viewer. A visual hiccup of this sort interrupts the flow, hence the pacing of the film, and pacing is a key factor in raising the viewer's involvement up to the highest possible level. Obviously, a series of such hiccups, recurring throughout the film, can be harmful indeed.

Let us probe this concept a bit more deeply. Practical filmmakers have long held that the viewer should remain completely unaware of technique—all technique, whether that of the actor, the cameraman, the writer, the director, or the cutter. In art, the obvious is a sin. Some aspects of this principle have already been discussed. Now let us examine a special case.

The setting is a desert road in New Mexico—John Ford country. A stagecoach rumbles toward the viewer, passes through and out of the scene. The cutter allows the shot to linger on the "painted desert" as the dust settles slowly to earth. If the viewer murmurs to himself, or to his companion, "What a beautiful shot!" we have stayed on the cut too long. The viewer is appreciating our "shot," not the film; he has become aware of our "cinematic composition," our technique.

However, it *is* possible to let the viewer savor the beauty of the setting as part of the film as a whole. If we *start* the shot with the same beautiful landscape, the viewer will appreciate it at least as much, but will be accepting it in the context of the story. Most probably, of course, the stagecoach will already be seen in the distance (an added plus to the composition). But even if it isn't, even if no action takes place on the screen as yet, the viewer, while reacting to the scene's beauty, will also be anticipating some action pertaining to the film—looking for the stagecoach, perhaps, thus again placing the scene into the context of the film. But by the time the coach passes the camera, the viewer is ready for a change of scene, which leads to:

Rule #4:   The "fresh" is preferable to the "stale."

If, for some valid reason, a few *frames* must be tacked onto the end of one cut or the beginning of the next, or if, because of the need for exposition or background establishment, as in the above example, a few *feet* must be added to the end of one cut or the beginning of the next, always choose to place the extra footage at the *beginning* of the new, incoming cut. The reason is obvious, but often ignored.

In the case of the stagecoach scene, the reason for adding the extra footage to the beginning of the shot is easily understood. In the case of the few frames, however, the logic may not be so easily grasped. But the same rule is at work in both instances. Let us return to the exit-entrance cut for our example.

The first cut has played itself out on the screen, and for the duration of the cut the set, or background, has been in full view, there to be seen, absorbed, and accepted. To linger on it after our actor has left the scene is to leave our viewer with cold coffee. The incoming cut, however, is new to the eye and to the mind; and if it is necessary to add a number of frames before the actor enters the scene, the viewer has at least a fresh setting to examine and integrate, which serves to keep his interest alive.

An understanding of rule #4 allows us to continue our examination of "static" cuts. The simplest, and most obvious, are the beginnings and ends of sequences and self-contained scenes.

Rule #5.   All scenes should begin, and end, with continuing action.*

Rule #5 is included not because its dictum is misunderstood or unknown, but because it is surprisingly often forgotten or ignored. It is a corrective procedure, and its message is simple.

The beginning of a scene (this is especially true of scenes at the start of sequences) should never reveal an actor preparing, or waiting, to act. An experienced director will, as a matter of course, give an actor the opportunity to "get into the scene" well before its usable beginning. If the scene is one of movement, the warm-up may be as simple as walking across the set, getting up from a chair or sitting down in one, hanging up the telephone, as though a conversation had just taken place, etc. The warm-up serves to keep the scene "alive" at the point of the cut, to subconsciously suggest to the viewer that he is seeing a fragment of continuing life, not a staged scene with a visible framework.

An inexperienced director, or one who "cuts in the camera," will often start his take just where the scene is meant to begin in the edited

---

* The word "action," as used here, does not necessarily mean movement. Resting is an "action" if it is part of the scene, as is sleeping.

film, which allows the cutter no room to maneuver. This is especially troublesome if the scene is to be used in a dissolve. The only cure is to cut into the body of the scene, even if it means starting the dialogue under the last part of the preceding cut.

A similar problem can arise at the end of a scene if the actor lets down immediately after his last line, his last bit of business, or if the director is too quick with his "cut!" Once more, the solution is to cut away while the scene is still alive, either by cutting to another player's reaction, to the "kitchen stove," or to the next scene, while overlapping the last bit of dialogue carried over from the shortened scene. You will be "saving" the director's film, and your "advanced" technique will probably elicit admiration. It will by no means be the first time that a last-ditch corrective measure has been hailed as a "creative" bit of editing.

Another common cut, seen many times in every film, is the "look off." Here is an example from *The Caine Mutiny.*

KEEFER

There's just one more thing and
you're finished. Climb that mast.

Willie and Harding look off, panicked.

LONG SHOT      POV MAST      FROM THEIR ANGLE

To Willie and Harding the mast seems at least a hundred feet high. There is a tiny square grille at the top.

MEDIUM SHOT      WILLIE, KEEFER, HARDING

WILLIE
(protesting)
What for? A mast is a mast.

(End of excerpt)

The "look off" here is quite clear. Less clear, however, is the last word in the writer's instruction: "Willie and Harding look off, panicked." There are situations where an actor's reaction to something the audience has not yet seen can be funny or effective. This is not one of them. Obviously, the panic would come *after* the shot of the mast, if at all. (It was not played that way in actuality.)

This cut-away seems quite simple and straightforward, but a good sense of timing is required. The actor looks off—but just how long does he look before we cut to what he sees?

The viewer, as a rule, will not accept the "fact" of a look until he sees the actor's eyes focus, or "freeze," on something off-screen.

At that point he, too, will look off, following the actor's gaze. By the time his own eyes have refocused, the actor's point-of-view (POV) shot should occupy the screen. To make the cut, then, we fix the frame in which the actor's eyes have "frozen," add three or four frames more to give the viewer time to react and move his eyes as he follows the actor's look, at which point the cut is made. After making 50 or 60 such cuts the routine will become almost automatic.

In the given example, however, *two* people look off, which complicates the cut. If they look off simultaneously, there is no problem— the two looks can be treated as one. But if the two actors have different reaction timing, which is more than likely, where do you cut? Which actor do you follow? Do you cut on the first fixed look, or do you wait for the second?

The not-so-simple answer is another question: whom is the viewer watching at the moment the cut should be made? If his attention is centered on the actor who looks off first, the viewer will follow his look and that determines the cut, regardless of what the other actor is doing. But if the viewer is watching the actor whose look is delayed, the second look now mandates the cut.

Another very common cut is introduced in the *Caine* example— the POV—in this case the shot of the mast. The length of such a cut is a matter of judgment. If an audience reaction to the cut itself is anticipated, the cutter will let it run long—long enough, as in this example, for the audience to appreciate the humor of the situation and to start a laugh which will continue to build (it is hoped) over the ensuing shot of the actors' reactions. If the cut is too short, the laugh will die aborning; if it is too long, the laugh may weaken beyond the power of the reaction cut to resuscitate it.

The only rule for such a cut is a paraphrase of Lincoln's answer to the joker who asked him how long a man's legs ought to be. "Long enough to reach the ground," said Abe. The POV shot should run just long enough to deliver its message, and not one frame longer: Never give the viewer the opportunity to say, "All right, already!" If the picture it presents is easily read, the cut can be as short as two or three feet. If, as occasionally happens, the cut is a repetition of an earlier shot with which the viewer is familiar, it might be shorter. On the other hand, if the picture is "busy," with its point of interest somewhat obscured (the mast, with its array of antennae, etc., was such a shot) longer viewing time is needed. *

If the cutter is really "with it" he will very gradually decrease

---

* The POV is one of the first victims of cutting nearsightedness. At each viewing the POV becomes more familiar and more dull, until it soon seems to run on forever. I have seen cutters "snip" a few frames off such a shot at each recut, until it had virtually no presence at all.

the length of such cuts as the film progresses—as the viewer's awareness becomes more acute, and he begins to understand the film's characters, to think and live with the people on the screen.

Another POV shot is the "insert"—a cut of any inanimate object. An insert containing reading matter requires a special kind of judgment. Since there are great differences in viewer's reading abilities, a compromise is in order, though the laggard should be favored. The fast reader will gain greater clarity from a second reading; the slow one will appreciate a fully delivered message.

Each cut in the POV category is on its own, its length determined by the cutter's evaluation of its content. Timing is all. Errors come easily. The POV, in whatever guise—insert, object, or scene—seems quite simple, but it can be a severe test of the cutter's mettle and gives the critical observer a good measure of his talent.

# 8

## *Try a Little Harder*

In our earlier discussion of action cuts we have been considering cuts made under perfect, or nearly perfect conditions. But conditions are rarely perfect, and not too often nearly perfect. A number of problems can raise their unattractive heads. Two scenes which ultimately will be cut together will often be shot on different days—sometimes weeks apart. Actors will have forgotten levels of intensity and the nature and speed of their movements.

For instance, in scenes shot for the exit-entrance cut, the actor may leave the first scene at a brisk pace and saunter into the next one, especially if the latter scene has been shot first. If an actor smokes a cigarette in the master shot, he will also smoke a cigarette in all the matching shots. But only a superhuman memory could enable him to recall exactly how he raised the Marlboro to his lips, or when; how deeply he inhaled or how deliberately he exhaled, just when he lowered it to flick off some ashes, and just how long he paused before raising it to his lips once more.

Most actors do their best to maintain consistency, as does the director, and the person especially responsible for helping the actor to match his wardrobe, his moves, and his demeanor—the script clerk. Unfortunately, her memory isn't perfect either, and her notes are sometimes inadequate. Besides, many directors refuse to allow their actors to be burdened with excessive detail, an attitude which I endorse. An actor who is conscious of the mechanics of his performance will usually perform mechanically. Freedom, spontaneity, and "being" go out the window if the player is required to devote more effort to matching his movements or "hitting his marks" than he does to making the scene come alive.

All this, of course, has to do with shooting, but it ultimately has a great deal to do with cutting; and the editor who is willing to "try a little harder" can contribute considerably to a film's "look" of consistency. Knowing how much is possible, I refuse to allow the script clerk to advise actors about their action matching unless they specifically request it. When a conscientious script clerk objects, which she often does, my response is always, "We'll fix it in the cutting room." And we always do, even if it takes some doing.

The "doing" is where many inexperienced or inexpert cutters make serious mistakes. Confronted with a bad match at the preferred cutting point, they ignore the proper cut and search out a point at which the action matches. Now, the substitute cut may be technically perfect, yet completely undesirable on at least two counts: (1) It may still jump because it comes at an illogical, therefore unacceptable point in the scene; and (2) what is more damaging, it may diminish the dramatic thrust of the scene, for the same reason. This leads to

Rule #6.    Cut for proper values rather than for proper matches.

If the dramatic demand at a particular moment in a scene dictates a cut from, say, a full shot (A) to a close shot (B), the cut *must* be made, regardless of a bad action or position match. The cut can be accomplished in a number of ways.

1. Ignore the mismatch! If the cut is dramatically correct it is remarkable how often the bad match will be completely unnoticed by the viewer. The important thing here, as in so many areas of cutting, is to know where the *viewer* will be looking. The mismatch that the cutter sees so clearly on the moviola is probably far from the viewer's center of interest. If the viewer is watching the actor's eyes, a mismatch of an arm or hand will be ignored nine times out of ten. I have often been able to obtain a perfectly smooth change of scene even though the action in the two cuts varied widely.

In *Murder, My Sweet*, I was faced with a closely related problem—a decided variation in lighting. Early in the film, Dick Powell as Phillip Marlowe is confronted by a menacing Moose Mulloy, played by Mike Mazurki. The tense scene was staged in a sketchily lit office at night. The only light source was the off-screen street lighting, dominated by a flashing neon sign positioned just outside the office window. Its on-off frequency of about four or five seconds was quite noticeable on the players' faces. The intermittent light effect was repeated, of course, in the two shot and in the tight "over-shoulders." None of these key shots was played at exactly the same pace, or with exactly the same sequence of movements. Although the light effect was started at the same point in each take, by the time the takes ended the light effects were completely out of sync with each other. Yet a good deal of intercutting was dramatically imperative. Obviously, the on-off light effect created a problem.

I decided to go for broke, and cut the sequence for its values, completely ignoring the light changes. I hoped for a miracle. It wasn't forthcoming. The lighting did *not* match. But the scene played exactly as it should, and no one, then or since, has ever objected to the lighting anomaly. Over the years this film, a prime example of "film noire," has been frequently run for students. Not one has noticed the lighting mismatches, not even through several reruns. Only when they are specifically pointed out are they finally recognized.

In short, the proper cut, to the proper shot, at the proper time, is always the cut of choice.

2. If, for some valid reason, the required cut from A to B *cannot* be made, a cut to a close-up, B', whose closeness omits the undesirable positioning or movement, will often do the trick. If no such close-up has been shot, all is not yet lost. Here is a stratagem that has saved quite a few difficult situations.

The close shot, B, can often be blown up into a close-up on the projection printer. The quality of the print may suffer a little, but only the cameraman will notice, and he will probably accede gracefully to the demands of the scene.

3. If all else fails, the cutter can always precede the desired cut to B with a shot replacing the latter part of cut A—say, a close shot of its main center of interest, whether it be the speaker in the scene, or an observer. The cut from such a replacement close shot will avoid the bad match and, although it might be criticized as a bit "cutty," it will serve its dramatic purpose.

To sum up, there is only one optimum way to cut a film, and the editor must overturn every stone in his effort to find it. Basically, it means showing, at any particular moment, that scene, set-up, move, or reaction which most effectively delivers its dramatic message. Compromises may be unavoidable, but they should never be accepted without a battle. It is good to remember that the obvious is not always the best and, if one keeps trying, the ultimate solution might be superior to the original intent. And most important of all, the film's dramatic requirements should *always* take precedence over the mere aesthetics of editing.

# 9

# *Cutting Dialogue*

Good drama* is never an essay, a lecture, or straight narrative. It is cause and effect, action and reaction, even when no physical activity is involved. A good dialogue scene is rarely a simple interchange of declarative lines, or overt plot exposition, no matter how brilliantly written; it contains conflict, surprises, "twists," and "food for thought"—something for the actor, as well as the viewer, to ruminate.

In all good films it is essential that the characters grow, or, to put it more accurately, develop—and such development is most effectively shown through their reactions, either to physical crises or to verbal stimuli. These are the "moments of transition" which every actor and director looks for in the script's scenes, whether or not they consciously identify them as such. And these are the moments of which every editor should be especially aware, the moments which he should treat with special care.

Such moments contain two elements—let us call them the "delivery" and the "reaction." Proper timing for each is of the greatest importance; where to cut *away* from the delivery and where to cut *to* the reaction may be most productively investigated in the context of dialogue scenes, since these are the scenes which, in the present state of the art, dominate most films.

But first, let us examine a typical cutting breakdown for such a scene without regard to the niceties of the editing. Our example is a single five-page scene excerpted from the shooting script of *The Carpetbaggers*. It is not only a good sampling of several types of cuts, it demonstrates a point made on page 419 of Chapter 2, Book IV.

---

* "Drama" is used here in the broad sense to cover all forms of theatrical presentation, whether tragedy, comedy, melodrama, musical, etc.

92.    (CONTINUED)

RINA

The invitations have already gone
out.

She starts toward Ellis, but Jonas stops her.

JONAS

Rina, sometimes you remind me
of me.

RINA

And so I ask myself, if I were
Jonas, what would I want in
return for this?

JONAS

You get an answer?

RINA

Yes—the other half of yourself—
me.

JONAS

Just don't forget to come when I
call.

They walk back toward Ellis.

DISSOLVE TO:

93.    INT. COMMISSARY—(FALSE DAWN)

The lights are still on in the dining room, though a little gray
light is struggling through the windows. Jonas sits at a table
in the executive dining room, with Nevada, Pierce, Norman
and Ellis seated around him. Rina sits a little behind Jonas,
who is eating breakfast. None of the others are eating, though
some may have coffee before them. Jonas speaks to the men.

JONAS

Rina, and Mr. Ellis—
(indicates with fork)

*Full Shot (1)*

*Cont.*

(CONTINUED)

93 (CONTINUED)

(1) cont.

showed me the picture.
>           (turns to Nevada, quietly)
Max Sand.

                NEVADA
The dossier, Junior. I put it to
script.

                PIERCE
Is there something here I don't
understand?

                NEVADA
It's a private joke, Dan, between
Jonas and me.

(2) 2 shot Nevada & P

Pierce retreats wisely. Jonas turns to Norman.

                JONAS
Why did you withdraw your
guarantee, Mr. Norman?

                PIERCE
              (interrupting)
Because he's an unprincipled,
thieving, son of a. . . .

(3) C.U. Jonas

                NORMAN
              (mildly)
Let's deal in business, not
personalities. Anger is for fools.

                PIERCE
You call ruining a man's life
"business"?

                NORMAN
I'm ruining nothing! This is
gambling! Some days we win,
some days we lose.

(4) 2 shot P. & Nor.

                PIERCE
You're the richest loser I know.

Jonas watches the two men carefully, sizing up the two men,
and the issue. Pierce indicates Nevada eloquently with a sweep
of his arm.
                        (CONTINUED)

cont.

93 (CONTINUED)

> PIERCE
> Look at him—the biggest star you
> have on the lot. . . .

> NORMAN
> The biggest cowboy star. . . .

> PIERCE
> Your bread and butter.

(4) 2 shot
P. & Nor.
cont.

> NORMAN
> I make other pictures!

> PIERCE
> Art pictures! That don't make a
> dime!

> NORMAN
> They add culture and dignity to
> the studio.

> PIERCE
> They add three starlets a week to
> your bed!

> NORMAN
> (stands up—angrily)
> I don't have to listen to this flesh
> peddler. . . .

> JONAS
> Please sit down, Mr. Norman—
> Mr. Pierce.

Pierce subsides and Norman sits back down in his chair. He is
obviously quite uncomfortable.

> JONAS (Cont'd)
> Now. . . .
> (to Norman)
> Why did you withdraw the
> guarantee?

(5) Full shot

> NORMAN
> Talking pictures, that's why. I
> can't sell The Renegade's Code for
> peanuts.

cont.

(CONTINUED)

93 (CONTINUED)

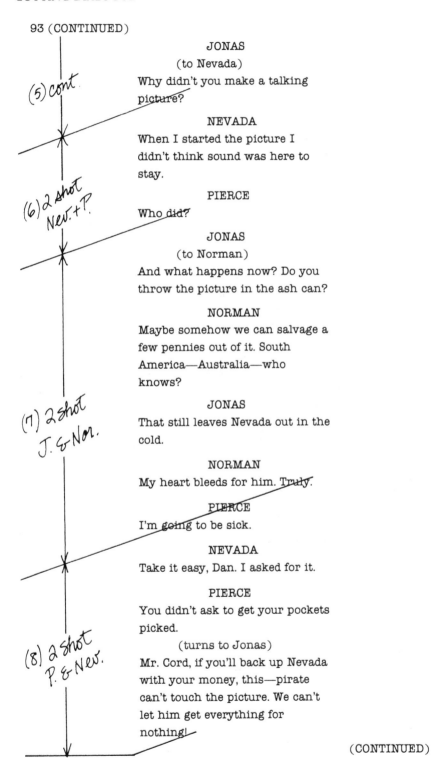

(5) cont.

(6) a shot
Nev. + P.

(7) 2 shot
J. & Nor.

(8) a shot
P. & Nev.

JONAS
(to Nevada)
Why didn't you make a talking picture?

NEVADA
When I started the picture I didn't think sound was here to stay.

PIERCE
Who did?

JONAS
(to Norman)
And what happens now? Do you throw the picture in the ash can?

NORMAN
Maybe somehow we can salvage a few pennies out of it. South America—Australia—who knows?

JONAS
That still leaves Nevada out in the cold.

NORMAN
My heart bleeds for him. Truly.

PIERCE
I'm going to be sick.

NEVADA
Take it easy, Dan. I asked for it.

PIERCE
You didn't ask to get your pockets picked.
(turns to Jonas)
Mr. Cord, if you'll back up Nevada with your money, this—pirate can't touch the picture. We can't let him get everything for nothing!

(CONTINUED)

93 (CONTINUED)

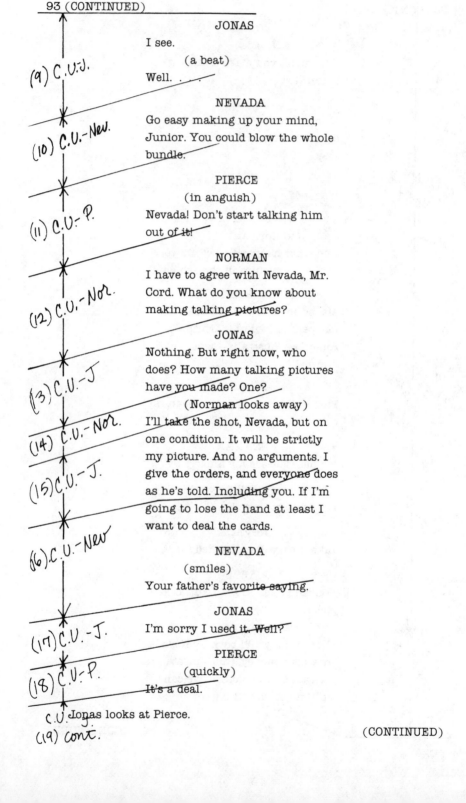

(9) C.U.-J.

JONAS

I see.
                    (a beat)
Well. . . .

(10) C.U.-Nev.

NEVADA

Go easy making up your mind,
Junior. You could blow the whole
bundle.

(11) C.U.-P.

PIERCE
                    (in anguish)
Nevada! Don't start talking him
out of it!

(12) C.U.-Nor.

NORMAN

I have to agree with Nevada, Mr.
Cord. What do you know about
making talking pictures?

(13) C.U.-J

JONAS

Nothing. But right now, who
does? How many talking pictures
have you made? One?

(14) C.U.-Nor.

                    (Norman looks away)
I'll take the shot, Nevada, but on
one condition. It will be strictly
my picture. And no arguments. I

(15) C.U.-J.

give the orders, and everyone does
as he's told. Including you. If I'm
going to lose the hand at least I
want to deal the cards.

(16) C.U.-Nev

NEVADA
                    (smiles)
Your father's favorite saying.

(17) C.U.-J.

JONAS

I'm sorry I used it. Well?

(18) C.U.-P.

PIERCE
                    (quickly)
It's a deal.

C.U. Jonas looks at Pierce.

(19) cont.

                                                    (CONTINUED)

93 (CONTINUED)

(19) C.U.-J (cont.)

JONAS

Don't think you've caught a
sucker, Pierce. By the time we
finish this picture you'll earn
your ten percent three times over.
First thing, line up all the good
talkies there are. I want to see
them. Then, get the writers in
and we'll start re-doing the script.

(20) C.U.-Nev

NEVADA

What's the matter with it?

JONAS

No women. In the real West I
hear there were a number of
them—real women. The kind men
killed each other for, robbed
banks to buy. The kind the real
Max Sand built a reputation
satisfying. It's time somebody
gave the West back to the
grownups.

(21) C.U.-J.

PIERCE

(chastened)

Anything else, Mr. Cord?

(22) C.U.-P.

JONAS

Mr. Norman, you will have to
make room for us.
(to Pierce)
Get the best sound man in the
business. Find a cameraman
who'd rather photograph women
than horses, and a dress designer
who doesn't use much cloth. And
Nevada, start looking like Max
Sand. Go out and get that suit
dirty.

(23) Tight Group

The phone rings. It is near Rina. She picks it up.

cont.

(CONTINUED)

93 (CONTINUED)

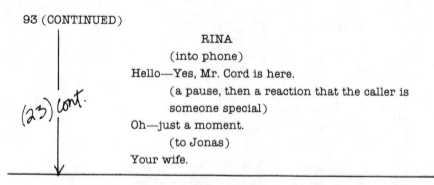

                                    RINA
                          (into phone)
                    Hello—Yes, Mr. Cord is here.
                          (a pause, then a reaction that the caller is
                          someone special)
                    Oh—just a moment.
                          (to Jonas)
                    Your wife.

The script was written by John Michael Hayes, at that time (1963) one of Hollywood's most highly regarded writers. It will be noticed that the five pages (the last half page is omitted as of no concern to us) are written as *one* master shot, even though the most cursory reading will reveal that a number of set-ups and cuts are required to properly develop the scene's several dramatic elements. (As the scene is broken down it consists of 23 cuts derived from 10 or 11 set-ups—specifically, 4 close-ups, 3 two shots, 2 or 3 group shots, and probably a reaction cut of Rina.) The custom of writing dialogue scenes in master shots is the rule rather than the exception.

Our scene is marked up (admittedly more neatly than in the working version) with the director's cutting instructions for the editor who is to make the rough cut. The cuts are numbered here for the convenience of the analysis, but the rest of the directions, including set-up identification (e.g., 2 shot—Nev. and P.) and the slanting lines which indicate cutting points are much as they were in the original breakdown.

On the whole this is a straightforward sequence; and even if I had not shot it and cut it some 20 years ago, I would, today, still probably break it down much as indicated. Of course, the proper cutting concept would have to be based on the cutter's knowledge of the characters as learned from previously filmed material. Lacking that knowledge, the cutting sequence might be quite different, even though the cutter had access to the script. Characters as written and characters as played are often surprisingly divergent.

In order to furnish "live" footage for the dissolve into the full shot (1), as well as to set up the scene and its personnel, certain "business," or action, not indicated in the script was extemporized when the scene was shot.

The cut to (2), a two shot of Nevada (Alan Ladd) and Pierce (Bob Cummings) enables us to accentuate a previously established "in" relationship between Nevada and Jonas (George Peppard). It also allows us, at the end of the cut, to use Nevada's meaningful look toward Jonas to slide more smoothly into cut (3), a close-up of Jonas.

This shot prepares us, gently, for Jonas' eventual domination of the situation, and the people involved in it, as it gets us back to the business at hand. Jonas' line, though spoken to Norman (Marty Balsam), brings an angry comment from Pierce, so:

Cut (4) is a two shot of Pierce and Norman. A close-up of Pierce at this point, even though he is the speaker, would probably confuse the viewer since Jonas in cut (3) has addressed Norman. The two shot allows us to see the person addressed and to catch Pierce's interruption without confusion. This is the second two shot which includes Pierce, and it serves to call attention to the director's responsibility for staging "cutting-compatible" set-ups. Nevada, Pierce, and Norman had to be placed in positions which would permit a two shot of Nevada and Pierce, and another of Norman and Pierce. Of course, these two "two shots" could never be directly intercut without Pierce "jumping" from one side of the screen to the other; but either could be used when needed by cutting away to a close-up, as in (2) to (3), or to another two shot of different people, as in (6) to (7). The third two shot (7) of Jonas and Norman further complicates the staging and the cutting, but the previously stated rule applies also to this set-up. If all this seems a touch complicated, rest assured—it is. Even experienced directors occasionally goof in such a situation.

To resume our analysis: Cut (4) is a scene of bickering conflict, rapidly paced, with dialogue overlaps (as shot). Since no reactions of special import are present, it plays well in the two shot. A group shot here would weaken the scene; and close-ups, as indirectly suggested by the writer's directions—"Jonas watches the two men carefully"—would have overstated the importance of the nattering and minimized the value of the close-ups to be used at the scene's climax. Cut (4) plays for a full page, some 40 feet at this rapid pace. The cut to (5) is made in movement, on Norman's rise.

This kind of "action cut", involving dialogue, is quite common—and often troublesome. The actor rises as he speaks, but rarely does he do so at exactly the same point in each take, or set-up, and rarely does the sound perspective of the two set-ups match. The best solution here is to cut for the picture match, allowing the dialogue from the two shot (4) to continue over the first part of the full shot (5). Even if the words do not synchronize exactly (and it would be a miracle if they did) the viewer's vision will not be sharply focused as it shifts with the action of the cut. By the time it is, that particular line (or phrase) of dialogue will have been completed and the next line, now properly that of the full shot (5), will have taken over. (An interruption here might be another complication—but more about that later.)

To resume, cut (5), a full shot, permits us to unruffle a few feathers, draw a deep breath, strengthen Jonas' position, and get back to the real business of the scene, while pulling away momentarily from what is really a secondary conflict, as we once again begin to build to a more dramatically sound (and inevitable) climax to the sequence.

With cut (6) we start to zero in on the real objective of the sequence: Jonas' take over of Nevada's film, which, in turn, will impel Jonas firmly into the motion picture business.

Cuts (7) and (8) continue our two shot build-up to what will be an extensive, rapid-fire intercutting of close-ups (9) through (22).

Cut (23) brings us back to earth. Associations and antagonisms which become major story developments have been firmly established; decisions, for good or ill, have been unalterably made. And to springboard us into the next sequence, the telephone rings, breaking the tension and bringing Rina (Carrol Baker) back into the scene.

Those, briefly, were the cuts, and the imperatives which led to them. Given the same set-ups and equal knowledge of the characters' earlier developments, half a dozen cutters, each assessing the sequence on his own, would probably cut it in much the same way, although minor variations would certainly occur. A TV cutter would undoubtedly use even more close-ups; an old timer perhaps not quite so many. But in this breakdown one important element has been temporarily set aside—*exactly where,* in each cut, does the cutter leave the scene, and *exactly where* does he start each incoming cut. It is in this area that the cutters' techniques might vary considerably; and it is here that such variations might enhance, or damage, the tone, the pace, and the impact of each cut separately and the sequence as a whole. Let us now retrace our steps and examine each cut as carefully as we can with this element in mind.

Before we can properly "handle" an exchange of dialogue, however, we must first understand the grammatical nature of our language.* In speaking English, preferred usage generally requires that the subject be placed near the start of a sentence, and that it be followed almost immediately by the predicate, whether simple or compound. The rest of the sentence, which might be quite long, usually consists of explanatory, modifying phrases or clauses. Certainly in the majority of cases, the *sense* of a statement is usually manifest before that statement is completed. This leads to a common and sometimes unjustly condemned habit—the habit of interruption.

In most conversations, often even in well-chaired discussions, people frequently, sometimes constantly, cut in on each other. A conversation without interruptions may be polite; it is also, quite probably, very dull. Interruptions are not necessarily a sign of rudeness, but of eagerness. Anticipating the finish of a speaker's sentence, the

---

* It is quite possible that the different structures of other languages would require different cutting techniques, but the principles to be discussed here, involving the use of English, can probably be modified by an intelligent editor to fit his native tongue.

listener is eager to respond, whether in assent or disagreement. Even if the listener remains silent, he will often react with a nod of approval, a grimace of doubt, or a frown of rejection, well before the end of the speaker's statement. And although a spoken sentence may occasionally deliver a surprise ending, in the great majority of instances that simply is not so.

This conversational glitch dramatically pinpoints one of the main differences between films and earlier forms of drama: The frequency of conversational interruptions in real life informs us of the number of times overlapping can and *should* be resorted to in a medium which is based on human interrelationships and interaction rather than on the *formal* presentation of ideas.

The cutter must remember that, whether with a verbal or a non-verbal response, the listener usually reacts *before* the speaker has finished speaking—*and so does the viewer.* He, too, is a listener, and it is the *viewer's* awareness of the listener's point of reaction which properly determines a dialogue cut.

With the foregoing in mind, let us more closely examine the cuts in our sample scene.

The cut-away from cut (1) should be made substantially as indicated by the diagonal line—somewhere in the middle of the word "Sand." The viewer is aware of its significance because of an earlier scene, and he is now interested in its effect on Nevada. To linger on the cut, as many cutters would, is to lag *behind* the viewer, and that is a cardinal sin.

The average film viewer is a highly conditioned animal. He has seen hundreds of films, thousands of "situations." Rarely does he experience a truly original scene. His grasp of dramatic situations is usually quite broad, and his reactions to an actor's line very swift indeed. His tolerance of the ordinary should not be mistaken for stupidity. Talking down to an audience is a fool's occupation. It is difficult enough to stay even with the viewer—one need rarely worry about being ahead of him. The filmmaker must always try (although only a few will completely succeed) never to fall behind. That way leads to boredom, inattention, and failure.

At the end of cut (1) many cutters will allow the out-going scene to run until they are sure the word "Sand" is quite finished. Since they do not, quite properly, want to risk cutting into the word, they give themselves a few extra frames for protection. This is good practice, as far as the *sound* is concerned, but there is no need to run the *picture* as long as the sound track. Picture and sound need never be cut simultaneously, and cutters who overlap infrequently are doing inferior work. In this particular example, it would mean that the cut has been made quite a number of frames *after* the proper *picture* cutting point (frame *t*, Figure 4) causing the viewer a moment's unwelcome distraction and an unnecessary lengthening of the cut. (Compare Figures 4 and 7.)

(Note: In the schematic Figures, the *frames* of the film are purely suggestive. In reality, many more frames would be involved.)

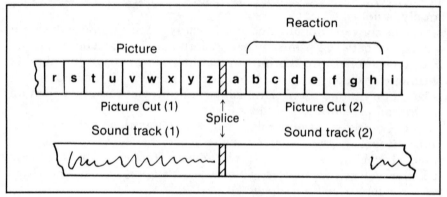

*Book IV - Figure 4*

The extra frames at the end of cut (1), frames *t* through *z*, combined with the three or four "empty" frames (see p. 489), at the beginning of cut (2)—frame *a*—can add up to as much as a full second of dead time between the point at which the viewer anticipates Nevada's reaction to Jonas' line, and the point at which the reaction is finally delivered. The "stall" is lengthened. And often, when the director or the producer pronounces, "It's twenty minutes too long. Cut it down!" the cutter, maintaining his straight across cut at the end of (1), will clip the beginning of the reaction in (2)—frames *a* through *h*. This will save some footage by bringing Nevada's *verbal* response closer to Jonas' line, but only at the expense of Nevada's *visual* response, his reaction, which, in classical film sense, is much more important. (See Figure 5.)

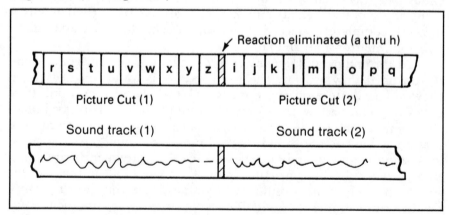

*Book IV - Figure 5*

Instead of eliminating the reaction frames (*a* through *h*), it is far better to eliminate the relatively unimportant frames at the end of cut (1): frames *t* through *z*. In order to keep the scene in sync, an equal amount of sound track must be cut from the beginning of sound track (2).

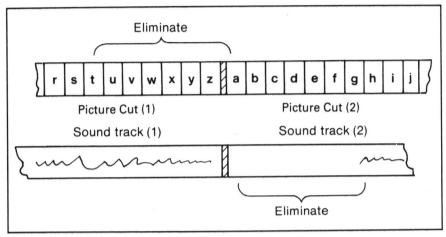

*Book IV - Figure 6*

This cut (Figure 6) saves the same amount of footage as in the straight across cut (Figure 5), while retaining the important elements of the scene. Figure 7 illustrates the final version of the proper overlapping cut.

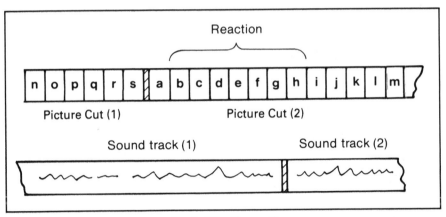

*Book IV - Figure 7*

By cutting from (1) to (2) at the point where the viewer looks toward Nevada, we are able to camouflage our cut without resorting to the "distraction" of physical movement. The movement here is mental on the part of the viewer, and self-willed, since he wants to see Nevada's reaction to Jonas' line. If we hit it exactly, we present

Nevada in the two shot just as the viewer's eyes refocus on the scene, showing him what he wants to see and, incidentally, rendering our cut invisible, since it is made as the viewer shifts his eyes. We are able to show Nevada's complete reaction (preceded by three or four empty frames), we shorten the pause between the two cuts, and we keep the dialogue flowing.

This is the key principle for cutting dialogue. There are exceptions, but the great majority of dialogue cuts can be made after this fashion. The advantages are obvious—the cut "goes with" the viewer's awareness, it hides our cut, it conforms to rules 4, 5, and 6, and it enables us to maintain a tighter pace and a smoother flow.

The three or four frames preceding the start of any reaction cut, which I have called empty frames, are mandatory. The practice is based on the principle stated in Chapter 6, Book IV (Figure 3). It provides the brief moment needed by the viewer to focus on the new scene. If the cut were to be made just one frame ahead of the start of the reaction, the viewer would miss it by catching it already under way, a most undesirable effect.

To proceed, the cut-away from (2) is not made as quickly as indicated. There is a moment's pause as Pierce "retreats wisely," then Nevada looks back at Jonas. The cut is made on the "look off" principle (Book IV, Chapter 7). We get to Jonas, in (3), in time for a slight reaction to the interchange in the previous cut, which is followed by the transfer of Jonas' attention to Norman. This close-up is also needed to separate the two two-shots, each of which pairs Pierce with a different actor (page 459). The cut-away from (3) returns us to the overlapping principle of (1), especially since Pierce actually cuts in on Jonas.

Cuts (4) and (5) have been covered earlier in the chapter. The cut-away to (6) employs the overlap since no time for thought on Nevada's part is necessary. The same is true for the cut-away from (6) to (7).

At the start of (7) time is allowed for Jonas to transfer his attention from Nevada to Pierce and Norman. Jonas probably has a brief reaction to Pierce's, "Who did?" before he shifts his attention to Norman. Here, too, as at the beginning of all cuts, the three or four empty frames preceding Jonas' reaction, no matter how slight, must be included.

The cut-away from (7) is overlapped by the beginning of (8). Pierce actually reacts to "for him," so this extends his reaction slightly. His line is a near-interruption of "Truly."

Cut (8) delivers the challenge to Jonas. Again we use the overlap, as indicated, to cut to (9).

Cut (9) starts a series of close-up intercuts. The first, on (9), is known in cutters' parlance as a "timed cut." Jonas takes a moment to digest Pierce's last remark. After "I see," he again pauses for thought and an ideational transition. His "well . . ." indicates the beginning of a decision which Nevada tries to forestall. Here the timing of the cut-away from (9) is instinctual. The cutter must guess at which point the viewer will look to someone for a reaction. A good cutter will guess right most of the time. The cut to Nevada (10) takes place during the look.

The cut-away from (10) is a natural overlap. We know that Nevada's line will cause Pierce some anguish, and we are eager to see his reaction in (11). From here on the cuts proceed at a rapid pace. The ends of all lines overlap—but the *reactions* at the *starts* of the cuts are important and must be carefully timed and protected. There is one cut-away to a silent reaction of Norman (14). This starts as an overlap on Jonas' word "made?" His next word, "One?," comes over Norman's close-up. Norman's reaction to the question is obviously important, since it drives home to him, but really to the viewer, a very vital point, one which makes Jonas' forthcoming decision seem quite inevitable. As Norman looks away, we cut back to Jonas (15). Here, the film is cut for looks and reactions—the sound track is secondary and can be extended (if necessary) to accommodate the picture cuts. Such extensions of timing are often required, and will be dealt with in a future chapter.

Cut (15) shows Jonas' full reaction to cut (14). It is important that he be aware of the effect of his put-down of Norman. The cut-away to Nevada (16) comes early, on Jonas' line "including you." This is a key condition—the "gauntlet." Nevada's reaction, by no means a foregone conclusion, is also important. Jonas' off-screen line is merely a restatement of earlier words, put in terms Nevada can easily understand and accept. Nevada's answer in (16) is a partial evasion, and also a slight getting even with Jonas. Nevada is trying to retain his dignity even though he knows, as does the viewer, that he must accept Jonas' terms. The cut-away from (16) is an overlap, especially since Jonas (17) reacts sourly to Nevada's implication. His question, "Well?," is overlapped by:

Pierce, in cut (18). His quick reaction and line is matched by an equally quick overlap to (19). From here on, the end of each cut overlaps the start of the following cut, down to the end of the sequence.

Before concluding this area of cutting, it is important to mention two exceptions to the quick overlapping technique. The first, already mentioned but not singled out, is not truly a dialogue cut, but it often comes up in dialogue situations. It is exemplified on page 453 in the cut-away from (2) to the close-up of Jonas (3). Although the dialogue in (2) has been completed, the viewer's attention is held by the visual interplay between Pierce and Nevada. The viewer must be allowed the time to absorb Pierce's important reaction of "retreat," at the end of which his attention is directed to Jonas (3) by Nevada's "look-off." In (3), Jonas continues the interplay briefly, then changes the subject of the conversation and the direction of the scene. The cut from (2) to (3) is based on the "look-off" principle, but the cutter must know which "look-off" to look for.

The second exception is of a different and much more subtle nature. It concerns the posterior *elongation* of close-ups in a flow-of-dialogue scene, especially where the lines and the reactions deliver different messages. This is best illustrated by an example from Leo McCarey's *Love Affair,* starring Irene Dunne and Charles Boyer.

These two play star-crossed lovers whose long-awaited rendezvous at the top of the Empire State Building is thwarted when Dunne, hurrying across a traffic-crowded street within sight of the meeting place, suffers a crippling accident. Unaware of the mishap, Boyer assumes he has been stood up. On her part, Dunne refuses to contact Boyer because she is now a quadriplegic.

In time, their paths cross, but under circumstances which still leave him ignorant of her condition. Piqued by their chance meeting and still very much in love, Boyer visits Dunne at her home. She successfully conceals her handicap by remaining seated throughout his visit. In the ensuing scene, Boyer's pride and Dunne's reluctance lead them both to avoid the truth as they recount their versions of the missed rendezvous. Yet this is the climax of the film, and it is mandatory that the truth emerge despite the fact that it is never voiced. Obviously, it could be done only through "attitude," or reaction, but not obviously.

Boyer and Dunne were masters of reaction. In this climactic scene their "looks" had to belie their words, but in a most subtle fashion. These looks came *after* the spoken lines, being, in a sense, reactions to *their own words.* Therefore, it was necessary to stay with each close-up after the speaker's line had been completed, if only for a brief moment. Only then could a cut be made to the necessary reaction and response, at the finish of which would come another subtly ambiguous look.

Since the viewer was completely aware of the situation, it was necessary to get him involved in a "game" of a sort—not *if,* since that was inevitable, but *how* and *when* will Boyer realize the truth. In this instance the viewer participated in the game willingly, enjoying the delayed looks and eagerly anticipating Boyer's "moment of truth." The beauty and genius of the scene lay in the fact that the denouement was brought about wholly by the "looks", or reactions, which followed completely plausible verbal deceptions.

Such scenes are rare because the teaming of such talent (including the writing and the direction) is rare. But now and then a line or two of this nature does surface. The editing of such a sequence demands as much timing sensitivity as does the staging. The cutter must "feel" the exact point in the delayed reaction at which the viewer will look for a counter-reaction, and a cut made at this point will inevitably be proper and smooth.

But cutting away from, and to, almost any reaction requires a finely honed sense of timing, which only practice can properly develop. However, a few hints may help and, in any case, this category deserves at least a brief consideration in its own right.

# 10

## *What Really Counts*

John Wayne was wont to say, "I don't act—I react." It was by no means an original phrase, and if it was meant as a self-assessment of his ability, he was short-changing himself. At its best, screen acting is a difficult art, whose subtleties often escape its critics; it demands great competence in all its aspects, of which, as the cliche indicates, reacting is one of the most important. In the theater, dialogue may be king—in films, the reaction is where most things happen.

Reaction is transition, change, movement—and movement is life. Reaction can reveal the birth and growth of awareness, show a quantum leap in levels of anger, or of love, discover to us the gathering of one's wits in thought, or a change in attitude or state of mind. It can express approval, doubt, or disbelief, and do so in a universal language—without words.*

In comedy it can range from the dead-pan reaction of a Buster Keaton, through the wicked leer of a Groucho Marx, to the broad distortions of a Jerry Lewis or a Martha Raye. In a more serious vein it may range from the steady, almost sly, look of a Spencer Tracy, to the baldly stated responses, whether snarling or smiling, of a Jimmy Cagney at his best. But, whether obvious or subtle, no screen actor can claim to have mastered his art until he has complete control over all his reactions. And no film editor can claim to have mastered his craft until he can effectively present those reactions to the viewer.

It can be argued that this is properly the concern of the actor and the director, and in a perfect world that would be so. But, unfortunately. . . . In most collaborative efforts, whether in art or in politics, a great deal of time is spent in disguising lapses in taste or judgment,

---

*Jane Wyman won the Academy Award in 1948 without uttering a syllable in *Johnny Belinda.*

in fleshing out missed opportunities, or simply in correcting mistakes. All this is "cutting territory."

On the more positive side, it is rarely that a writer, an actor, or a director exhausts all the useful possibilities and nuances of even the finest script—which always leaves a "little something" for the editor to deal with. If he is willing to look for, and accept, the challenge, this aspect of the craft can be a good deal more rewarding and pleasurable than the amelioration of a film's mistakes. But in both of these areas creative "handling" of reactions can be a rich and productive field.

Now, let us begin at the beginning—understanding the *need* for a reaction, finding it, then timing it. Writers are aware of the importance of the reaction as a vital element in communication. Some screen writers, in particular, know that a good reaction can eliminate a lot of words—but full and accurate instructions are difficult to write in script terms. Besides, the actor and the director hate to be "written down to" as much as does the intelligent viewer. So the writer usually delivers his instructions in a conventional form. Here are three actual examples:

(1)     From The Left Hand of God.

MARY YIN
(a small shrug)
Why not? Rice wine—and a
woman—

(2)     From The Caine Mutiny.

WILLIE
(desperately)
But, mother—

(3)     From A Walk on the Wild Side.

DAVE
(grinning)
How about upstairs?

A weakness of this convention is that it often leads to redundancy. Many writers are taught, or conditioned, to be playwrights: They feel that reactions must also be expressed through dialogue since they can't always be seen at the back of the theater. An example:

JEAN
(nodding)
Yes - of course. . . .

But Jean is a fine actress, and her nod can say it all. In our example (1) the "small shrug" *says* "why not?" There is no need to verbalize it. A moment's thought will make clear how the line in example (3) could also be eliminated, although this would have to be worked out on the set. As for example (2), the "desperation" was quite explicit in the whole scene; the instruction here was quite unnecessary.

A good director combs his script and carefully monitors his rehearsals for such obvious tautologies. And though most actors love their lines, the best of them have learned the value of acting through reaction and are eager to cooperate. Spencer Tracy, who could "read the lyrics" better than any actor of his day, was always happy to see one eliminated, and one of his reactions could replace a page-full of words.

The great majority of reactions are easily identified; consequently they are often taken for granted. But when cutting, even a procedure as simple as finding the *start* of the reaction requires close and careful examination. The moviola does not necessarily tell the whole story, and often only the "big screen" will reveal whether or not the cutter has included the complete reaction in his cut.

That reaction is not always heralded by a movement of the facial muscles. The most subtle reactions may show a barely discernable "glint," or change, in the expression of the eyes, especially if the actor is listening, as he should be, and not just waiting for a cue. The *very first frame* where the change begins must be marked, then preceded by the several empty frames mentioned earlier. (See Book IV, Chapter 9).

Obviously, the *length* of a reaction can have a decisive bearing on a scene's impact, but many filmmakers are not aware of how easily that factor can be manipulated. One quick example will illustrate the point.

> Scene: A woman exits a building. As she nears the curb, a car pulls up and a man steps out. He wears a hat.

MAN WITH THE HAT

(quietly)

Hi, Molly. Hop in.

CLOSE-UP     MOLLY

> Now Molly can react in a number of ways. We will examine the two extremes.

(1)

MOLLY

(without hesitation)

All right.

> And she gets into the car.

Since there is no hesitation in Molly's reply, or in her reaction, the viewer will assume that the situation is routine, and that nothing especially dramatic is about to happen.

(2)     CLOSE-UP     MOLLY

> She hesitates, looking closely at the man in the hat. After a
> long beat, she speaks:

                              MOLLY
                      All right.

When the viewer sees Molly hesitate for a measurable length of time, he *thinks with her*, and a number of possibilities cross his mind. Is the man a near-stranger? Is he someone she knows, but fears? Is he an ex-husband with vengeance on his mind? Is he going to "take her for a ride"? Or does the man represent an inner temptation? Her eventual "All right," although spoken exactly as in version (1), will now have one of several possible meanings. Even the *sound* of her response will seem different because the viewer's imagination has been nudged into activity.

It *is* still possible to extract audience participation, and a good deal of that possibility can be contrived in the cutting room.

Let us examine two such manipulations which share similar solutions.

1.  In the previous example, let us assume the scene was shot with the shorter version (1) in mind. During editing sessions it is decided to add a little suspense to the scene, either for comedic or for melodramatic purposes. (Such decisions are made more frequently than one might imagine.)
2.  A screen character is thinking his way through to an important decision. He is fully aware of his alternatives, which have been laid down in earlier scenes, and he makes up his mind expeditiously. However, the cutter knows that the *viewer's* awareness of the alternatives has been dimmed by the intervening sequences, and he undertakes to give him more time to recall them to mind than the actor's reaction allows.

In both examples, extra footage preceding the actor's reaction is required, and such footage is usually available. It is in that part of the reactor's close-up, immediately preceding his reaction, which shows him *listening* to the speaker who has supplied the "food" for his thought. As a rule, the listener does not move or react prematurely, and an extension of considerable length can be obtained from the "listening" footage.

An actor need not be "emoting" to supply the cutter with a reaction. Stillness, too, can be a vital expression. (Read E.A. Poe's *Silence—A Fable*). If the close-up comes at the point where the actor should react to a given stimulus, the very absence of movement can show our listener lost in thought. When the mobile reaction finally comes, we know he is reaching a conclusion.

There are occasions, as would be quite likely in example (1), where no footage for extension is available in the footage shot. The cutter still has a trick or two up his sleeve. He can "freeze frame" the close-up immediately preceding the reaction (unless, of course, there is background movement). If the actor's move, when the "live" action begins, is not too sharp, no viewer will be aware that a foot or two of film has been "frozen" from one selected frame. The cliches "rooted to the spot" and "frozen in amazement" describe such a reaction accurately, and they have a most dynamic connotation.

Another alternative is to find a suitable reaction from another sequence in the film, which is not as unrealistic as it sounds. (I once found a usable close-up reaction in another film!) If the shot is close enough to avoid showing too much clothing (which might be different) and the hair is not dressed too differently (usually no problem with males), such a borrowed scene can be quite satisfactory, even if originally shot in another setting. The background of a large close-up is usually unidentifiable at best.

There is an important lesson here for every beginner, one that every good editor has learned—*never give up*. If it is necessary to correct a fault, or if it is possible to improve the dramatic quality of a sequence, and the proper material is not at hand, explore *all* possibilities, or invent a few. The odds that some workable solution can be found are so overwhelming that one should never stop trying, no matter how difficult the problem. Always remember that film is the art of illusion, and the most unlikely things can be made to seem real.

# 11

# *If You Can't Make It Smooth, Make It Right*

So far we have discussed "smooth" cutting techniques—matches in movement, exit-entrance cuts, "look-off" cut-aways, reaction timing, and the use of properly timed anticipation in dialogue interchanges. However, even a superficial examination of almost any film will reveal a number of cuts which do not fall into any of these categories. They appear to be made arbitrarily and are seen, as a rule, in visual sequences such as fights, chases, contests, or scenes of suspense, in montage sequences, or in dialogue scenes which offer no thought transitions or opportunity for "mulling over," and where no essentially new information is being presented.* Such scenes, or sequences, are usually developments of established plot lines, goals, or characterizations, and their purpose is to move the story toward some minor or major resolution or climax.

This aspect of cutting, more than any other, tests the cutter's instinct for proper pace and timing. If his cuts are too quick, or "choppy," the viewer may be confused or irritated; if they are too long, the film lags, along with the viewer's interest. Each sequence of this kind presents its own special hurdles—rarely do they repeat themselves exactly—but a generalized discussion is possible through the use of hypothetical examples.

Let us examine the opposite of the precisely timed dialogue scene of substance, say an argument between two characters in which maximum pace is desired. The basis for the conflict has been established earlier in the film, and additional information would be redundant;

---

*I find it impossible to resist the comment that this sentence aptly describes the total contents of the majority of today's films.

attack, defense, and counterattack follow each other at breakneck speed. Since the dialogue carries most of the dramatic burden and individual reactions are hardly subtle, many such scenes are filmed in master shots or, if broad movement over a considerable amount of space is called for, in a series of connecting master shots. Cutting such a sequence would be relatively easy. But let us assume that the sequence is lengthy and a point is reached where intercutting of swiftly paced close-ups will accentuate the verbal battle.

When the close-ups are shot, the mixer and the cutter will invariably request that the dialogue in each close-up be recorded "cleanly," i.e., without dialogue overlaps. Most directors will accede to this request. Overlaps make proper cutting difficult (though not impossible) and often "fix" the timing beyond the cutter's power to manipulate.

Cutting such a sequence entails a certain amount of labor, but few creative problems. The easiest, and best, approach is to use the *picture* as the guide.

An aside: With the exception of certain musical sequences, the cutter should work primarily with the picture in practically *all* situations. Even in dialogue scenes it is the image of the speaker, the listener, or the reactor which is important. The images change, interrelate, grow, or diminish; the sound track is, in a sense, an accompaniment, a continuous flow (even though its intensity and perspective may vary) much like the musical theme which underscores a sequence. The listener's hearing is continuous—his viewing is not— and the cutter's greatest efforts are always involved with the image.

This is not meant to imply that the creative possibilities of sound should be overlooked although, aside from the compulsory dialogue and sound effects, they usually are. One of the weaknesses of modern film is that the creative use of sound has been ignored by filmmakers even more than the creative use of images.

Back to the argument: The cutter, or director, will break down his sequence diagrammatically, much after the pattern described on pages 452 through 457. But now he will pay little attention to reactions. Instead, he will run the first close-up, say of character A, up to the point at which he wants character B to interrupt. At this point he cuts to B, allowing only the few empty frames to precede the start of the dialogue.*

In order to avoid cutting into A's line, two tracks will be set up, track *a* and track *b*, which will carry the lines of A and B respectively.

---

*Most editors are good lip readers, and a cutter can save time and effort by cutting the picture without the accompanying sound, resorting to the "sound head" only if the actor's lips cannot be seen. When the cut is completed he, or more likely his assistant, will cut the tracks *a* and *b* to synchronize with the edited picture.

This enables the cutter to run A's line to its completion on track *a*, while B's interruption runs simultaneously on track *b*. B's line, in turn, will continue in full on track *b* even when *a* eventually cuts in on B. A's second line will, of course, be placed on track *a*, as will all of his following lines.

When the sequence is cut to the editor's satisfaction, he will get a "temporary dub," combining tracks *a* and *b* into one master track which takes its place in the work print. Tracks *a* and *b* are set aside for possible later recutting, and as a guide for the final dubbing of the film.

There are minor variations of this technique for cutting rapid-fire, overlapping dialogue, but the one outlined here is probably the simplest, the most accurate, and by far the least messy. It will also, with a little additional effort, accommodate additional interruptions from additional speakers on additional tracks.

The cutting of a physical battle, whether in the ring or in an alley, presents few new problems, especially if its set-ups have been well planned by the director. Normally, a fight has to be choreographed, much as a dance number would be. Anyone who has watched professional bouts on TV understands how much dead time there is in most such contests. Many fights will feature no more than two or three solid blows in an entire three-minute round. Even well-regarded pugilists have often saved their maximum efforts for the last 15 or 20 seconds of each round in the belief that a furious finish will make the greatest impression on the judges—which it often does.

This should not be too difficult to understand. Unless he is a slugger who prides himself on his quick K.O. (and there are few of these, especially in the lighter classes), the fighter must pace himself for a long battle. On frequent occasions he will rest during the action, clinching while he catches his breath, or moving out of range while ostensibly exhibiting his "fancy" footwork. But this, though real, does not make for a good film fight. Here, the viewer wants constant action which can be clearly seen, and that means that the action must be carefully planned. In truth, unplanned action can lead to accidents and injuries which may delay shooting.

Fortunately, actors can rest between takes, most of which last no more than a few seconds. However, when a number of these short cuts are strung together to make a full round, the participants will appear to be the unexhaustible superfighters the viewer wants to see.

So, in the great majority of film fights, each cut is planned and used to show a particular blow, or combination of blows, in a specific action "routine." The planning, of course, is always done before the shooting, and the cutter's job usually consists of lining up the takes in their proper sequence, selecting the best angles for each separate bit of the routine, then cutting them together by using the "action match" technique—there is always an overabundance of matching action to cut on. But if, for some reason, the director has overlooked the required action overlap, a cut-away to one of the "corners," the referee, or (less desirable) someone in the crowd, can serve as the "kitchen stove."

Unless the cutter uses a shot of someone fully involved in the drama, a cut-away to an audience shot is not, as a rule, a wise move. The principle at work here is identical to that discovered in cutting early musicals. It is this: The viewer does not care to be told what his reaction should be by being shown a model reaction of our own choice. (The viewer is constantly manipulated, to be sure, but not in so brash a manner.) Once the "number" is under way the viewer is the audience, and a cut to the filmed audience can be distracting, especially if the viewer's reaction and the filmed reaction do not coincide. Only if the filmed reaction is important to the plot (for instance, its approval of a "new" or substitute performer) is such a cut properly in order.

The same holds true for a staged fight. Only if the crowd reaction is an essential element in the story is it of any real value. Otherwise, it is wiser to let our viewer react to the action and accept it as a real experience, exactly as one hopes he will with any and every other kind of sequence in a well-made film.

A street fight should also be carefully planned, for much the same, though more extreme, reasons. Although the dramatization of such a battle can be directorially very different from the more formal prize fight, the planning and the cutting follow the same pattern.

Since few, if any, blows and kicks of any weight actually land in a film fight, a few cutting tricks can help to manufacture reality. Not all actors can "time" or "take" a punch properly. Let us say that in a full shot the "puncher" misses the intended target, his opponent's chin, by an unacceptable margin. On top of that, the "receiver's" reaction is a shade too late. If, just as the fist, in the full shot, should meet the chin, we cut to a close-up of the "punchee" and see his head snap back as we hear a loud, dubbed-in "smack" of the fist, the illusion of a solid blow can be made to seem very real indeed. In cutting such a sequence I have often found myself wincing at the imagined moment of contact, even though I knew that no actual physical hit had been made. Practically all film fights are a succession of such cutters' tricks—examples of the magic of screen illusion at its most convincing, if not necessarily at its best.

It is wise to withhold judgment on the effectiveness of such sequences until temporary sound effects are incorporated. The sound of the punches can make a world of difference in their appearance and believability; and though cutting in temporary effects demands a good deal of additional time and labor, it more than pays for itself at the eventual editorial runnings.

A first cut always has a great deal missing, especially in the area of sound effects and music. It is unfortunately a fact of the business that many directors and producers, in spite of their claims to the contrary, cannot truly judge a rough cut on its anticipated merits. But it is difficult for even the most experienced filmmakers to accurately visualize the film as it will look and sound after all the experts—the sound effects creators, the composers, the musicians, the rerecording and dubbing mixers, and the film timers—have had their turns at the film.

As an editor, I found it much easier to "sell" the directors, the producers, and the executives, if I did as much temporary cosmetic work as I could possibly manage. It must always be kept in mind that they, too, have bouts of insecurity. Key sound effects and "library" music can markedly increase a film's dramatic, suspenseful, or romantic effects. As a matter of practical fact, the inclusion of temporary music is useful in another most important way.

Properly scored musical background serves to *increase* the apparent pace of most sequences. Therefore, if the cutter is moderately certain that a particular scene will eventually carry a musical background, he must edit his film accordingly. This means he will opt for a slower pace than he expects the sequence will ultimately achieve. If he cuts the film to its maximum pace *without* music, it will probably seem hurried after the music is added. So he must keep his "otical" illusion in mind and resist the "itchiness" if the sequence in its rough version seems a touch lethargic. The presence of a temporary musical score will help to ease the situation.

This one more instance of the creative importance of an editor's instinct for timing.

# 12

# *Know Your Audience*

The sharp-eyed reader may have noticed an occasional reference to "the viewer" or "the audience." If he is especially discerning he may have reached the conclusion that I regard the viewer as something more than a passive observer. He would be quite correct.

We have often heard, or read, some artist proclaiming proudly, if somewhat arrogantly, "I create only for myself." Overlooking its possible sour grapes aspect, this statement usually emanates from an artist who has not, at least not *yet,* caught the public fancy.

I am acquainted with no honest artist who does not want an audience, who doesn't pray for an audience, and who isn't bitterly unhappy if he can't attract one. Whether one is preaching, teaching, "illuminating," or just entertaining, an audience, especially a paying audience, means acceptance; and acceptance, in one form or another, is an innate desire in every human being. But beyond this, from a purely practical point of view, creating for oneself alone is a luxury no filmmaker can afford—unless he has the wealth of a Howard Hughes.

This does not mean that a filmmaker must pander to his audience. On the contrary, the creator must always "do his thing," but he must make it appealing. The ability to appeal, whatever the subject matter, separates the successful creator from the artistic failure.

Aside from the satisfaction of being "heard," there is an important technical aspect to the creator-viewer relationship. The viewer is an observer, but he is also a reactor, and just as the filmmaker must understand the character's potential multiplicity of reactions, so he must understand those of his audience. Audiences are seldom fickle, but our knowledge of them is often incomplete. An artist who does not adequately read his audience can lose it as quickly as he once gained it. (And occasionally, he *wants* to.)

It is essential to understand that there is more than one type of audience; and though an audience as a unit is curiously monolithic, one monolith may differ from another. A youthful audience, for instance, will accept information or entertainment in the areas of humor, sex, suspense, and social attitudes which older audiences will view with distaste. Further differences will be found between rural and urban viewers, between residents of the Bible belt and those of the two coasts, between people of the deep South and the far North and, of course, between audiences of different social strata or different cultures.*

Once an editor arrives at a good understanding of his audience he can start learning how to use it. For instance, you are cutting a scene for a laugh—but what *sort* of laugh? There are many kinds of laughs, and an understanding of them is obligatory. If the most you can expect is a chuckle, you do not time your cuts or play your reactions for a guffaw. If you are letting out the stops in a sentimental scene, at what point does emotion become maudlin, or sentiment turn into mawkishness?

The editor will find that previews offer him the best opportunities to study audiences. Previews are useful not only in the re-editing of a film—*objective* attention to audience reaction enables the perceptive editor to develop techniques for strengthening viewer participation in the film as a whole. (One must also be aware that an audience, as a bloc, may respond quite differently than an individual. For that reason, one must be wary of accepting reactions of individuals or small groups as indicative of eventual audience response.)

Once more I must stress the importance of *objectivity*. Many a film has suffered because of wishful thinking. Reluctance to properly evaluate, or even admit, an unfavorable reaction has often precluded constructive re-editing. Occasionally, an unforeseen reaction can be so completely negative that no remedial action can save the film, but in most instances corrective measures can be taken. These may involve a full or partial elimination of the objectionable material, a decisive change in editing, or a rewriting and reshooting of some, or all, of the offending scene or sequence. But the customary first recourse is an attempt at re-editing—and quite often, if the scene's shortcomings are examined with complete objectivity, such attempts are successful.

One of the most important (but, unhappily, most ignored) lessons to be learned from audience analysis is the value of silence. Very early in my editorial period I discovered that viewers are more attentive to silent sequences than they are to dialogue scenes.** This seemingly illogical phenomenon came as a complete surprise. I had assumed that

---

*A film which is a hit in Los Angeles will often be a total flop in San Francisco.
**Every good mystery or suspense film demonstrates this point repeatedly.

the presence of dialogue would obligate the viewer to listen; whereas silence, which removed that obligation, would allow him freedom to indulge in occasional comments. Not so. When the screen talked, so did the viewer—when the screen was silent (except for possible underscoring) so was the audience.

Later, the development of recorders enabled me to tape preview reaction. The tapes generally confirmed my earlier findings. Even in substandard films, silent scenes commanded attention—as the cliche has it, "you could hear a pin drop"—while dialogue brought diminishing attention.

The silent sequence is most often seen in suspense films, whether they be mysteries, private-eye or police versions, in horror stories, which cover a wide field today, in action films, also ranging broadly from gangster to Westerns, and in docudrama, seen almost exclusively on TV.

Chase sequences, like fights, are always choreographed, either by the director or by his stunt coordinator. A knowledgeable director will plan his set-ups, or angles, to show every move, or series of moves, as he visualizes them. There will be few protection shots, and the cutter's job will consist mainly of finding the best action matches for stringing the cuts together. Later editing may require deletions of portions of the action, which can easily be accommodated by cutting to the kitchen stove—in most instances a shot of one or more of the onlookers.

An inexpert or insecure director will cover himself with an excess of material. This places the responsibility for careful selection on the shoulders of the editor—a responsibility most cutters welcome even though the time and labor involved is multiplied by a large factor.

Chases usually feature a number of exit-entrance cuts, e.g., a car will exit one scene to be immediately picked up at the start of another, which once more brings the car toward the camera or shows it moving off into the distance. Furthermore, chases almost always involve more than one participant, and many of the cuts are merely alternating shots of the pursuer and the pursued. But when a series of two or more cuts of one of the principals is called for, the technique recommended for exit-entrance cuts (see Book IV, Chapter 6) should be applied. For instance, a car hurtles toward and past the camera. The next cut is a close shot of the driver, shot from inside the car. Here the windshield in the first cut assumes the role of the face and eyes in the earlier exit-entrance cuts. As the car's windshield moves half-way off the screen, the cut to the vehicle's interior will be completely unnoticeable. To the viewer it will seem that the camera simply passed through the windshield into a close shot of the driver. Try it. It works every time.

The cut-away from the interior will probably be made on the

driver's look, or reaction, much like the average look-off cut. If, on the other hand, a series of full shots are cut in sequence, the applicable cutting technique is similar to one used in editing sequences of suspense.

In a suspense sequence the most important ingredient, by far, is *mood*. Only rarely is character or plot development a consideration. The characters have usually been adequately developed and the basis for the suspense has been introduced. The stalking or hovering menace, whether human, animal, or extra terrestrial, is known to the viewer, if not always to the screen character. The cutter's obligation is to establish a mood which will convey the subdued terror of suspense to the audience.

The special technical aspects of suspense-invoking set-ups, lighting, and use of lenses are, of course, the responsibility of the director and the cameraman, but the juxtaposition of the cuts to obtain the greatest possible audience involvement is the responsibility of the editor.

What must be understood here is that it is the *viewer* who must be caught up in the mood. Showing a frightened actor will be of purely academic interest if the viewer himself does not feel the menace of the scene. If the viewer is to empathize with the character on the screen he must be emotionally involved even if that character is not yet fully aware of his predicament. Otherwise, the viewer may consider the character somewhat foolish when he finally reacts with fear to a stimulus which he, the viewer, has not yet accepted.

Fortunately, the cutter has a wide field of reference on which to base his cutting conception. Every person has, not infrequently, felt terror. The sound of following footsteps on a dark and deserted street at night has triggered a sudden flood of fear in all of us as children (and even as adults). The heart-stopping sense of an unwelcome presence in a darkened house as we enter it late at night is a universal experience. And parapsychological fears lie shallowly buried in the subconscious minds of even the most cynical skeptics.

This potential for arousing the viewer's emotional responses makes the suspense sequence the most sure-fire attention-grabber in films. The cutter needs only to intelligently select and properly align the most effective shots, or set up the most effective sound effects, most effectively timed, to have the audience reacting at his will. A shot of an empty street, whose cleverly contrived shadows conceal hiding places for unnamed menaces, or a suddenly billowing curtain in the absence of the slightest breath of wind, can raise the hackles on all but the most insensitive necks.

Sound, whether direct or off-beat, can be most important. In one of Val Lewton's suspense films *(Cat People)* a potential victim of an escaped black panther walks nervously through a cemetery. (The setting is obvious, but effective.) Suddenly, there is a harsh growl, and an immediate audience reaction to the probable presence of the man-eater. Without pause, the roar turns into the harsh grinding noise of an automobile self-starter. Relief gives rise to nervous laughter, but the suspense, the certainty that the next such moment will be decisive, continues to grow. This incidental deception renders the panther's real attack, which occurs a short time later, even more terrifying.

The trick is to *never let go*—to pile effect on effect, to continually enhance the mood, to maintain peak viewer attention. A shot must be long enough to deliver its desired effect—it must never last so long that the viewer can start to analyze the components which make it work, not even for a brief instant. And it should *never* be repeated. No clever magician repeats an illusion at the same performance; neither should the film editor. A truly effective set-up loses at least some of its punch the second time around. (This holds true for all shots, not only in scenes of suspense.) Just as "milking a gag" weakens a comedy scene, so repeating a clever shot weakens its total effectiveness.

As in other instances of arbitrary cutting, the selection, arrangement, and timing of the cuts is a judgment call; it depends on the cutter's instinct and skill. The "feeling" for the viewer's attention span is all-important. Although, when cutting for suspense, reaction cuts are usually longer than normal to allow for the build-up and penetration of fear and/or terror, these cuts should stop just short of the point at which the viewer might become aware that he is being manipulated. Then, leaving the viewer at the height of his interest, each cut should be followed by another which will continue and, ideally, increase that interest to a new high.

It is, of course, essential that the cuts should be aligned in optimum order. Since build-up is extremely vital, a close analysis of each cut must be made. An effective shot at the climax may fail in the film's introduction; a cut which may be useful in the build-up may produce a let-down at the denouement.

With this in mind, all cuts should be lined up, analyzed repeatedly, realigned where necessary, over and over again, until the cutter is completely satisfied that he has arrived at the best possible sequence of cuts. Only then should they be spliced together.

# 13

# Dissolves: Why, How and If

From time to time certain techniques become fashionable and are considered "in" by filmmakers, including cutters. Every fad carries an inherent weakness which outweighs any possible benefit: A fashionable movement usually has one creator, or trend-setter; all others are necessarily imitators, or followers. In films, the fad is also self-indulgent, ignoring the viewer, who will usually react most favorably to the most effective technique rather than one which happens to be chic. Beyond that, it limits the cutter's options.

In films, the fashion phenomenon has surfaced in a number of ways, e.g., in the craze for indiscriminate camera movement and in the use of dissolves. Camera placement, whether mobile or static, is the responsibility of the director; but the decision to use or eliminate dissolves is frequently in the hands of the film editor.

The function of the dissolve is mainly to facilitate transition. In its simplest form it can carry us from one place to another or from one time to another. In complex clusters, like the Hollywood montage, the dissolve is the filmmaker's "time machine," transporting the viewer instantly backward or forward in time and location at his will. In more sophisticated usage, dissolves aid greatly in the manipulation of pace and mood.

Before "talkies," most fades and all dissolves were made in the camera, a rather awkward and unwieldy operation. Shortly after the advent of sound it became fashionable to eliminate the dissolve by cutting directly from the end of one sequence to the beginning of the next, no matter how extensive a transition was required. However, the development of the projection printer, with its ability to manufacture effects of all shapes and styles, brought the dissolve back into universal use. Much later, TV rediscovered the straight-cut technique and, to a considerable extent, this fashion still persists. In both instances dissolves were eliminated because of technical shortcomings and economic considerations, but the practice continues largely because of the working of the fashion syndrome.

At one time or another I have used all of the techniques—I do not disapprove of any of them. I do, however, disapprove of the cutter who disregards suitability, who voluntarily limits his range by adopting only those techniques which are currently in fashion. There are occasions when the oldest cliche is entirely apropos, and attempts to avoid it lead only to circumlocution. Properly used, the dissolve is an asset; improperly used, it is a time waster and a distraction.

Before discussing the various transition techniques, it might be beneficial to define the dissolve. This effect is not fully understood by many students or, surprisingly, by more than a few who certainly know their way around a movie lot.

A dissolve is not a "fade-out" or a "fade-in". Those two terms are adequately self-descriptive (although "black-out" and "black-in" might be more accurate.) In the fade-out, always used at the end of a sequence or a section of film, the screen image grows progressively darker over a number of frames, usually three or four feet, until the screen is a dead black. The fade-in which follows reverses the process. Because of today's tighter story construction, fades are now rarely used except at the start and the finish of the film. However, if the story breaks down into markedly disassociated episodes, fades can still be useful, giving the viewer a brief pause to catch his breath and gather his senses for the incoming section. Just as an unusually long novel may be separated into "books," so a film can be divided into discrete sections by fades—out and in.

A dissolve, on the other hand, has the opposite effect. It *connects* the outgoing and the incoming sequences, welding the two disparate sections into one. The second image does not displace the first instantly, as in a straight cut, but over a period of time which may be as short as a quarter of a second or as long as a minute or more. The dissolve allows the two images to be seen concurrently, as in a double exposure. As the outgoing scene dims out, the incoming scene grows correspondingly brighter until, at the end of the dissolve, the first scene has disappeared entirely and the second scene is seen at full exposure. There is never a period of blackness. In fact, the intensity of the exposure of the two scenes always adds up to 100 percent. In other words, when the printing intensity of the outgoing scene is 80 percent, that of the incoming scene is 20 percent. At the midpoint of the dissolve, each scene should have an intensity of 50 percent. And so it continues, until the outgoing scene registers 0 and the incoming scene 100.

Leo McCarey enjoyed telling of the tyro director who asked for a few words of general advice before making his first film. Only half in jest, Leo answered, "If you find yourself in trouble—dissolve!" McCarey saw the finished film at its preview. "It was, scene—dissolve, scene—dissolve," he laughed, "from the start of the film until its sorry finish."

This rather sad anecdote illustrates one of the dissolve's remedial functions—one which, it is hoped, most cutters will have little use for. But it also serves to bring out a more positive point: The dissolve is of especial value in welding two possibly unrelated sequences into one continuous whole when obvious juxtaposition of content or image is undesirable.

There is a vast array of dissolve patterns to choose from, of which the most exotic are seen in TV commercials and film trailers. A spinning helix can wipe out scene A as it brings on scene B, or small squares of the first scene can be replaced in rapid, random succession by similarly sized squares of the second scene, until the latter occupies the entire frame. If something fancier is called for, the cutter need only ask. If he can dream it up the dissolve technician can bring it into being. But for most feature films the dissolves of choice are more sedate.

The most commonly used and, while still effective, the most unobtrusive, is the true, or "lap" dissolve. This has been described earlier in the chapter, where both scenes are seen in their entirety while their relative intensities change in reverse proportion.

Following the "lap" in order of popularity and usefulness is the "wipe," or "barn-door" dissolve. (Some purists do not include "wipes" in the dissolve category.) In this effect scene A is "wiped" off the screen, in any desired direction, disclosing scene B. Used as a "hard" wipe, i.e., where a visible dividing line can be seen sweeping across the frame, it can help to convey a sense of swiftness and action. For instance, in scene A a character walks off screen left. As he moves, the entire frame is swept off the screen, right to left, at the speed of his movement; while scene B, showing the same character, or another, against a different background, is swept onto the screen from the right. This is shorter than an exit-entrance cut by a number of frames and imparts a feeling of speed to the scene transition.

"Soft" wipes, in which the sweeping line is invisible, are practically unnoticeable, but impart a much more subtle effect than a straight cut can supply.

The lap dissolve, however, is the most flexible and, consequently, the most useful. The normal lap runs three or four feet. (I prefer the longer version.) But for special situations, the length can vary considerably. For example, in *The Reluctant Saint* Maximillian Schell, playing Joseph, a lay brother, is summoned by the abbot and told that his beloved father has died. As the camera moves gently into a close-up of the stricken Joseph, the scene dissolves into a shot of a tolling church bell, but it does not disappear completely. Instead, Joseph's image remains on-screen for some 40 feet until, with the bell still superimposed, it dissolves to a long shot of the front yard of Joseph's home. Only then does the shot of the bell slowly fade away, leaving us with a clear full shot of Joseph and his mother driving a donkey cart into the open yard.

This series of dissolves (three in number) over the long super-imposition gives the viewer a chance to experience Joseph's silent anguish while it establishes a mood which allows us to by-pass his return home, the father's funeral, etc. Into 30 seconds we compress days of actual time while still allowing the viewer to feel Joseph's emotions and absorb the mood of the occasion.

On the other hand, a transition in *Give Us This Day (Christ in Concrete)* called for more speed and shock. As the leading couple expresses relief at the near-attainment of a long-sought financial goal, the camera moves up to a close shot of a calendar, informing the viewer that it is October 23, 1929. Pausing just long enough for the significance of the date to begin to sink in, a quick dissolve (probably two feet long) discloses a moving tray full of apples, the recognizable symbol at that time of the great depression. The camera pulls back to show the tray being carried by a shabbily dressed woman as she crosses in front of a group of men lounging listlessly outside the union hiring hall.

The double image of the calendar date and the apples throws us full force into the depression, still a vivid memory in the minds of most of the viewers at the time the film was made (1949). Dramatically, shock was demanded here—mood followed slowly and inexorably. If the film had been made in 1979 I might have used the straight-cut technique, but probably not. Regular dissolves were more applicable in the greater part of the film, and a sudden change in style might have appeared to be self-conscious—a sin all filmmakers should avoid.

Whether straight-cut or dissolve, the main consideration here is that the cutter's decision should not be casually made. Each sequence transition should be carefully studied, and the optimum effect selected, while two considerations are kept in mind: (1) each transition calls for the effect which best suits that particular situation; yet (2) the overall style of the film must never be disregarded. The two requirements may seem inconsistent, but the great variety of dissolves available make it quite possible to find a constructive compromise.

And one thing to remember: Situations which permit experimentation will occasionally arise. Such opportunities should never be rejected. But the cutter must always make sure that the final choice in no way unfavorably disturbs the flow, the mood, or the content of the film as a whole.

A word of warning: There must be enough working footage in the film used for the dissolve to keep the scene alive even when the image is fading out (or in). In poorly made commercials one often sees an actor waiting for his cue to move, or to start speaking, as the scene dissolves or fades in on the screen. Unfortunately, one sometimes sees the same gaffe in a feature film, where it is far less excusable. The effect of such carelessness can be devastating, completely spoiling mood, effect, and the viewer's concentration.

This error is always the result of a slovenly approach to one's work and can easily be avoided by giving dissolves the same T.L.C. one would expend on any other cutting problem.

Dissolves are essential, of course, in the construction of montage, but this field requires a chapter to itself.

# 14

# *Editing—Simple and Pure*

Editing is to cutting as architecture is to bricklaying; one is an art, the other a craft. Not all architects are brilliant, nor all architecture high art, but at its best it is undeniably creative. So is editing. But in the realm of film the "architect" may also be the "bricklayer" or, more properly, vice versa; the cutter may be the editor, but not necessarily so.

It must be understood that the editing or re-editing of a film is not always the standard procedure. Some scripts are well written and minor changes, if any, are made during production. Scenes are well staged, well acted, and well shot. The cutter's job is then relatively simple; he needs only to join the relevant portions of the selected takes together in the most efficient and properly paced manner.

In a fair percentage of cases, however, it isn't quite that easy, and not nearly so straightforward. Especially on the more ambitious projects, problems, not always unforeseen, will arise. Films such as *Reds, Lawrence of Arabia, Gone with the Wind, Dr. Zhivago,* or my own *The Young Lions* carry such complex plots and are inhabited by so many characters, that intelligent story decisions cannot always be made at the script or even the shooting stage. Some scenes may be shot "on spec," and final judgment as to their worth deferred until after the first cut has been viewed. Then the work begins. It is by no means unusual for that work to take two, three, or even four times as long as the actual shooting.

When deletion starts, the speculative scenes or sequences are not always the first to go. Contributions of the director and/or the actors may have changed values, relative importance, or even story direction during the course of photography. Even everybody's favorite scene (in the script) may turn out to be expendable on the screen. An opening scene, for instance, written for purely expository purposes, may turn out to be redundant if the characters, due to brilliant interpretation on the set, have been more fully developed throughout the film than they had originally been visualized. Or, not infrequently, a re-alignment of a scene may help to clarify a circuitous plot or a fuzzy character.

All this is not too different from the contribution of a literary editor whose authors have a leaning toward longwindedness.* But there is one marked dissimilarity. Film is not as malleable, nor as cheap, as print. If a segment of a novel is deleted, a sentence or two may be all that is needed to fashion a proper bridge or transition. In a film, the required replacement for that sentence or two will probably not have been shot, and retakes or added scenes cost many thousands of dollars. The saving of those thousands of dollars can sometimes be accomplished by the application of ingenuity at the least, or creativity at best. Let us now consider a few examples of the different types of "editing" as opposed to "cutting" that may be required.

The first example is a segment from the early pages of *The End of the Affair*, Lenore Coffee's screenplay of the novel by Graham Greene. The changes in this short scene do not result in any measurable short-ening of its length, and the material was all at hand from the original shooting. But, since the continuity was now altered, special care had to be taken to ensure a smooth, noncontradictory flow of images.

Figure 8 (three script pages in length) shows the scene as it ap-peared in the shooting script. (It will be noted that it was written as a master scene.) Figure 9 shows the same pages marked out for the new alignment, i.e., the sections which follow each other are desig-nated (1), (2), (3), etc. Figure 10 presents the rearranged scene, with the cuts which made the rearrangement possible now indicated in script terms. The apparent increase in length is due to the insertion of the angle descriptions. In reality, the scene was shortened by a few seconds, but that was not the purpose of the alterations. First, study Figure 8. Then study the changes as indicated in Figure 9.

*Book IV - Figure 8*

| 6.       HENRY'S STUDY                                    (Script page 5) |
| :--- |
| As Henry comes in he pokes up the fire until it burns brightly. It is a quiet, studious room, with leather chairs and a great many uniform volumes of books on the shelves, and an oil painting or two. Bendrix comes in and stands looking at the room.<br><br>(CONTINUED) |

*Thomas Wolfe is perhaps the best-known example of such writing and, cur-rently, James Clavell freely confesses that his editor is his "life-saver."

*Book IV - Figure 8 (continued)*

6 (CONTINUED)

> BENDRIX
>
> I don't think I've seen this room
> before.

> HENRY
>
> It's my study.

> BENDRIX
>
> Spend much time in it?

> HENRY
> (leaving the fire)
> A good deal. That is, whenever
> Sarah's out.

Henry stands irresolutely. Bendrix looks at him with a
friendly, mocking air.

> BENDRIX
>
> What's troubling you, Henry?

> HENRY
> (with sudden helplessness)
> Bendrix—I'm afraid.

> BENDRIX
>
> What is it you're afraid of?

Henry crosses to his desk and picks up a letter lying face
down. His face is filled with disgust.

> HENRY
>
> I've always thought the worst
> thing a man could do—the very
> worst—

He is unable to continue. Bendrix replies smoothly—

> BENDRIX
>
> You know you can trust me,
> Henry.

(CONTINUED)

*Book IV - Figure 8 (continued)*

6 (CONTINUED)

(Script page 6)

> HENRY
> I haven't done anything about it,
> but this letter has sat on my desk
> reminding me. It seems so silly,
> doesn't it, that I can trust Sarah
> absolutely not to read it, though
> she comes in here a dozen times
> a day, and yet I can't trust—
> She's out for a walk now—a walk,
> Bendrix . . .

He breaks off with a gesture of despair.

> BENDRIX
> I'm sorry.

> HENRY
> They always say, don't they, that
> a husband is the last person to
> know—
>          (thrusts letter toward Bendrix)
> Read it, Bendrix.

Bendrix takes the letter with no inkling of its contents, and
increasing surprise as he reads it aloud.

> BENDRIX
>      (reading)
> 'In reply to your inquiry, I would
> suggest you employ the services
> of a fellow called Savage, 159 Vigo
> Street. From all reports he has
> the reputation of being both able
> and discreet—'
>          (he reads on a bit, then looks up,
>           genuinely startled)
> You mean that you want a
> private detective to follow Sarah?
>      (Henry nods)

(CONTINUED)

*Book IV - Figure 8 (continued)*

6 (CONTINUED)

Really, Henry, you surprise me.
One of His Majesty's most
respected Civil Servants. . . .
             (Bendrix looks incredulous)
Funny—I imagined your mind was
as neatly creased as your trousers.

                                        (Script page 7)

                    HENRY

I thought when I saw you in the
Square tonight that if I told you,
and you laughed at me, I might be
able to burn the letter.
             (hopefully)
You do think I'm a fool, don't
you?

                    BENDRIX

Oh, no, I don't think you're a fool,
Henry. After all, Sarah's human.

                    HENRY

You mean, you think it's
possible?

                    BENDRIX

             (shrugs)
Why not go and see this Mr.
Savage—then you'd know.

Henry stands indecisively, the letter in his hand.

                    HENRY

And I always thought you were a
special friend of hers,
Bendrix. . . .

                    BENDRIX

I only said it was possible—I
didn't say anything about Sarah.

                                        (CONTINUED)

*Book IV - Figure 8 (continued)*

---

6 (CONTINUED)

                    HENRY
          I know. I'm sorry.
                (with a burst of feeling)
          You can't think what I've been
          through all these months. I never
          know where she is or what she's
          doing. She's away at all hours,
          Bendrix—and no explanation.

                    BENDRIX
                (almost impatiently)
          Then see Mr. Savage.

                    HENRY
          But just think—sitting there in
          front of a desk, in a chair all the
          other jealous husbands have sat
          in—

    Henry gives a shudder of distaste. Bendrix looks at him with
    an odd smile.

                    BENDRIX
          Why not let me go, Henry?

---

Now study the changes as indicated in Figure 9.

*Book IV - Figure 9*

---

                                             (Script page 5)

6.      HENRY'S STUDY

        As Henry comes in he pokes up the fire until it burns brightly.
        It is a quiet, studious room, with leather chairs and a great
        many uniform volumes of books on the shelves, and an oil
        painting or two. Bendrix comes in and stands looking at the
        room.

                                             (CONTINUED)

---

*Book IV - Figure 9 (continued)*

6 (CONTINUED)

> BENDRIX
>
> I don't think I've seen this room
> before.

> HENRY
>
> It's my study.

> BENDRIX
>
> Spend much time in it?

> HENRY
>
> (leaving the fire)
> A good deal. That is, whenever
> Sarah's out.

Henry stands irresolutely. Bendrix looks at him with a
friendly, mocking air.

> BENDRIX
>
> What's troubling you, Henry?

> HENRY
>
> (with sudden helplessness)
> Bendrix—I'm afraid.

> BENDRIX
>
> What is it you're afraid of?

Henry crosses to his desk and picks up a letter lying face
down. His face is filled with disgust.

> HENRY
>
> I've always thought the worst
> thing a man could do—the very
> worst—

He is unable to continue. Bendrix replies smoothly ---

> BENDRIX
>
> You know you can trust me, Henry.

(1)
cont.

(Script page 6)

> HENRY
>
> I haven't done anything about it,
> but this letter has sat on my desk
> reminding me. It seems so silly,

(3)

(CONTINUED)

*Book IV - Figure 9 (continued)*

6 (CONTINUED)

>           doesn't it, that I can trust Sarah
>           absolutely not to read it, though
>           she comes in here a dozen times
>           a day, and yet I can't trust ----
>           She's out for a walk now—a <u>walk,</u>
>           Bendrix . . .

*(3) cont*

He breaks off with a gesture of despair.

>                    BENDRIX
>           I'm sorry.

*out*

>                    HENRY
>           They always say, don't they, that
>           a husband is the last person to
>           know ---

*(5)*

>                    (thrusts letter toward Bendrix)
>           Read it, Bendrix.

Bendrix takes the letter with no inkling of its contents, and
increasing surprise as he reads it aloud.

>                    BENDRIX
>                    (reading)
>           'In reply to your inquiry, I would
>           suggest you employ the services
>           of a fellow called Savage, 159 Vigo
>           Street. From all reports he has a
>           reputation of being both able and
>           discreet—'

*(2)*

>                    (he reads on a bit, then looks up,
>                    genuinely startled)
>           You mean that <u>you</u> want a
>           private detective to follow Sarah?

*(4)*

>                    (Henry nods)
>           Really, Henry, you surprise me.
>           One of His Majesty's most
>           respected Civil Servants . . .

*(6)*

>                    (Bendrix looks incredulous)
>           Funny—I imagined your mind
>           was as neatly creased as your
>           trousers.

*cont*

(CONTINUED)

*Book IV - Figure 9 (continued)*

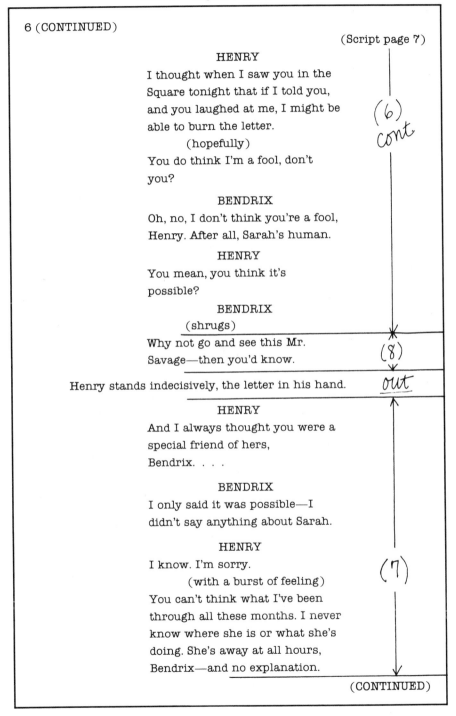

6 (CONTINUED)

(Script page 7)

HENRY

I thought when I saw you in the
Square tonight that if I told you,
and you laughed at me, I might be
able to burn the letter.
   (hopefully)
You do think I'm a fool, don't
you?

BENDRIX

Oh, no, I don't think you're a fool,
Henry. After all, Sarah's human.

HENRY

You mean, you think it's
possible?

BENDRIX

   (shrugs)
Why not go and see this Mr.
Savage—then you'd know.

Henry stands indecisively, the letter in his hand.

HENRY

And I always thought you were a
special friend of hers,
Bendrix. . . .

BENDRIX

I only said it was possible—I
didn't say anything about Sarah.

HENRY

I know. I'm sorry.
   (with a burst of feeling)
You can't think what I've been
through all these months. I never
know where she is or what she's
doing. She's away at all hours,
Bendrix—and no explanation.

(CONTINUED)

*Book IV - Figure 9 (continued)*

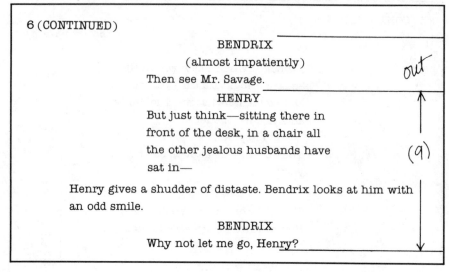

Since the purposes of the changes are by no means clearly evident on even careful examination, a rationalization is in order.

The chief aim of the realignment is to break up Bendrix's continuing speech on script page 6 (numbers (2), (4), and the first part of (6) ). This operation is needed to allow more give and take in the dialogue, to eliminate the image of Henry standing dumbly (and unnaturally) while Bendrix ambles through his lines, his reactions, and his transitions, and to camouflage the expository nature of the last part of Bendrix's speech (beginning of (6) ).

Now, the rationalization in detail. Script page 5 of the excerpt stands as is—no changes are needed. It quite satisfactorily establishes the tension of the moments that follow.

On script page 6 it seemed more honest to have Henry present the letter promptly rather than beat about the bush with his oblique reference to some obscure problem. As it stands in the original, Bendrix takes Henry's line (3) in stride, ("I'm sorry") as if he knows exactly what Henry is talking about. As far as the viewer is concerned, he doesn't. We find out as the scene progresses that Henry's only purpose in bringing Bendrix into his home is to discuss with him the letter and the situation which gave it birth. To show Henry behaving like a bashful schoolboy before getting to the point works against the character.

Instead, the new alignment allows us to understand, as Bendrix reads the opening paragraph of the letter, what Henry has on his mind. Now, speech (3) has an altogether different thrust. It is no longer a puzzling circumlocution but a somewhat indirect allusion to the reason for the letter's intent; he mistrusts his wife—and it hurts.

As a consequence, Bendrix's next line (4) does not seem so gratuitous. Even though the line is a question, he is not guessing but making a positive statement.

Line (5) is a further development of Henry's sense of guilt and impropriety—again, not arbitrarily made, but in shamed answer to Bendrix's attacking question.

Now, (6), Bendrix has had time to put his thoughts, reactions, and emotions into place, and he continues the scene with a mocking chiding of Henry, a chiding that is really expository. But though the line tells us a good deal about Henry, its expository nature is concealed by its more apparent purpose—a gentle put-down and a quick puncturing of Henry's mounting self-pity. As Henry's answer indicates, this is exactly what he has been looking for as a way out of a degrading situation. It also gets the conversation back to a more hopeful direction (for Henry), only to have him jolted once more by Bendrix's cynicism ("After all, Sarah's human").

The changes on script page 7 are made, first, to make Henry's protest—"And I always thought you were a special friend of hers, Bendrix . . ."—come in answer to Bendrix's cynical shrug rather than to the suggestion that he see Mr. Savage, and second, to diminish the line's expository nature by making it a deeper expression of the drama of the scene. In other words, Henry's reply seems a logical reaction to Bendrix's shrug rather than a line inserted only to inform us that Bendrix knows Sarah.

The third purpose of the realignment is to eliminate Bendrix's "impatient" urging. Too much insistence on his part should make Henry suspicious, something both we and Bendrix are clever enough to avoid.

Figure 10 should now be read through nonclinically in order to absorb the flow and feeling of the realigned scene. At first reading the effect of the changes may seem slight but, as indicated in the foregoing paragraphs, they have a considerable bearing on the believability of the scene and the honesty of the characters in it.

*Book IV - Figure 10*

---

6.    HENRY'S STUDY

As Henry comes in he pokes up the fire until it burns brightly. It is a quiet, studious room, with leather chairs and a great many uniform volumes of books on the shelves and an oil painting or two. Bendrix comes in and stands looking about the room.

(CONTINUED)

*Book IV - Figure 10 (continued)*

6 (CONTINUED)

                          BENDRIX
              I don't think I've seen this room
              before.

                          HENRY
              It's my study.

                          BENDRIX
              Spend much time in it?

                          HENRY
                    (leaving the fire)
              A good deal. That is, whenever
              Sarah's out.

Henry stands irresolutely. Bendrix looks at him with a
friendly, mocking air.

                          BENDRIX
              What's troubling you, Henry?

                          HENRY
                    (with sudden helplessness)
              Bendrix—I'm afraid.

                          BENDRIX
              What is it you're afraid of?

Henry crosses to his desk and picks up a letter lying face
down. His face is filled with disgust.

                          HENRY
              I've always thought the worst
              thing a man could do -- the very
              worst --

He is unable to continue. Bendrix replies smoothly --

                          BENDRIX
              You know you can trust me,
              Henry.

7.      CLOSE-UP      HENRY

He thrusts the letter toward Bendrix.

                          HENRY
              Read it, Bendrix.

                                          (CONTINUED)

*Book IV - Figure 10 (continued)*

8.     CLOSE-UP    BENDRIX

He takes the letter with no inkling of its contents. He reads it aloud with increasing surprise.

                  BENDRIX
               (reading)
        'In reply to your inquiry, I would
        suggest you employ the services
        of a fellow called Savage, 159 Vigo
        Street. From all reports he has
        the reputation of being both able
        and discreet ---'
            (he reads a bit more, silently, then looks
            up, startled)

9.     CLOSE-UP    HENRY

                  HENRY
        I haven't done anything about it,
        but this letter has sat on my desk
        reminding me. It seems so silly,
        doesn't it, that I can trust Sarah
        absolutely not to read it, though
        she comes in here a dozen times
        a day, and yet I can't trust ----
        She's out for a walk now—a walk,
        Bendrix. . . .
            (breaks off with a gesture of despair)

10.    CLOSE-UP    BENDRIX

                  BENDRIX
        You mean that you want a
        private detective to follow Sarah?

11.    CLOSE-UP    HENRY

                  HENRY
        They always say, don't they, that
        a husband is the last person to
        know ---

                            (CONTINUED)

*Book IV - Figure 10 (continued)*

12.        TWO SHOT        BENDRIX AND HENRY

                              BENDRIX
                 Really, Henry, you surprise me.
                 One of His Majesty's most
                 respected Civil Servants . . .
                        (Bendrix looks incredulous)
                 Funny—I imagined your mind
                 was as neatly creased as your
                 trousers.

                              HENRY
                 I thought when I saw you in the
                 Square tonight that if I told you,
                 and you laughed at me, I might be
                 able to burn the letter.
                        (hopefully)
                 You do think that I'm a fool, don't
                 you?

                              BENDRIX
                 Oh, no, I don't think you're a fool,
                 Henry. After all, Sarah's human.

                              BENDRIX
                 You mean you think it's possible?

        Bendrix shrugs.


13.        CLOSE-UP        HENRY

                              HENRY (cont.)
                 And I always thought you were a
                 special friend of hers,
                 Bendrix. . . .


14.        CLOSE-UP        BENDRIX

                              BENDRIX
                 I only said it was possible—I
                 didn't say anything about Sarah.

                                              (CONTINUED)

*Book IV - Figure 10 (continued)*

---

15.     CLOSE-UP     HENRY

                        HENRY
              I know. I'm sorry.
                  (with a burst of feeling)
              You can't think what I've been
              through all these months. I never
              know where she is or what she's
              doing. She's away at all hours,
              Bendrix—and no
              explanation. . . .


16.     CLOSE-UP     BENDRIX

                        BENDRIX
              Why not go and see this Mr.
              Savage -- then you'd know.


17.     TWO SHOT     HENRY AND BENDRIX

                        HENRY
              But just think—sitting there in
              front of a desk, in a chair all the
              other jealous husbands have sat
              in --

              Henry gives a shudder of distaste. Bendrix looks at him with
              an odd smile.

                        BENDRIX
              Why not let me go, Henry?

---

The next example is a scene from *A Walk on the Wild Side,* a film written by a number of writers, based on Nelson Algren's novel of the same name.

In this scene the problem is twofold: first, to shorten it as much as possible, since too much time is taken to deliver its simple message; and second, to eliminate as much as possible of its mawkish flavor.

Figure 11 presents the scene as written.

*Book IV - Figure 11*

13    FULL SHOT   INT. GERARD SUNROOM   DAY

As Dove enters, the object that first pulls his eyes with
irresistible power is the painting over the fireplace. The
painting is impressionistic, unsparingly real—a face wreathed
in some mysterious and indefinable pain. Dove stares at it in
confusion. Suddenly Eva breaks the spell.

> EVA
> It's a self-portrait.

> DOVE
> It -- it looks like Hallie -- and yet
> it doesn't.

He turns toward Amy with an abrupt, pleading urgency.

> DOVE (cont.)
> Miss Gerard, where is she?

> AMY
> (flatly)
> My condolences on the death of
> your father.

> DOVE
> (desperately)
> Where is Hallie, Ma'am?

> AMY
> Her whereabouts are no business
> of yours.

> EVA
> Amy . . .!

> AMY
> My niece is not for you, Mister
> Linkhorn. Hallie was born and
> raised in Europe—in Paris. She's
> had everything—known
> everything. Beside her, what are
> you? An uneducated dirt farmer.

(CONTINUED)

*Book IV - Figure 11 (continued)*

13 (CONTINUED)

> DOVE
> (fighting back)
> I'm through with farming. I mean
> to look into other things. . . .

Amy makes a scoffing noise.

> DOVE (cont.)
> Pa used to say no man can be
> sure of his callin' till he's thirty.
> That's when Christ got started.

> AMY
> Sounds like Fitz Linkhorn, all
> right.

> DOVE
> (bursting out)
> Tell me where Hallie is, Miss
> Gerard.

A flush of anger touches Amy's cheek. Her knuckles tighten
on the arm chair.

> AMY
> Hallie! Hallie! You understand
> nothing about Hallie! A self-
> centered, unpredictable girl—even
> to herself!
> (she regains control)
> Mister Linkhorn—my niece was
> bored that summer—visiting us
> in this dustbin of a town. You
> were an entertainment—a
> novelty. . . .

> EVA
> Amy! Don't be cruel! Please. . . .

> AMY
> . . . and she diverted herself with
> you!

(CONTINUED)

*Book IV - Figure 11 (continued)*

13 (CONTINUED)

For a moment Dove gazes at Amy. Then he speaks quietly, but forcefully.

DOVE

Maybe it's you who can't
understand her—or anything
that's got to do with love. Livin'
in this tomb, you. . . .

AMY

(rising in anger)

Get out!

But Dove is carried away now. He pulls some letters out of his pocket and rapidly, urgently, he opens one, seeking out a paragraph to read. He finds what he's looking for.

DOVE

(desperately)

Listen—listen to this. It's from
Hallie. . . . 'Sometimes when
night comes, it terrifies me and I
cry out, "Where is Dove?" Dove
and love! The words go together—
get mixed up. Where is love? And
I cry for that lost, lovely
summer. . . .'

He stops reading, takes a moment to rein in his emotions. Amy gazes at him grimly, intently. Finally:

AMY

Where is that from?

DOVE

New York. I got twelve letters --
one every two, three days . . .

AMY

And then?

DOVE

Nothing! I've written twenty times
since then, and my letters come
back marked 'Address Unknown.'

(CONTINUED)

*Book IV - Figure 11 (continued)*

---

13 (CONTINUED)

                              EVA
                    Poor boy . . .


                              AMY
                         (cutting in harshly)
                    Obviously, my niece has lost
                    interest in you.


                              DOVE
                    No! That can't be. I only read you
                    part of the letter. Each one is
                    more needful of me than the one
                    before.


Amy watches him a moment—seems to soften.

                              AMY
                    I'm sorry, Dove. But I can't tell
                    you where she is.


                              DOVE
                    You mean you're her only living
                    relatives and you don't know
                    where she is?


                              AMY
                         (hard again)
                    I'm not used to being sassed in
                    my own house, young man. I'll
                    ask you to leave.


Dove hesitates, looking at her with pure hatred.

                              AMY (cont.)
                    What are you waiting for? The
                    sheriff?


Abruptly, Dove turns and leaves. With a sudden, nervous
rapidity, Eva follows.

Figure 12, which follows, indicates the proposed cuts. In this instance the alignment of the retained portions follows the original sequence, with the deletions accomplished by cutting to angles which were originally shot. The re-edited version is more than one-third shorter and immeasurably less maudlin.

*Book IV - Figure 12*

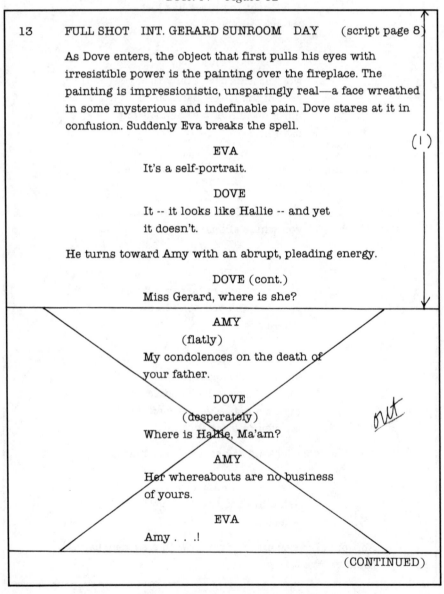

13      FULL SHOT   INT. GERARD SUNROOM   DAY      (script page 8)

As Dove enters, the object that first pulls his eyes with irresistible power is the painting over the fireplace. The painting is impressionistic, unsparingly real—a face wreathed in some mysterious and indefinable pain. Dove stares at it in confusion. Suddenly Eva breaks the spell.

(1)

EVA
It's a self-portrait.

DOVE
It -- it looks like Hallie -- and yet
it doesn't.

He turns toward Amy with an abrupt, pleading energy.

DOVE (cont.)
Miss Gerard, where is she?

AMY
(flatly)
My condolences on the death of
your father.

DOVE
(desperately)
Where is Hallie, Ma'am?

AMY
Her whereabouts are no business
of yours.

EVA
Amy . . .!

out

(CONTINUED)

*Book IV - Figure 12 (continued)*

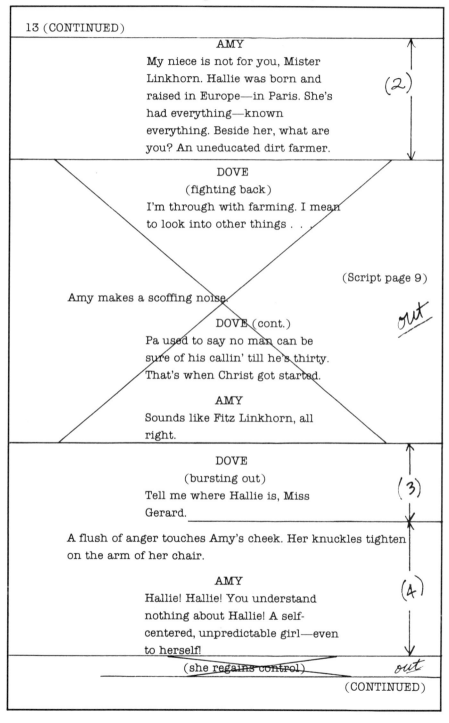

13 (CONTINUED)

AMY

My niece is not for you, Mister
Linkhorn. Hallie was born and
raised in Europe—in Paris. She's
had everything—known
everything. Beside her, what are
you? An uneducated dirt farmer.

*(2)*

DOVE
(fighting back)
I'm through with farming. I mean
to look into other things . . .

(Script page 9)

Amy makes a scoffing noise.

DOVE (cont.)
Pa used to say no man can be
sure of his callin' till he's thirty.
That's when Christ got started.

*out*

AMY
Sounds like Fitz Linkhorn, all
right.

DOVE
(bursting out)
Tell me where Hallie is, Miss
Gerard.

*(3)*

A flush of anger touches Amy's cheek. Her knuckles tighten
on the arm of her chair.

AMY
Hallie! Hallie! You understand
nothing about Hallie! A self-
centered, unpredictable girl—even
to herself!

*(4)*

(she regains control)

*out*

(CONTINUED)

*Book IV - Figure 12 (continued)*

13 (CONTINUED)

Mister Linkhorn—my niece was
bored that summer—visiting us
in this dustbin of a town. You
were an entertainment—a
novelty. . . .

EVA

Amy! Don't be cruel! Please. . . .

AMY

. . . and she diverted herself with
you!

*out*

For a moment Dove gazes at Amy. Then he speaks quietly, but
forcefully.

DOVE

Maybe it's you who can't
understand her—or anything
that's got to do with love. Livin'
in this tomb, you. . . .

AMY

(rising in anger)

Get out!

*(5)*

(Script page 10)

But Dove is carried away now. He pulls some letters out of his
pocket and rapidly, urgently, he opens one, seeking out a
paragraph to read. He finds what he's looking for.

DOVE

(desperately)

Listen—listen to this. It's from
Hallie. . . . 'Sometimes when
night comes, it terrifies me and I
cry out, "Where is Dove?" Dove
and love! The words go together—
get mixed up. Where is love? And
I cry for that lost, lovely summer
. . .!

*out*
*(cont.)*

(CONTINUED)

*Book IV - Figure 12 (continued)*

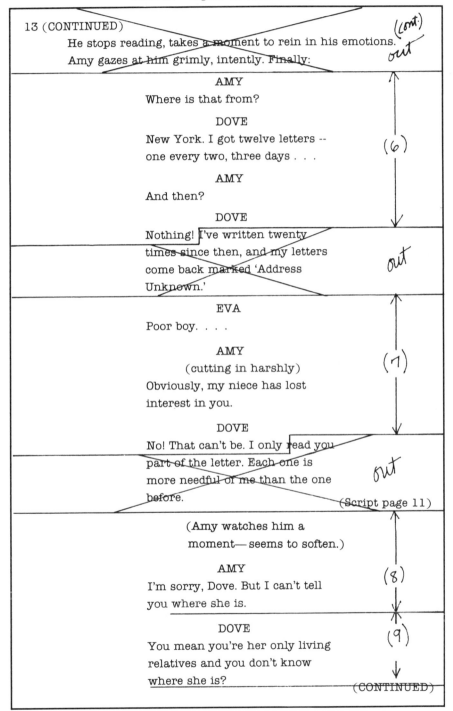

13 (CONTINUED)
He stops reading, takes a moment to rein in his emotions. *(cont.)* out
Amy gazes at him grimly, intently. Finally:

AMY
Where is that from?

DOVE
New York. I got twelve letters --
one every two, three days . . .

AMY
And then?

DOVE
Nothing! I've written twenty
times since then, and my letters
come back marked 'Address
Unknown.'

(6)

out

EVA
Poor boy. . . .

AMY
(cutting in harshly)
Obviously, my niece has lost
interest in you.

DOVE
No! That can't be. I only read you
part of the letter. Each one is
more needful of me than the one
before.

(7)

out

(Script page 11)

(Amy watches him a
moment— seems to soften.)

AMY
I'm sorry, Dove. But I can't tell
you where she is.

(8)

DOVE
You mean you're her only living
relatives and you don't know
where she is?

(9)

(CONTINUED)

*Book IV - Figure 12 (continued)*

---

13 (CONTINUED)

> AMY
> (hard again)
> I'm not used to being sassed in
> my own house, young man. I'll
> ask you to leave.
>
> (10)
>
> Dove hesitates, looking at her with pure hatred.
>
> AMY (cont.)
> What are you waiting for? The
> sheriff?
>
> Abruptly, Dove turns and leaves. With a sudden, nervous
> rapidity, Eva follows.

---

The first deletion, on script page 8 of figure 12, gets Amy directly to the point, which is consistent with her character and with her attitude toward Dove.

Amy's line in (2) is pure exposition, but its nature is camouflaged to some extent by using the information as a basis for making the scene one of conflict.

The next deletion, following (2), eliminates Dove's attempt at self-defense, an attempt which weakens his position and his character. His ignoring of Amy's attack lends him dignity, and his persistence drives Amy into her brief outbreak, which tells us all we need to know at this point about her feelings toward her niece and possibly a little about Hallie.

The deletion after (4) eliminates an unnecessarily cruel, and therefore unbelievable, reaction on Amy's part.

The cuts on script page 10 are quite obvious. Dove's maudlin speeches are not only corny (since they come so early in the film that neither the story's basic situation nor Dove's character are yet established); they also tend to present him as a weak, unattractive person.

Figure 13 shows the scene as re-edited, with the necessary angles indicated. This kind of editing will not make a bad scene great, but it can make it acceptable and useful. Since unfortunately few films, or film scripts, are perfect, an editor who can skillfully accomplish this kind of corrective manipulation will never lack a professional home.

*Book IV - Figure 13*

13    FULL SHOT   INT. GERARD SUNROOM   DAY

As Dove enters, the object that first pulls his eyes with
irresistible power is the painting over the fireplace. The
painting is impressionistic, unsparingly real -- a face
wreathed in some mysterious and indefinable pain. Dove
stares at it in confusion. Suddenly Eva breaks the spell.

EVA
It's a self-portrait.

DOVE
It -- it looks like Hallie -- and yet
it doesn't.

He turns toward Amy with an abrupt, pleading urgency.

DOVE (cont.)
Miss Gerard, where is she?

14    TWO SHOT   AMY AND EVA

AMY
My niece is not for you, Mister
Linkhorn. Hallie was born and
raised in Europe -- in Paris. She's
had everything -- known
everything. Beside her, what are
you? An uneducated dirt farmer.

15    CLOSE SHOT    DOVE

He ignores the put-down.

DOVE
Tell me where Hallie is, Miss
Gerard.

16    CLOSE SHOT    AMY

AMY
Hallie! Hallie! You understand
nothing about Hallie! A self-
centered, unpredictable girl—even
to herself!

(CONTINUED)

*Book IV - Figure 13 (continued)*

17     GROUP SHOT     DOVE, AMY, EVA

For a moment Dove gazes at Amy. Then he speaks quietly, but
forcefully.

                         DOVE
              Maybe it's you who can't
              understand her—or anything
              that's got to do with love. Livin'
              in this tomb, you . . .

                         AMY
                    (rising in anger)
              Get out!

But Dove pulls some letters out of his pocket and opens one,
seeking out a paragraph to read. He finds what he's looking
for.

                         DOVE
                    (with some urgency)
              Listen—listen to this. It's from
              Hallie. . . . 'Sometimes when
              night comes it terrifies me and I
              cry out, "Where is Dove?" Dove
              and love! The words go
              together. . . .

18     CLOSE SHOT     AMY

                         AMY
                    (cutting in)
              Where is that from?

19     CLOSE SHOT     DOVE

                         DOVE
              New York. I got twelve letters --
              one every two, three days. . . .

                         AMY'S VOICE (O.S.)
              And then?

                         DOVE
              Nothing!

                                              (CONTINUED)

*Book IV - Figure 13 (continued)*

20      GROUP SHOT      DOVE, AMY, EVA

                          EVA
                Poor boy. . . .

                          AMY
                    (cutting in harshly)
                Obviously, my niece has lost
                interest in you.

                          DOVE
                No! That can't be. I only . . .


21      CLOSE SHOT      AMY

                          AMY
                    (cutting in)
                I'm sorry, Dove. But I can't tell
                you where she is.


22      CLOSE SHOT      DOVE

                          DOVE
                You mean you're her only living
                relatives and you don't know
                where she is?


23      GROUP SHOT      AMY, DOVE, EVA

                          AMY
                    (hard again)
                I'm not used to being sassed in
                my own house, young man. I'll
                ask you to leave.

        Dove hesitates, looking at her with hatred.

                          AMY (cont.)
                What are you waiting for, the
                sheriff?

        Abruptly, Dove turns and leaves. With a sudden, nervous
        rapidity, Eva follows.

# 15

# *Rescuing the Actor*

One more important area remains to be discussed—selective editing of inadequate acting. Not *bad* acting: The only ameliorative measure a cutter can take in such a circumstance is to diminish the misery as much as possible, but acting which for one reason or another fails to hit the mark.

The best example of corrective treatment in my experience was the result of serendipity rather than of creative ability—of an effort to make the best of a difficult situation rather than a rationally conceived and executed editing accomplishment.

*Ruggles of Red Gap,* directed by Leo McCarey, starred Charles Laughton and Charlie Ruggles. Laughton had a "rubber" face and, though certainly a fine actor, was occasionally guilty of severe attacks of "mugging," especially in moments of high emotional involvement. I was forced to cut around or away from much of his face-making, but one sequence presented a nearly impossible problem. The scene was set in a western saloon. Laughton, playing Charlie Ruggles' very English butler (won in a poker game from a British lord) has accompanied his new boss to the bar. At one point, Ruggles wishes to quote from Lincoln's Gettysburg Address, but can't remember the speech. Neither can any other member of his party, nor any of the saloon's habitués.

Suddenly, Ruggles' attention is arrested by Laughton, who is murmuring, "Four score and seven years. . . ." Amazed to learn that the Englishman knows the words, Ruggles encourages him to continue.

Laughton was highly emotional and extremely nervous. Filming this shot alone, in medium close-up, occupied a day and a half. McCarey patiently shot the scene some forty or fifty times, rarely getting a complete take, and never a perfect one. Finally Laughton, with tears streaming from his eyes, dropped to his knees and begged for mercy. McCarey decided to postpone further shooting.

At this point I suggested that it might be possible to patch together a complete sound track by using the best parts of a number of takes. McCarey agreed. To begin with, I worked only with the sound track, checking out all of the 15 or 20 printed takes and an even greater number of "outs." Using a line here, a phrase there, sometimes only a word or two, I pieced together a complete version of the speech. McCarey listened to it, liked what he heard, and asked me to comlete it.

So far my efforts had been little more than routine. Now came the hard part. Fitting the picture to the track brought chaos, since each sound cut needed a matching picture and there were dozens of cuts. Only one solution presented itself. The speech was started in a set-up over Laughton's back, followed by cuts of the reactions of others in the saloon—first, Charlie Ruggles and his table companions, then other onlookers as, one by one, they left their stools and walked over for a closer look and listen. Off-screen, the butler's voice grew in strength as he gained confidence, and the speech ended triumphantly to the bar-keeper's "Drinks on the house."

Dramatic logic holds that at least a large part of the speech should have been played on the scene's central character, the butler. But every matching cut of Laughton showed his rather generous lips blubbering, his eyes turning upward in their sockets, and huge tears rolling down his cheeks. So, except for two short cuts, the entire speech was played over shots of the onlookers.

At the executive running, Ernst Lubitsch, then head of Paramount production, suggested that since the scene belonged to Laughton we should see more of him. McCarey agreed, and I was outvoted. I selected a pair of the least objectionable cuts and added them for the sneak preview.

*Ruggles of Red Gap* turned out to be one of that year's top films. At the preview it played beautifully—up to the Gettysburg Address. The scene started, the players reacted, everything went well. Then came the first cut of Laughton, tears streaming down his cheeks as he spoke. Americans admire the Gettysburg Address, but they don't cry over it. The audience burst into laughter, which continued to build throughout the rest of the now inaudible speech. But laughter, at the expense of Lincoln's noble phrases, was not what we were looking for. One of the film's key scenes had been torpedoed.

As we left the theater after the preview, McCarey said, "Put it back the way you had it." I did, and the next preview confirmed our original judgment. This time there was no laughter. The audience listened attentively and applauded Laughton's performance. From that day until the end of Laughton's life, hardly a Lincoln's birthday passed without one of the major radio networks inviting him to once again deliver the Gettysburg Address.

This example illustrates not only the part luck can play in the editorial construction of an important sequence, it focuses attention on what may be the most difficult and perhaps (in my opinion, at least) the most creative and potentially useful editing technique of the future—the old art of *montage*.

# 16

# *The Montage*

There are two basic types of montage. What is sometimes referred to as the "Hollywood" montage differs substantially from the "European" montage. The latter, developed to its highest level by the Russian filmmakers of the 1920s, used a carefully designed and edited series of straight cuts to develop story, situation, and character; it is most effectively demonstrated in the celebrated "Odessa steps" sequence in Eisenstein's *Battleship Potemkin.*

The Hollywood montage, on the other hand, is almost invariably a transition. It, too, is composed of a number of silent cuts, often in a series of dissolves, and always musically underscored; but there its similarity to its foreign cousin ends. It is, in truth, simply a more complicated, and often more pretentious, version of a straight dissolve.

A familiar example: As a sequence ends, the camera dollys in to a shot of a window. Through it we see a tree in full summer foliage. Now the scene dissolves to another shot of the same window (often an exact duplicate of the preceding set-up) but the tree is now bare. The next shot shows the tree and the surrounding terrain covered with snow. The final dissolve discloses the tree heavily loaded with blossoms; and, as the camera pulls back to a full shot of the interior of the room and a new scene gets under way, the viewer knows that approximately one year has elapsed.

A similar series is often used to convey transition in space. A shot of New York's skyline dissolves to the cornfields of the middle west, then to a spectacular shot of the Rocky Mountains, and finally to a shot of the Golden Gate Bridge, taking us pictorially across the breadth of the United States. It may not be as economical as a shot of a character saying, "I'm flying to San Francisco," but it's a lot prettier and, when constructed in less hackneyed style, it is better story-telling. (Obviously, the preceding time transition montage would not work for *Hawaii Five-O*, nor would a location transition connecting less well known places have any meaning. Problem: How would one devise a seasonal transition for a tropical location, or a location transition transporting the viewer from Riyadh to Timbuctu?)

The Hollywood montage is also used as a means of exposing a character's unspoken thoughts, or to pictorialize his subconscious experiences, as in dreams or nightmares. Such montages are really moving collages, and their effectiveness depends in great part on the creativeness and dramatic skill of the editor.

Much ingenuity has been expended in countless efforts at originality, but the weight of past accomplishments make such efforts increasingly difficult to realize. In many instances the efforts are abandoned, and the desired objectives are achieved through a simple exchange of dialogue, or in a sometimes desperate throwback to earlier times, by the use of titles. But each new film presents new opportunities and, in the words of the old pro, "Whatever the technique—if it does the job, use it."

It is unfortunately true that many screen writers, especially those schooled in TV, still think in terms of dialogue when constructing a transition in time or place, but the recent experiments with the old techniques seem to indicate that the viewer would rather see it than hear it. Expository dialogue is still anathema to any filmmaker with talent or taste, and a good editor with a bent for resourcefulness and an eye for imagery can please the viewer's visual sense, develop the situation, and still save time by creating a pictorial transition.

Even in Hollywood films the opportunity to build a montage which carries the developmental potential of a regular sequence does occasionally present itself. Such opportunities arise most frequently in suspense films, and an effective one is found in *Murder, My Sweet*, the 1944 version of Raymond Chandler's *Farewell, My Lovely*.

At one point in the film Phillip Marlowe, played by Dick Powell, is laid low by the usual blow on the head. A recurring effect, an engulfing black cloud, wipes out the scene. It clears up to show a somewhat distorted shot of Marlowe being dumped into an elevator. The next cut shows him regaining consciousness just as the elevator tips forward to send him sliding through the open door. Now the camera falls with him as he flails away at empty space while the isolated elevator car accelerates off into the abysmal background. Next, Marlowe laboriously climbs a steep flight of stairs, only to be confronted by the gigantic, menacing faces of his tormentors. Whether drugged or frightened into a panic, he grabs for the stair railing, only to have it melt under his hand. Once more he falls headlong into a black, bottomless pit. Now Marlowe approaches a series of doors—door frames, really—set out in empty space. As he stumbles through them, leisurely pursued by a man in a white lab coat, each succeeding door is progressively smaller until, as he reaches the end of the line, he can barely squeeze his head through the opening. (This effect was borrowed from one of my own recurring nightmares.)

The man in the white coat, seen for the first time in the film, has kept pace with Marlowe by walking through the doors as if they weren't there. He carries a syringe. As Marlowe thrusts his head through the last tiny door frame, he looks up to see the sardonic face of his pursuer. Marlowe raises his hand in a feeble gesture of defiance and we cut to a close insert of a giant-sized syringe as it plunges toward the camera. Marlowe falls away once more, and the whole picture goes into a rapid spin which, as it slows to a stop, turns out to be a ceiling light fixture seen through a tattered screen of smoke. The camera pulls back to disclose Marlowe lying on a small bed in a sparsely furnished room. Although the smoke effect continues to diffuse the scene, we know we are now looking at reality as seen through Marlowe's drug-bemused eyes.

(For the technically minded, here is a breakdown of the montage. It starts from the center of the black-out effect.)

| | | Time | Total time |
|---|---|---|---|
| | | | (in seconds) |
| 1. | Marlowe is dragged into elevator | 10 sec. | |
| 2. | Marlowe regains consciousness— slides out of elevator | 5.8 sec. | 15.8 sec. |
| 3. | Marlowe falls away from elevator | 4.2 sec. | 20.0 sec. |
| 4. | M.S. Marlowe climbs stairs toward camera—large heads of Moose and Marriot appear in B.G. | 4.3 sec. | 24.3 sec. |
| 5. | Close O.S. shot of Marlowe—in B.G. large C.U. of Marriot dissolves into large C.U. of Moose. Moose reaches out for Marlowe | 4.4 sec. | 28.7 sec. |
| 6. | C.U. Marlowe—reacts to vision | 1.1 sec. | 29.8 sec. |
| 7. | O.S. Marlowe—C.U. Moose in B.G. continuation of shot #5 | 1.0 sec. | 30.8 sec. |
| 8. | M.S. Marlowe—leans back over melting handrail—falls | 3.8 sec. | 34.6 sec. |
| 9. | Marlowe falls through space | 6.6 sec. | 41.2 sec. |
| | A wavering dissolve to: | | |
| 10. | L.S. Line of doors—Marlowe enters shot—stops at first door—looks back over his shoulder | 4.2 sec. | 45.4 sec. |

|  |  | Time | Total time |
|---|---|---|---|
|  |  |  | *(in seconds)* |

With this shot a superimposition begins—
a ragged cobweb effect—which continues
over all shots to the end of the montage.)

| 11. | C.U. Moose—dissolves to—C.U. man in a white lab coat | 2.6 sec. | 48.0 sec. |
|---|---|---|---|
| 12. | C.U. Marlowe—reacts and starts through the first door | 2.0 sec. | 50.0 sec. |
| 13. | Full shot—from behind Marlowe—as he goes through first door. Man in white follows through closed door | 9.5 sec. | 59.5 sec. |
| 14. | Front M.S.—Marlowe through 2nd door (in F.G.). Man in white follows | 4.0 sec. | 63.5 sec. |
| 15. | Close O.S. shot—Marlowe reaches last door—looks back at pursuer | 2.2 sec. | 65.7 sec. |
| 16. | C.S. Man in white walks toward Marlowe | 1.1 sec. | 66.8 sec. |
| 17. | O.S.C.U. Marlowe—starts through last door | 1.2 sec. | 68.0 sec. |
| 18. | C.U. Marlowe—comes through door toward camera—sees: | 1.4 sec. | 69.4 sec. |
| 19. | C.U. Man in white confronts Marlowe | 1.4 sec. | 70.8 sec. |
| 20. | Insert syringe | 2.0 sec. | 72.8 sec. |
| 21. | Marlowe falls back through door | 0.7 sec. | 73.5 sec. |
| 22. | Marlowe falls through spinning hole DISSOLVE TO: | 6.5 sec. | 80.0 sec. |
| 23. | Spinning ceiling light—when it stops, the cobweb effect has subtly changed to a moderately heavy frozen smoke effect. (To stop of spinning . . . | 6.5 sec. | 86.5 sec. |
|  | Note: In general, the cuts become shorter as the montage builds to a climax. |  |  |

This series of dissolves and straight cuts lasts less than a minute and a half, but in that short time we are able to cover a passage of days, to introduce a new face, that of the spurious psychiatrist, whose character and purpose are immediately clear, and to develop a new plot situation—all without resorting to a single line of dialogue.

This montage was originally intended to be a concoction of surrealistic scenes, in the style of Salvador Dali, but at the last moment it was decided to use more translatable imagery. Dramatizing the commonly experienced dream sensations of falling, spinning, and claustrophobic spaces encourages the viewer to identify with Marlowe's state of mind; and avoiding the explicit encourages him to share Marlowe's bewilderment, to live with him through his moments of terror, rather than to regard them from a distance with a clinical eye.

The building of such a pictorial sequence, with its sense of personal creative involvement, evokes some of the feeling of early "story-on-the-back-of-a-menu" days and affords the editor a very special pleasure. It is the nearest thing we have to that triumph of ingenuity over ignorance, the "creative editing" of Kuleshov, Eisenstein, Pudovkin, et al.

In the first quarter of this century the screen was dumb. In illiterate areas of the world, titles were useless. There was, of course, an alternative, but pantomime, though a fine art, is the antithesis of screen acting which must present at least the appearance of reality. Working within this limitation, the Russian filmmakers were occasionally able to construct amazingly real films by creating montages of carefully shot and cleverly juxtaposed images. Their techniques have been fully described and analyzed by the creators and practitioners of the art and by many of their admirers. Here I will offer an example or two, and draw some conclusions as to their possible value for modern films.

In an oversimplification typical of early films, Eisenstein's *The Old and the New (The General Line)*, shows an instructor demonstrating the use of a mechanical cream separator to a skeptical audience of backward peasants.* The success or failure of the instructor's demonstration will determine his success or failure in organizing the collective.

The ragged peasants, some 20 or 30 in all, are assembled in a bare room, staring at a covered object some five feet in height. A number of group shots and close-ups of the doubting Thomases, interspersed with cuts of the somewhat anxious instructor, create anticipatory suspense. Then, with the flourish of a magician disclosing a mysteriously manifested cage of white doves, the instructor uncovers the separator.

In an unusual sequence of cuts, the act of flipping off the machine's covering is played in two separate and different set-ups. The

* Few students today will know what a cream separator is. It need only be known that it separates whole milk into two of its components—cream and skim milk. Centrifugal force is the operating principle, and each of the milk components issues out of its own separate spout.

movement at the beginning of the second cut actually overlaps, or repeats, the movement of the last half of the first cut. In the continuation of the action, the drape's landing on the floor is played in three separate and similarly overlapping cuts.

This series of cuts creates an interesting effect—it gives an "entrance" to an inanimate object. Drawing out the action of the removal, the tossing aside, and the landing of the drape supplies the climax dramatically demanded by the suspense which leads up to the separator's introduction. It also lends greater emphasis to the subsequent scenes.

For now a new suspense build-up begins. The instructor laboriously starts to crank the heavy fly wheel which, through a chain of gears, spins the milk-containing chamber. When it has acquired a bit of momentum he turns the job over to a young, eager peasant. A long series of cuts follows, with the action roughly divided into three parts. First, close-ups and group shots of the peasants, intercut with the shots of the revolving fly wheel, spinning gears, and whirling milk, establish and build the peasants' growing skepticism as cuts of the spouts show no results. Interestingly, in this section only the machine moves—the reactions of the humans are fixed in still shots, each one a portrait worthy of a gallery showing. The symbolism of the static peasants opposed to the dynamism of the machine is obvious but effective.

But soon the watchers' aloof disdain turns to laughter and sneers—the reactions of the instructor and his two peasant supporters show increasing anxiety. As their frustration deepens, movement number 2 begins. A cut of one of the nozzles shows what might be a pulsating drop of white liquid just beginning to form. Now the shots of the instructor and the peasants mirror the expected change in attitudes as further cuts to the machine disclose that the skim milk and the cream are indeed beginning to ooze out of their respective spouts. These cuts build slowly—several cuts of the spouts are needed to convince the peasants (and us) that the white liquid is really starting to flow.

The third development is triumphant. The machine pours out streams of skim milk and cream; the instructor, his young helper, and the peasant woman who has been the prime mover in the demonstration are ecstatic. The peasants are now all firm believers. A few gratuitous shots of leaping fountains of water dissolve us through to the next sequence, which shows milk cows being delivered to the now organized collective—naturally.

This sequence is some six minutes in length, and in those six minutes the viewer is completely convinced that the once skeptical peasants are ready to give up their "old" practices of manual labor for the "new" mechanization of their daily work.

A montage of this sort is truly a realization of the old adage, "One picture is worth a thousand words." A successful demonstration is always more convincing than a verbal argument, as any good salesman knows. Obviously, few people today are interested in cream separators, but the principles involved in the sequence have a wide application. Every dramatic structure of movement depends on change—change of attitude, of action, or of direction—and those changes must be found understandable and acceptable by the viewer, who cannot be conditioned as arbitrarily as a character in a script.

Let us create another example of the power of an image to clarify a subtle thought or idea, this one from the world of science. Most people are aware that matter is supposed to consist of submicroscopic particles whirling at great speed in relatively vast areas of space. Yet it is very difficult to convince a person that the hardwood coffee table on which he props his feet is almost complete emptiness. He will hear your words but his senses will call you a liar. So let us develop a series of images, or cuts.

First, a shot of a bicycle, placed upside down as if about to be worked on. Next, a shot of a stationary bicycle wheel. This, and the following series of artfully composed close shots of the wheel's spokes, show that they occupy only a minute percentage of the space between the wheel's hub and rim. A shot of a child playing, poking a finger between the spokes, then repeating the action with a pencil, which he bounces off the sides of the slender steel struts in complete safety. Now, a hand moves the bike's pedal—slowly the wheel begins to turn. Succeeding cuts show the wheel picking up speed, the spokes gradually losing their identity until they become a transparent blur, a diffused area between rim and hub which seems quite empty. Again, a hand tries to poke a pencil through this empty space, only to find a shattered stub in its grasp. The wheel is now not only as solid as the top of the coffee table—it is many times more dangerous.

This exercise is an oversimplification but, properly presented, it can help a viewer to understand how an apparently empty space can become rock hard when rapid movement is involved—even if the moving "pieces" themselves are invisible.

The foregoing example may be somewhat removed, but so are many problems of human interrelations which are the building blocks of drama. Just as a free, rapidly deflating toy balloon can tell you more about jet propulsion than most textbooks, so Hitchcock's murder-in-the-bath montage (in *Psycho*) is far more vivid and immediate than any verbal or normal pictorial rendering could possibly be. If clever cutting can make a star out of a cream separator, or furnish a useful explanation of atomic movement, think of what could be done with a scene in which the central figures were Paul Newman and. . . .

Which brings us back to the present and a vividly dramatized scene in *The Verdict*. It is quite short, and not a true montage, but it approaches that technique in its creative use of the image as a substitute for dialogue.

Newman must find a particular nurse to testify for him in a wrongful death trial. Her testimony is of vital importance—his case, his reputation, and his future as a lawyer all depend on it. Yet the nurse is so frightened for her own safety that she has moved to another town, changed her name and her job, to avoid any involvement in the proceedings. Obviously, obtaining her cooperation will be difficult— probably impossible.

Newman finally locates her but, in order to see her, he is forced to disguise his purpose, his profession, even his place of residence. His deceptive approach has barely begun when she sees, carelessly exposed in his breast pocket, the shuttle flight envelope which shows he has come from Boston, the scene of the crime and the trial.

In a close-up, she looks at him, traumatized, her eyes showing her fear and her awareness of his true mission. In his close-up, in turn, he pleads wordlessly. Back to her—her eyes fill with tears as she begins to cry quietly. Now Newman speaks, "Will you help me?" And the sequence ends. We know that she will cooperate, whatever the consequences, though not a single word relating to the true purpose of the confrontation has been uttered.

It is great acting, but it is also a brilliant series of cuts, an example of "movies" at their best. No playwright, past or present, could, with dialogue, have presented a scene half as concise; and no other theatrical medium could even have begun to duplicate its effectiveness. It is a rare example of the aborted art of montage, an oasis in the desert. And if, to quote Lindgren once more, "The development of film technique has been primarily the development of editing," and I believe it has, then a reinvestigation of the art of "creative editing" is the only way to reach the green fields beyond.

# *Epilogue*

Rule #7.   Substance first—then form.

Mikhail Baryshnikov's comments on young performers today have already been quoted (see Postscript, Book III). He stands by no means alone. Film critic David Denby writes, "[Y]oung film-school graduates, often without any literary or theatrical training at all, have taken over the directors' seats."[*] And Norman Cousins, in one of his perceptive editorials, wrote, "We are turning out young men and women who are superbly trained but poorly educated. They are a how-to generation, less concerned with the nature of things than with the working of things. They are beautifully skilled but intellectually underdeveloped. They know everything that is to be known about the functional requirements of their trade but little about the *human situation* that serves as the context for their work."[**] (Italics added.)

Seven years of teaching have made me acutely aware of the truth of Mr. Cousins' words, and the last twenty years of gradually diminishing film viewing have led me to anticipate Mr. Denby's. They have also convinced me that the conditions they all describe derive not only from the students' desires but also from the teachers' aims. Which leads me, at the risk of being charged with redundancy, to write a few final words of advice. This book has persistently stressed technique and has urged the pursuit of perfection in its use. But the "human situation," in all its guises, it what good films are all about, and technical skill counts for nothing if it is used only to manufacture films which have little to do with humanity.

For ten years I was a film editor at Paramount, the only Holly-

[*] "Theaterphobia," *The Atlantic*, January 1985.
[**] *Saturday Review*, May–June 1983.

533

wood studio which assigned its cutters to the set, there to help with editorial and set-up decisions—*if* the director invited such assistance. Throughout the thirties I worked with some of that decade's best filmmakers. Actually, since many of them were extremely protective of their images, I spent a good deal of my time on the set watching, listening, and occasionally wrestling (in my mind, of course) with some problem confronting the director. Eventually I found myself winning the fall more often than losing it and, with the cockiness of youth, I grew to feel I knew most of what there was to know about filmmaking.

When I directed my first film I was shocked to discover that although I had learned a good deal about the technical aspects of directing, I had been aware of only a very small part of what went on in the director's minds. Processes involved in the making of their creative decisions had never been openly discussed. I now know that no such discussions were possible, except in the most general terms, since most such decisions are made intuitively, and intuition is hardly a "teachable" art.

However, although it is true that talent can't be taught, it *can* be made aware, and it is only in the area of awareness that this book is meant to wander. To increase that awareness, a truly dedicated film student will do a great deal of outside reading. Herewith, are some suggestions—no specific authors, since there is a mountain of material in all the recommended categories, but only subject matter.

To understand the architecture of the screenplay, you must study not only the best films, past and present, but the structures of the novel, the short story (apropos because of its ability to develop character and situation in a limited amount of space and time), and musical composition, since its techniques of pacing, emphasis, prestatement and development of theme parallel good film structure to a surprising degree.

To understand the character of man, you should study anthropology, animal behavior, and sociobiology. To understand what shapes the minds of your characters and establishes their standards, study philosophy and religion—*all* religion. To understand what minds so conditioned have done with their world, look into history.

On a more practical level, to obtain hints on audience manipulation and to learn how to draw the most and the best out of your crew and your cast, study psychology, of course.

Above all, study the world around you, and the people in it—all people, the short and the tall, the thin and the fat, the beautiful and the ugly, the biased and the generous of mind, but especially the "average." Most craftsmen can make some kind of dramatic fare out of the extremes, but if you can uncover those elements which touch the heart and make high drama out of the "ordinary", you will be an artist indeed.

# Filmography
## of
# Edward Dmytryk

THE HAWK     (Ind)     (1935)
TELEVISION SPY     (Para)     (1939)
EMERGENCY SQUAD     (Para)     (1939)
GOLDEN GLOVES     (Para)     (1939)
MYSTERY SEA RAIDER     (Para)     (1940)
HER FIRST ROMANCE     (I.E. Chadwick)     (1940)
THE DEVIL COMMANDS     (Col)     (1940)
UNDER AGE     (Col)     (1940)
SWEETHEART OF THE CAMPUS     (Col)     (1941)
THE BLONDE FROM SINGAPORE     (Col)     (1941)
SECRETS OF THE LONE WOLF     (Col)     (1941)
CONFESSIONS OF BOSTON BLACKIE     (Col)     (1941)
COUNTER-ESPIONAGE     (Col)     (1942)
SEVEN MILES FROM ALCATRAZ     (RKO)     (1942)
HITLER'S CHILDREN     (RKO)     (1943)
THE FALCON STRIKES BACK     (RKO)     (1943)
CAPTIVE WILD WOMAN     (UNIV)     (1943)
BEHIND THE RISING SUN     (RKO)     (1943)
TENDER COMRADE     (RKO)     (1943)
MURDER, MY SWEET     (RKO)     (1944)
BACK TO BATAAN     (RKO)     (1945)
CORNERED     (RKO)     (1945)
TILL THE END OF TIME     (RKO)     (1945)
SO WELL REMEMBERED     (RKO-RANK)     (1946)

CROSSFIRE     (RKO)     (1947)
THE HIDDEN ROOM     (English Ind.)     (1948)
GIVE US THIS DAY     (Eagle-Lion)     (1949)
MUTINY     (King Bros.-U.A.)     (1951)
THE SNIPER     (Kramer-Col)     (1951)
EIGHT IRON MEN     (Kramer-Col)     (1952)
THE JUGGLER     (Kramer-Col)     (1953)
THE CAINE MUTINY     (Kramer-Col)     (1953)
BROKEN LANCE     (20th-Fox)     (1954)
THE END OF THE AFFAIR     (Col)     (1954)
SOLDIER OF FORTUNE     (20th-Fox)     (1955)
THE LEFT HAND OF GOD     (20th-Fox)     (1955)
THE MOUNTAIN     (Para)     (1956)
RAINTREE COUNTY     (MGM)     (1956)
THE YOUNG LIONS     (20th-Fox)     (1957)
WARLOCK     (20th-Fox)     (1958)
THE BLUE ANGEL     (20th-Fox)     (1959)
WALK ON THE WILD SIDE     (Col)     (1961)
THE RELUCTANT SAINT     (Col)     (1961)
THE CARPETBAGGERS     (Para)     (1963)
WHERE LOVE HAS GONE     (Para)     (1964)
MIRAGE     (Univ)     (1965)
ALVAREZ KELLY     (Col)     (1966)
ANZIO     (Col)     (1967)
SHALAKO     (Cinerama)     (1968)
BLUEBEARD     (Cinerama)     (1972)
THE HUMAN FACTOR     (Bryanston)     (1975)

# Filmography
## of
# Jeanne Porter Dmytryk

**Film**

SONG AND DANCE MAN     (20th C-Fox)     (1935)
TOM SAWYER     (David O. Selznick Prod.)     (1936)
HEART OF THE RIO GRANDE     (Republic)     (1937)
HELLIZAPOPPIN'     (Univ)     (1937)
SAN FERNANDO VALLEY     (Republic)     (1938)
THE UNDER PUP     (Univ)     (1938)
STRIKE UP THE BAND     (MGM)     (1939)
HENRY ALDRICH FOR PRESIDENT     (Para)     (1939)
ONE MILLION B.C.     (Hal Roach)     (1939)
BABES ON BROADWAY     (MGM)     (1940)
KISS THE BOYS GOODBYE     (Paramount)     (1940)
ABOUT FACE     (Hal Roach)     (1940)
FALL IN     (Hal Roach)     (1940)
NASTY NUISANCE     (Hal Roach)     (1941)
CALABOOSE     (Hal Roach)     (1941)
THE YOUNGEST PROFESSION     (MGM)     (1942)
ANDY HARDY'S BLONDE TROUBLE     (MGM)     (1942)
YOUNG IDEAS     (MGM)     (1943)
BATHING BEAUTY     (MGM)     (1943)
ABBOT AND COSTELLO IN HOLLYWOOD     (MGM)     (1944)
EASY TO WED     (MGM)     (1945)
WHAT NEXT, CORPORAL HARGROVE     (MGM)     (1945)

TILL THE END OF TIME      (RKO)      (1946)
BETTY CO-ED      (Col)      (1946)
SWEET GENEVIEVE      (Col)      (1947)
TWO BLONDES AND A REDHEAD      (Col)      (1947)
LITTLE MISS BROADWAY      (Col)      (1947)
THAT HAGEN GIRL      (Warner Bros.)      (1948)
CRY DANGER      (RKO)      (1949)
KENTUCKY JUBILEE      (Lippert Prod.)      (1950)
G.I. JANE      (Lippert Prod.)      (1950)
RACING BLOOD      (Independent)      (1950)
THE LEFT HAND OF GOD      (RKO)      (1955)

**Television**

A regular on the RED SKELTON COMEDY HOUR (1954–1955)
A regular in the ABBOT AND COSTELLO FILMS made for TV
      (1945–1946)
Live TV HALLMARK THEATER      (CBS)      (1955)
Live TV NINETY MINUTES      (CBS)      (1956)
Live TV ODYSSEY      (CBS Special)      (1957)
Guest Star on many TV weekly shows